BALL THE WALL

Nik Cohn in the Age of Rock

Introduced by Gordon Burn

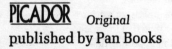 *Original*
published by Pan Books

Some of these articles first appeared, in slightly different form, in *Cream* magazine, *Harpers and Queen*, *King Magazine*, *New York* magazine, *Playboy* and *Queen* magazine.

First published in Picador 1989 by Pan Books Ltd,
Cavaye Place, London SW10 9PG

9 8 7 6 5 4 3 2 1

This collection © Nik Cohn 1989
Introduction © Gordon Burn 1989

ISBN 0 330 29970 0

Photoset by Parker Typesetting Service, Leicester
Printed and bound in Great Britain by
Richard Clay Ltd, Bungay, Suffolk

'To all who pass
That they may see –
Rock 'n' roll
Was a part of me.'

JOHNNY ANGELO

For Michaela

Contents

Author's note

'Ball the Wall', the title of a record by Professor Longhair and his Shuffling Hungarians, is a New Orleans phrase that means exactly what you think it means.

Introduction

'Tell us a story.'

'It was in Waterloo Place that I entered an amusement arcade, put a nickel in the slot and placed my eye up close against the Scopitone, where Little Richard was pounding the piano, performing 'Tutti Frutti', and his trouser-cuffs billowed out like sails. Right then I discovered the truth.'

'What was the truth?'

'Awopbopaloobop Alopbamboom.'

'Awopbopaloobop?'

'Alopbamboom.'

(I Am Still The Greatest Says Johnny Angelo, 1967)

Nik Cohn was a prodigy of sorts. *Market*, his first novel, was published when he was seventeen. His second, *I Am Still The Greatest Says Johnny Angelo*, was published three years later. By then he was also established as the best writer on pop music and sixties' 'teendream' culture in Britain, arguably the world.

When he was twenty-two, Cohn returned to Ireland, where he had spent the first part of his life, and knocked out what still remains the classic utterance on Pop, in a little over a month. *Awopbopaloobop Alopbamboom* (originally published as *Pop From the Beginning*) was dedicated to Jet Powers, Dean Angel and Johnny Ace, and was a hymn to the Golden Age when all that counted was 'the endless and perfect and changeless beat' – mindless and yet epic Superpop uncontaminated by self-consciousness and significance.

What Cohn loved – James Brown, Little Richard, P. J. Proby and, most of all, Elvis – he loved to distraction. What he hated – performers who were 'white, sleek, nicely-spoken and phoney to their toe-nails', the later Beatles, Bob Dylan – he hated with a vengeance.

'Nik is no obituarist', Kit Lambert, co-manager of the Who, wrote in the introduction to *Awopbopaloobop*. 'But if he did write your obituary you'd be better off dead.'

Cohn's talent though was never really as a hatchet-artist. He was an enthusiast and was unrivalled in selling his enthusiasms. 'He had pop off by heart, he thought in it instinctively – no sermonizing, no crap,' Cohn once wrote of Pete Townsend. It is just as true of his own prose.

Cohn not only wrote *about* the teendream but actually achieved the impossible and embodied the spirit of Pop in his best work. Cohn's writing style is 'full of conscious hipnesses', as he himself once wrote of somebody else. But it stands as living proof that seriousness doesn't always have to equal pompousness and pretension and using fifteen rhubarb words when five simple ones will do.

Until I met him to discuss putting together this collection, I had met Nik Cohn only once, many years before. It must have been the early seventies, 1971 or '72, by which time he was already describing himself on the jackets of his books as 'a writer, pin-ball artist and pig farmer', and living with his wife and young daughter in a thatched cottage within easy striking distance of the West End. I was, and still am, a fan; and Cohn, then as now a gentleman and an exotic, didn't disappoint.

He was wearing a three-piece suit made of Donegal tweed, with hairy socks, a tie with Da-glo cricket bats on, and drinking from a jug of Abbot Ale. Lunch consisted of beef dripping on doorsteps and selections from Aretha Franklin, Billy Fury, the Penguins, Professor Longhair, Johnny Otis and the Monotones played loud enough to loosen the wattle. At 1.45 precisely the Dansette was switched off and for the next fifteen minutes we listened to the Archers. Afterwards, we walked the dog across the adjacent fields.

Fifteen years or so later, we met again for lunch. This time it was in the red flock-and-gilt, *haut bourgeois* restaurant in Leicester Square where, newly arrived in London from Newcastle at the age of seventeen, Cohn had wandered by mistake into the Ladies, found two of the waitresses *in flagrante delicto*, and realized instantly that this was the life.

Although amused to have his greatest hits collected together in a single volume, he was wary from the beginning about what this part of it might consist of. 'Let's keep it', he said, peering out of the plastic shrubbery framing his now slightly greying curls, and betraying not a sign, in either his appearance or his accent, of the many years he has spent living in the United States, 'Can't we keep it . . . *you* know . . . a bit mythic?'

For a while, back in the 1960s, Cohn was 'the kid of the moment', to use a Lillian Hellman phrase. In his white dude suits and maximum velour fedoras, his opal stick-pins and yellow kid-leather shoes, he was big on image. And, no less important, his timing was spot-on. Furthermore, he could write.

'He was subtle and vacuous, bizarre and familiar, emotional and strictly commercial, all at once; he stole from everyone he could and was still completely original,' Cohn writes in his marvellous profile of Phil Spector, and that was true of the best of his own work as well.

'They read like slogans and a series of posters', Cohn now says of *Market, I Am Still The Greatest Says Johnny Angelo* and *Awop-bopaloobop*, the books he wrote between the ages of sixteen and twenty-two. Maybe. But they did what they set out to do. They trapped an instant and preserved it for all time.

They are heroic pulp. But, as Cohn himself has written of Townshend's early songs for the Who, they relate to *real* pulp in roughly the same way that Roy Lichtenstein's Pop Art paintings of about the same time relate to the original comic strips on which they are based. They are simple *and* intelligent.

'Violence and glamour and speed, splendour and vulgarity, danger and gesture and style – these were the things that he valued, nothing else,' one of Cohn's leading *doppelgängers*, 'Arfur', says of another, 'Johnny Angelo'. 'Everywhere that he travelled, everything that he did, he existed in one unending movie. Inside the movie, I joined him.'

And that is what the reader who wants to get the most out of Cohn must be prepared to do too. Like the music that provided the soundtrack to his life and pulses through his work, Cohn demands total surrender. Nothing less. It's no use riding with one foot on the ground.

'You are either hot or cold', in the words of Jerry Lee. 'If you are lukewarm, the Lord will spew you out of his mouth.'

'He showed up about 1965', Kit Lambert, his friend and mentor, wrote of Cohn. 'The Beatles were into their first million, the disgruntled Rolling Stones were touring USA circuses, billed virtually as a freak show, and a nervous Carnaby Street tailor had just refused to put his scissors into a large Union Jack, which was meant to wind up as stage clothes for the Who, when a thin young man – he looked about fourteen – wearing carefully dirtied-down sneakers, grabbed me in Wardour Street and informed me that he was writing an article for *The Sunday Times*. I believed him a lot. He landed up in a Chinese restaurant, interviewing the Merseybeats . . . He is very bright, he knows too much, and he *still* doesn't shave.'

Market, Cohn's first novel, was published later in 1965. 'Johnny Angelo' was already on the stocks. Fuelled by a prodigious intake of bottled stout and amphetamines, and by an unswerving confidence in the messages his own nerve-ends were sending back to base, he swept like a tornado through Cultureburg and clubland and along the Street of Shame.

Superficially at least, Nik Cohn was one of the storm troopers of Tom Wolfe's new 'literature of fact'. This was a small but dedicated corps, almost exclusively American, who were intent on taking the ground for so long occupied by the old school of literary movers and shakers and arterio-sclerotic writers of 'faded Aubusson prose'.

And it is true that Cohn reported back from the frontline, from the boutiques, the salons, the recording studios, the clubs, the riots and the busts in a way that happily violated what Orwell called 'the Geneva conventions of the mind'. But social realism, the motor-power of Wolfe's prose and the New Journalism's fundamental aesthetic, was never really what turned him on. Myth-making – making things up, in other words – was always more his natural bent.

Cohn was – and, as far as one can tell, still is – an incurable romantic, with passions that burned deep. He has never been one to let truth stand in the way.

That was the fundamental difference between him and the other trailblazers of the New Journalism. One point on which Tom Wolfe was always most insistent was that facts were sacred; you never took liberties with the facts.

Cohn never went along with that. 'Not having been to a place never stopped me from *describing* it,' he says. 'Any more than not meeting someone stopped me talking about my interview with them.'

'Doesn't truth get tiresome?' the Doctor asks Johnny Angelo. 'When lies are so much fun.' And, reading it collected together for the first time, this is the message of all Cohn's work, whether masquerading as fiction or journalism.

Behind the mythification, however, certain basic facts may be gleaned. Born in '46, Cohn grew up in Northern Ireland, moved to Newcastle in his teens, had a brief and abortive fling as a would-be tenor sax man and finally, at seventeen, deciding that writing looked less like real work than anything else in prospect, bought himself a secondhand typewriter and descended on London.

Over the next decade or so, his output was virtually non-stop. Apart from *Awopbopaloobop Alopbamboom*, there were four novels; *Today There Are No Gentlemen*, a study of the style revolution in dress and the cultural shift that had spawned it; *Rock Dreams*, a collaboration with the Belgian Guy Pellaert; and an avalanche of stories, reviews and features for *The Observer* and *The Sunday Times*, *Rolling Stone*, *Playboy*, *Queen*, the *New York Times*, et al. Then, just as suddenly as the onslaught had begun, it ceased and desisted.

The reason was simple – The Golden Age, Cohn reckoned, was done, a dead letter. The English scene in particular, once so vital, now seemed completely atrophied. So in '75 he moved to New York, hoping, in Satchell Paige's phrase 'to angry up his blood again'. Joining *New York Magazine* he wrote 'Another Saturday Night', the story that would be filmed as *Saturday Night Fever*. But the cure, on the whole, refused to take. Even in America, he sensed a prevailing exhaustion, as of a once-inexhaustible theme now grown feeble, used up.

One last story for *New York Magazine*, '24 on 42', about staying alive in Times Square, completed the odyssey. Leaving the Street, after almost twenty years, he felt as if he could no longer escape the unbeautiful facts behind his beautiful lies. He had balled the wall long enough.

It was, in a sense, a fall to Earth, but that didn't mean that Cohn now embraced reality. On the contrary it is exactly his impatience with the mundane and with its literary equivalent, the standard clichés of English, that has fed his obsessions and shaped his writing style. Like his heroes and alter egos – Jerry Roll Morton, Willie Pastrano, Elvis, Jet Powers, the black disco dance champion Tu

Sweet – he has always been hooked 'on image, on heroics'. Anything less he can't help but find life-diminishing and almost physically offensive.

Cohn has spent his life in pursuit of the fast and the apocalyptic. Sometimes – as in the case of those listed above – he has found it. Most times, however, he hasn't. And when he hasn't, he has been obliged to make it up.

'Two sorts of writers make bold to present a collection', Norman Mailer has written in the introduction to one of the collections of his own work. 'The first kind writes sufficiently well to induce his publisher to put together his very separate pieces, and they are printed as a convenience for his readers. In such collections there is a tendency for the attitude to belong to the subject more than to the author – professional football is seen as professional football and ladies' fashion as ladies' fashion.

'The other kind of writer can be better or worse, but the writings always have a touch of the grandiose, even the megalomaniacal: the reason may be that the writings are parts of a continuing and more or less comprehensive vision of existence into which everything must fit. Of course, if the vision is interesting, the fit can be startling, dramatic, illuminating, nourishing, or arouse a desire for more, but good or poor, the unspoken urge is to find secret relations between professional football and ladies' fashion and bring them alive as partners to the vision. Such writers are of course rare, and everything they (write is) part of one continuing book – the book of their life and the vision of their existence.'

There seems no doubt to me that Nik Cohn is a writer of the second stamp. A number of other reasons could be put forward to justify the existence of this book: that Cohn presaged, for example, many of the 'movements' of the seventies and eighties, from the Sloanes and Young Fogies to Malcolm McLaren and Punk; that he was writing about 'style' a decade and more before people know what either style (as in 'style editor') or subculture (as in 'the meaning of style') were.

But that single fact alone – that the writings constitute 'a continuing and more or less comprehensive vision of existence' – seems to me enough. And, besides, we're treading perilously near – may already, in fact, have blundered into – the slender territory where Pop and 'Art' overlap. Cohn made his feelings on this clear many years ago, and they haven't changed.

'While it lives off flash and outrage, impulse, excess, and sweet teen romance, it's perfect. But dabble in Art and it immediately gets overloaded . . . the words of Little Richard summed up what Pop was about in 1956. They sum it up now and always:

AWOPBOPALOOBOP ALOPBAMBOOM'

Cohn is a dandy in an age of hackery. He has a burning sense of the present but doesn't bend with the winds of fashion. He is a one-off. It's enough.

GORDON BURN

ONE

Juvenile
Delinquencies

1946
–66

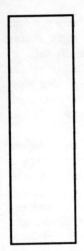

In Derry

T he winter I turned eleven I came upon a certain snake in the street. This was in Londonderry, Northern Ireland, where I grew up and where no snakes should have been.

Time has blurred the context. Exactly what led me to the snake in question, how I even happened inside its neighbourhood, I can't now imagine. All I remember is walking by myself on an empty backstreet after dark and this street was dim and shuttered, curfew-silent, the way that all good Protestant streets in Derry were meant to be. It must have been a Thursday, the day we ran cross-country at school, because my feet ached. Anyhow. At a given moment I turned a blind corner, and I blundered on the snake.

It didn't register right away. Just at first I was dazzled by bright lights, and by the enormity of what I'd done, where I was. For my feet had brought me out into the one place in town where no soul that hoped to be saved must ever venture – Waterloo Place, at the downtown end of The Strand, on the borders of Bogside, the Papist war zone.

What made it such a plague-spot I had no idea. I only knew that a plague-spot it was. Tiggle, the janitor, said as much. So did McAlee, the man who did the drains. In the walled fastness of Magee, the college at which my father taught French, it was freely referred to as an MKS, for Mobile Knocking Shop.

And here I was, smack dab at the heart of it. After dark. By *daylight, on the few furtive occasions I'd glimpsed it before, it had only looked shabby, terminally depressed. But by night it was transfigured into a style of place I hadn't dared to dream existed.*

Directly across the street from me sat a perfect neon Inferno, as brightly lit and self-contained as any stage-set: Rock 'n' Roll blasting from the open doors of coffee ba..; beehive blondes with sky-blue or scarlet glitterskirts and bright-orange lipstick; sailors hunting in packs; leather boys, motorbikes, the reek of diesel.

Nothing had prepared me, not remotely. Derry in that era, before the Provos and long before Bloody Sunday, was very much a backwater, some thirty to fifty years adrift of the moment, and proud of it. As for Magee itself, its isolation was almost monastic. Nobody owned a TV, precious few a gramophone and, though my father read The Irish Times *each morning in the college library, my own grip on reality was confined to what I might glean from* Dandy *and* The Eagle, *Dan Dare had landed on Mars, Wyatt Earp was Sheriff in Tombstone and Desperate Dan had made himself ill by devouring a box of six-inch nails, believing them to be sweet cigarettes.*

Once when I was four I'd caught a whiff of 'Put Another Nickel In', Teresa Brewer, courtesy of a passing bus, and my mother had had to drag me off the street by main force. But at the moment I stumbled on to The Strand, at the turn of 1957, the only Pop singer I'd heard of was Ruby Murray, and then only because she came from Belfast.

I froze. If I'd been transported here by time machine, I could not have been worse out of place. Instinctively, I understood that my role was as voyeur, a worshipper at one remove, and I snuck back inside an unlit doorway, from which safety I could watch unobserved – see, and not be seen.

Only then did I notice the snake. From deep inside the chasm of the Roseland Café, a jukebox let loose with 'Tutti Frutti', Little Richard, and on the pavement outside an impromptu jitterbug broke out. Teenagers in fancy dress, whom I later learned were Teddy Boys, began to jive with each other, males with males, in a craze of flashing fluorescent socks and shocking-pink drapes, drainpipes and blue suede shoes; and as they whirled they kept passing the snake, which I took at first to be a whip or a length of elasticized tubing, back and forth between them like a baton.

When the music died out, so did the dancing. But the snake remained in view, dangled beneath a streetlamp, neatly framed and backlit by the Roseland's plate-glass window; and now I could see it clearly.

From across the street, seen out of darkness into light, it appeared to be about two foot long, with a tapering greenish coil for its body and a great black-hooded skull. Something between a cobra and a python, I guessed, and it twirled and corkscrewed, stretched and contracted in rhythm, twined around a blue mohair sleeve with a purple velvet cuff.

It didn't seem a discovery, exactly. That was not the right word. Rather, my main feeling was simply of recognition. It was as if there was something I had always known deepest down, only I'd forgotten or misplaced it, let it escape me, and now the snake, and everything that went along with the snake, had restored it.

The something in question had no name, of course. And I did not try to give it one. All that I thought consciously was that I now possessed a secret, and this secret made me powerful, in some way superior.

It was not a familiar feeling. In all of my pre-Strand existence, secret power was the last thing I'd thought to possess. On the contrary, I was consumed by not belonging, having no true place, either in Derry or anywhere else on Planet Earth.

In this last view, I had widespread support: 'Unfit to fit', some kindergarten confrère *once carved into the lid of my desk, and the motion seemed to be carried by acclamation.*

Part of the problem was genetic. By birth and upraising I was an Anglo–Tuetonic–Russian–Menshevik–Agnostic–Jew, and pretty much typical of the type. Born in London, weaned in Scotland and South Africa, I didn't arrive in Ireland till past my fifth birthday, and somehow I never fully acclimatized. Certainly not in native eyes, at any rate. My father wrote books about heretics, my mother had an accent, and I myself was neither Protestant nor Catholic, not Irish but nothing definable else. In the context of Derry, and in particular of Foyle, the moth-eaten Presbyterian shrine in decline where I went to school, I might as well have come from Mars – the man who fell to Earth and, abysmally, failed to bounce.

Magee completed the curse. In theory it was a training school for

Calvinist ministers; in reality, with its high stone walls and imported tutors, more like an unarmed encampment; and its isolation from the town was absolute. Dimly one was conscious of the hatred outside, with its perpetual roundelay of Catholic ambuscades and Protestant reprisals, Black Masses and Orange parades. But they seemed to carry no reality. Even when I was blown out of my bed by the concussion of a detonated radio tower, or when a pitched battle raged at the army camp and an RUC (Royal Ulster Constabulary) sergeant had the lobe of his left ear shot off by an IRA sniper, it felt like some yarn out of Hot Adventures. *If it had not been for Tiggle, the aforesaid janitor, my only link to life as endured beyond Magee's walls, I would hardly have been aware that men, when shot, did actually bleed.*

Always the key was that I myself took no part. From my very earliest remembrance, in which my twenty-month self enticed a five-year-old gardener's daughter into climbing up a tree and getting stuck – thus allowing me to study from below the effects of light and shade on her sky-blue knickers, her sweating spun-gold legs all covered with scabs, ripe and pickable as currants baked into damp bread, also the way in which her screams caused her thighs to shimmy and shudder like blancmange in a gale – intuition told me that my best role was not to perform but always to watch, preferably from a safe distance.

There was one exception. At Magee, down by Tiggle's cottage and the tennis court where he died, there was an outhouse with a long and flat cement exterior wall and up against this wall, every rainless afternoon after school, I used to bat a tennis ball. Sometimes I would hit it with a rot-gutted racquet as flaccid as a butterfly net, sometimes with a sawn-off broomstick or the flat of a cricket bat, and sometimes, when times were tough, with a cabbage-stalk soaked in brine; and as I hit, I counted.

The formula never varied. First I would attempt to execute one hundred strokes on my forehand, then another hundred backhand, then forehand again, then backhand, and so interminably on, until at last I miscued, at which point I'd go back to the beginning, start over from Stroke One.

What was the use? I couldn't have explained it then; I'm still not sure today. No special target was involved, no astronomical figure whose attainment would somehow release me. Equally, there was no question of athletic prowess. On the contrary, in my passion not to flub, I kept all my shots as passive and pattycake as possible, never dared the slightest variation. Avoidance of error was not the main thing, it was the only thing, and so metronomic was the thud of ball on wall, I might have been marking time.

In the face of such utter futility, the mildest of men and divinity students seemed goaded beyond enduring. With time I acquired a regular gallery of hecklers, beseeching me, just once, to give the ball a free and hearty whack. But I never did. The very soullessness of this unending putt-puttery was its perverse pleasure. One afternoon, half-way through my seventh hundred on the forehand, Tiggle keeled over in mid-imprecation, belly-up and purple-headed at my back, with the palest pink froth about his lips like the lees of lemonade sherbet. There were murmurings of manslaughter, and these I took as a compliment.

For years the ceremonial never varied by one beat. Then I came out into The Strand, observed the snake and later, safe back in the sanctuary of Magee, I went down directly to the outhouse wall. Even though it was pitch dark, I grabbed up a rusty coal shovel, whirled it like a shillelagh; and I began to smash the balls at random.

I hit out, blindly, possessed. Exploding all about me like so many hand grenades, balls ricocheted into my face and eyes, my belly; knocked me backwards, drove me to my knees. Ball the wall, indeed I did; and the tarmac beneath me, and the air, and all of the darkness, too.

I didn't quit till every last ball I owned had been splatted or for ever lost. Then I hurled the shovel as far as my mean strength could launch it, and I never played that game again.

I took to travelling, instead. Of a sudden Magee no longer seemed a refuge, only a confinement, and I invented numberless excuses to be free of it, to go out scavenging.

There were, for instance, my feet. Claiming incipient droopage of the instep, I won permission to pay a weekly visit after Friday school to one Bernard Dinty, a cobbler turned foot-healer.

Dinty's office, a bare, white room above a flesher's on Shipquay Street, lay deep within the walled city, overlooking Bogside, and it hid behind drawn blinds, with a hurricane lamp for shadowing. There I would be marched back and forth across a narrow strip of linoleum, one full hour by the clock, practising posture, balance and what Dinty termed tone of gait.

This office, it was rumoured at Foyle, doubled as a front for a butter-smuggling ring. And it's true, there was something rancid and furtive in its air, a smell of dirty little secrets. As for the healer himself, a rumpled little squit of a man, all polka-dot bow tie and stained white medico's coat, he liked to soundtrack my perambulations with lectures on the evils of masturbation, also of patronizing brothels, or, as he preferred, the Temples of Venus. 'Fallen arches today, fallen women next Saturday', was his pet motto and, each time he delivered it, he would touch my bare short-trousered leg above the knee, not so much sweating as oozing, clammily steaming, like an overheated jam pudding in melt-down.

My compensation was that, by the time I won release, it would be after dark, all the streets would have changed for night, and then the straightest, safety way home would lead me directly past the Roseland Café.

The snake itself, I never saw again. But the Teddy Boys, its votaries, were regulars, and they came to embody everything I sensed, everything that I still couldn't spell.

In their daytime incarnations, I understood, the Teds were only Papist scum, the delinquent flotsam and jetsam of Bogside. As such, their life prospects were nil. Foredoomed, the dispossessed, they had traded away the Free for the Welfare State, and now they had no work, no homeplace, no future hope whatever, unless it be the fleeting glory of an IRA martyrdom. They were, in every common sense, non-persons. And yet, here on The Strand, in the neon night by Rock 'n' Roll, they were made heroic. In every flash of fluorescent sock or velvet cuff, every jivestep swagger for Chuck Berry, every leer and flaunt of their greased pompadoured ducktails, they beggared the fates, made reality irrelevant.

The second step was Elvis.

Again, I had Bernard Dinty partly to thank. Late of one Friday dusk, headed for my weekly treadmill and not overkeen to arrive, I let myself loiter outside the flyblown windows of McCafferty's, Journals & Uncommonly Fine Books, Inc., and there sat a copy of

Titbits, *a weekly yellow tabloid barred by my mother as 'cheap and nasty', therefore a jewel beyond price to myself. On its cover was a head-and-shoulders glossy of the King.*

In the first shock of impact I was only conscious of the mouth, in particular the upper lip. This seemed to loom disembodied, in the style of a Cheshire Cat grin, only twisted and lopsided, as serpentine as any real or rubber snake, so that its smile became a sneer. And this sneer said: 'Oh, yeah?', to which echo answered: 'Oh, yeah!'

In that instant I accepted Elvis Presley to be my personal living saviour and nothing has happened since to change my mind, bruise my faith one iota.

What I saw in him, beyond sheer physical gorgeousness, was the possibility of the impossible. The upper lip, the sneer, were a direct extension of the Teddy Boys and Roseland. For Elvis, I sensed at once and soon discovered for a fact, came from the same unregarded stable. He too had started out foredoomed, dispossessed, the most hopeless of White Trash. In pubescence, I read, his ambition had been to grow up a truck driver. Specifically, he'd lusted after the peaked mesh caps that truckers affected; he'd thought these made them look daring. But such heroics, he understood, were beyond him. In the crunch, he was too soft-skinned, too scared, too much a mother's boy. A true trucker he could never be. So he became a Messiah, instead.

An earnest pilgrimage began. But it did not prove easy going. For Protestant Derry, homeplace of the Apprentice Boys, and Rock 'n' Roll were mutual poison. The Teddy Boy riots over Blackboard Jungle *and Bill Haley in England had triggered a panic all over loyalist Ulster. It was not merely as if a teenage rebellion loomed but as if the massed forces of Satan had been unleashed, threatening to wipe out all sanity, ditto sanctity: 'Civilisation as we know it', in the words of* The Derry Sentinel.

For quite some time, all Rock shows, artifacts and films were outlawed. And anyone who challenged this suppression was in for a bumpy ride. Mary Fadden, a comely fifth-former at Northlands, the local girls' school, was expelled for secreting a picture of Jerry Lee Lewis in her desk; discs and posters fuelled bonfires; and Elvis himself was ceremonially torched in effigy at the Brandywell Football Grounds, nailed to a flaming cross. Only Catholics, since idolatry was their nature, were free to devil-worship in peace.

What to do? There seemed only one solution. So my feet took a turn for the worse. In reality, I had ceased to frequent Dinty after a session at which, suggesting that I might benefit from being fitted with metal instep supports, he insisted on taking my inner-thigh measurements. For public consumption, however, I now increased my visits from weekly to almost nightly and, with the freedom thus gained, I went exploring.

Across the river, in Waterside, there was a disused funeral home at which, three nights a week, at 6d a shot, contraband Teen movies could be sat through and sometimes seen, according to the state of the projector. One drawback was that a cross-pollination of embalming fluid and scented wax flowers still hung in the air, an intimation of mortality sickly sweet enough to turn the most fanatic stomach. Still, hunched in the suffocating dark, I drowned myself in Don't Knock The Rock, The Girl Can't Help It *and* I Was A Teenage Werewolf, *had a crush on Eddie Cochran but chose to marry Sheree North.*

The Crypt, as it was aptly named, was just the start. At the gatehouse in Donegal I discovered that by perching myself atop a step-ladder, then balancing the family steam-wireless on a stack of Encyclopaedia Britannica, *1911, in thirty-four volumes, I could jam my left ear up tight against the soundbox, four inches below my bedroom ceiling, and so receive the faintest static-riddled crackling of Radio Luxemburg, a thousand miles away across Europe; at Thos. Mullen, Tonsorial Artist, on Ferryquay Street, back copies of* Titbits *and* Men Only *tutored me in the hit parades, also in anatomy ('Petunia, 19, is an artists' model and this is one pulchritudinous petal that any Old Master would be proud to pluck'); and at last one night at the Palace, the first cinema in town openly to dare show an Elvis film, half-way through the 'Teddy Bear' sequence in* Loving You, *I heard a siren shrieking above, looked up from my lair in the back stalls and saw the balcony overhead shaking, literally buckling, from sheer humping tonnage of wet-knickered nymphs. 'Earthquake!' the inevitable alarmist hollered and a minor stampede ensued, cravens of all persuasions scrabbling wholesale for the exits, like so many extras from* The Last Days of Pompeii.

But I myself failed to budge. For this, I knew well, was no earthquake or even holocaust – it was the end of the world. Or leastways, of civilization as we knew it.

SHELTER ISLAND,
NEW YORK,
JUNE 1988

Mad Mister Mo

This is a true story about Mo.

Mo smelled of chalk all over and he wore a ragged black gown with holes in it. When he walked, he gathered his black gown in tight around him like a shroud. Mo was my history master when I was ten years old, and his clothes and his skin and his breath all smelled of chalk. My father said Mo was a madman, I called him Mad Mister Mo. When he left school at the end of the day, he took off his torn black gown and put on a black overcoat and black hat instead.

My father saw him standing on the edge of the bomb site in the rain. Some small boys were playing football and Mo walked up close to them without making a sound, he just stood there and watched them and didn't speak to them. He was wearing his black overcoat with the collar turned up and his black hat pulled down low over his eyes to protect them from the rain. He stood there and looked at the boys and didn't go away. 'What are you doing?' my father said. 'I'm frightening them,' said Mo, his voice blurred against his collar. 'I'm making them run away.'

Mo was about fifty years of age but he looked older. He had a dark-brown sallow skin that was pulled tight across his cheekbones, and he wore make-up to make his eyes look hollow and agonized. His eyes were yellow and he painted his eyelids with mascara to make them heavy. At the end of the term, when there was no more work to be done, he took a leather-bound copy of *Oliver Twist* out of his desk and read us the bits about Fagin over and over again.

Mo lived in a big greystone mansion house on the outskirts of town and he built a high wire fence all around it. The house was big and square and set in its own gardens, and he lived in it alone with his mother. His mother was blind and crippled; she used to sit out on the front porch in summer and face the garden. I stood outside the wire fence when it was beginning to get dark and I saw her. There were beds of roses and tulips and Mo wouldn't let anyone touch them, they were his own private possessions and he protected them from everyone. He wore his black overcoat and his black hat, he knelt down beside each bloom in turn and made sure that they were all right. It was a slow ritual and it took all afternoon. His blind mother sat on the front porch in her wheelchair and faced towards the smell of flowers. I was shut out of it all, beyond the fence, and I watched everything that happened. Mo knelt down by his yellow and red and pink roses and handled them tenderly.

I stood outside his fence in winter, when it was dark and very cold, and I watched Mo pacing up and down his upstairs room. He left his light on deliberately and he left his curtains wide open, I stood outside his wire fence and watched him. He paced up and down inside his room, his shoulders hunched and his hands clasped behind his back, and I could imagine the glint of his yellow eyes, imagine the white dusty smell of chalk on him. He stood at his lighted window, he must have known I was watching from beyond his fence. And he was silhouetted big and black against his room. He looked out into the dark and didn't move. I watched him and he stood without moving for half an hour on end, black, hunched, staring out.

In class, he wrapped his gown in tight around his body and walked up and down the room. He stood over me and questioned me and, when I couldn't answer, he poked me in the ribs with his forefinger. I stared very hard at the initials carved on my desk and Mo leaned in close, just above me, and breathed chalk on me until my eyes watered. He asked me again and I still didn't know the answer and he lifted me out of my seat by the tufts of hair behind my ears. Everybody turned round to watch us. Then I cried and Mo told me not to be a girl and he kept poking me in the ribs with that long bony forefinger.

I told my father of him and my father complained. Mo said I was wild and sacrilegious and it was impossible to control me. He said that I had no religion and I would suffer for it later. I could flaunt my evilness and think that I was smart but there was no place for smartness in heaven and I would be paid back.

I thought he meant it. I believed that everything he did was serious. One morning I was early into class and I told him I had recanted and Jesus Christ had led me to the light. Mo laughed at me. And he threw out his arms like a mad messiah and he preached me lust and thieving and blasphemy. He shouted at me and he said that religion was bad and murder good, love was bad and hate was right. He preached me the triumphant victories of evil. I looked at him without understanding and nearly cried. When he saw the tears come into my eyes again, he threw a book at my head and went out of the room, gathering his gown around his shoulders. I sat at my desk and did nothing. Then later he came back and laughed at me, but this time he was more gentle. He dug his finger into my ribs and smiled and he told me I was stupid.

In class, Mo declaimed on the destruction and betrayal of villains. 'Remember Rasputin,' he said. 'Think of the way he was killed. Imagine him in the Petersburg palace in all his magnificence, surrounded by enemies and deceivers. He was at a banquet given specially in his honour and was drinking bottle after bottle of red wine, he was wearing a flowing white robe and his long black beard had been combed and he was laughing with pleasure. His enemies were standing all around him and they too were laughing, but they were laughing with malice and not with pleasure. Rasputin was laughing with love in his heart because he had come to marry the beautiful princess, and the princess was there with flowers tied in her hair.

'Now Rasputin walked round the great banquet table and picked up a chocolate. He ate it and it was filled with poison but he didn't seem to notice and he ate another. There was a big box of chocolates and Rasputin ate them all, laughing and thinking of the lovely princess who was shortly to become his bride. When he had finished all the chocolates, he raised his glass of wine and proposed a toast to the princess. The glass had also been filled with poison but Rasputin drank all the wine and still he was behaving quite normally. Then he laughed. His enemies were still standing all around him but they weren't laughing now, they were frightened out of their wits.

'Finally the archduke pulled out a pistol from under his tunic and emptied it into Rasputin's stomach. And then all the other guests did the same and one after another they fired their pistols at the defenceless Rasputin. Rasputin gave one great roar and then he fell down on his back. The archduke gave a smile of triumph and knelt down beside the body to make sure that it was quite dead. But Rasputin wasn't dead, he began to rise from the floor and once again all the nobles had to shoot him. This time he fell down immediately and didn't move.

'The nobles lifted him up and carried him out of the palace down to the River Volga, which was iced over because it was winter. Then they threw Rasputin into the river and, as he fell, he came back to life. He would have escaped but he came up under the ice and there was no way out. Still, with his phenomenal strength, he could have forced his way out, but as he swam along under the ice he remembered his enemies and the way his beautiful princess had betrayed him, and decided to die after all. So he allowed himself to sink to the bottom and there he stayed. When they found him, his hand was frozen into the sign of the cross. And that was how Rasputin died.'

Mo was talking very quietly. He stood behind his desk and watched us through his yellow eyes. 'Please, sir, I thought he was the villain,' I said. 'I thought Rasputin was a bad man.'

Mo laughed. He threw his head right back and he roared and shook with laughter. He laughed so much that it made him cough. Then he quietened down and he sat down at his desk and took out an old dog-eared notebook. He read through it for a bit and finally he wrote in it. 'Look,' he said. 'Take a look at what I've written.' He had scrawled all over the page and I couldn't read his writing. His dirty fingernail pointed to the right place. I spelled it out letter by letter: 'Rasputin was a bad man,' it said. That was all.

'Richard III,' Mo said. 'Imagine him without an army, without a friend, without his kingdom, without even a horse to escape on. He has been hounded down. He has been hunted and beaten and he has been robbed of his crown. He has been brought to his death by the plotting of his enemies. Richard III can see no route of escape. He sinks to his knees in the grass still wet with blood and he prepares to meet his death.'

Mo stopped talking and he looked at me. I was watching the tree outside his window and I didn't want to return his look. He walked up and down in front of my desk and he was smiling at me but he wasn't friendly. He was standing beside me and pressing me lightly in my ribs. 'I think you ought to know,' Mo said, 'Richard III was a bad man, too.'

I told my father about Mo and Rasputin and Richard III. My father said that Mo was mad and a bad influence and he ought to be locked up. He said that Mo was pretending to be the same as Rasputin and Richard III, and that he was frightening us because he wanted to be a villain. An unhappy and betrayed villain like Rasputin, my father said.

On Sunday morning I went walking all through the dockside markets, past the cheap dresses and candy flosses and the travelling salesmen standing on orange crates. I began to walk up the hill back into the city and I came to St Columbus. Mo stood on the steps outside the barred doors and he was shouting but I couldn't understand what it was all about. There were old men and children sitting on the steps in front of him, and Mo stood out in front of the bombed church and looked down into the river and city and the bright dockside market. I sat at his feet with my cap in my hand and I listened. His black coat trailed out behind him, the black hat hid his eyes. I looked up at him and his head was back, his arms were out wide in his favourite stance, and he was weeping.

The old tramps all around him were chewing grass and dried tobacco and took no notice of him. Mo seemed to be drunk, he stood overlooking the bowl of town and water and cheap pink dresses and he tottered. And one moment he was screaming and swearing and then he would suddenly go quiet and say things too soft for me to hear. He shook his fist at the sky and tears rolled down his leather cheeks. I sat on the steps below him and watched. He wouldn't be quiet and the words kept coming but I couldn't understand him.

It was cold and windy and Mo's black coat blew out behind him. He crouched over me and spoke to me softly, urgently, pointing down at the river and the stalls of the market. The black hat covered us both. He was speaking into my ear and his voice was thick. I still couldn't make him out but he was swearing and complaining and crying. He turned towards the bombed shell of the church and tried to spit but he only succeeded in dribbling down his own chin. He was talking about God. The wind blew grit into our eyes and the tramps chewed their own cuds. I think he was swearing and blaspheming against God. He was shaking his fist at heaven and I think he said that God was a whore.

I went home to my father and told him all about it. My father laughed. He said that Mo was a disgusting old drunk and a big ham actor. My father said he was despicable, I wasn't to be frightened of him or take any notice of him.

The last time I saw Mo was on Hallowe'en night, when we all lit fireworks. There was a big lawn opposite our house and high bank on the far side of the lawn. I lit the fireworks on the lawn and then I ran up the bank to watch them. My parents and all their friends stood in rows on top of the bank and their feet got slowly colder as the night went on.

The fireworks and us made a little patch of warmth in the middle of the dark. The Roman candles went up, red and green and yellow and blue, flew up into the air and burst. They flared up and something moved behind them. I lit a catherine wheel and it threw yellow flames across the dark and I could see a black shape moving somewhere in the background. The shape moved around the flames, turned towards us and it changed into a human body. It came slowly across the lawn and up the bank, and we huddled together in a tight little ball of warmth and waited. It was Mo. He walked towards us and the fireworks shone on his yellow eyes. I put my arm across my mouth, bit on the sleeve. Mo walked straight up to me and looked at me and he didn't have any expression on his face. Mad Mister Mo. The fireworks went bang bang behind his head. And I could smell the chalk on him. He stood there and looked at me and then he walked away. Moved slowly away and through the flames again and back into the dark.

He looked at me and then he went away. The next morning I went to school but Mo had gone away to another town and I never saw him again. Inside my desk, his notebook was open at a page, I looked at it and read. It didn't take me long. Eighteen letters, five words. 'Rasputin was a bad man,' it said.

I Am Still The Greatest
Says Johnny Angelo

A t the age of four, Johnny owned a red suit, a bright-red suit. It had tight, red trousers that tapered gently to the ankle, and a chunky-cut jacket, low-hung to below the waist, which was given added style by its bulky shoulder-padding. Attached was a matching red hood and, on top of this hood, there was a brilliant white pompom.

Again, the whiteness of the pompom was echoed by a white scarf, twirled once, twirled twice around his neck and then slung casually over his left shoulder to trail half-way down his back.

At the far end of his mother's back yard, there was a high brick wall, ten foot high by thirty foot long with a thickness of nine inches across the top. It was a crumbling and weather-beaten wall. And one day Johnny did a catwalk on top of it.

He climbed the wall in his red suit. He climbed it painfully, by centimetres and millimetres, inching up and falling back again, crawling up it by his fingertips. Twice he fell back to the bottom again. On the third attempt, he made it.

His head appeared over the top, the shrewd fat face of a baby, puckered with concentration and framed by the big red hood with the white pompom.

It was a very windy day. His mother was hanging out

washing in the yard below, sheets and blankets that were caught by the wind and billowed up in her face. And the wind blew grit in Johnny's eyes, but he pulled himself up by his shoulders, until first his left knee and then his right were wedged solidly on top of the wall. Then he stood up and dusted himself.

He looked around. He had never been so high in his life. His mother was working in the yard below and Johnny shot her down with his forefinger. Then he did the catwalk.

His knees were stiff and his back was straight, his head was held high, his eyes looked straight ahead. His red suit shone.

He marched from one end of the wall to the other, then back again, then back once more. He marched stiffly, in the style of the Nazis, his leg held rigid at knee and hip. His white scarf billowed behind him in the wind.

Mrs Canning from 23 was the first to see him. She was washing her windows and she saw him on the wall, a child aged four, fat and squat, very solemn. She threw up her window and yelled at him. 'Johnny! Johnny! Come down off that wall!'

Johnny took no notice. He turned once more at the end of the wall and began the slow march back. His mother looked up and saw him. Then everyone knew and windows were raised all along the street. *Come down, Johnny, come down. Come down off that wall*. But Johnny didn't.

He kept on walking still. Once his foot slipped, a brick broke from the wall and fell and split in two. Johnny Angelo marched from one end of the wall to the other in his bright-red suit. He looked tiny and he had a very long way to fall. His mother began to weep.

Then Mr Stein from 34 came down in his shirtsleeves and tried to climb the wall. He was too heavy, he couldn't make it. Then the other people arrived and stood in the yard, shouting instructions. And Johnny walked above their heads and wouldn't come down.

They stood in clusters and watched him. The whole street was awake. A ladder was placed against the wall and Mr Parkes from 8 began to ascend. But the wood was rotten, a rung gave way and Mr Parkes fell heavily, turning his ankle.

Johnny Angelo wasn't reachable.

At the age of four, he walked the wall and everyone watched. His white scarf was whipped by the wind, his red suit gleamed and, when he was bored, he swung his legs over the side; glanced once at the crowd below and shinned down to the ground.

Then they all went home to tea.

Mrs Angelo was forty-one years of age. She was thin and tired and grey-faced. She coughed in the mornings and gasped for breath and stopped to hold her side half-way up a flight of stairs. Johnny Angelo didn't like her: she smelled of exhaustion.

She wore a white housecoat that was stained to grey and brown. It was frayed at the hem and almost worn through at the elbow. She wore it in the kitchen when she read the paper. She was wearing it in the morning when Johnny came out to school and she was still wearing it when he come home in the late afternoon.

Her home fell into disrepair. There was a front room and a back room. The back room was the centre of everything. It was the kitchen and the washroom and the dining room. Johnny slept in it with his two sisters while his mother and his father slept in the front room, which was the best room. Then there was the back yard and there was also an attic, where Johnny Angelo was alone.

When he was six, he began to be disgusted.

The brown paint peeled off the back room walls and nothing was done to put it right. Johnny was ashamed to return from school. The beds weren't made, the sink was stacked with dirty washing, the drains were blocked. There was a sad sick smell everywhere.

His father was a silent man who worked in the docks. He used to spend all his spare time in his allotment and not come home until dark. Then he sat in an armchair and didn't speak.

Johnny's mother woke up coughing. He heard her scuffle in the front room, gasping for breath. When she came through into the back room, her flesh was grey and her hair hung all in rats' tails about her neck. She lit a cigarette. The milkman knocked on the door, his mother turned a blank face towards the noise. The tap was running. Then Johnny Angelo rolled over and turned against the wall.

The same thing, day after day. The exact same faces and expressions, the same walls – Johnny Angelo was bored and he walked the wall in his bright-red suit.

He was sent to bed at seven.

His sisters, who were older, played card games on the kitchen table. Johnny lay in his bed, pretending to be asleep, but his eyes were open.

Inside the front room, his mother was talking to his father but his father didn't reply. The door was closed: light came through the cracks.

Each time a card hit the table, there was a slapping sound. Johnny Angelo waited for it. Five seconds passed and a card hit, slap. Then the two sisters watched each other across the table and Johnny waited. In between each slap, there was a silence and then another card hit, slap, and then another, slap, and the sisters watched each other and there was silence and Johnny watched from beneath the bedclothes.

Then his sisters saw him and were angry: 'Johnny, go to sleep.'

'Johnny, you are watching.'

'Johnny, I will tell.'

At the age of six, that's when Johnny Angelo retreated to the attic upstairs.

It was dirty, dank and damp, ten foot by seven. The roof slanted in on him and the attic was filled with discards of every description, with thrown-out clothes and books and broken toys. Rain came in through the roof, the skylight rattled in its frame. Everything smelled of dust and Johnny sat cross-legged on the floor, counting. This was his personal property.

He climbed up to his attic by rope ladder and drew it up behind him. He drilled a peephole in the trapdoor and squatted on the attic floor, his eye to the hole, watching.

He saw the people who came to visit. He heard his mother coughing, he knew his father was sitting in the armchair. Then he watched his sisters playing cards, he watched the cards slap on the table and he heard his sisters singing.

His mother shouted when his dinner was cooked. *Johnny, come and eat. Come down.* But Johnny stayed where he was and didn't come down.

He turned into a jackdaw.

He stole anything that he came across and hoarded it in his attic. Books, caps, football boots. Toy cards, comics, badges, popcorn, spanners, socks and saucepans. Each item sorted and catalogued, as follows: one dumdum thirty-eight; one cowboy hat; three spotted handkerchiefs; one hundred bangbang caps; one Dan Dare mask, flawed.

He filed everything, stored them in order, then gloated on them in the secrecy of his attic. What did he want? He wanted more.

In particular, he wanted turnip watches. Big flat turnips with umpteen hands. When he opened them up, it was like dissecting a frog, there was so much to notice, to study and compare. Hands that turned fast and hands that turned slowly, the ticking of engines, the whirring of motors. And miniscule cogs that interwove, that twined and drew apart, over and over. Then he closed them up again and the fronts were smooth and smug, very fat and it was a comforting thing, a turnip, to jiggle in his hand. To look at in the attic. To keep as a pet.

When he had collected twenty watches, Johnny Angelo took them all to pieces and, using the very best parts of each, he manufactured a turnip of his own design. It had five hands and they all went round at different speeds. They kept their own time, they moved in private cycles, 11 or 18 or 29 hours to their day.

In this style, Johnny made his speeds the way he wanted them, he retreated inside a secret pace and, when he was eight years old, he went thieving in the market.

He was tall for his age, pretty and he had soft gold hair that fell across his eyes. His eyes were big and black. He fluttered his lashes, bit his lip and old gentlemen adored him.

In the Sunday morning markets, he cruised. Fruit markets and flower markets and fish markets. There were winkles and eels and cockles and whelks. Canaries and mockingbirds and nightingales. Fields of yellow silk and the stalls all thrown together in a heap, everything mingled, where the market flowed on like a river. Then Johnny Angelo turned around and turnips winked at him from everywhere he looked, sitting all snug inside their pockets. His hand snaked out and plucked them one by one. Round and smooth and sleek and warm, they nestled like white mice in the palm of his hand.

Back inside his attic, he had a mirror in a gilded frame. He set it up against the slanting roof, jammed between the ceiling and the floor. Then he studied himself.

The skylight rattled in its sockets, rats skittered in the walls. And Johnny Angelo had a black Gladstone bag, inside which there jingled a dozen assorted turnips of varying description.

For instance, he selected a golden watch with silver engravings and he held it flat in his right hand. He smiled in the mirror, he frowned, he winked. Or he chose a heavy silver turnip with a false compartment for photographs and a sepia snapshot of a man with curled moustaches, then he placed it in his breast pocket so that the winder just peeped out coyly over the top. He looked soulful. He turned down the corners of his mouth and he drooped his nostrils. He sat cross-legged and watched himself. His mother was calling him for tea. He sat with his back to the mirror and sneaked glances at himself over his shoulder. He had golden hair and golden flesh: he was considered beautiful. He had many watches all laid out in a row.

His tea was burned. The back room was filled with smoke and the windows were steamed over. Johnny's father sat in the armchair and didn't speak. This man had worked in the docks for twenty-eight years. When he reached retiring age, he would be given a silver turnip watch.

At seven o'clock, directly after he'd finished his tea, Johnny was sent to bed. Motorbikes were revving up in the streets outside. His sisters were playing dominoes at the kitchen table, his mother was sitting by the fire with her eyes shut. The fire was on her face; fire and shadow, sound and silence. The dominoes rattled on the board and Johnny's eyes were opening and shutting. The back room was very dark and he folded his knees into his belly. His eyes were opening and shutting all the time.

When he woke up, it was three in the morning and everything was still. Johnny rose up and climbed into his attic. Then he picked out five of his very finest turnips and arranged them in a line before the mirror. Then he sat down cross-legged behind them.

Johnny Angelo and a row of five watches: it made him happy and he sat watching for a very long time. He thought it was something quite beautiful and he wanted to keep it for ever, to trap it in his hand.

So he went out and stole a camera. At four o'clock in the morning he hurled a brick through a shop window and listened to the crash of falling glass. No one came. Johnny reached his hand through the hole and picked out the best-looking camera in the shop. He enjoyed this. He liked in particular the shattering of the glass, the jagged circle of the hole and the silence that surrounded him. And he walked home with his camera tucked openly under his arm, straight down the centre of the empty High Street.

Almost at dawn, he took pictures of his own reflection. Pictures of the five watches in a row and him sitting cross-legged behind them, pictures of him smiling and pictures of him looking sad. Pictures of Johnny Angelo.

At the age of fourteen, Johnny Angelo was a heart-throb.

He had three-inch sideboards and he wore his hair swept high in a golden quiff, from which one lock detached itself and fell forward into his eyes. His smile was lopsided. And his mouth was full of the whitest teeth.

This is what he wore: scarlet silken shirts, open at the neck, and tight torero pants; white kid shoes with golden buckles; a photograph of Elvis Presley right next to his heart; a silver crucifix. All over his neighbourhood, he was known as Speedoo.

He was loved. Every morning, when he walked into class, all the little schoolgirls hung out of their windows and strained to catch a glimpse of him. Their skirts were rucked way up beyond their knees, their ponytails swung low. Waiting for Johnny Angelo, they scrawled his name in lipstick, one hundred times.

He was also greatly hated. On the far side of the schoolyard, right opposite the girls, there were classrooms full of young boys. And the things that the girls so adored, the white kid shoes and the lopsided smile, these were the exact same things that the boys most abhorred.

Each day, Johnny was late.

Five minutes, then ten, then fifteen: he sauntered down slow and everyone waited. And he used a special walk, known as Shooting the Agate, where he hooked his thumbs inside his belt and he hunched his shoulders, he flicked his ankles out sideways at every step and, of course, there was a cigarette slouching from his bottom lip.

When he came into the schoolyard, he carried his books in a luncheon box, tied up in red braces, and he moved very slow, not looking to left or to right.

On one side of the schoolyard, the young girls stretched out their arms and pelted him with Jelly Babies; on the other, the boys took aim with their pea-shooters and shot him right between the eyes. Either way, Johnny kept on walking still.

But when he reached the portals, right before he disappeared, he half-turned. For the girls and the boys alike, he let one small smile flicker in the corner of his mouth, he let one hand trail behind him, fingers outstretched, and he Shot the Agate.

Somebody screamed.

Then he was gone.

He bought a pair of blue suede shoes and they filled his life. Sitting at the back of the classroom, he put his feet up on the radiator and he couldn't stop staring, his eyes were dazzled by blue and these shoes had pointed toes, sharp steel tips, pure white stitching.

Each night, he spent thirty minutes cleaning them with a soft felt brush, one hundred strokes with his left hand, one hundred strokes with his right. Then he wrapped them in chamois leather and took many pictures of their reflections. And the time came soon when he didn't even wear them but carried them around in his luncheon box, tied up in red braces.

When nobody was looking, he took them out and held their softness against his cheek. He was happy then. But one morning he came into class and dirty words were scrawled on the blackboard: *Goodbye Blue Suede Shoes*.

Sure enough, the afternoon arrived when Johnny was working out in the swimming baths, diving off the high board, swooping like a swallow, and then he came back into the changing rooms and the blue suede shoes were destroyed. They had been scuffed and splayed and spat upon, abused in every way imaginable and, scarred across the toes with a rusty penknife, there was an epitaph, as follows:

'*Adios Amigo*.'

Then a certain ritual was established, by which Johnny's enemies hid up an alley and each afternoon, when he walked home from school, they jumped out and hit him.

Each morning, he was screamed at; in the afternoon, he was beaten up. But Catsmeat truly loved him.

Who was Catsmeat?

Catsmeat was a mental deficient, who wore orange fluorescent socks, and he was an albino, with flesh as shapeless and soggy as sourdough. And one morning, when he leaned out of his window, he saw Johnny Angelo come into the schoolyard and he saw the blue suede shoes, the scarlet shirt, the crucifix, and Johnny half turned, half smiled, one lock of his hair fell over his eyes and his mouth was full of the whitest teeth. And Catsmeat said nothing but turned aside and he wept.

Inside the gymnasium, Johnny turned circles on the horizontal bar, beautiful slow parabolas, and Catsmeat watched him through the window, his nose splayed flat against the glass. He had a crewcut, he had pink piggy eyes. Every time that Johnny passed through a door, it was Catsmeat who held it open.

But Johnny didn't notice, he was busy thinking of his bright-red suit, his blue suede shoes. He combed his hair in the mirror. He practised his lopsided smile. He sat on the schoolyard wall, reading *Elvis Monthly*, and young girls surrounded him but he felt no lust, he went to the movies instead.

*

Down in the market, he payed his rent with his fingertips and his table was piled high with silver cigarette cases, cufflinks, diamond tiepins. Soon he grew wealthy and he ordered double portions of froth on his coffee, he bought a cut-throat razor with an ivory handle.

The jukebox was silver and gold, it had coloured spangles that twinkled as it played. Johnny Angelo sat in the corner booth, and Catsmeat told him jokes, performed tricks, darned his socks, while good hard rock swept over them.

Then it was Friday night and *Jailhouse Rock* was playing at the Roxy.

The Roxy was a motion-picture coliseum of 1931, B. De Mille baroque, complete with sweeping stairways and marbled pillars and mighty Wurlitzers, cupids and gargoyles. These last years, however, it had begun to decline. The stucco was crumbling, the Wurlitzer was no longer used, rats ran in the aisles. Most nights, it was three quarters empty, it was cold as a morgue and rain fell through the roof.

But on this Friday night, the queues stretched three times round the block and many hundreds were turned away. Only the leather boys were admitted, their pockets all bulging with rocks and knives and bicycle chains, brass knuckles and the final equalizer.

Tonight there was no popcorn sold, no drinks on a stick and there were no lovers holding hands. Instead there were policemen patrolling the runways, torches in their hands, and policemen on the balconies and policemen at all the doors. And then there were the leather boys, who divided up into blocs, some saying that Bill Haley was King and others saying No, it was Elvis.

Johnny Angelo was up on the second balcony, crouching in the dark, and he was combing his hair, he was smiling all lopsided. Then the lights went down and the screen was filled by pictures of Elvis.

Jailhouse Rock: Elvis played a truck driver who kills a man in a fist fight and gets himself sent to the penitentiary. Inside the prison barbershop, his hair is shorn and his sideboards razored off entirely.

And the first lock of his hair to fall, this was the precise moment that the riot began in the Roxy.

High up among the gargoyles, the leather boys stamped their feet and the policemen flashed their torches. Elvis's sideboards were sheared down to the bone and girls began to weep and there was the noise of flick-knives snapping open. Then Elvis emerged with a crewcut and somebody jeered, saying Bill Haley is Best, and the very next thing his flesh was slashed with razors.

Johnny Angelo rose up, and Catsmeat beside him, and everyone began to stampede. The policemen formed into lines and swung their truncheons. Girls screamed and klaxons sounded and great hunks of stucco crashed down into the stalls, a gun went Bang and all this time the leather boys were chanting: El Vis, El Vis, El Vis.

Then Elvis was singing 'Jailhouse Rock' itself, and his hair was long again, his sideboards black and shiny, and he switched his hips, he leered across his shoulder. Dancing on a rampart, sliding down a drainpipe, he squirmed and shook and shuddered, he strutted all over and this is what he meant: Fuck You.

Everyone was moving in the dark, and Johnny Angelo put his knee through the seat in front of him, the wood exploded, and he slashed at the cushions with his razor, and the stuffing came spilling out in handfuls, all grey and musty, and then someone was running towards him, a Bill Haley fan, wishing to hurt him but Johnny reached out real slow and he stuck a thick wad of stuffing straight down his attacker's throat, choking him.

There was blood on the floor. Catsmeat reached down and touched it. It was slippery in his fingers and, meanwhile, Johnny reached the edge of the balcony and went clean over the edge, grabbing a gargoyle by its throat, shinning down the stucco, and then he leapt into the runway, his knife still in his hand, and Elvis was leering, and Elvis was squirming, huge motion pictures, and a policeman was dying, his skull smashed in with a hammer.

Johnny Angelo stood still.

And Elvis was saying Fuck You.

So Johnny ran hard up the aisle and there was a great confused mass of flesh across his path but he smashed straight through, out the other side and on, until he came into a doorway and then there was a policeman, his face loomed up white and he swung his truncheon, he yelled for Johnny to stop. But Johnny didn't, he held his knife out in front of him and he kept right on, he ran directly through the lawman's guts. His knife went in deep and twisted. Then Johnny pulled it out again and the policeman fell down. Then Johnny went out in the street.

Outside in the street, it was empty and silent and still. Johnny's heels clattered down the pavement, he ran up an alley and he hid behind some trashcans. He sat down in the slops and wiped the blood off his knife. His knife had an ivory handle.

Johnny combed his hair.

'Fuck you,' said Johnny Angelo, and he lived in a cold-water room on Bogside, the hallway was full of cats and he smiled his lopsided smile. He flicked his ankles out sideways. He hid his eyes behind big black shades. He turned the jukebox way up high.

Most nights he went inside a club called Heartbreak Hotel, down in the docklands. High above his head, there was a disused church, where vagrants and derelicts stayed, and motorbikes were stacked in rows along the quays. The wind cut sharply off the river, blowing back Johnny's quiff like a plume. Everything was silent. Everything was still.

Heartbreak Hotel was a cellar, filled with a livid purplish light, and all the girls sat stiff-backed along one wall. Tight dresses and lipstick, they sported high-heeled shoes but the boys ignored them, preferring to huddle in their own tight circles, where they told dirty jokes and snickered, where they smoked cigarettes.

In particular, there was a rider named Ace, the leader of the pack. He wore a black leather jacket with silver studding down the back, tight black leather pants, high black boots and he had a face like a weasel, all skinny and shifty and starved.

Why was he the leader? Just because he smoked a cigarette with perfect style and, down in Heartbreak Hotel, this was the only thing that counted.

The elegance with which the smoker inhaled; the length of

time that the smoke remained in the lungs; the smoothness with which it was then expunged through the nostrils; the condition of the smoker, e.g. the absence of gasping or watery eyes; and, finally, the wrist-action with which the smoker dispatched the ash – all of these things were crucial and Ace was an artist, he couldn't be topped.

Johnny Angelo challenged him.

A beer crate was placed in the middle of the floor and Johnny crouched on one side. Ace on the other. Twenty cigarettes were laid out between them, a lighter and an ashtray, and all of the leather boys ranged in ranks behind Ace, and Catsmeat stood behind Johnny.

These were the rules: the contestants took turns to inhale and they continued to smoke without a pause until one of them cracked.

And Johnny was flash.

His style was full of flourishes, allusions, baroque embellishments. Just the way that he flared his nostrils and the smoke poured forth so smooth, this alone was enough to draw murmurs of admiration from the leather boys and Ace seemed crude by comparison. Nonetheless, he had lungs like indiarubber, he had stamina that was infinite and eight cigarettes were smoked in succession but neither Johnny nor Ace gave ground.

Nobody spoke, no one moved: Johnny Angelo blew smoke rings, then poked his finger through the hole, very idle, and a purple haze hung over everything. Ace sucked deep and Johnny watched him, stared him down until he sweated and his face was pinched like a ferret.

The tenth cigarette was completed, then the eleventh and Johnny kept watching, and Ace kept sweating. Flicking ash, Johnny yawned and stretched and, half-way through the twelfth cigarette, Ace just suddenly upped and quit. He ground out the butt beneath his heel, he walked away into the docklands. Then everyone sighed and the jukebox started playing, while Catsmeat wept.

At the age of fifteen, Johnny led the pack.

The leather boys drifted round the beer crate and formed a ragged circle around him. Then Johnny let a very small smile flicker in the corner of his mouth, he let one hand trail behind him, fingers outstretched, and he led a parade of motorbikes.

At three o'clock in the morning, he emerged from Heartbreak Hotel and nothing stirred. All the ships were tied up, all their crews were down in the cabins and the quays were quite deserted. Very far away, the derelicts whimpered in their sleep.

Right then, out of silence, there came an explosion like an earthquake, a sudden howl of engines, and the whole of the docklands shook. Windows rattled in their frames, loose bricks fell crashing into the street and then, out of the debris, Johnny Angelo came riding on a motorbike, a black monster on a black machine.

So many years, he'd listened to the bikes revving up in the alley and now he rode out front, black leather and black helmet, a yellow dragon emblazoned on his back and one word, ELVIS, spelled out in silver studding.

Very slowly, soberly, the riders moved out of the docks and into Bogside and on through all the city. Everything was empty, all the streets were stilled and this was a solemn procession, Johnny Angelo first, then Catsmeat, then all of Johnny's followers, fanned out in formation, and they passed through like ghosts, not looking to left or to right.

'I am the greatest,' said Johnny Angelo and, when he was twenty-four, he rode on a golden Cadillac.

Entering a city, he wore a suit of golden velvet, shoes of golden suede and his hair fell to his shoulders. Standing on top of his Cadillac, he waved and smiled and blew kisses and, all around him, there were black-leather riders on black motorbikes, known as the Mighty Avengers.

Behind the golden Cadillac, there came a long black limousine, in which sat Johnny's intimates, Catsmeat and Yolande, and his hair-stylist, his masseur and his valet, his astrologer and his tennis coach, plus a selection of pretty young starlets.

And behind the black limousine, there came an open wagon, which was filled with varied performers, Johnny Angelo's private circus, complete with clowns and jugglers and tumblers, belly dancers and dwarves, contortionists and bearded ladies and, also, his mother, his father and his two older sisters.

Finally, behind the open wagon, there came a series of trailers, in which were caged wild animals, who roared and shrieked and howled, who screamed abuse through the bars.

Very slowly, this cavalcade nosed through the crowds and, when it reached the heart of the city, the wagon opened its doors. Music played loudly, the voice of Johnny Angelo boomed from a dozen hidden loudspeakers and out rushed freaks of every description, hunchbacks and midgets and spastics, stringbeans and albinos, who ran among the crowd and showered them with confetti, and pulled faces, turned somersaults and gave out countless autographed pictures of Johnny Angelo.

Raised high upon his Cadillac, meanwhile, Johnny held a single white rose. Smiling rather sadly, he cast it high into the air where it hung for a moment, hovered, and then it dropped down in the street, where it was torn apart by a thousand clutching hands, while Johnny passed by.

Once inside his dressing room, he took two full hours to prepare himself. Everywhere that he performed, it was his habit to send a team of interior decorators ahead of him, who equipped his rooms with gilded mirrors and chandeliers, Persian rugs, Egyptian tapestries and a satin *chaise longue* for Johnny himself, on which he now reclined, sucking on a liquorice stick.

And first, his stylist combed his hair, one hundred strokes with the left hand, one hundred strokes with the right, and then drew it back in an eighteenth-century ponytail, tied up with a black velvet bow.

Second, his beautician painted his eyes, using liner and shadow and thick mascara, and coated his teeth with sparkling white oil, and powdered his golden flesh, and lastly touched his mouth lightly with lipstick.

Third, his manicurist shaped his fingernails, and his masseur toned up his muscles, and Catsmeat read him poetry, and Yolande licked inside his ear.

Finally, his valet dressed him in a suit of baby-blue velvet, with pants so tight that it took him five minutes to get them on, and buckled blue suede shoes, and white knee socks, and his jeweller hung him heavy with monogrammed bracelets, diamond earrings and, of course, a silver crucifix.

In Johnny Angelo's life, everything was a ritual and, just before he went on stage, he faced his astrologer, who consulted charts and Tarot cards. If these turned out badly, the whole performance was cancelled. But if the omens were auspicious, nothing on earth could stop him and he smiled his golden smile, Sun God Johnny Angelo.

On stage, his followers were already raging and the auditorium was filled with entertainments of every kind. Simultaneously, there were trapezists and trick cyclists and high-wire artists, trampolinists who bounced into the balconies, belly dancers who strutted their stuff by candlelight, and wild animals who prowled the aisles, chimpanzees and llamas and baby leopards, and there were liveried servants who scurried everywhere, distributing capons among the audience, sweet-meats and guavas, pomegranates and fat black grapes, and that wasn't all, there were also sword-swallowers, human torches, boxing kangaroos and, most important of all, there were goatskins full of rough Algerian wine, which were passed from hand to hand, until everyone was flushed and roaring, howling for Johnny Angelo and then, without warning, the lights went out.

In a single mauve spotlight, Catsmeat emerged from the shadows and climbed up into a podium, a pulpit. He wore a white silk suit, a pink carnation in his buttonhole, and he was round like a human doughnut, he had pink piggy eyes.

Inside this auditorium, there were ten or twenty or fifty thousand small girls, all of whom lived for Johnny Angelo, and now they began to scream, they began to weep and wring their hands. Lost in the dark, they called his name, they fainted, they bayed. Down on their knees, they prayed.

For several minutes, Catsmeat said nothing. Basking in his pool of purple light, he felt no urgency, he was happy here. Smirking, he picked his nose and, even when he finally made his announcement, it carried no hysteria, it was almost conversational: 'Johnny Angelo,' he said.

Somewhere in the wings, trumpets played a Purcell fanfare, very stately, and Johnny was revealed, standing motionless on top of his golden Cadillac, one arm raised, just like the Statue of Liberty.

Solemn and slow, he travelled across the darkened stage and nobody screamed, every sound was stilled. Very stern, he froze the audience and he held them like that, he permitted no kind of levity. But then, without warning, he suddenly jack-knifed and he jumped up high in the air, he flew and, in that instant, even as he was airborne, everything exploded.

Lights flashed and flames leaped up and mirrors glinted all over the auditorium, blinding and distorting, and a hundred musicians thumped, strummed and blew, and bass drums rolled like thunder, and electric guitars wailed like sirens, and then Johnny hit the ground, his legs began to tremble.

The noise was frightening: out of the dark, there came wave after wave of a sound that was screaming, yet resembled no scream that you'd ever heard. It had no rise and fall, no variation, almost no emotion, and it shattered all the windows, so that the audience was showered with splintered glass, and it went on for ever, it was quite relentless.

And this was the truth of Johnny Angelo, that he was all things at once, masculine and feminine and neuter, active and passive, animal and vegetable, and he was satanic, messianic, kitch and camp, and psychotic, and martyred, and just plain dirty.

He twitched and squirmed and shuddered. He ran his hand down inside his thigh and tickled. His head was tucked in against his shoulder, very coy, and he pouted, he fluttered his eyelashes. He blew fat kisses from red wet lips. He staggered with emotion. He fell down on his knees, grovelling in the dust, and then his hips rose up and over, he raised himself, and his baby blue pants split open from knee to crotch, the girls glimpsed golden flesh. Or he sang songs of heartbreak and he buried his face in his hands, moving very slow, like a man in an underwater dream. Or he leered and he scowled, he ground his groin and every defenceless virgin in the world was raped, he beat them and he whipped them, he kicked them in the guts and stomped them underfoot and fucked them till they fainted.

Or he minced. Or he slithered his legs like serpents, he stretched them out like tentacles, and he bent them back double, he tied them up in knots, and he sprawled them all over the stage, nothing else existed. He blasphemed. He wept. He cowered, begging for mercy: 'Am I clean?' he said.

And the screams got louder and louder and louder. Down in the darkness, the small girls were rending their hair, were tearing their own flesh and they writhed in religious ecstasy, and their bodies were racked by spasms, their eyes rolled up, and there were some that pissed themselves, there were others that were covered in vomit. A sordid detail, but true, there were many that ripped the legs from their seats and thrust them under their skirts, mauling themselves most horribly.

Johnny Angelo's hair was undone, it tumbled down around his shoulders, and he was dripping sweat. His mascara ran, his lipstick was smeared all over his face. His clothes were torn in many places and his golden flesh was soggy and his face became a swamp. His eyes went blind. His mouth hung open. When he was twenty-four, he was ugly.

He was pelted with jelly babies and hairclips and cigarette butts, teddy bears and coins. A gilt bracelet hit him full on the mouth, splitting his lip, and blood flowed over his face. Blood stained his blue velvet suit, blood fell on the stage, blood got in his eyes and he stumbled, he collapsed in a heap.

On his knees, he clutched at his heart and, taking out a white silk handkerchief, he soaked it in his blood, he let it fall into the audience.

With a last convulsive effort, he tried to rise. Just for a moment, he almost made it, he staggered three steps forward but then he suddenly crumpled and fell down on his back, spreadeagled, his arms and his legs stretched out in the shape of crucifixion.

Catsmeat ran on in his white silk suit, and others behind him, and they carried Johnny Angelo, limp and shattered from the stage. Just as they reached the wings, however, he revived and he threw them all off, he came storming back on his stage and he grabbed the microphone and he reached out with his blood-stained hands: 'Am I clean?' he said. 'Can you touch me?'

*

There follows a transcript of a press conference given by Johnny Angelo, sitting in his suite at the Hotel Excelsior, on 14 April 1964:

'What is your favourite colour?'

'My favourite colour is baby blue.'

'Are you pleased to be here?'

'It's wonderful to be back.'

'How do you feel about your latest record?'

'I'm so very happy to see it in the charts, it's a thrill, and I wish to thank all my loyal fans, who put it there and make my life worth while.'

'How is your tour going?'

'Great business. Just great business.'

'Any amusing incidents?'

'Just one so far: in Decatur, a little girl came to the stage door and asked to see me. Of course, I try to meet my fans whenever possible, I make it my duty, but imagine my surprise when in came a very small child, no more than eight years old, who was clutching a battered teddy bear, and she curtsied, she stepped right up to me, bold as brass, and she said to me, "Johnny Angelo," she said, "please will you give teddy a kiss, because teddy wants to marry you." '

'Are you happy?'

'I am very happy.'

'Why aren't you married?'

'I believe that the right girl has not yet come along. Someday I hope to meet my dream and fall in love but, until that happy time, I will endure by myself.'

'Are you very rich?'

'My wealth is beyond all reckoning.'

'What is your temperament?'

'I am very sensitive. Sometimes almost too sensitive – I am a leaf blown by the wind, a naked nerve, and the merest breeze may bring me pain.'

'What is the nature of your appeal?'

'I am the world of dreams, the Thousand Nights of Arabia, and I am all things at once, all heroes and all villains. I am the Wonderful Wizard of Oz, the sneaky Doctor Strange, the secret Count Mordo, who flies by night, and the glamorous Mr

Universe. I provide, and you may quote me on this, a teenage fulfilment of fantasy.'

'In other words?'

'I fuck.'

'What are your ambitions?'

'My personal ambition is happiness; my professional ambition is likewise.'

'Who do you admire?'

.'Among my favourites are Lord Byron and Elvis Presley, the Mad Monk Rasputin, Howard Hughes and Our Lord Jesus Christ.'

'What are your hobbies?'

'I am partial to pinball.'

'Where is your family?'

'My mother is dead, my twin brother is also dead and my father is an oil tycoon, who lives by himself on a very large estate. When I was only five years old, he ran away with a waitress and I was left to keep us alive. For years, we scrabbled and starved in a rat-infested basement, until my mother died of TB and my brother ran off to sea and my two sisters turned to alcohol, sousing themselves in gin, the first sad step on the road to prostitution. By God's good grace, I was spared and I persevered until things began to break my way. When I was twenty-one, I rode on a golden Cadillac, I was worshipped by millions and I travelled to my father's distant estates. For three days and nights, I drove without stopping, until I arrived at a long winding driveway and, at the end of this driveway, I drew up in front of a house like a palace. I knocked on the door. For some minutes, I waited in the cold but then the lock turned and a face appeared, the face of my father. I looked deep into his eyes. I smiled. Just as I was going to embrace him, however, he suddenly shrank back and his eyes were blank. "Who are you?' my father said.'

'What happened then?'

'I went away.'

'Did you weep?'

'I returned to my fans, who love me, and I learned to live again.'

'Do you believe in God?'

'I do.'

'What is your preferred foodstuff?'

'My most favourite is knickerbocker glory de luxe, which consists of vanilla ice-cream, chocolate and coffee and strawberry, poured over with hot chocolate sauce, and crushed pineapple sauce, and butterscotch and melba sauce, plus a turret of fresh whipped cream, sprinkled with pistachio and topped with a morello cherry, the whole thing combining into a fantasia.'

'What do you value?'

'It is sacred to be clean.'

'How many cars do you run?'

'I own seven cars.'

'Are you paranoid?'

'I am fastidious. I am a creative artist, which means that I am condemned to solitude, for inspiration is loneliness, and I am repelled by squalor, I cannot live with ugliness or tedium.'

'Do you sleep in the nude?'

'I refuse this question.'

'Are you lonely?'

'All men are lonesome.'

'Do you like women?'

'I do not.'

'Why not?'

'In my view, a woman is a vulture and she is full of shit, she's a wheedler and whiner and twister. The man that trusts her consigns himself to hellfire and she will gobble him up like popcorn. Plus, her body disgusts me and the way that she fucks is distasteful, all the ways that she screams and scratches and smells, with no sense of dignity – these things repel me and it is also true that a woman will destroy you, casting you aside as soon as you're squeezed dry, and she is dirty in her habits, her flesh is soft and sloppy.'

'Have you ever been in love?'

'Once, I was worshipped by a girl named Astrid, who sat with me in the soda fountain, and we drew Love Hearts on the steamed-up window sipping Coca-Cola, one bottle, two straws. Very soon, she wore my highschool ring and I kissed her lips by moonlight, I wished upon a star.'

'What went wrong?'

'Her folks did not agree. A child of the ghettoes, I came from the wrong side of town and I rode a motorbike, I wore black leathers. When her father saw me, he locked Astrid up in her bedroom and threw away the key.'

'Are you embittered?'

'I am saddened.'

'Do you hate?'

'I am weary of bullshit, for not a day goes by without some fresh plots being laid against me, some flagrant fabrication, which tries to sabotage my records, my concerts, my private life and will not quit until I am dead.'

'Why don't you fight back?'

'I am a pacifist.'

'Who are your friends?'

'My oldest companion is Catsmeat, who acts as my MC, my jester and general factotum. Even though he's a retard, his loyalty is boundless and I cherish him, I do indeed.'

'What is your sign?'

'I am an Aquarius.'

'Do you prefer blondes or brunettes?'

'Just so long as they're female, I'm satisfied.'

'Are you frightened of death?'

'I am frightened of nothing: death tracks everyone, after all, it is insatiable but I believe I am prepared. When it shows its face at my window, I will not hide beneath the bedclothes.'

'Do you believe in magic?'

'Ask me another.'

'Do you have any heroes?'

'I recall with affection my twin brother, Jason, who became a missionary and disappeared in the African jungles. Roaming through the swamps, he was caught by headhunters and his brains were sucked out through his ears.'

'Are you serious?'

'I am.'

'What will you do next?'

'I may become a leader of men. Riding on my golden Cadillac, I would bless the crowds and bring them wealth, good luck and happiness. Just like my fans, they would love me very much and, in return, I would treat them as my children.'

'Do you like oysters?'

'I enjoy the sensation when they slip down my throat, soft and slimy as the sperm of a worm, but they also make me sick to my stomach.'

'What is your most especial quality?'

'I am a magnet. Every time I walk in a room, the people turn and stare, they can't help themselves, and I draw them on behind me, a Pied Piper of Hamelin.'

'Do you have many servants?'

'My circus numbers fifty-three.'

'Will you live for ever?'

'I don't believe so.'

'What do you think of fun?'

'This is my philosophy: live for today, tomorrow may not come and, therefore, I party every single day, feasting and carousing, travelling the highways, causing riots everywhere I go.'

'Tell us a story.'

'It was in Waterloo Place that I entered an amusement arcade, put a nickel in the slot and placed my eye up close against the Scopitone, where Little Richard was pounding the piano, performing 'Tutti Frutti', and his trouser-cuffs billowed out like sails. Right then, I discovered the truth.'

'What was the truth?'

'Awopbopaloobop Alopbamboom.'

'Awopbopaloobop?'

'Alopbamboom.'

'What are your beliefs?'

'I believe in God, I believe in my fans, I believe in Johnny Angelo. I also believe that a time will come when we will overwhelm all obstacles and no more squalor will survive, only style.'

'What are you like?'

'I am terrible, I am tender.'

'Do you run from adversity?'

'I spit on it.'

'What is your favourite sport?'

'I am fond of chess and karate, archery and wrestling but,

most of all, I am thrilled by motorbike jumps.'

'What is a motorbike jump?'

'The method is as follows: riding on my black machine, I roar up a long ramp and fly straight off the end, hurtling over a line of ten cars, placed end to end, and landing safely on the other side, a jump of more than forty yards.

'Isn't this dangerous?'

'I have broken my leg in three places, fractured my wrist, dislocated my shoulder and, next time, it may well be my neck.'

'Why do you do it?'

'Coming in to land, just for one moment, it's true that I touch infinity.

'Are you frightened of the dark?'

'I am.'

'Why do you cause riots?'

'I'm fond of fun.'

'Are you evil?'

'Among the cripples of Waterside, horrified by their suffering, I touched my silver crucifix and I caused the lame to walk, I caused the blind to see.'

'Do you eat sweets?'

'I love chocolate bon-bons.'

'What is your stance on drugs?'

'I abhor them and hold them in contempt, since they befuddle the brain, rot the bones and poison the bodily fluids, until the user becomes a travesty of life.'

'Are you left-handed?'

'I am.'

Sixty miles from Gulch City, eighty miles from Magdalena, Armadillo was nothing but sand; but here, with the remnants of his great fortune, Johnny built a neon sculpture, a monstrous effigy of himself.

A hundred and eight feet high, it glowed with sixteen colours and it wore a suit of baby blue neon, it was hung with a neon crucifix and, high above everything, visible at a range of a hundred miles, it featured a flashing neon sign, and the slogan it spelled was as follows: JOHNNY ANGELO in silver, I AM THE GREATEST in gold.

Furthermore, this was not just a monument, it was a lived-in palace and, the moment that he entered its toe, the visitor was lost in a world of neon delight.

All the organs of Johnny's body were traced in appropriate colours, red for the bloodstream and blue for the lungs, gold for the flesh, puke green for the intestines and purple for the heart. And in the liver, there was a gambling salon and, in the pancreas, a cinema and, in the bladder, a discotheque. In the brain, there was a lecture hall. Inside the genitals, predictably, there were scented boudoirs.

Everywhere that the visitor turned, he was dazzled by bright lights, which formed pretty pictures or spieled strange messages, and music blared in every limb, kaleidoscopes unfurled at every corner and, twenty-four hours a day, the name JOHNNY ANGELO kept flashing overhead.

As for Johnny himself, his bedroom was placed in his own left eye, and hour after hour, he gazed out across the desert, brooding, while his circus disported and roistered down below, having the time of their lives.

In his thighs and arms and belly, his disciples lived for fun alone. They swam up and down in his arteries, they prayed in his armpits and orgied in his scrotum and, everywhere that they went, neon flashed and flickered constantly, so that nothing looked the same, not ever.

From time to time, overwhelmed by sensation, a strongman or bearded lady would go insane and leap screaming through the vents of Johnny's suit, tumbling sixty feet to their death. In general, though, morale was very good and the circus endured through all disasters, even when the fuses blew or sandstorms whipped in their faces or, once, when the whole of one kidney exploded, killing five outright and injuring fourteen others.

Nor did Johnny Angelo absent himself entirely. Once a week, he described the sweeping stairway of his throat, a single white rose in hand, and he strutted on his collarbone. Again, he snarled and squirmed and grovelled on his knees, twisted his legs like rubber bands, buried his guitar in his groin. Yet again, he smiled his golden smile and then, launching himself without looking, he swooped and soared and ricocheted, span and trampolined, all the way down to his diaphragm.

And this much was true: once inside the movie, he was caught for ever. At the age of twenty-six, excess was his life, to which he was committed, and it was too late now to change. 'I will die as I have lived,' he decided, very solemn, and swore to turn his back on doubt and all analysis.

From his bedroom, he watched the moon and thought dark thoughts. Gnawing at the end of his pencil, he wrote small sad poems, which took him nowhere, and he played his old hit records, relics of his golden age.

And then, when he was almost twenty-seven, he looked in the mirror and there, unmistakably, he saw the first fine wrinkles forming round his eyes, the first sag beneath his chin. When his stylist dressed his hair, he noticed clusters of golden hair in the comb and, swinging like Tarzan on the hairs of his neon chest, he had a blackout, he lost his fingerhold and dropped like a stone. If it hadn't been for a budding paunch, which broke his fall, he would certainly have plunged to his doom.

On the following morning, he called a meeting of all his followers and, seated on his lower lip, he swung his legs, he kicked his heels. He wore a white silk suit, white kid shoes, a pink carnation in his buttonhole. With every word that he spoke, his neon mouth moved in time and, smiling, he made a speech, as follows: 'I am sick and tired of tedium.'

After that, he felt more serene. Now that the die was finally cast, he relaxed, he combed his hair and made out his will. Also, he wrote a letter to Astrid, his teenage dream, all full of passionate lovewords, and he composed his epitaph: *To all who pass that they may see – Rock and roll was a part of me.*

Down in the duodenal tract, meanwhile, casting craps against the wall, Catsmeat was humming tunelessly and Johnny tousled his hair, cuffing him like a lapdog. 'When I'm dead,' Johnny said. 'Will you visit my grave?'

'I will,' replied Catsmeat.

'And will you shed tears?'

'Yes, I will.'

'And will you bring me flowers?'

'I will bring yellow roses and I will lie down beside your tombstone, I won't move until I'm dead myself.'

In all the years of their acquaintanceship, almost half of their lifetimes, this was the most conversation that they'd ever had. Catsmeat and Johnny together, and now, while Catsmeat wept, Johnny Angelo stroked his cheek, quite tender.

Then he was calm. He was almost content.

Outside La Collina, there was a very long driveway, more than five hundred yards in length, which led to the electric gates, and Johnny Angelo walked down it slowly, his hands above his head. Beyond the gates, the federals did not move.

On either side of the driveway, there were parklands that were tangled like a jungle, all full of swamps and creeper and monkey trees and, through the undergrowth, there roamed many animals, badgers and rodents and skunks, felines and doves. High above everything, the mansion hung like a shroud and, for fully five minutes, Johnny went on walking.

About fifty feet from the gate, he stopped. The federals stared at him, he stared back at the federals and neither side made any move. Time passed.

At last, growing bored, the federal captain stepped forward, a man in a scarlet uniform: 'Are you coming out?' he asked. 'Or do we come in?'

Then Johnny Angelo dropped his hands, whipped his Colts from out of their holsters and let fly without looking. In the space of a second, twelve shots were fired and twelve federals fell down in the dirt, where they died.

There was a silence.

Then the federals fired back and Johnny was hit in the shoulder, in the thigh, in the hip and in the guts but he wasn't killed outright, he was only maimed and he crawled along the ground, crablike, until he reached the shelter of his golden Cadillac, which was parked just inside the gates.

Behind the Cadillac, he wiped the blood from his lips and, both slowly and painfully, he began to reload. Everything was still and he listened to the animals moving in the jungle, he was surrounded by secret stirrings. Just for one moment, he shut his eyes and was still. Then he stood up. 'I am still the greatest,' said Johnny Angelo, and he started to shoot from the hip.

TWO

Awopbopaloobop Alopbamboom

Kit Lambert's Introduction to the English edition of *Awopbopaloobop Alopbamboom*

N ik Cohn has chosen a grim and appropriate moment to make this brilliantly clear, aerial survey of the Pop World. Out in the audience, too many British teenagers are listening dutifully to their Government-approved diet of ballads and recipes: on stage, the scene is a little brighter. Key musicians are playing for other key musicians. The Beatles and the Stones, seemingly, have become too vast and trunkless ever to play at all. I hope this book will not be thought of in five years' time as the definitive history of a forgotten age. Fortunately, Nik is no obituarist: anyway, if he did write your obituary you'd be better off dead.

He showed up about 1965. The Beatles were into their first million, the disgruntled Rolling Stones were touring USA circuses, billed virtually as a freak show, and a nervous Carnaby Street tailor had just refused to put his scissors into a large Union Jack, which was meant to wind up as stage-clothes for the Who, when a thin young man – he looked about fourteen – wearing carefully dirtied-down sneakers, grabbed me in Wardour Street and informed me that he was writing an article for The Sunday Times. I believed him a lot. He landed up in a Chinese restaurant, interviewing the Merseybeats.

But a major article did appear quite soon in The Sunday Times. It revealed a knowledge of Pop (and a rudeness about it) which was fairly frightening. Then came a series of tough and highly partisan record reviews in Queen. He mastered the art of the loving clinch which turned into the killing punch, making enemies along the line. There were accusations of intellectual – even cash – payola. But Nik just got forgiven without getting cynical.

He has been described as the speed-writer of Pop. Half-martyr to his own myth, he sprints across the gilded landscape, although his feet are bleeding inside the carefully dirtied-down sneakers. At least,

Ball the Wall

I hope they are: you see he is very bright, he knows too much and he still doesn't shave.

KIT LAMBERT

in partnership with Chris
Stamp, manager of the Who,
Thunderclap Newman, the
Crazy World of Arthur Brown
and Arfur, and director of
Track Records.

1 LET IT ROCK

Roots

MODERN POP BEGAN WITH ROCK 'N' ROLL IN THE MIDDLE FIFTIES AND basically, it was a mixture of two traditions – Negro rhythm 'n' blues and white romantic crooning, coloured beat and white sentiment.

What was new about it was its aggression, its sexuality, its sheer noise; and most of this came from its beat. This was beat, bigger and louder than any beat before it, simply because it was amplified. Mostly, Pop boiled down to electric guitar.

Of course, electric guitars were nothing new in themselves; they had been around for years in jazz and R & B, and had even been featured on some white hits, notably those by Les Paul, but they had never before been used as bedrock, as the basis of a whole music. Crude, powerful, infinitely loud, they came on like space-age musical monsters and, immediately, wiped out all of the politeness that had gone before.

Pre-Pop, from the thirties on, dance music had got bogged down in the ballroom age – the golden era of the big bands, when everything was soft, warm, sentimental. When everything was make-believe.

It's one of the clichéd laws of showbiz that entertainment gets sloppy when times get tough, and what with the depression, the war, and its aftermath, times had got very tough indeed. Hemmed in by their lives, people needed to cling tight in the dark of dance halls, to be reassured, to feel safe again. Reality they could very well do without.

Always, that's the kind of situation that Tin Pan Alley thrives on; songs about moonlight, stardust, roses and bleeding hearts were duly churned out by the truckload. The big bands lined up strict and formal in penguin suits, the crooners slicked their hair back heavy with grease, the close harmony groups went oo-wah oo-wah in the background, and everybody danced. It was warm and snug like a blanket.

Sometimes, the big band era caught an odd freshness, an innocence, an atmosphere a bit like a Fred Astaire film. But when it was bad, which was almost always, it was only dire. The worst thing was that it all dragged on so long without changing. Most dance eras last a few years, a decade at most, but the war froze everything as it was, gave the big bands a second life; by the early fifties, the scene had come to a standstill.

All this time, the music industry was controlled by middle-aged businessmen, uninterested in change of any kind. They were making money as things were, so they made no effort to find anything very new. They'd switch a few details, dream up some small novelty gimmick, and leave it at that. And the only reason they got away with it was that nobody offered any alternatives. Mostly, showbiz survived on habit.

There was no such thing as teenage music then, nothing that kids could possibly identify with. The business was structured in such a way that singers were generally well into their thirties by the time they made it. There'd be occasional novelties, cute comedies, but basically teenagers had to put up with the same songs their parents liked.

The nearest thing to an exception was Frank Sinatra.

In the early forties, when he first happened, Sinatra was still in his middle twenties, a novice by the standards of that time, and he was the first heart-throb.

He was hardly a teen idol – he was a conventional balladeer, he was backed by an ordinary big band, he sang the same songs as everyone else. But he was also good looking, he had soulful eyes, and almost all of his fans were women. They screamed for him, rioted for him, even swooned for him, and this was something new. Of course, film stars had always been treated like that.

Sinatra was the first singer to join them, that's all.

As a prototype for Pop, though, Johnnie Ray was much closer, the Nabob of Sob, the Million Dollar Teardrop himself.

Born in Oregon, 1927, he was tossed high in a blanket at the age of ten, landed on his head, and became about fifty per cent deaf. According to his press releases, he also changed from a happy, well-adjusted child into a full-time introvert, solitary and sad. At any rate, by the time he became a singer, he was wearing his neurosis like a badge. The gimmick was that when he got towards the climax of his stage act, he would collapse into helpless sobs. Not just once or twice but every time he performed. It was a ritual.

His big breakthrough year was 1952, and the record that did the trick was a double-sider: 'The Little White Cloud That Cried' on one side and just plain 'Cry' on the other, titles that more or less summed him up.

Anyhow, he caused riots, real live ones – he had his clothes ripped off, his flesh torn, his hair rumpled – and the police kept having to rescue him. He sang the same trash as everyone else, even a bit worse, but he contorted himself, he buckled and gulped, and that released an intensity of aggression that nobody else had stirred.

Johnnie Ray upped his earnings to four thousand dollars a week and sold records by the million – and all this time, he did nothing but cry. 'I've no talent, still sing as flat as a table,' he said. 'I'm a sort of human spaniel: people come to see what I'm like. I make them feel, I exhaust them, I destroy them.'

He was underrating himself. He couldn't sing, true enough, but he generated more intensity than any performer I ever saw in my life, and it was impossible not to feel involved with him.

He was a very skinny man, and when he moved, his limbs jerked out sideways as clumsily as puppet strings. He'd start his act slowly, out of tune, and he'd be almost laughable, whining and amateurish, gangling around the stage like some fevered crab. But then, just when you'd dismissed him, he'd launch himself into one of his major agonized ballads, and suddenly everything would come alive.

He'd hunch up tight into himself, choke on his words, gasp, stagger, beat his fist against his breast, squirm, fall forward on his knees and, finally, burst into tears. He'd gag, tremble, half strangle himself. He'd pull every last outrageous ham trick in the book, and he would be comic, embarrassing, painful, but still he worked, because under the crap, he was in real agony, he was burning, and it was traumatic to watch him. He'd spew himself up in front of you, and you'd freeze, you'd sweat, you'd be hurt yourself. You'd want to look away and you couldn't.

Frail as he was, thin and deaf and sickly, his fans would be twisted into paroxysms of maternal hysteria by him, and they'd half kill him. All around, it was the kind of orgiastic exhibition that simply hadn't happened before, and it was entirely pop. The music wasn't; the atmosphere was.

Ironically, considering that he'd helped pave the way for Pop, he was destroyed by it. As soon as Rock came in, he sounded hopelessly dated and melodramatic, and he stopped having hits. He kept on touring, but he sagged.

He had bad publicity, too: in Detroit, 1959, he was charged with soliciting a man in a bar. Amid frantic ballyhoo, he was acquitted, and having heard the verdict, he fainted dramatically on the court-room floor. When he came around, he cried, 'My prayers have been answered.' 'Oh, that poor boy,' said the jury forewoman. And Ray fainted again.

In theory, he'd triumphed – but then it turned out he'd been found guilty on a similar charge in 1951, and that did him no good whatever.

Still, he keeps going in cabaret, and when he turns it on, he's as fierce and agonized as he ever was.

All the time that moonglow ballads were dominating the white market, black music, as always, was bossed by the Blues. The old country Blues, raw and ragged and often wildly emotional, had been increasingly replaced by rowdy big city Blues, by electric guitars and saxes, and right through the forties and early fifties, the movement had been towards more noise, more excitement. Beat came in, passion went out, and somewhere along the line, the new style became known as rhythm 'n' blues, R & B.

What this usually involved was a small band – five or six pieces, maybe more – belting out a succession of fast twelve-bars. Styles varied, of course, but generally the trend was towards the jump Blues, loose-limbed stuff played by people like Louis Jordan, Lloyd Price, Wynonie 'Mr Blues' Harris and Fats Domino.

It was good-time music, danceable and unpretentious, and by

comparison with the mushiness of white music in the same period, it was like a window opened to let out some bad air.

It was straight about sex; it used no euphemisms about hearts and roses. A lot of the time, in fact, it was downright filthy: Hank Ballard's 'Work With Me Annie', Billy Ward's 'Sixty Minute Man', and the Penguins' 'Baby Let Me Bang Your Box' were typical. All of them were big hits in the R & B charts, and predictably, all of them got banned by the white radio stations.

Just the same R & B somehow began to filter through to white kids, and they liked it. In 1951, a DJ called Alan Freed launched a series of Rhythm Reviews at the Cleveland Arena and immediately drew crowds three times the capacity.

These shows featured coloured acts but were aimed at predominantly white audiences, and to avoid what he called 'the racial stigma of the old classification', Freed dropped the term R & B and invented the phrase Rock 'n' Roll instead.

Right through the early fifties, white stations persisted in blocking R & B off their airwaves, and the biggest names were still people like Doris Day, Perry Como, and Frankie Laine.

Black hit songs were usually covered and castrated for the white market – Pat Boone did Fats Domino's 'Aint That A Shame', for instance, and Dorothy Collins assassinated Clyde McPhatter's 'Seven Days' – and even multimillion R & B sellers like Joe Turner, Ruth Brown, and Bo Diddley never made the pop charts.

Pop and R & B apart, there was also, throughout the South, a massive market in Country 'n' Western, jogalong stuff to be sung through the nose. In England, this was thought of as cowboy music and didn't sell much. But in the States, people like Hank Williams, Slim Whitman, Eddy Arnold, and Tennessee Ernie Ford rated as big as anyone and often appeared in the top ten.

Each of these musics – Country and R & B and Tin Pan Alley – had its own hit parade. Sometimes, of course, these would intertwine – La Vern Baker's 'Tweedly Dee' was a hit in both pop and R & B markets – but mostly they ran independently, and it was quite possible for someone like Eddy Arnold, say, to sell fifty million records and still mean hardly anything on the national charts.

So these were the musical ingredients that made Pop happen – the white ballad tradition, the exhibitionism introduced by Johnnie

Ray, the elaborate sentimentality of C & W, the amplified gut-beat of R & B. Among them, they would have been enough to produce a major craze.

What made Rock 'n' Roll more than a craze, what turned it into a small social revolution, was nothing to do with music.

Basically, it all came down to the fact that the affluent society teenagers now had money. If they were white, if they came out of anything but the worst slums, they weren't going to go hungry. More likely, they were going to get solid jobs and make money. They were even going to get time to spend it.

Even more important than any factual economic changes was the shift in atmosphere. For thirty years back, both in America and Britain, most working-class kids had come out of schools with a built-in sense of defeat. They might be headed for some dead-end job, they might be sent off to win wars, they might wind up in bread lines. Whatever happened, they weren't going to have much fun.

By comparison, the fifties were lush. Of course there was always the chance that everyone would get blown sky-high by an H-bomb, but that was too huge a concept for most to grasp, and at least there, was no depression now, no blitz, no rationing. It wasn't just a matter of keeping afloat any more – teenagers could begin to call the cards.

The only snag was that, when they went looking for things to spread their bread on, they found absolutely nothing. They had no music of their own, no clothes or clubs, no tribal identity. Everything had to be shared with adults.

It was tough. After all this time, teenagers had finally made it through to the promised land, and they'd found it barren. Definitely, it was frustrating. They had all this money, nothing to do with it, and they went spare.

Always, the moment of maximum revolt comes just when things are beginning to get better, when the first liberalization sets in. When kids had had nothing at all, they had somehow accepted it. Now life was easier; and, especially in England, they began to riot.

They weren't quite like any movement that had happened in earlier decades. There were so many of them and they were so aimless; they'd roam around in packs, brawling and smashing at random. A bit later, they dressed up in black leather and rode motorbikes. And still all they did was break things, windows and locks and bones. There was nothing else to do, and right through the fifties, the gangs held command; they were the only action going. If you didn't want to join them, you had to sit indoors and vegetate.

There was something else: businessmen had never before seen teenagers as independent commercial units, as having entirely separate needs and tastes from the rest of the community. Now the possibilities hit them like a prophetic vision, and they moved in fast, fawning like mad.

Predictably, kids bought just about anything that was put in front of them: motorbikes, blue jeans, hair oils, ponytails, milkshakes, and, most of all, music. All you had to do was label something Teen, and they had to have it.

In music, the one snag was that the record companies had no idea what teenagers really wanted. All they could do was release noise by the ton and see what caught on best. It was only a matter of time before they struck gold.

This was solid thinking: in April 1954, an ageing Country & Western singer called Bill Haley made a record called 'Rock Around the Clock'. By 1955 it was a hit in America, and then it was a hit in Britain, and then it was a hit all over the world. And it just kept on selling; it wouldn't quit. It stayed on the charts for one solid year.

By the time it was finished, it had sold fifteen million copies. It had also started Rock.

Bill Haley

BILL HALEY WAS LARGE AND CHUBBY AND BABY-FACED. HE HAD A kiss curl like a big C, slapped down on his forehead with grease and water, and he was paunchy. When he sang, he grinned hugely and endlessly, but his eyes didn't focus on anything. Besides, he was almost thirty, married, and the father of five children. Definitely he was unlikely hero food.

Just the same, he was the first boss of rock. At his peak, he made a film called *Rock Around the Clock*, and when it was shown in the summer of 1956, audiences danced in the aisles, ripped up cinema seats, hit each other, and destroyed anything they could lay their hands on. In one shot, it crystallized the entire rock rebellion.

The main plot of the film was that Bill Haley grinned. He picked his guitar, and his kiss curl wobbled. He sang the title song, and the beat stoked up, and kids everywhere went berserk.

In England, said kids were called Teddy Boys – the Teds – and a spotty lot they were. Nourished on rationing, they tended to be underfed, rat-faced and, when roused, they took out their switch-blades and stabbed each other. Because of this, the movie *Rock Around the Clock* was banned in some towns.

Up to now, the Teds had been very much a minority, but once they'd rioted, the press discovered them as copy and decided that they spelled full-scale revolution. For the first time, the concept of

Teenager was used as news, as a major selling point, and in no time, everyone else was up on the bandwagon. Churchmen offered spiritual comfort, psychologists explained, magistrates got tough, parents panicked, businessmen became rich, and Rock exploded into a central issue.

Of course, teenagers weren't slow to respond. There were more riots, more knives, even a few killings. And the papers hollered harder, the panic got greater, the circle kept spinning; suddenly the generation war was open fact. It wasn't an undertone, it wasn't just a novelty any more. It really mattered. Above all, it meant money.

As for Bill Haley, he was a trouper and kept right on grinning. Born in the suburbs of Detroit, 1927, he'd started playing guitar for a dollar a night at the age of thirteen. Later, he fronted a Country & Western group and buzzed around the Midwest, busily getting nowhere. Then he put in six years playing on a small-time radio station until finally, around 1951, he got wise, abandoned country music for good, and swung across to commercial R & B.

First, he listened hard to the biggest-selling coloured blues of the time, Louis Jordan and Wynonie Harris, and copied the beat. Second, he watered down the lyrics, the sexuality, of the original and made it acceptable to white audiences. Third, he changed his group's name to the Comets ('It sounded kind of far-out, wild') and worked out some acrobatic stage routines. Then he got moving.

In 1951, under the new format, he had a minor success with 'Rock the Joint'. The next year he did even better with 'Crazy Man, Crazy', and in 1954 he finally made it big with 'Shake Rattle and Roll' which was a straight cover of Ivory Joe Hunter's big hit in the R & B charts. Later that same year he made 'Rock Around the Clock'.

Musically, he was pretty dire. He was a fair country guitarist, but he wasn't remotely a singer, and his Comets sounded like they all had concrete boots. The beat was lumpish, dull. Alone of all the early rockers, Haley has no charm now, not even nostalgia value. 'Rock Around the Clock' became a minor hit again in 1968, but, to me, it just sounds bad period.

'Rock Around the Clock' was no better and no worse than most of his work. The song was laughable, the arrangement nonexistent, but the beat was there and Haley shouted quite loud. In honesty, it was a dog – but it was also first, and that's where it won. It had no competition.

Originally, it sold as a novelty, as a joke almost. Then the press took it up, hammered it, called it anti-music, and suddenly it became a big generation symbol, a social phenomenon on its own. By the end, it was the source of an entire new music and Haley was automatically leader. He'd been lucky, of course, but he'd been around a long time, and no one could reasonably begrudge him his break.

Soon he was featured in a film called *Blackboard Jungle*, a corny old soapbox about juvenile delinquency and generalized teen hang-ups. The opening sequence showed school kids jiving debauchedly in the playground, and Bill Haley was singing 'Rock Around the Clock' on soundtrack. It all helped – the film was successful, caused fuss, helped sell records. Above all, it cemented the fiction of a uniquely teenage way of life with Bill Haley as its leader.

Through 1955 and on into 1956, he held complete control. He racked up another million seller with 'See You Later Alligator' and had another monster film in *Don't Knock the Rock*. He was everything – singer, face, prophet, explorer – and no one else counted. But all the time he was on a raincheck; he was doomed. He'd jumped the gun, and he was ahead only as long as it took the rest of the field, younger, tougher, sexier, to catch him and swamp him.

Don't Knock the Rock was the signal. It was Bill Haley's film, but he lost it; he had it torn right out of his hands by Little Richard, a guaranteed genuine rock howler out of Macon, Georgia. Little Richard was the real thing. Bill Haley wasn't. Haley kept grinning, but he sounded limp by comparison, looked downright foolish.

But what really did him in was the coming of Elvis Presley. The moment Elvis cut 'Heartbreak Hotel', Haley was lost. Suddenly his audience saw him as he was – ageing, married, corny, square, deeply boring – and that was that. Within a year, he couldn't get a hit to save his life.

In early 1957, he toured England. By this time, he was already sagging on the ropes in America, but Britain hadn't yet caught on, and his arrival spelled bonanza time. He rode from Southampton to London in state on the Bill Haley Special, laid on for him by the Daily Mirror, and at Waterloo he was met by three thousand fans, many of whom had waited all day for him. He grinned. 'It's wonderful to be here,' he said. 'I'm going to like England just fine. I only hope it likes me back.' The only stroke he missed was the bit about our English policemen being wonderful.

On 12 February, he played the Dominion, Tottenham Court Road. It was the prototype of all Pop concerts since. The music was drowned out by screaming, whistling, stamping, and roaring; the gallery shook so much that people below could see the floor buckling above their heads. All you could hear was the beat, the amplification, the non-stop thump. The big beat, the monster. That was all there was.

The only trouble was Haley himself. Instead of a space-age rocker, all arrogant and mean and huge, he turned out to be a dated vaudeville act. The saxophonist squealed, honked, and blowing madly all the time, leaned over backward until his body was parallel with the floor, his head almost touching the stage. The bass player lay on his instrument, climbed up it, used it like a trampoline. Haley grinned.

It was really quite bitter. After all, he was everyone's first try at Pop, and having him turn out like this was very much like getting drunk, losing one's virginity, and then waking up in an empty bed the next morning.

Haley took it philosophically. He kept plugging away, made new singles, toured, plastered his kiss curl down with grease water, picked guitar, and grinned at all times. In 1964, he was back in England, almost unchanged. This time nothing much was expected of him; he was seen as a historical curiosity and was received with some affection. At thirty-seven, he was attractive in his resignation. 'I'm old now,' he said, 'But I've been around. I sure have been around.' And he shook his head slowly as if he had truly seen everything there was to see.

Elvis Presley

WHAT ROCK NEEDED TO GET IT OFF THE GROUND WAS A UNIVERSAL hero, a symbol, a rallying point. Someone very young, private, unshareable – exclusive teenage property. Someone who could crystallize the whole movement, give it size and direction. Obviously, Bill Haley didn't measure up. Equally obviously, Elvis Presley did.

Elvis is where Pop begins and ends. He's the great original and, even now, he's the image that makes all others seem shoddy, the boss. For once, the fan club spiel is justified: Elvis is King.

His biggest contribution was that he brought home how economically powerful teenagers really could be. Before Elvis, Rock had been a gesture of vague rebellion. Once he'd happened, it immediately became solid, self-contained, and then it spawned its own style in clothes and language and sex, a total independence in almost everything – all the things that are now taken for granted.

This was the major teen breakthrough and Elvis triggered it. In this way, without even trying, he became one of the people who have radically affected the way we think and live.

Superficially, there was nothing special about him – he was stolid, respectable, unambitious. He liked trucks. He was country, naïve, very religious. Beyond that, he played a bit of guitar, sang some.

Definitely, he was young for his age – collected teddy bears, ate ritual peanut butter and mashed banana sandwiches last thing before he went to sleep each night and loved his mother to the point of ickiness. In fact, he was cutting an amateur record of 'My Happiness' as a birthday present for her when he first got discovered.

Later, he was signed to Sun Records, a local label, and went out on the small-time Southern circuit, playing school dances, country fairs and so forth.

And his first record, 'That's All Right', was quite marvellous. Elvis had been exposed to a lot of different musics – coloured R & B, fundamentalist preachers, country ballads – and his singing was a mixture of all of them, an improbable stew to which he added sex. His voice sounded edgy, nervous, and it cut like a scythe, it exploded all over the place. It was anguished, immature, raw. But, above all, it was the sexiest thing that anyone had ever heard.

By May 1955, he had a manager, Colonel Tom Parker (the title was honorary). If nothing else, Parker was a man of experience. At forty-nine, he'd been through peepshows, carnivals, patent medicine, the Great Parker Pony Circus and just about anything else before Elvis came along. Canny but unsophisticated, he hadn't been unsuccessful and he managed some successful Country stars but, then again, he'd hardly struck gold either. On all known form, he was an unlikely revolution-maker.

Under Parker, Presley was moving up. His records were selling quietly but well round Memphis and the girls had just begun to scream at him. His singing was as good now as it was ever going to get and he kept moving his hips, wriggling and, every time he did that, there was some kind of riot.

Early 1956, Elvis was signed by RCA–Victor and made a record called 'Heartbreak Hotel'. It sold a million and a half straight off. By the end of six months, he'd sold eight million records, worked up to ten thousand fan letters a week and raised the shrillest, most prolonged teen hysteria ever. It really was as fast, as simple and complete as that. By the next year, he had grown into an annual twenty million dollar industry.

He would come out on stage standing on a golden Cadillac. He wore a golden suit and, on his feet, he had golden slippers. His sideboards reached down to his earlobes and his hair, heavy with grease, came up in a great ducktail plume off his forehead. He had a lopsided grin and he used it all the time.

When the music started, he'd begin wriggling and he wriggled so hard that quite a few cities banned him for obscenity. 'Elvis Presley is morally insane', shrieked a Baptist pastor in Des Moines and that just about summed it up.

He was flash – he had four Cadillacs, a three-wheeled Messerschmidt, two monkeys, much jewellery. He built himself a house for one hundred thousand dollars and it glowed blue and gold in the dark.

On stage, he sang hymns in between his hits. With strangers, he was invariably charming, boyish, immensely courteous. He'd smile shyly and mumble. He'd call men 'sir' and women 'ma'am', drop his eyes, look around frequently for approval. And, of course, this was all tremendously flattering. In these ways, he had real talent for handling people, for making himself liked.

At the centre of everything was his mother. But, shy and deferential as he was, whenever he got pushed into fights by passing madmen, he'd invariably take them apart. No question, he was a very Southern boy.

Always, he came back to sex. In earlier generations, singers might carry great sex appeal but they'd have to cloak it under the trappings of romanticism, they'd never spell anything out. By contrast, Elvis was blatant. When those axis hips got moving, there was no more pretence about moonlight and hand-holding; it was hard physical fact.

With crooners, with people like Sinatra and Eddie Fisher, girls had suffered crushes and they'd sigh, swoon and sob gently inside their handkerchiefs. Always, they'd been romantic and quite innocent.

With Pop, though, it's all been down to mainline sexual fantasy. Sitting in concert halls, schoolgirls have screamed, rioted, brawled and fainted. They've wet themselves and they've masturbated. According to P. J. Proby, they've even ripped the legs off their chairs and mauled themselves. They've done all kinds of outrageous stuff that they'd never do anywhere else and they've been so uninhibited because there has always been a safety belt, because the Pop singer himself has been unreachable, unreal, and nothing could actually happen.

In this way, it's all been sex in a vacuum – the girls have freaked themselves out, emptied themselves, and then they've gone back home with their boyfriends and played virgin again. As rituals go, it's not been beautiful but it's been healthy, it's acted as a safety valve. Screaming at Elvis or the Beatles or the Rolling Stones, has been as good as saying confession or going to an analyst.

At the same time, off-stage, Elvis read the Bible, loved his mother. 'He's just like a paperback book,' one of his girl fans explained. 'Real sexy pictures on the cover. Only when you get inside, it's just a good story.' He looked dangerous but ultimately was safe and clean. This is what young girls have always wanted from their idols, an illusion of danger, and Elvis brought a new thrill of semi-reality to the game.

With all his peacockery, his implied narcissism, he was also a major pose-maker for boys. A lot of the time he sang conventional romantic lyrics but some of his biggest hits were breakaways – the harshness and contempt for women in 'Hound Dog' was typical.

'Blue Suede Shoes' was even more to the point. This had been a hit for Carl Perkins in 1956 but Elvis took it over the following year and gave it wholly new dimensions. It was important – the idea that clothes could dominate your life. Girls and money didn't count. All that mattered were shoes, beautiful brand-new blue suede shoes. It was the first hint at an obsession with objects – motorbikes, clothes and so on – that was going to become central.

By 1958, Elvis had ruled for two years solid and the hysteria showed no signs at all of dying down. He'd gone into movies – *Love Me Tender*, *Loving You*, *Jailhouse Rock*. He had racked up twenty million sellers worldwide. Still, he had some long-term problems. He was already twenty-three, he couldn't go on being a teen idol for ever. The difficulty was how to turn him from an adolescent rebel into a respectable establishment figure without his fans feeling cheated.

At this point, a godsend: Presley's army draft came through and he went on ice for two years. It meant losing a lot of money but Elvis took it philosophically. As for Colonel Parker, he was delighted.

From here on in, Elvis got more and more saintly. On army training, he was a paragon of diligence, cheerfulness, humility. His officers praised him warmly, the press swung behind him. Adult

America was much reassured – the monster had shown that it was only kidding.

In August 1958, his mother took sick, had a heart attack and died. At the funeral, Elvis was hemmed in tight by reporters, jotting down every word he said, noting every last sob and whimper. 'She was the sunshine of our home,' Elvis moaned. 'Goodbye darling. We love you. I love you. I love you so much. I lived my whole life just for you.' Next morning, his ramblings were splashed syllable by syllable across the papers. It was diseased, ghoulish, but it finally cemented the new Presley image. The boy was all right.

There was even a record about it all, 'New Angel Tonight' by a certain Dave McEnery. The first verse went:

> There's a new angel tonight
> Up in heaven so bright,
> The mother of our Rock 'n' Roll King –
> And I know she's watching down
> On her boy in Army brown,
> In her angel mother's heart remembering.*

By the time he was shipped out to Germany, Elvis was everything that an all-American boy ought to be, working and playing hard, dating but not too much, visiting spastics, drawing emotional tributes from rugged GI buddies. He wound up a Specialist Fourth Class, a rank equivalent to corporal and worth $122 a month. The whole operation was a triumph.

By the time that he came back to civilian life again, he was almost as respectable as an Andy Williams or a Perry Como. Predictably, his first new record was a ballad 'It's Now Or Never', an inflated up-dating of 'O Sole Mio'. Also predictably, it was his biggest seller yet, doing more than nine million worldwide.

He never again went back on the road. Instead, he hid himself away in vast mansions in Hollywood or Memphis and there he has stayed ever since. He hasn't toured in years. He lives a life of almost total privacy, kept company only by his wife, his small daughter and twelve ex-GIs, who amuse him and fetch him drinks and play touch football with him. Whatever he does, whatever

*Words of 'New Angel Tonight' by permission of Southern Music Publishing Co. Ltd, London.

fires him, he's discreet about it – nobody knows for sure what he thinks or wants to do. He gets slightly lonely, we're told. That's all.

Most of his time is spent in churning out an endless series of safe and boring musicals – *Kissin' Cousins*, *Clambake*, *Frankie and Johnnie*, *Harem Scarum*, *Girl Happy* – and each one seems worse than the one before. Elvis himself is thirty-four, paunchy, slow and his voice has lost its edge, until he now sounds a bit like Dean Martin. His songs are drab, his scripts are formula-fed and his sets look as if they've been knocked together with two nails and a hammer. He still makes a fortune but his singles sell patchily and his films break no box office records.

To be fair, he's shown recent signs of getting back into business. He issued three strong singles running – 'Big Boss Man', 'Guitar', 'US Male' – and did a much-publicized TV spectacular on which he sounded tougher, more raunchy than he'd done in years. Whether this will grow into any major revival remains to be seen.

As far as his fans are concerned, he could just as well be on another planet. From time to time his gold Cadillac is sent out on tour across America and they come to see it, touch it. His annual earnings are around ten million dollars. He has sold the best part of a hundred and fifty million records. And somehow his fans accept his absence and have come almost to like it.

The point is that he has passed beyond the edge of criticism, that he's somewhere out of reach on a plateau of showbiz untouchability. The obvious parallel is with Frank Sinatra – both of them have changed so much, have earned such astronomical money, have so dominated the entertainment worlds of their time that what they do for the rest of their lives has become largely immaterial. They have run out of challenges.

All that's left now is the image, the vision of him as he was when he was twenty-one, twenty-two, strutting and swivelling and swaggering, hanging his grin out, putting on the agony, riding on the top of his Cadillac, gold on gold, and freewheeling through everything. He was magnificent then, he really was. And his whole story has been an ultimate perfection of the Hollywood romance, an all-time saga of what happens to sexy little boys when they get fed into the sausage machine.

So Elvis now is a godhead – unseen, untouchable, more than

human. The demon lover has turned into a father, an all-powerful figure who can rule a fan's life without actually having to be there. His remoteness is a positive advantage, his present badness is irrelevant, and there's no reason why it should ever end. Worship is a habit that's hard to break.

Classic Rock

ROCK 'N' ROLL WAS VERY SIMPLE MUSIC. ALL THAT MATTERED WAS the noise it made, its drive, its aggression, its newness. All that was taboo was boredom.

The lyrics were mostly non-existent, simple slogans one step away from gibberish. This wasn't just stupidity, simple inability to write anything better. It was a kind of teen code, almost a sign language, that would make Rock entirely incomprehensible to adults.

In other words, if you weren't sure about Rock, you couldn't cling to its lyrics. You either had to accept its noise at face value or you had to drop out completely.

Under these rules, Rock turned up a sudden flood of maniacs, wild men with pianos and guitars who would have been laughing stocks in any earlier generation but who were just right for the '50s. They were energetic, basic, outrageous. They were huge personalities and they used music like a battering ram. Above all, they were loud.

It was a great time – every month would produce someone new, someone wilder than anything that had gone before. Pop was barren territory and everything was simple, every tiny gimmick was some kind of progression. Around 1960, things evened out and much of the excitement died out. Pop had become more sophisticated, more creative, more everything. But the fifties were the time when Pop was just Pop, when it was really something to switch on the radio and hear what was new right that minute. Things could never be so good and simple again.

For instance, the first record I ever bought was by Little Richard and, at one throw, it taught me everything I ever need to know about Pop.

The message went: 'Tutti frutti all rootie, tutti frutti all tootie, tutti frutti all rootie, awopbopaloobop alopbamboom!'* As a summing up of what rock 'n' roll was really all about, this was nothing but masterly.

Very likely these early years are the best that Pop has yet been through. Anarchy moved in. For thirty years you couldn't possibly make it unless you were white, sleek, nicely spoken and phoney to your toenails – suddenly now you could be black, purple, moronic, delinquent, diseased or almost anything on earth and you could still clean up. Just so long as you were new, just so long as you carried excitement.

Most of the best early rockers came out of the South: Elvis from Mississippi, Little Richard from Georgia, Buddy Holly from Texas, Jerry Lee Lewis from Louisiana, Gene Vincent from Virginia. These were the states where the living had always been meanest, where teenagers had been least catered to, and where, therefore, the Rock kickback was now most frantic.

Anyhow, the South was by far the most music-conscious section in america. it always had been. It had huge traditions in R & B; country, trad, and gospel, and its music was in every way more direct, less pretentious than that up North. Mostly, it had a sledge-hammer beat and pulled no punches. Down here, rock was an obvious natural.

The only innovation was that the rockers made use of all the sources around them. Up to this time, whites had used country, Negroes had used R & B, and the two had never remotely overlapped. Now everyone incorporated anything they could lay their hands on, and it was this mix-up of black and white musics that gave southern Rock its flavour.

*Words of 'Tutti frutti' printed by kind permission of Burlington Music Company Ltd.

Of all the great southern rockers, just about the most splendid was the aforementioned Little Richard Penniman out of Macon, Georgia.

He was born on Christmas Day 1935, one of thirteen children, and had a predictably harsh childhood. At fourteen, he was singing solos with the local gospel choir. At fifteen, he was blues-shouting, dancing, and selling herb tonic in a medicine show. From there, he got into a variety of groups, made a sequence of nothing records, and finally in 1955, when he was twenty, sold a million copies of 'Tutti Frutti'.

He looked beautiful. He wore a baggy suit with elephant trousers, twenty-six inches at the bottoms, and he had his hair back-combed in a monstrous plume like a fountain. Then he had a little toothbrush moustache and a round, totally ecstatic face.

He played piano, and he'd stand knock-kneed at the keyboard, hammering away with two hands as if he wanted to bust the thing apart. At climactic moments, he'd lift one leg and rest it on the keys, banging away with his heel, and his trouser rims would billow like kites.

He'd scream and scream and scream. He had a freak voice, tireless, hysterical, completely indestructible, and he never in his life sang at anything lower than an enraged bull-like roar. On every phrase, he'd embroider with squeals, rasps, siren whoops. His stamina, his drive were limitless and his songs were mostly total non-songs, nothing but bedrock twelve-bars with playroom lyrics, but still he'd put them across as if every last syllable was liquid gold. He sang with desperate belief, real religious fervour: 'Good golly, Miss Molly, you sure like a ball – when you're rockin' and rollin', I can't hear your momma call.'*

As a person, he was brash, fast, bombastic, a sort of prototype Mohammed Ali ('I'm just the same as ever – loud, electrifying, and full of personal magnetism'), and right through the middle fifties he was second only to Elvis. Most of his records sold a million each: 'Long Tall Sally', 'Lucille', 'The Girl Can't Help It', 'Keep A Knocking', 'Baby Face'. They all sounded roughly the same: tuneless, lyricless, pre-neanderthal. There was a tenor sax

---

*Words of 'Good Golly; Miss Molly' by permission of Southern Music Publishing Co., Ltd, London.

solo in the middle somewhere and a constant smashed-up piano and Little Richard himself screaming his head off. Individually, the records didn't mean much. They were small episodes in one unending scream and only made sense when you put them all together.

But in 1957 he suddenly upped and quit. No warning – he just stopped touring, stopped making records, and went off to play piano in a Seventh Day Adventist church off Times Square.

Apparently, he'd been in a plane and a fire had broken out. Richard got down on his knees and promised that if he was spared, he'd give up the devil's music for ever and devote himself to the gospel instead. 'And God answered my prayers and stopped the fire.'

So he announced that he was giving up, but his entourage thought he was crazy and laughed at him. Then Richard, in a typically flash performance, took his many rings from his fingers and flung them into the sea. Almost $20,000 worth: 'I wish I'd seen the face of the man that caught those fish. A king's ransom, all courtesy of Little Richard.' And he quit on the spot. At least, that's the story he tells, and it might be true. Some of his stories are.

Five years he kept it up, made no records, gave no interviews. But in the early sixties he began to cut gospel records, and from there it was inevitable that he'd go back to rock again. He didn't get any further hits, but he was still a name. Several times he toured Britain, and each time he went down a storm.

The first time I saw him was in 1963, sharing a bill with the Rolling Stones, Bo Diddley, and the Everly Brothers, and he cut them all to shreds. He didn't look sane. He screamed and his eyes bulged; the veins jutted in his skull. He came down front and stripped – his jacket, tie, cuff links, his golden shirt, his huge diamond watch – right down to flesh. Then he hid inside a silk dressing gown, and all the time he roared and everyone jumped about in the aisles like it was the beginning of rock all over again.

Objectively, he didn't even do much. Anyone else that has a great stage act always has an obvious selling point: James Brown has speed, Johnnie Ray has pain, Elvis has sex. Little Richard had none of that. All he had was energy.

He howled and hammered endlessly. On 'Hound Dog', he

dropped down on his knees and grovelled, and still he howled. It was all gospel – 'that healing music, makes the blind to see, the lame to walk, the dead rise up.' He kept it up so long, so loud, it made your head whirl. Good hard rock; he murdered it and murdered us. When he was through, he smiled sweetly. 'That Little Richard,' he said. 'Such a nice boy.'

Fats Domino came from further back. In fact, he was almost pre-pop. As early as 1948, he cut a big hit called 'Fat Man', and he'd already tucked about ten smashes under his belt by the time that Bill Haley came along.

At this period, he sold mostly around his home town of New Orleans and worked for a strictly Negro market. The music he peddled was a nicely relaxed line in R & B, backed by tightly-knit small bands, and everything he did was casual. Fats himself wrote the songs, played piano and sang.

When rock came in and R & B was acceptable, the fat man very quickly cashed in. He had whole strings of American hits and by 1960, he'd sold upwards of fifty million records. Fifty million is a lot of records. Officially, he's also credited with twenty-two individual million sellers, which puts him ahead of everyone outside of Elvis and the Beatles.

Mind you, it has to be said that these figures make him sound a lot bigger than he ever was. Most of his alleged million sellers were only regional hits and he never made much sustained impression on British charts. All the same, he was a figure. More important, he made good records.

The way he was so lazy and good-humoured, he was a bit like an updated Fats Waller. Most of his best songs – 'Blue Monday', 'I'm Walkin', 'Blueberry Hill' – were dead simple, straight ahead, and Fats sang them as if he was having himself a time. When he was at his best, he conjured up small-time coloured dance halls on Saturday night – he played a bit, sang a bit and everyone got lushed. Good-time music, that's all it was and it hit the spot just right.

In 1967 he did a Sunday night show at the Saville in London and the audience was made up of rockers from way back – all greased hair, drainpipes and three-quarter coats. Fats weighed in at sixteen stone and smiled all the time. He ran through his hits and diamonds glittered on his fingers and he wore bright orange socks.

When he came to his finale, he went into an endless and very corny workout on 'When The Saints Go Marching In'. It went on and on and on. Fats glistened and gleamed all over, his band cavorted like circus clowns and it was all a bit embarrassing. At the end, Fats got up and started to push his piano across the stage with hard thumps of his thigh. He was past forty and not fit and it was a very wide stage. By the time he was half-way across, he was flagging. The music rambled on and Fats was bent almost double with effort. It was a very ludicrous situation – the rockers stormed forwards at the stage, willing him on, and he kept heaving, he wouldn't give up. And it took him maybe five minutes but finally he did make it and everyone cheered like mad.

Two of the rockers jumped up on stage and lifted his hands holding them aloft like he was a winning fighter. They were big kids and Fats, for all his weight, is quite squat. He stood shaking between them and he looked vulnerable, almost old. Everyone was rioting. Fats streamed sweat and kept smiling but he also looked a bit confused. Very likely, no one had gone quite that wild for him in ten years.

Another noble rocker was Screamin' Jay Hawkins, who had been around ever since the middle forties. He wore a zebra-striped tailcoat, a turban, polka dot shoes. He began his act by emerging flaming from a coffin, and he carried a smoking skull called Henry; he shot flame from his fingertips; he screamed and bloodcurdled. At the end, he flooded the stage with thick white smoke, and when it cleared, he was gone.

'I used to lose half my audience right at the start, when I came up screaming out of my coffin,' he said. 'They used to run screaming down the aisles and half kill themselves scrambling out of the exits. I couldn't stop them. In the end I had to hire some boys to sit up in the gallery with a supply of shrivelled-up elastic bands, and when the audience started running, my boys would drop the elastic bands onto their heads and whisper 'Worms'.

Jay's biggest hit was the original version of 'I Put a Spell on You', and he had other triumphs with things like 'The Whammy' and 'Feast of the Mau Mau'. Actually, he had quite a pleasant baritone, but on stage, he'd only screamed and ghouled. 'I just torment a song,' he said. 'Frighten it half to death.'

Then there were the Coasters, who had the most sly-sounding lead singer in the whole business, not to mention the most lugubrious bass. The lead, Carl Gardner, played the school bad boy. He sang like he had some bubble gum permanently stashed away inside his cheek, and everything he did was sneaky, pretty hip. Then he was a loudmouth, a natural-born hustler, and all the time the bass groaned and grumbled below him, the voice of his conscience speaking. The lead took no blind notice.

Mind you, they could hardly miss. For a kickoff, they had the most prolific songwriters in Rock going for them: Jerry Lieber and Mike Stoller, a partnership that hustled upward of thirty million records in five years. Lieber and Stoller also wrote some of the best early Elvis hits, notably 'Hound Dog' and 'Jailhouse Rock', but they were natural humorists, and Presley was just a bit straight for them. The Coasters were ideal.

Lieber and Stoller churned out stuff that was inventive, wry, and sometimes very shrewd – a running commentary on the manifold miseries of being teenage – and the delinquent talents of Carl Gardner did the rest with no sweat. Between them, they came up with some very funny records.

The format was simple: they got a fast shuffle going, reeled off the assembled lyrics, and then stuck a frantic yakety sax chorus into the middle. It was a comforting scheme of things. You always knew what was coming and could relax. So the lead snickered, the bass moaned, and everyone was happy.

Probably their most classic effort was 'Yakety Yak', a knock-down and drag-out row between a bullied teenager and his monstrous parents. The teenager, of course, is seen as martyr. He spends his whole time tidying his room, doing homework, washing, generally flogging himself.

From there they went on to further explorations of teenage hell 'Charlie Brown' ('Why's everybody always picking on me?'), 'Poison Ivy', and 'Bad Blood'. Each one was perfect in its own way, but the whole style was completely geared to Rock attitudes, and when times changed, they were among the first to slip.

They're still around, though, and occasionally a new single

filters through. Nothing vital is changed. The lead still sounds maybe fifteen years old and carries himself as if he's just seen his geometry coach slip on a shrewdly planted banana skin. The bass still groans. They live in a cut-off private world and everyone is sweet sixteen for ever.

Chuck Berry was a bard; Classic Rock's definitive chronicler, interpreter and wise-guy voyeur. He wrote endless Teen Romance lyrics but sang them with vicious, sly cynicism and this is the clash that makes him so funny, so attractive.

His most perfect song was 'You Never Can Tell', an effort that gets a lot of its flavour from the knowledge that it was made soon after Chuck had served a hefty jail sentence for transporting a minor across a state boundary without her parents' consent. Its full lyrics went:

It was a teenage wedding and the old folks wished 'em well,
You could see that Pierre did truly love the mademoiselle,
And now the young monsieur and madame have rung the chapel bell –
C'est la vie, say the old folks, it goes to show you never can tell.

They furnished off an apartment with two rooms, they were all by
themselves,
The coolerator was crammed with TV dinner and ginger ale,
But when Pierre found work, the little money coming worked out well –
C'est la vie, say the old folks, it goes to show you never can tell.

They had a hi-fi phono, boy did they let it blast,
Seven hundred little records, all rockin', rhythm and jazz,
But when the sun went down, the record tempo of the music fell –
C'est la vie, say the old folks, it goes to show you never can tell.

They bought a souped-up Jidney, was a cherry-red '53,
They drove it down to New Orleans to celebrate their anniversary.
It was there where Pierre was wedded to the lovely mademoiselle –
C'est la vie, say the old folks, it goes to show you never can tell.*

A jangle piano rambled away legato in the background and there were great swirling sax riffs and Chuck himself more intoned than sang, sly and smooth as always, the eternal sixteen-year-old

*Words of 'You Never Can tell' by permission of Jewel Music Publishing Co. Ltd, London.

hustler. That was it – the Teendream myth that's right at the heart of all Pop and 'You Never Can Tell' expressed it more exactly, more evocatively than any of the other fifty thousand attempts at the same theme.

Of course, this is all very naïve and undeveloped by comparison with what has come since, but then Bogart proved thirty years ago that, in mass media, you don't need to be a monster intellectual to be great. In fact, it's a definite disadvantage if you are. What you do need is style, command, specific image and these are the exact things that Chuck Berry has always been overflowing with.

Basically, what it boils down to is detail. Most pop writers would have written 'You Never Can Tell' as a series of generalities and it would have been nothing. But Chuck was obsessive, he was hooked on cars, rock, ginger ale and he had to drag them all in. That's what makes it – the little touches like the cherry-red Jidney '53 or the coolerator.

Chuck was born in California in 1931, grew up in St Louis and, when he was older, got to be a hairdresser. By nature, he was an operator and he was always going to be successful. The only question was how. So he tried singing, he wrote, he made progress. In 1955, he had his first national smash with 'Maybelline' and from then on he was a natural Mister Big.

As a writer, he was something like poet laureate to the whole Rock movement. He charted its habits, hobbies, hang-ups or celebrated its triumphs or mourned its limitations and he missed nothing out. 'School Days' pinned down exactly that schoolkid sense of spending one's whole life listening for bells and 'Johnny B. Good', guitarslinger, created a genuine new folk hero and 'Roll Over Beethoven' should have been adopted as the universal slogan of rock. But almost best of all was 'Sweet Little Sixteen'. Nothing summed up better the twinned excitement and frustration of the time:

> Sweet little sixteen, she's just got to have
> About a half a million famed autographs.
> Her wallet's filled with pictures, she gets 'em one by one,
> Becomes so excited, watch her, look at her run
>
> Sweet Little Sixteen, she's got the grown-up blues
> Tight dresses and lipstick, she's sportin' high-heeled shoes
> Oh but tomorrow morning she'll have to change her trend
> And be sweet sixteen and back in class again.

> They're really rocking in Boston, in Pittsburg, PA,
> Deep in the heart of Texas and 'round the Frisco Bay,
> All over St Louis, way down in New Orleans,
> All the cats want to dance with Sweet Little Sixteen.*

Beyond his writing, he played a very fair blues guitar, Chicago-style, and sang in a voice as waved and oily as his hair. On stage, his speciality was the duck walk, which involved bounding across the stage on his heels, knees bent, body jackknifed and guitar clamped firmly to his gut. Then he would peep coyly over his shoulders and look like sweet little sixteen herself, all big eyes and fluttering lids. He had a pencil moustache and had the smoothness, the cool of a steamboat gambler. A brown-eyed handsome man, in fact.

Just when things were going so well for him, he made his mistake with the minor and was put away. By the time he got out again, in 1963, rock was finished but the British R & B boom was just getting under way and he was made blues hero number one by the Rolling Stones, who started out playing almost nothing but Chuck Berry songs. Almost as a matter of course, he'd landed on his feet.

He was brought over and made much of but turned out to be hard to deal with. He was arrogant, rude. When he liked to turn it on, he could be most charming but often he couldn't be bothered. First and last, he was amazingly mean.

There's an authenticated story about him that, on his first British tour, he used to study the evening paper nightly and check to see if there had been any fluctuation in rates of exchange. If there was any deviation in his favour, no matter how small, he'd demand payment in cash before he went on. On one night, this supplement came to 2s. 3½d.

By and large, white rockers were a lot less impressive than their coloured counterparts. After the wildness of Little Richard, the lyricism of Chuck Berry, they sounded samey and half-hearted. As personalities, too, they were less colourful, less articulate. Mostly, they were plain boring.

The major exception was Jerry Lee Lewis, a pianist and shouter

---

*Words of 'Sweet Little Sixteen' by permission of Jewell Music Publishing Co. Ltd, London.

from Louisiana. He used R & B and country in about equal doses and attacked the keys in very much the same style as Little Richard, bopping them with fists, feet, elbows and anything else that was handy. Towards the end of his act, he'd climb on top of the piano, hold the mike like a lance and stay up there until the audience got hot enough to dash forward and drag him down.

His great gift was that, no matter how frantic he got, his voice remained controlled and drawling country. He seemed to have a lot of time to spare, an unshakeable ease, and this gave him class.

He had long yellow crinkly hair that fell forward over his eyes when he worked and a thin, slightly furtive face. He always reminded me of a weasel. And when he got steamed up, he'd sweat like mad and his face would collapse into nothing but a formless mass of heaving, contorting flesh. Still, his voice would be strong, easy. As stage acts go, it was hardly pretty but, definitely, it was compelling.

After he'd rampaged through his earliest hits (the apocalyptic 'Whole Lotta Shakin' Goin' On' and 'Great Balls of Fire') he did a 1958 tour of Britain and immediately plunged neck-deep into trouble. He had brought his young wife with him. His very young wife, as it turned out. Her name was Myra and Jerry Lee said she was fifteen. Later, he admitted that she was only thirteen. He also said that, at twenty-two, this was his second marriage. His first had been at fourteen ('Hell, I was too young').

The British press duly disgraced itself. It howled blue murder, screamed babysnatcher, and finally got the tour cancelled. Jerry Lee flew out in disgrace. 'Hell, I'm only country,' he pleaded, but no one took any notice.

Before the cancellation, he'd had time to do two concerts and, doomed by so much bad publicity, they were disasters. In the first, Jerry Lee dashed out in a pillar-box red suit and smashed straight through two numbers without let-up. He was brilliant, by far the best rocker Britain had then witnessed, and he half won his audience round. Then, before going into the third, he took out a golden comb and very delicately swept his hair back out of his eyes. It was a fatal move. Someone yelled 'Cissy!' at him and from there on in it was solid murder. Finally, Jerry Lee just upped and walked off stage. The curtain came down. Pandemonium.

All of which goes to show how superficial the Rock revolt had really been. On paper, Jerry Lee's marital junketings were exactly calculated to improve his prestige, make him into an even better symbol of rebellion. In practice, it only took a fast burst of pomposity in the papers and the kids were just as appalled as their parents. And when Jerry Lee left his hotel, he was hissed and insulted and spat upon.

Jerry Lee wasn't downcast. Arriving back in New York, he announced that his concerts had been 'Great, just great' and that, as he'd left, 'three thousand stood and cheered'. There are people around who'll tell you that he's the greatest Pop figure ever. I wouldn't agree, but he certainly rates. I also like his attitude. 'You are either hot or cold,' he says. 'If you are lukewarm, the Lord will spew you out of his mouth.'

Buddy Holly was really called Charles Hardin Holley and first came out of Lubbock, Texas, with broken teeth, wire glasses and halitosis, plus every last possible kind of country southernness. He wasn't appetizing. In fact, he was an obvious loser.

On the other hand, he had a voice, he wrote natural hit songs, and what's more, he was by no means prepared to sit tight in the background and churn out smashes for other artists. He said he wanted to sit in his front room and watch his face singing to him out of the television screen. He was very firm about this. So a man called Lloyd Greenfield, a tough, no-nonsense agent, took him up and changed him into another person. Buddy had his teeth capped, his breath cleaned, his hair styled, his wire glasses exchanged for big impressive black ones, his voice toned. Then he was put into high-school sweaters and taught how to smile. Suddenly, he was all-America.

The whole saga was straight out of Stan Freberg – Holly sang lead with a group called the Crickets and promptly cut a succession of monster hits with them: 'That'll Be the Day', 'Oh Boy', 'Maybe Baby'. By 1958, growing big-time, he had dumped the Crickets and gone solo, clocking up a further sequence of million-sellers on his own: 'Peggy Sue', 'Rave On', 'It Doesn't Matter Any More'. He was smooth, he was clean. He had a smile straight off a toothpaste ad, and his new black glasses were major trend-setters. In every detail his career was perfect, and in February of 1959, just to round it off, he got killed in an air crash at

Fargo, North Dakota. He was then twenty years old.

Long-time Rock fans have always been bitterly divided about him. He wasn't a hard core rocker, being too gentle and melodic, and this eccentricity can be construed either as back-sliding or as progression. Even ten years after his death, it isn't an academic question; I have seen Rock preservation meetings reduced to brawling knuckle-dusted anarchy about it. On the wall of a pub lavatory in Gateshead, there is a scrawled legend: 'Buddy Holly lives and rocks in Tijuana, Mexico.'

He was all adenoids – twanged them like a catapult, propelled each phrase up and out on a whole tidal wave of hiccoughs and burps. As sound it was ugly, but at least it was new. It was also much copied; Adam Faith, for one, built his early career largely around his variations on it. For that matter, so did Bobby Vee.

Holly's breakthrough, in fact, was that he opened up alternatives to all-out hysteria. Not many white kids had the lungs or sheer hunger to copy Little Richard, but Holly was easy. All you needed was adenoids. The beat was lukewarm, the range minimal – no acrobatics or rage or effort required. You just stood up straight and mumbled. Even the obvious beaters, things like 'Rave On' or 'Oh Boy', were Neapolitan flowerpots after 'Tutti Frutti'.

In this way, Buddy Holly was the patron saint of all the thousands of no-talent kids who ever tried to make a million dollars. He was founder of a noble traditon.

Killed in the same air crash that took care of Holly were Ritchie Valens and the Big Bopper. Valens, at seventeen, had already made some of the direst records in Pop. The Bopper, on the other hand, had made one of the all-time best: 'Chantilly Lace'.

His real name was J. P. Richardson; he was a Texan disc jockey, and 'Chantilly Lace' was his only hit. A fat man in his late twenties, he wore vast baggy striped suits, the jackets half-way down to his knees and the trouser seats big enough to hide an army in, and he owned a grin of purest lip-smacking lechery, a monster. 'Chantilly Lace' is his testament.

He's in a phone booth, ringing some girl, and he's having to hassle like mad to get a date out of her. He sweats, he giggles, he groans. He drools, overflows himself.

You can feel him wriggling his fat shoulders in delirium, his joke suit around him like a tent, his eyes bugging and his bottom lip hanging slack: Chantilly lace and a pretty face, giggling talk, wiggling walk, pony tail hanging down, Lord, makes the world go round round round, makes him feel real loose like a long-necked goose. And all this time he's melting.

He's getting nowhere, of course, but he doesn't give up; he campaign shouts like a southern Democrat. The result doesn't matter anyhow; it's the performance that counts. 'Ooh, baby,' he howls. 'You know what I like. You KNOW.'* And when he says that, he bursts, he just disintegrates.

Eddie Cochran was pure Rock.

Other people were other kinds of Rock, country or highschool, hard, soft, good or bad or indifferent. Eddie Cochran was just Rock. Nothing else. That's it and that's all.

There's not much fact on him: he was born in Oklahoma City, October 1938, youngest out of five children. His family moved to Minnesota, then to California. He grew up to be one sweet little rock 'n' roller, a nice looker, and he made records and had hits. He played good guitar and worked on sessions in Los Angeles. He wrote songs, got to be quite big. He even toured England. And on 17 April 1960, he was killed in a car crash on the A1. He was then twenty-one years old.

As a person, there's even less on him. He looked like another sub-Elvis, smooth flesh and duck-ass hair and a fast tricksy grin, the full uniform. He was quiet, a bit inarticulate, a bit aggressive, and he cared mostly about his music. He was polite to journalists, helpful even, but had nothing much to tell them. I was once told that he had a deep interest in toads but I have no evidence on it. He was nothing special. He just came and went.

What made him such pure Rock? In a way, it was his very facelessness, his lack of any detailed identity. With so little for anyone to go on, he seemed less a specific person than an identikit of the essential rocker, a generalized '50s' blur, a bit pretty and a bit surly and a bit talented. Composite of a generation.

But he was something more than that, his songs were perfect

---

*Words of 'Chantilly Lace' by permission of Southern Music Publishing Co. Ltd, London.

reflections of everything that Rock ever meant. They were good songs, hard and meaty, but that wasn't it. In every detail, they were so right. So finally rocker.

'Summertime Blues', 'My Way', 'C'mon Everybody', a few more – there were only maybe half a dozen things that did him full justice but, between them, they added up to something more than somewhat.

There is almost a continuous storyline running through them. Eddie is still at school and hates it. Lives at home and hates it. Works in his holidays and hates that worst of all. Still, he's a pretty ready kid, can handle himself. And he runs in some kind of gang, he's leader of the pack. Eddie Cochran, no punk or palooka of '59.

When he gets very lucky, his father gives him the car for the night and then things are wild. Of course, after he gets back home, four in the morning, bushed and busted, he is kept in for a fortnight but that's the name of the game: he can't win. The world rides him. When he works, he's paid chickenfeed. When he enjoys himself, he is automatically punished. Tough.

Still, when he walks down the street so nice and slow, his thumbs hooked into the belt-loops of his blue jeans, his hair all plumed and whirled, the girls look up from their chewy mags, sip Coke through a straw and they think he's cute, real cute. Sure good-looking, he's something else.

And that's about where it ends: that was Rock, those were the great rockers.

Looking back through what I've written, I'm struck hardest by two things – just how good the best of Rock really was, and just how sadly most of its practitioners have ended up.

I suppose the trouble was only that Rock was such committed music, such a very specific attitude, so tied to its time, it wasn't possible for real rockers to ever move on. Of course this is a stock problem in any field – revolution so quickly becomes boring – but the thing about pop is that its generation cycles last five years at the very most.

Never mind: the best Rock records stand up still as the most complete music that Pop has yet produced. Everything about it was so defined – all you had to do was mix in the right ingredients, stir well, and you had a little Rock masterwork on your hands. It was that simple, that straightahead, and finally, that satisfying.

Of course, classic Rock wasn't ever anything like as complex, as creative, as the music is now. Does that matter? It was Superpop. On its own terms, it was quite perfect.

2 TEENDREAMS

Highschool

SOUTHERN ROCK WAS HARD ROCK, NORTHERN ROCK WAS HIGH school. Stan Freberg made a record that summed up Northern Rock exactly. In it, he's a record-producer-cum-manager and he discovers a totally talentless kid who wants to be a rock 'n' roller. So he takes this kid and records him, standing behind him with a sharp stick to help him hit the high notes. And all that the boy has to do is sing the word *highschool* over and over again. His record is an instant hit.

Highschool wasn't a musical form; it was an attitude, and that attitude read: 'We go to high school. We dig rock 'n' roll. We date and go to parties and yes, we sometimes neck but no, we never pet. We also fall in love and that really burns us up. Then we pass notes in class and don't eat and even cry at night. We also drink Coke, and hamburgers are really neat. We wear sneakers, short shorts, high-school sweaters. The girls have pony tails and the boys are crew cut. Our parents can be kinda draggy at times, but gee whiz, they were young themselves once and they're only trying to do their best for us. Finally, we dig America. We think it's really peachy-keen.'

There's a Pop film that has been made maybe a hundred times over, and it is the absolute epitome of everything highschool. A girl from a nice home falls for a singer in a rock 'n' roll group. He had a mean childhood; therefore he's a bit surly and sad, but really he's a nice kid. The girl's father hears about this and orders them to break up. There is much tragedy and heartburn all around. Finally, the Rock singer finds some way of convincing the father that he's all right. Everyone is happy. In the last scene, all the kids jive while the father gently fox trots. Everybody laughs.

Where Southern Rock introduced something new to popular music – noise, violence, the mixing of R & B and Country, gibberish, semi-anarchy – highschool was basically a continuation of existing white traditions. The solo singers were pretty boys, very much in the tradition of Sinatra, Eddie Fisher or Vic Damone, and the groups sang harmony roughly in the style of the Inkspots, the Four Preps, the Hi-Los or the Four Freshmen. All that was changed was that highschool catered solely for a teenage market and that it had no conception of quality whatsoever. It was lousy. Its concentrated badness, in fact, is what made it attractive.

Another big difference was that Southern rockers, by and large, had been their own bosses. They had business managers, but they conceived their records, worked out their stage acts, built their images all by themselves. Highschool rockers were almost always puppets.

Hype is a crucial word. In theory it's short for hyperbole. In practice, though, it means to promote by bribery, hustle, pressure – even honest effort if necessary – and the idea is that you leave nothing to chance. You slip some cash to radio stations, maybe some to TV producers, maybe some more to the trade press. You also throw nice parties and do all the conventional publicity strokes. In short, it's the art of the possible.

Hype has become such an integral part of Pop that one hardly notices it any more. There's hardly any major Pop star in the world who has never laid out some capital as insurance. From certain angles, it's justifiable; you believe in your product, and you spend money on promoting it in any and every way. You have faith. Of course, it's not ethical or even legal, but then what business is?

At any rate, the '50s were the golden age of hype. There was a huge scandal about it in 1959 – the payola fuss – and a lot of people came crashing down, including Alan Freed, the DJ who'd put on the first Rock shows in Cleveland back in 1951. Things have never been the same since. In the four years before the fall, however, everyone had themselves a carnival.

Highschool, in fact, is where the stock pop satire comes from – moronic groups, fat cigar-smoking agents, crooked managers, and all the rest. Things have changed, or at least they've got more complicated. In highschool, the caricature carried a lot of truth.

At the core of highschool was an unlimited assortment of face-less spotted groups. Mostly they made one big smash right off and then disappeared without trace. Sometimes they hung on for maybe a year. They hardly ever lasted longer.

The names and songs were virtually interchangeable: 'Short Shorts' by the Royal Teens ('Who wears short shorts? We wear short shorts.'*); 'At the Hop', by Danny and the Juniors ('Let's go to the hop, oh baby, let's go to the hop.'); 'Little Darlin'' by the Diamonds: 'When' by the Kalin Twins, and so on *ad nauseam*. Almost all of them used a bass voice like a foghorn at the bottom, an anguished falsetto over the top, and much mumbling in the middle. They cavorted and bounded and frolicked. They smiled constantly and they died cruel deaths.

*Words of 'Short Shorts' by permission of Essex Music Ltd, London.

California

CALIFORNIA IS TEEN HEAVEN. IT IS THE PLACE THAT POP WAS created for. Chuck Berry did a song about it called 'The Promised Land', and like always, he knew what he was talking about.

This California is hugely enlarged reality, verges on complete fantasy. In Pop, it is the joob-joob land far beyond the sea, where age is suspended at twenty-five and school is outlawed and Coke flows free from public fountains and the perfect cosmic wave unfurls endlessly at Malibu. The home of the lotus eaters. That's what it is for, kids who live in grey cities, tenement blocks, and it keeps raining and they know this can't be right; there must be something better. California is the something better.

No drag lives there but only sun, sun, sun. Surf in the morning, hot rod later, and maybe a barbecue at night – isn't that the way life should be? Surf City, two girls for every boy. Drive-ins and Muscle Beach Party. California dreaming: that's what Chuck Berry meant.

To fit these fantasies, Californian Pop has always been like comic strips, continuing images of sand and sea and sun, everything drawn bright and clean and simple.

It hasn't ever properly grown out of highschool. As late as the middle '60s, West Coast heroes were still pictured sitting in class all term, passing sly notes to the school iceberg. At night they went to drive-ins and necked. On weekends they bombed up and down the coastline in their hot rods. Eddie Cochran would have understood it perfectly. And when summer came and school was out, they went down on the beaches, surfed, barbecued steaks, and danced barefoot in the sand. That's when they also fell in love, happily or unhappily, and they stayed that way till fall. Then they went back to school and started all over again.

It was a tightly limited world, very compact, very safe, and there are people around who see it as a vision of hell, but I'm not one of them.

Anyhow, it was a storyline that never seemed to run out of steam, and from 1960 on, which was about the time that California developed a specific Pop identity, separate from all other high-school, it was variously used by the Beach Boys, Jan and Dean, the Hondas and the Ripchords and the Rivingtons, Ronnie and the Daytonas, Dick Dale, and umpteen others. The market was inexhaustible. All you had to do was throw in the right dream words, wipe-out and woody and custom machine, and you were home. Californians bought you out of patriotism, and everyone else bought you for escape. The more golden your visions, the more suntanned your sound, the better you sold. It was almost that simple.

Musically, as well as emotionally, it was all updated highschool, big bass voice at the bottom and careening falsetto up above. All that was new was the efficiency with which it was done.

Californian Pop tended to be competent. Almost professional. Sometimes it used quite complex arrangements, lines inter-weaving, voices unexpectedly juxtaposed, even a bit of half-baked counterpoint. More, nearly everyone sang in tune. As Pop, it was light and flexible and fast. Vastly attractive. And it was perfected by the Beach Boys.

In the first place, the Beach Boys were three brothers, Brian and Dennis and Carl Wilson, and one cousin, Mike Love, rounded out by a local boy soprano called David Marks. All five of them lived in Hawthorne, California, and went to school and surfed.

This was the beginning of the '60s, and surfing was everything; it was the maximum West Coast cult. It had been a major world sea sport ever since the war, a bottomless box of myths and remembered afternoon heroics, a sunshine pool-shoot, but it had been mostly adult, mostly the property of hairy athletes in their mid-twenties. Now, by the early '60s, schoolboys had finally got wise to it, and they were altogether hooked.

It was understandable hysteria – imagine yourself riding waves, everyone watching you, girls gawking, and you have this one small board under your feet, that's all, but still you swoop and soar, fly free, and nothing can bring you down. You walk the water. And so fast – what speed, what poise, what godlike splendour. No wonder bikinis pop. No wonder your classmates turn their heads away (boy, were their faces ever red?!). And at the end, you tuck your surfboard under your arm like some briefcase and walk up the beach so cool and easy, not looking to left nor right, not even caring. Still the greatest. Then you lie down in the sand and starlets cluster to feel your muscles. That's surf fantasy. No more peacock sport was ever invented.

Anyway, the Wilsons surfed like everyone else, and Dennis, who was a light-golden colour, who was good looking and fit and always made out with girls, was very smart at it. But Carl and Brian were overweight and weren't so hot. Carl was the youngest and even-tempered by nature, and he didn't mind too much. But Brian was the eldest, the most intelligent, the most talented, and he didn't like fatness one bit.

Around 1962, the Wilsons formed themselves into a group – their father was a long-time songwriter, and it was almost inevitable that they'd get involved with pop – and Brian, being the cleverest, became their writer. What he wrote about was surf.

Amazingly, this was the first time that any specifically surf music had been written, the first time that California was given its own pop identity. Out of nowhere, though, Wilson wrote songs with titles like 'Noble Surfer', 'Surfin' Safari' and 'The Lonely Sea', and they were wild.

He worked out a loose-limbed group sound and added his own falsetto. Then he stuck in some lazy twang guitar and rounded it all out with jumped-up Four Freshman harmonies. No sweat, he'd created bona fide surf music out of nothing. More, he had invented California.

In 1963 he adapted Chuck Berry's 'Sweet Little Sixteen' and called it 'Surfin' USA'. This was the great surf anthem: the clincher, a hymn of unlimited praise. He did 'Surf City' for Jan and Dean, and it was a national number one. So surf was suddenly

American big business, and Brian Wilson ruled it.

It made sense. Maybe he did have flab problems, maybe he wasn't Mister Surfing Universe – but he wrote the songs, did the real work, and Dennis just sat at the back playing drums. Other kids surfed much better, but only Brian Wilson articulated it all, made pop poetry from it, got rich off it. Inside very few years he could afford to hide his belly inside the Rolls-Royce he'd bought from Brian Epstein.

Very quickly he expanded from surf to hot rod, the other major West Coast obsession, and then further into generalized pop. He handled things well, kept progressing all the time. By the time any fad burned out, the Beach Boys were inevitably long, long gone.

His car songs were beautiful. Hot rods brought out a huge sentimental streak in him, and he wrote real flowerpots. When his cars won out, he celebrated them like monster heroes, and when they broke down, he mourned them like dying lovers. His great maudlin falsetto quavered and ached, the harmonies behind him went dirge-like.

There was no subject too soap-opera for him to take on. He churned out 'A Young Man Is Gone', an ode to the departed James Dean, and 'Spirit of America' and 'Be True to Your School'. At the same time he did some fine rejoicings, full of energy and imagination: 'Shut Down', '409', 'Little Deuce Coupé'. Fine rock and roll music but brought up to date, kept moving and not left to atrophy. Best of all was 'I Get Around'.

What Brian Wilson was doing now was making genuine Pop Art. Not camp word-plays on Pop, but the real thing. He was taking the potential heroics that surrounded him and, not being arty, not being coy in the least, turning them into live music.

Simply, he'd taken highschool and raised it to completely new levels; he'd turned it into real myth, and as far as I'm concerned, this was his best period.

Personally, he wasn't easy. He was arrogant, solitary, and very self-involved. He understood well that he *was* the Beach Boys, that the rest of the group were virtually only his assistants, and he wasn't too gentle about it. Also, everyone told him how clever he was, how talented, and he believed them. He began to see himself as an artiste.

By now, he had established the Beach Boys as the most successful group going, and he was tired. He had all the songs to write, all the decisions to make; at the same time, he was on the road, travelling and losing sleep, huddling in cockroach dressing rooms – generally hustling himself half to death. Then, from late 1964 he was under pressure from Beatlemania, and the Beach Boys went through a bad slump, their records selling less. So he thought he needed time to reflect, space to stretch in, and he decided he'd stop touring. He'd stay home in California and write masterworks instead. As for the rest of the group, they could go right on touring and earning. That's what he thought and, no arguments allowed, that's what he did.

Since that time, he has been increasingly withdrawn, brooding, hermitic. He has developed strong mystic traits, runs in no gangs. Occasionally he is to be seen in the back of some limousine, cruising around Hollywood, bleary and unshaven, huddled way tight into himself. Most secret and enigmatic: a pop Howard Hughes.

The Twist

'I'M NOT EASILY SHOCKED BUT THE TWIST SHOCKED ME ... HALF Negroid, half Manhattan, and when you see it on its native heath, wholly frightening ... I can't believe that London will ever go to quite these extremes ... the essence of the Twist, the curious perverted heart of it, is that you dance it alone': Beverley Nichols reporting from New York in January 1962.

It's strange the way the Twist got so fussed about. Realistically, it was the least sexual dance craze in forty years. With old faithfuls like the jitterbug and the jive, after all, the girls spun like tops and everyone got fast flashes of panties. With the Twist, you got nothing. Just Chubby Checker telling you to imagine that you'd had a bath and were towelling your back. Approximately as carnal as cornflakes.

Well, Pop was now sunk neck-deep in pigshit and needed something violent, something quick, to pull it out again. Never mind if it be real or phoney, straight or hyped, just so long as it could hit. And it happened that there wasn't anything real available at the time, so hyped it had to be.

And the Twist was lying around. Most often it would have been a stock grade-C fad, maximum span of six months. Another hula hoop. But 1961 was parched, was really desperate. So first Chubby Checker had a hit record. Second, New York smart society decided that the Twist was cute and started to hang out in the

Peppermint Lounge. Third, the gossip columnists jumped aboard. Fourth, the whole industry started hyping. And fifth, madness set in.

At this point, enter something like Beverley Nichols on a white horse, and suddenly you get visions of kids copulating on dance floors, mass national debauch, and the breakdown of all known moral standards – the collapse of Western civilization. Strong stuff: that's the way the money grows. So now you finally have a story, a phenomenon. All right, so nobody really gives a damn and nobody ever will. That isn't quite the point.

'The Twist' wasn't even new. Hank Ballard, who had been around on the R & B scene ever since the early fifties, wrote the original song in 1958 and had a specialized hit with it. Dance-craze records have always been a stable part of the Negro market, and nobody paid much attention.

Two years on, Chubby Checker re-recorded it and got himself a national breakout. Checker was Ernest Evans from Philadelphia and had been a chicken-plucker. He looked something like a young Fats Domino, and he played it up; he even bowdlerized the fat man's name (Fats Domino = Chubby Checker: ya dig?). Truthfully, he wasn't much talented, but happy to toil: he found himself with a hit on his hands and he hammered it. He twisted like a maniac. Demonstrated it on television, diagrammed it in the papers. Lost thirty-five pounds in a year just pretending to towel his back. So the Twist seemed almost fun, and it caught on. Journalists satirized it gently, how ludicrous and freak it was. The Peppermint Lounge, just off Times Square, hired a group called Joey Dee and the Starliters, and they played Twist all night every night. Chubby Checker cut 'Let's Twist Again'. Even Elvis had a number one Twist song, 'Rock-A-Hula-Baby'. This was all getting to mean big business.

Here's where something odd happened. New York socialites, truly smart people, started to haunt the Peppermint Lounge. Elsa Maxwell and Greta Garbo and Judy Garland, Noel Coward and Tennesee Williams, the Duke of Bedford. Everyone, as they say, who was anyone. All of them twisting like there was no tomorrow and looking very foolish indeed. Inside weeks, you had to spray twenty-dollar bills like confetti even to catch a glimpse of the dance floor.

This was only odd because no jetsetter had ever shown any remote interest in pop before. Not a flicker. In the '50s, it had seemed hip to like the more refined end of modern jazz – Miles Davis, the Modern Jazz Quartet, even Thelonious Monk. But not rock and roll music. Anything but that. The thing to be was cool and there was nothing cool in Pop. Certainly not in fat Negro chicken-pluckers from Philadelphia.

But the '60s were something different, and it was suddenly fashionable to be frantic again. It was like the '20s, the Scott Fitzgerald thing, the Charleston, all that dazzle and fevered decadence. So Pop was permissible. Amusing. Jackie Kennedy was rumoured to Twist. In London, Margot Fonteyn shook it down in public. In Paris, so did Jean Cocteau.

This is where it started, the hysterical adulation of Pop singers by the rich and trendy all over the world. It became hip to know Joey Dee, hipper to know Checker. Huge status to be publicly snubbed by Phil Spector. A bit later it was paradise to be entirely ignored by the Beatles. And by 1966, Mick Jagger was the most wanted guest in the world, the final face, the ultimate. For one pout of his red lips, any millionairess hostess going would have promised away her life.

Anyhow, once the Faces had showed at the Peppermint Lounge, the Twist ballooned almost instantaneously from a fad into an industry. The papers pissed themselves. Big money got invested. Very quickly, there were Chubby Checker T-shirts and jeans and ties, Chubby Checker dolls. Or Twist skirts and Twist raincoats and Twist nighties. Conveyor-belt Twist movies. Ballrooms had their biggest boom in decades. Everyone cleaned up. And the insanity was that, even now, nobody really cared. Try finding one truly hooked twister and you'd have had quite some search. No competition, the Twist was the most total hype ever.

The one thing remotely interesting about it, as Beverley Nichols pointed out, was that you danced it alone. Suddenly, dancing hadn't anything to do with romance any more, nothing to do with companionship or fun. Instead, it became pure exhibitionism, a free platform for sexual display, and down among the teenybops, that passed for kicks.

Certainly, the Twist's appeal had nothing to do with its music, which was always drab as hell; its cuteness was simply that it allowed kids to do something that would have got their faces slapped for them in any earlier generation; namely, to stand up in public and promote their ass. And all right, so it looked foolish, but it felt illicit; that was the full equation.

The Twist itself didn't last long. Well, it wasn't really meant to. In any case, it was replaced by other dances, other campaigns, and the same people went on making money. In the absence of any dominant individuals, dance-crazes bossed pop right up until the Beatles broke. There was the Hully Gully, the Madison, the Fly, the Pony, the Popeye, the Mashed Potato, The Dog, the Monkey. A bit later, the Slop and the Waddle and the Frug. The Jerk and the Block. Right on into these last years and the Boogaloo, the Philly Skate, the Sanctification, the Beulah Wig. The inspired Funky Broadway. That's not all. Endless and interchangeable steps. Go to a club one week; go back the next, and everyone is moving different. There are kids who devote all their lives from sixteen to twenty-one in mastering dances that nobody else is up to yet. It's a full-time career. More than a career – an art almost. At the least, a vocation.

Dancing was a focus. So was radio. Between them, they made up the hard centre of early sixties' American teen romance. They bossed.

Millions of kids up in front of their bedroom mirrors, getting hip to the Pony with the Good Guys on Station WMCA. Or out in the park on the Hully Gully from the All-Americans on WABC. Or sipping Coke through Murray the K's Monkey on 1010 WINS. That's the way the fantasy went. It was a self-contained cycle, twenty-four hours each day, DJs spieling like maniacs all across the nation, and music splintering and feet shuffling, butts twitching by the megaton. It didn't ever have to end; it needed no improving. It was perfection.

Radio was a big surprise comeback. Television had completely taken over in the '40s, the '50s, but now steam was huge all over again. Not to be listened to, not like before TV, but as an endless burble background for teenage daydream. It was all music, no speech and no interruptions allowed – kids didn't like talk; they flipped dials fast to another station. So the only way a DJ could survive was to develop a spiel so fast, so smooth, that it became music on its own. No message, no sense to impart. It was pure noise: 'So hit me one time, that's a groove, that's nice, baby, ooh mammy-o, lay it down, sock it to me, John, George, Paul, and Ringo, Fab Four, babydoll, it's what's happening, baby, and bam bam bam –' starting as a rumble and rising gradually to an unending Hitlerian scream. It was like electricity, it was like glass. It was just there.

Murray the K was king jockey. Of all DJs ever made, he spieled hardest, fastest, loudest, and longest. Hustled the biggest deals and pulled the biggest strokes. In his hysteria and unflagging speed, in his total shamelessness, in his haste to cash in and equal haste to later opt out, he entirely epitomized the phase.

He wasn't hip or heroic in the least, but he won out on brashness alone. He was in his late thirties, a sturdily built businessman, and he wore Stingy Brim straw hats, tight pants, lurid shirts. He could have been a successful insurance salesman from Ohio going berserk on Hawaiian vacation. But still he talked blind streaks and never ran out of wind.

His catch phrase was 'It's what's happening'; he used it all the time. And he rocked in his seat, he roared and hollered, pounded, went purple in the face, but he never once stumbled in his spiel. Never ever. He was surrounded by tapes: commercials, one-shot interviews, trains, cavalry charges, explosions, weirdbeard laughs, end of the world screams. In between, he even played records. Everything was impetus. Murray the K, wham bam thankyou mam. Interminable shows like roller-coaster rides: he's what's happening.

He outstayed all rivals, beat them blind when it came to cunning. In the very early sixties, he was unchallenged top dog, and then naturally, because American DJs hardly ever last, he began to flag. By early 1964, he was definitely on the slide.

Right then the Beatles flew in for their first American tour. At this moment, they were at their utmost peak; they had the top five records on the American charts, and they were the hottest properties ever. And when they touched down at Kennedy Airport, they went straight into press conference, there to be interviewed by the cream of the nation's journalists. And, strangely, by Murray the K.

It wasn't ever a fair contest. The journalists huddled together and fired questions. But Murray the K somehow wriggled through their legs and got right to the Beatles' feet, crouched there and just about crawled up them. Stingy Brim hat, maniac leer, and his stick mike pushing upward, ever upward. His mouth shooting questions all the time. And he stole it, he broke it up. He turned a formal occasion into farce. So Paul McCartney looked down at him. 'Murray the K,' said Paul, 'cut out the crap.'

Immortality: the nation's pressmen got routine, Murray the K got exclusives. 'Cut out the crap.' That's all. Nirvana. Quite possibly, it was the scoop of the century.

From there, he hounded the Beatles like Charlie Chan. He roomed with George Harrison and taped his thoughts just before going to sleep, just after waking. Dubbed himself the Fifth Beatle and got away with it, because who could resist such nerve, who could fail to be secretly impressed? So Murray came back to New York with a mountain of exclusive tapes and played them endlessly. Sample – Murray the K; 'What's happening, baby?'

Ringo Starr: 'You're what's happening, baby.'

Murray the K: 'You're happening, too, baby.'

Ringo Starr: 'OK, we're both happening, baby.'

By the end of the tour, Murray was right back on top again and stayed that way. He made one hundred and fifty thousand dollars a year. Sold Murray the K T-shirts and hosted albums of Murray the K's Golden Gassers. And his resourcefulness is such that he might never end. He summed it up himself. 'I'm not riding the Beatles' coattails,' he told Tom Wolfe once. 'If they go, I'm going to be ready for the next person that comes along.'

3 THIS ENGLAND

Six Five Special

BRITISH POP IN THE FIFTIES WAS PURE FARCE.

Nobody could sing and nobody could write and, in any case, nobody gave a damn. The industry survived in a state of perpetual self-hyped hysteria, screaming itself hoarse about nothing in particular. There was much assorted greed, schnidery and lunacy. Trousers dropped like ninepins. Sammy Glick would have had the time of his life.

Before this, in the early fifities, the biggest stars were people like Dickie Valentine and Anne Shelton and Joan Regan. Mostly they had come up through dance bands and, once they had established themselves, they were safe for life. Nothing changed from year to year. The stuff they sang was just as maudlin and meaningless as its American counterpart. Worse, they didn't even have that certain flair and style that made Sinatra or Como or Tony Bennett half-way bearable. They didn't have anything.

At this time, records weren't too important. The really big money was in stage performances and sheet music sales and, accordingly, the business was controlled by agents and publishers. Especially publishers. They had a long-term agreement with the BBC by which they paid fixed rates to get songs plugged. In return, the BBC ensured that at least half of every popular music programme was made up of songs that had been paid for.

What it meant was that nothing got hard-sell plugging unless

'The Industry' willed it. Effectively, this was monopoly and, until the system was abolished in the middle fifties, it wasn't possible to have a hit song without falling meekly in line.

In these years the industry was structured around the massed publishing offices of Denmark Street, England's Tin Pan Alley. The men in control were mostly middle-aged, and they ran a slow business, very cautious. If they had to be cut-throat, they were always sentimental with it, and many of them did truly believe that they were turning out quality. They tended to be married, with children. They had great sense of tradition. If you asked them, they'd probably tell you that there was no biz like showbiz.

Rock knocked all of that on the head. Records took over as the main focus of interest and, because of this, publishers found themselves increasingly fazed by managers, producers, engineers.

Rock brought in operators who were younger, faster, tougher, cleverer, nastier. More complicated and more neurotic. In every way, more interesting. They were young hustlers who had probably been hanging around in some other trade, films, or journalism or crime, and immediately saw rock as a gold-mine dream come true. Sometimes they genuinely liked pop and sometimes they didn't. Either way, they cleaned up.

Most of them were homosexual. They'd see some pretty young boy singing in a pub, take a liking to him, and sign him up. They'd bed him and then they'd probably very quickly get bored with him.

The boy would fade and disappear again. Or, every now and then, he would turn out to be a stayer after all, and he'd somehow keep himself afloat. It was this scrabbling, this desperate jockeying for favour, that made the fifties such black comedy.

I haven't brought this up purely as a tidbit: the managerial queerness of this time has had an indirect but strong and lasting effect on teen life in general.

What happened was that managers decided what their protégés should wear on stage, and not surprisingly, they went for effeminacy, for flash and flamboyance. They chose things that would previously have been worn only by exhibitionist queens. Then the singers went out in all this outrageous tat, and some of them were successful, and their styles were copied. Private sexual fantasy turned into minor public cult. From there, things snowballed like mad and, by the early sixties, the movement had been enshrined in Carnaby Street. So now millions of kids all over the country are wearing pure homosexual regalia as a matter of course, and nobody gives it a second thought.

Of course that's a simplification, and there were many other factors at work in the swing toward flamboyance. Still, early managers have a lot to answer for.

The first attempt at a major British rocker was Tommy Steele, and a sad flop he turned out to be. Launched in 1956, he was eighteen years old, came from Bermondsey, and had been a merchant seaman. He had a lot of curly blonde hair and a grin as deep and wide as the Grand Canyon.

He was discovered singing in a Soho coffee bar, the 2 I's, by a man called John Kennedy, a New Zealander in his late twenties. Kennedy had been around in a variety of trades and had flair, invention and a fast mouth.

Give him due credit: Tommy did his best to live up to the spiel. On stage he squirmed and wriggled in all the right places, strummed his guitar till his fingers went numb, snarled animal, generally did the whole bit. Still, he wasn't really cut out for it. The trouble was, he wasn't evil enough. He was amiable, perky. Almost sweet, and that wasn't any good to anyone.

As it turned out, he was natural showbiz. He had instant charm going for him; he was photographed with his mother, and he kept right on flashing that bottomless grin. He was all hair and teeth. Adults took one look at him and weren't remotely fooled – the boy was all right. So he moved on from Rock as fast as he could and turned to ballads, comic recitations, novelties. He played Shakespeare at the Old Vic and studied tap dancing and squeezed himself into evening dress. He even combed his hair.

Naturally, teenagers were much disillusioned and switched allegiance. It didn't matter: he was an all-around family entertainer now, that mythical beast, and he couldn't miss. He sang and danced and quipped. He was much loved by everyone. And he was that all-time showbiz cliché, the lovable Cockney, always merry and bright.

Compare his saga with the Elvis story and you have the precise difference between the great American and the great British entertainment epics. Elvis became God. Tommy Steele made it to the London Palladium.

Terry Dene was next in line. He wasn't talented; he had smooth features, and he sang Rock without giving it any personal flavour at all. What happened to him sums up the '50s very well.

He had bad nerves. He'd come from roughly the same background as Tommy Steele, had emerged out of the Elephant & Castle, but he wasn't anything like as brash or self-assured; he wasn't remotely tough. He was plain petrified in fact.

He had a round face, unformed, childish, and he always looked as if he was on the point of bursting into tears. Very often he did just that, which made him ideal maternity food for those who liked it but poisoned him for just about everyone else. No question, the boy was cuddly.

All the time he had troubles. He wasn't much of a singer and often got the bird. This upset him. He'd brood until he got out of control, and then he'd have some form of breakdown. He'd be told to take a rest and he'd return glowing, earnestly promising reform. Things would go all right for a bit, but inevitably he'd slip back. Then the cycle would begin again.

He didn't even get many hits. Factually, he was never more than a minor success, but the press found him fascinating – his breakdowns and comebacks, his almost weekly crises – and they plugged him like mad. This way, even by Pop standards, he grew into a figure out of all proportion to anything he'd ever done.

In July 1958, aged nineteen, he married a singer called Edna Savage, a few years older than himself, and it was the fuss wedding of that year. The papers picked it up as a signal that even rockers were human, were capable of finer feelings, and ran it huge. The whole industry glowed with reflected pride. Terry Dene wept with happiness.

Predictably, it didn't work out. Edna Savage quickly got disgruntled and threatened to leave, reasons not disclosed. Just when things were coming to a head, Terry got his draft notice.

The press yelled bonanza again. The comparisons with Elvis were most lavishly drawn, the image of pretty young rocker giving up a fortune and selflessly marching away to fight for king and country was nudged home with a bulldozer. Terry himself was quiet and dignified. Edna Savage was proud of him; his mother was proud of him. For one week, he was a hero.

As Rifleman 23604106, he smiled for cameras, waved for weeping fans. He kissed Edna Savage goodbye and flashed a thumbs-up sign. A few hours later, though, having realized exactly what he was taking on, he burst into tears and collapsed. 'It was grim, man, just grim,' he said. 'I was standing up there with my tin tray, having my bit of food plonked down in front of me like all the others. The thought of me in that little bed with fifteen other blokes around – I felt real sick.'

Two months on, he got his medical discharge and made his ritual comeback. This time it didn't work. Edna Savage left him and nobody was proud of him any more. His records didn't sell. 'This time I'm older, sadder and much wiser,' he promised but no one believed him. He retired and came back, retired and came back again. He had a couple of years in badly paid tours and everything was rough. Finally, he dropped out of sight.

That wasn't all: a couple of years later, he was seen standing on a Soho street corner, preaching the gospel with the Salvation Army. What he preached was repent your sins, change your ways before it's too late. Nobody much stopped to hear him.

He looked much older, greyer. But he said he was happy and fulfilled. He didn't want publicity, he wouldn't give interviews. For some reason, he didn't trust the press.

What's more, he stuck it out, he didn't break down. He went on the road and, as far as I know, he's still out there, preaching as he goes.

Tommy Steele and Terry Dene were the heavies. Wee Willie Harris, Vince Taylor and Screaming Lord Sutch added slapstick.

Wee Willie had his hair dyed flaming pink and wore a polka-dot bow tie like elephant's ears. Also baggy candy-striped Big Bopper suits and neon shoes. All set off by an unchanging idiot grin.

Vince Taylor was black leather and chains, the final rocker. High boots and studs and black greasy hair. He did all right in England and then cleaned up in France, where British rejects always go over big. the '60s finished him. Last thing I heard about him, he had turned mystic and hung out in a big room in Soho with a gaggle of disciples. He saw himself as prophet. In his big room, there were two telephones. One he used for ordinary calls. The other was his hotline to God.

Screaming Lord Sutch was nobody's idea of a genius musician either. He didn't need to be, because he was a tireless self-publicist instead. Basing himself very much on the antics of Screamin' Jay Hawkins, he pulled all the standard stunts of the time – clambered out of coffins or dressed up like a caveman. What made him a standout was his persistence.

His gift was that, whenever he looked like fading, he always managed some stroke. He stood for Parliament, got engaged, grew his hair long, tried some new form of fancy dress, hustled like mad. As stunts they were lousy, but they were also endless, and their cumulative effect wasn't resistible.

He had real staying power. He has never had hits, but he's outlasted everyone and still goes out for good money now. He's an institution. These days he has transformed himself into Lord Caesar Sutch and rides on stage in a chariot. Why the change? 'You have to move with the times,' says Sutch.

In all this chaos and foolishness, the only man who had any remote awareness of what was really happening was a TV producer called Jack Good. Everyone else saw Pop as a one-shot craze and rushed to cash in on it fast before sanity returned and everything returned to normal. By contrast, Good realized it clearly as a major phenomenon.

I suppose he was the first Pop intellectual. He'd been to Oxbridge, had letters after his name and could spell words of more than three syllables. More, he knew that Pop was going to boss the entertainment industry from here on in, that it was the product of real social change rather than publicity hype, that its possibilities were just about limitless.

As a producer, he was responsible for *Six Five Special*, *Oh Boy* and the other major Rock TV shows of the fifties. In the '60s, he emigrated to America and produced *Shindig*, their best pop showcase ever.

He sent P. J. Proby to Britain in 1964. He dreamed up a musical version of *Othello*, Muhammed Ali to take the title part and Proby himself to play Iago. He even made a great record called 'I Sold My Heart To The Junkman' by Lyn Cornell, an English version of an American hit, out-of-tune and hopeless but quite amazingly exciting, a little joke masterpiece. In every job he tried, he did something good.

I can remember hearing him interviewed on the radio once, sometime in the late '50s. He said that Elvis Presley was a genius and that he'd go down as one of the major artistic figures of our century. Even now, that would hardly go unchallenged. In its time, it was total anarchy. And his willingness to be outrageous, to shoot his mouth off at a sceptical audience was a big help in getting rid of Rock's built-in inferiority complex.

The next figure to come along was Larry Parnes, who was a very big-time manager indeed and sold Pop in bulk. He handled whole battalions of singers and gave them marvellous technicolour names – Billy Fury, Cuddly Duddley, Marty Wilde, Vince Eager, Johnny Gentle, Dickie Pride, Duffy Power, and so forth.

Parnes was the perfect '50s manager – meaning that he was shrewd, fast-witted, and had natural publicity flair – but didn't go further. He had limited imagination, didn't plan years ahead, and didn't bother his head too much about art or progression. Instead, he made money and avoided stupid mistakes. He was a good businessman.

His first major property was Marty Wilde, who tried hard, had many hits, and was a thoroughly likeable man but didn't have the magnetism to bring him right through. Billy Fury was different.

Fury was the closest that Britain ever got to producing a genuine rocker, someone almost in the class of Eddie Cochran.

For one, he was a face: high cheekbones and moody little eyes and a comma of hair drooping down on his forehead. For two, he was a mover, he rolled his hips like he almost meant it.

Originally, he was a Scouse called Ronald Wycherley and, when he was in his middle teens, he wanted to wear drainpipe jeans but his father wouldn't let him. So he'd sneak out of the house into the back yard and hide his drainpipes in the outdoor lavatory. Then, when the time came to go out, he'd saunter away all innocent in his baggy flannels, whip round the corner, up over the back lane wall, rescue his drainpipes from the can and finally hit town in full splendour. That was determination. That was his exact difference – could anyone imagine Tommy Steele or Terry Dene going to all that trouble just to be an image rocker?

He was a merchant seaman but did some singing and song-writing on the side, and the way he was discovered was very typical of the period and of the way that Larry Parnes functioned. In 1958, he got the ferry to Birkenhead, where Marty Wilde was doing a one-nighter, and played a few songs in Marty's dressing room. Larry Parnes overheard him.

Five minutes later, Ronald Wycherley was Billy Fury and was playing bottom of the bill. When he came off stage, he dashed back home, packed his case and joined the tour. Real Eddie Cantor stuff – no fuss, no messing about, no nothing. Just go out there and sing and get paid. The rest, as they say, is history.

On stage, he was best at agonized balladeering, face contorted and hand clutching at nothing, thin body all racked and buckled with sadness. When things got going, he'd wrap himself around the microphone like a python and rape it. This got him banned in Ireland and fussed about even in England. So he toned down. Still, just for a moment, he'd been wild in there.

He was strange. When he was at his peak, around 1961, he moved into the country and took up bird-watching. Ornithology became his great driving passion. He said that he couldn't talk deeply about himself to people, couldn't relax with them but he felt much happier with animals. 'I'm an introvert and an extrovert', he said. 'I'm an exhibitionist on stage but I can't tell anyone about myself, I freeze up. I don't want anyone to know.'

When he talked, he mumbled and stared at his hands. He was tense and, in some odd sense, genuinely innocent.

Fury was one prong of the triumvirate that dominated British Pop from about 1959 until the Beatles first broke through in 1963. The other two were Cliff Richard and Adam Faith. Of the three, Fury was the most exciting, Faith the most intelligent, Richard the most competent. What they had in common was that they were all articulate, smooth, composed. In every way, they were presentable. They had tidy smiles and noncommittal accents and nice manners. They tended not to make fools of themselves in public. Among them, they made Pop singing almost respectable.

Cliff was easily the most successful. His great secret was that he was like some magic slate, a pad on which almost anyone could scrawl their fantasies and rub them out and try again. He was the nice boy that girls could be proud to date, the perfect son that mothers could be proud to raise, the good guy that schoolboys could be proud to have as a friend, the earnest youth that intellectuals could be proud to patronize, the perfect flesh that homosexuals could be proud to buy drinks for, the showbiz smile that hipsters could be proud to despise, and so on. It was a format that Tommy Steele had used first and that the Beatles were later to perfect. It is the classic British way of making it: be a clean white wall and let everyone write graffiti on you.

There were other big successes at this time: Frank Ifield, a large hunk of Australian baritone with an alarming line in yodelling; Helen Shapiro, who had a truly foghorn voice but was badly over-publicized and didn't sustain; Eden Kane, who growled; David Jacobs, compere of the long-running TV show *Juke Box Jury*, the last word in Mister Smooth; Emile Ford, who was excellent but who was also Black and that, ten years ago, was just about that; and Norrie Paramor, a small middle-aged man with glasses, mild and harmless, who produced hits for Cliff and the Shadows.

The best of the bunch was Adam Faith, who was at least an original. He was a marvellous face, classic bone structure, but he was also very short and had to wear monstrous high-heeled boots if he wasn't to be dwarfed by his infant fans. He didn't have much of a voice either, he was all nose and tonsil, a poor man's Buddy Holly. What he did have, though, was good management, good song-writing, good plugging and, most important, a certain persisent oddity, a real individuality.

His first number one, 'What Do You Want?' was one continuous hiccough, a dying fit, agonized and agonizing, the words contorted almost beyond recognition. He spewed up the word 'baby' as 'biybee', choking horribly on each vowel, and that was the major hook. So all right, maybe it wasn't any profound insight into the human condition but it was catching; it made him. One word mispronounced and he had his whole career going for him.

Natch, he flogged it hard, spluttering and expiring like a man inspired, and he did very nicely. In retrospect, his big hits – 'Poor Me', 'Someone Else's Baby', 'How About That?' – stand up as the best, most inventive British records of that time, the only truly POP music we were producing then. They still sound active now.

But the most important thing he did was to introduce the concept of Pop Singer as Thinker, now so popular with documentaries and the Sunday papers.

Originally, he got interviewed by John Freeman on *Face To Face*, a chore he shared with such as Jung, Gilbert Harding and Tony Hancock. Freeman put up a series of nice slow lobs for him and Adam fended them off very capably – his favourite composers were Sibelius and Dvořák, he said, and his favourite book was *Catcher In The Rye*; sincerity was the quality he would most like to be admired for, that and being an individual; thirty was about the right age to get married. That kind of thing. Hardly sensational but he spoke it neatly, smoothly. He was strictly non-moronic.

Soon, he was to be heard discussing morals, sex before marriage, just about anything solemn that got thrown at him and this was where Pop began to go up in the world. Slowly and humbly, admittedly, but upwards just the same. All through the '50s Pop had been desperately unfashionable, the last word in non-chic. Outside its immediate public, it was seen simply as a joke.

Now, mostly because of Adam, it was getting to be accepted. It was becoming something of a fashionable status symbol and that, of course, is where the Beatles cashed in.

The Beatles

IN THE BEGINNING, I SHOULD SAY, THE BEATLES WERE THE QUARRYMEN, and then they were the Silver Beatles, and there were five of them: John Lennon, Stuart Sutcliffe, Paul McCartney, George Harrison, and Pete Best. All of them came from working-class or lower-middle-class backgrounds in Liverpool, and the only ones with any pretensions to anything were Paul McCartney, who had racked up five 'O' levels, and Stuart Sutcliffe, who painted.

The heavies at this time were Sutcliffe and John Lennon, who were at Art School together.

Sutcliffe was something like an embryo James Dean, very beautiful looking, and he wore shades even in the dark: he was natural image. Of all the Beatles at this stage he was the most sophisticated and the most articulate; Eduardo Paolozzi, the painter, who taught him for a time, says that he was very talented indeed.

As for Lennon, he was a roughneck. His father, who was a seaman, had left home when Lennon was still a small child; his mother had died, and he'd been brought up by his Aunt Mimi. And by the time he got to Art School, he'd grown into a professional hard-nut, big-mouthed and flash, notorious for his great skill as a thiever; and he rampaged through Liverpool like some wounded buffalo, smashing everything that got in his way. He wrote songs with Paul McCartney. He had hefty intellectual discussions with Sutcliffe. He was rude to almost everyone, loud and callous and brutally funny; his put-downs could kill. A lot of people noticed him.

The Beatles, at this time, were still total Teds: they wore greasy hair and leather jackets and winkle pickers; they jeered and got into fights and were barred from pubs. Mostly, they're remembered as thugs.

The music they played then was souped-up rock, much influenced by Eddie Cochran and Buddy Holly, not notably original, and they were less than an explosion. In 1960 they managed a tour of Scotland with Johnny Gentle, one of the lesser figures in the Larry Parnes stable, but mostly they alternated between random gigs in Liverpool and seasons at the Star Club in Hamburg, where they played murderous hours each night and half-way starved to death.

At this point, Stuart Sutcliffe left the group to concentrate on his painting and, soon afterwards, died of a brain tumour. He was twenty-one. Meanwhile, the Beatles had begun to move up a bit – they'd made some records in Germany, bad records but records just the same, and they'd built themselves a solid following, both in Germany and at home. And musically, they'd become competent and they had their own sound, a crossbreed between classic rock and commercial R & B; they were raw, deafening, a bit crude, but they were really exciting. At least, unlike any other British act ever, they didn't ape America but sounded what they were – working-class Liverpool, dirty-mouthed and scruffy, unfake – and that's what gave them their strength; that's what made Brian Epstein want to manage them.

Epstein was the eldest son in a successful Jewish business family, and he ran a Liverpool record store. In his early twenties he'd wanted to be an actor and he'd gone to the Royal Academy of Dramatic Art, but now, approaching thirty, he'd resigned himself to being a businessman. Intelligent and loyal and neurotic, painfully sensitive, he was nobody's picture of a hustler, but he was civilized, basically honest, and he had capital. So he asked the Beatles to let him be their manager and they agreed.

Soon after this, Pete Best, the drummer, got flung out and was replaced by Ringo Starr. Best had laid down a loud and clumsy beat, quite effective, but he'd been less sharp, less clever, less flexible than the other Beatles and they'd got bored with him; they wanted him out. Characteristically, though, they saddled Epstein with the job of telling him.

Ringo Starr's real name was Richard Starkey, and he'd been playing with Rory Storme and the Hurricanes, Liverpool's top group of that time. Actually, he wasn't too much of a drummer, and he had rough times at the hands of vengeful Pete Best fans; he was given a fierce baptism, and the Beatles themselves mostly ignored him – he didn't belong. But he had his own defences, a great offhand resilience and a deadpan humour, and he survived.

Meanwhile, Epstein acted like a manager. Privately he had huge inhibitions about hustling, but he fought them down and sweated. The Beatles roasted him any time he showed signs of flagging (Lennon in particular was merciless), so Epstein had demos made and touted them around the record companies; he pleaded and spieled and harangued. And having first been turned down by Dick Rowe at Decca, the King Dagobert of Pop, he finally got a contract with EMI and everything began.

From there on in, it was fast and straight ahead: the first single, 'Love Me Do', made the top thirty; the second 'Please Please Me', made number one; the third 'From Me To You', also made number one (louder), and the fourth 'She Loves You', was the biggest hit that any British artist had ever cut. All of them were written by Lennon and McCartney.

By spring of 1963, they had taken over from Cliff Richard in Britain, and by autumn they were a national obsession. At the beginning of 1964, given the most frantic hype ever, they broke out in America and stole the first five places solid on the chart. That summer, they released their first movie, *Hard Day's Night*, and it smashed, and that just about rounded things out. Altogether, it had taken two years from first big push to last.

At the end of all this, they had become the largest, Elvis apart, phenomenon that Pop had yet coughed up, and even more remarkably, they've hardly slid since. To the time of writing, they have sold upward of two hundred million

119

records, and they're coming up for their twentieth straight number one.

Beyond that, they had made millions of dollars for themselves and many more millions of dollars for their government; in reward, they were all given the MBE for their contributions to the export drive. This was a clincher – assorted retired majors and jumped-up clerks sent their own medals back in protest, but everyone else was delighted. That's how respectable Pop had become, and it was the Beatles who'd made it like that.

One side effect of Beatlemania was that there was a hysterical boom in Liverpudlia. Two days after 'Please Please Me' had crashed number one, the collected managers and agents of Britain hit Merseyside like a plague, and they didn't leave again until every last able-bodied guitar picker in town had been hijacked. They were pure Hollywood, straight out of *Mad* Magazine – smoked cigars, drove limousines, waved shiny contracts, and conned everyone blind. They slavered greed from their throats, lust from their nostrils, hype from their eyeballs, and inside six months they'd run the city clean. Nobody left but women, children and crips. Total wipe-out.

In the first wave alone, there were the Searchers, Gerry and the Pacemakers, Billy J. Kramer and the Dakotas, the Mojos, the Swinging Blue Jeans, the Undertakers, Tommy Quickly, the Merseybeats, and the Big Three. Without exception, they had a few fast hits and then, without exception, they blew up.

Liverpool is a strange town; it gets obsessed by everything it does. It's a seaport made up of different races, a city full of neighbourhoods, full of gangs, and outside of Glasgow it's the rawest, most passionate place in Britain.

It has a certain black style of its own, a private strength and humour and awareness, real violence, and it is also grim, very much so. After the pubs close down, everyone stands out on corners and watches what happens and has nowhere much to go. Clubs are small, sweaty, and dumb. Kids don't move by themselves or they get nutted by the guerrillas. This is ghetto America in England: a night out ends almost inevitably with a punch on the nose, or worse.

In such an atmosphere, hungry and physical, Pop could

hardly miss. It exploded. It took over completely, it turned everyone fanatic, and by the early sixties there were upward of 350 groups around, more getting born each day. Almost always, they were musically dire, quite dreadful, but that wasn't the point – they were loud, crude, energetic, and they weren't faked.

Of course, in the normal run of things, almost none of them would ever have happened, but this was no normal run; the Beatles had smashed, Liverpool was a national obsession, and suddenly they couldn't lose.

Quality wasn't remotely relevant here – all they had to do was open wide, let those lush scouse accents out, and they were home in one; they had walkovers. In this way, the charts got filled with musical assassination. But it was a fierce time; at least it was rowdy, and nobody was bored.

Individually, nobody came to much: the Searchers were the most melodic, the Swinging Blue Jeans the most frantic, the Merseybeats somehow the most archetypal. Outside of that, nothing.

As for the Beatles, beyond their music itself, their greatest strengths were clarity of image and the way they balanced. It's a truism that no Pop format is any good unless it can be expressed in one sentence, but the Beatles went beyond that; they could each be said in one word: Lennon was the brutal one, McCartney was the pretty one, Ringo Starr was the lovable one, Harrison was the balancer. And if Lennon was tactless, McCartney was a natural diplomat. And if Harrison was dim, Lennon was very clever. And if Starr was clownish, Harrison was almost sombre. And if McCartney was arty, Starr was basic. Round and round in circles, no loose ends left over, and it all made for a comforting sense of completeness.

Completeness, in fact, was what the Beatles were all about. They were always perfectly self-contained, independent, as if the world was split cleanly into two races, the Beatles and everyone else, and they seemed to live off nobody but themselves.

There is a film of their first American press conference that expresses this perfectly. Hundreds of newsmen question them, close in and batter and hassle them, but the Fab Four aren' reached. They answer politely, they make jokes, they're most charming — but they're never remotely involved, they're private. They have their own club going, and really, they aren't reachable. They are, after all, the Beatles.

The Rolling Stones

IN LIVERPOOL ONE TIME, EARLY IN 1965, I WAS SITTING IN SOME PUB, JUST next to the Odeon Cinema, and I heard a noise like thunder.

I went outside and looked around but I couldn't see a thing. Just this noise of thunder, slowly getting closer, and also more faint, another noise like a wailing siren. So I waited but nothing happened. The street stayed empty.

Finally, after maybe five full minutes, a car came round the corner, a big flash limousine, and it was followed by police cars, by police on foot and police on motorbikes, and they were followed by several hundred teenage girls. And these girls made a continuous high-pitched keening sound and their shoes banged down against the stone. They ran like hell, their hair down in their eyes, and they stretched their arms out pleadingly as they went. They were desperate.

The limousine came up the street towards me and stopped directly outside the Odeon stage door. The police formed cordons. Then the car door opened and the Rolling Stones got out, all five of them and Andrew Loog Oldham, their manager, and they weren't real. They had hair down past their shoulders and they wore clothes of every colour imaginable and they looked mean, they looked just impossibly evil.

In this grey street, they shone like sun gods. They didn't seem human, they were like creatures off another planet, impossible to reach or understand but most exotic, most beautiful in their ugliness.

They crossed towards the stage door and this was what the girls had been waiting for, this was their chance, so they began to surge and scream and clutch. But then they stopped, they just froze. The Stones stared straight ahead, didn't twitch once, and the girls only gaped. Almost as if the Stones weren't touchable, as if they were protected by some invisible metal ring. So they moved on and disappeared. And the girls went limp behind them and were quiet. After a few seconds, some of them began to cry.

In this way, whatever else, the Stones had style and presence and real control. They are my favourite group. They always have been.

To begin with, they used to play the Crawdaddy Club in Richmond and they laid down something very violent in the line of rhythm 'n' blues. They were enthusiasts then, they cared a lot about their music. Really, that was the only thing that linked them because they'd come from different backgrounds, very different situations, but they'd all grown up to the Blues and, for a time, they got along.

At this point, they were only archetypal drop-outs. I mean, they weren't art students but they should have been, they had all the symptoms, that aggression, that scruffiness and calculated cool, that post-beat bohemianism. And in these very early '60s, before the age of T-shirts and baseball boots, the heavy art-school cults were Ray Charles and Chuck Berry and Bo Diddley, Muddy Waters, Charlie Mingus and Monk, Allen Ginsberg and Jack Kerouac, Robert Johnson. If you were pretentious about it, you might stretch to a paperback translation of Rimbaud or Dostoyevsky, strictly for display. But the Stones weren't pretentious – they were mean and nasty, full-blooded, very tasty, and they beat out the toughest, crudest, most offensive noise any English band had ever made.

At any rate, the Stones were at the Crawdaddy, peddling stuff about midway between the bedrock Chicago Blues of Muddy Waters and the Pop-Blues of Chuck Berry, and they built themselves a following. Naughty but nice, they were liked by Aldermaston marchers and hitch-hikers, beards and freaks and pre-Neanderthal Mods everywhere. Simply, they were turning into the voice of hooliganism.

As groups go, they were definitely motley: Mick Jagger, who sang, came out of a solid middle-class background and had been to the London School of Economics; Keith Richards came from Tottenham and was quite tough; Brian Jones wasn't tough at all – he was from Cheltenham, very safe, but he was insecure, neurotic, highly intelligent.

Charlie Watts had worked in an ad agency and, being a drummer, never talked; Bill Wyman was older, was married – he didn't quite belong.

Anyhow, the thing about them was that, unlike the Beatles, they didn't balance out but niggled, jarred and hardly ever relaxed. At all times, there was tension to them – you always felt there was a background chance of a public holocaust. That was partly what made them exciting.

In 1963, Andrew Loog Oldham became their manager.

Oldham, without doubt, was the most flash personality that British pop has ever had, the most anarchic and obsessive and imaginative hustler of all. When he was good, he was quite magnificent.

His father having been killed in the war, he'd grown up with his mother, quite rich, and he was sent to public school. By the time he was sixteen, he was doing window displays for Mary Quant, the clothes designer, and then he spent a year bumming round the South of France before he came back to work in the cloakroom at the Ronnie Scott Club and be a publicist with Brian Epstein's NEMS. And that was the whole sum of his achievement at the time he first met the Stones. He was then nineteen years old.

What he had going for him was mostly a frantic yen to get up and out: he loathed slowness and drabness, age and caution and incompetence, mediocrity of all kinds, and he could not stand to work his way up steady like anyone else.

Instead, he barnstormed, he came on quite outrageous. He slabbed his face with make-up and wore amazing clothes and hid his eyes behind eternal shades. He was all camp and, when he was batting off nothing at all, he still shot fat lines and always played everything as ultimate big-time.

The great thing was the way he pushed himself, he could either clean up or bomb completely. He couldn't possibly get caught by compromise.

Anyhow, the Stones were obviously just his meat. He caught them at Richmond and got hooked by their truculence, their built-in offensiveness. Also, he struck up immediate contact with Mick Jagger, who was greatly impressed by him and became almost his disciple, his dedicated follower in the ways of outrage.

So Oldham brought in Eric Easton, who was his partner and had capital. Easton, a stock businessman who handled such showbiz stuff as Bert Weedon and Julie Grant, wasn't unimpressed. 'But the singer'll have to go,' he said. 'The BBC won't like him.'

As manager, what Oldham did was to take everything implicit in the Stones and blow it up one hundred times. Long-haired and ugly and anarchic as they were, Oldham made them more so and he turned them into everything that parents would most hate, be most frightened by. All the time, he goaded them to be wilder, nastier, fouler in every way and they were – they swore, sneered, snarled and, deliberately, they came on cretinous.

It was good basic psychology: kids might see them the first time and not be sure about them, but then they'd hear their parents whining about those animals, those filthy long-haired morons, and suddenly they'd be converted, they'd identify like mad.

(This, of course, is bedrock pop formula: find yourself something that truly makes adults squirm and, straightaway, you have a guaranteed smash on your hands. Johnnie Ray, Elvis, P. J. Proby, Jimi Hendrix – it never fails.)

So their first single, 'Come On', got to the edge of the twenty, and then 'I Wanna Be Your Man' was number ten, and 'Not Fade Away' was number three and, finally, 'It's All Over Now' was number one. Their initial album did a hundred thousand in a week and, by this time, they were running hot second to the Beatles and they kept it like that for two years solid. Later on, in America, they even temporarily went ahead.

All this time, Oldham hustled them strong: he was hectic,

inventive, and he pulled strokes daily. Less obviously, he was also thorough, he worked everything out to the smallest spontaneous detail. Well, the Stones were really his fantasy, his private dream-child and, healthy narcissist as he was, he needed them to be entirely perfect.

The bit I liked best, about both Oldham and the Stones themselves, was the stage act. In every way, both individually and collectively, it expressed them just right.

Charlie Watts played the all-time bombhead drummer, mouth open and jaw sagging, moronic beyond belief, and Bill Wyman stood way out to one side, virtually in the wings, completely isolated, his bass held up vertically in front of his face for protection, and he chewed gum endlessly and his eyes were glazed and he looked just impossibly bored.

Keith Richards wore T-shirts and, all the time, he kept winding and unwinding his legs, moving uglily like a crab, and was shut-in, shuffling, the classic fourth-form drop-out. Simply, he spelled Borstal.

Brian Jones had beautiful silky yellow hair to his shoulders, exactly like a Silvikrin ad, and camped it up like mad. He did the whole feminine thing and, for climax, he'd rush the front of the stage and make to jump off, flouncing and flitting like a gymslip schoolgirl.

And then Mick Jagger: he had lips like bumpers, red and fat and shiny, and they covered his face. He looked like an updated Elvis Presley, in fact, skinny legs and all, and he moved non-stop, so fast and flash he flickered. When he came on out, he went bang. He'd shake his hair all down in his eyes and he danced like a whitewash James Brown, he flapped those tarpaulin lips and, grotesque, he was all sex.

He sang but you couldn't hear him for screams, you only got some background blur, the beat, and all you knew was his lips. His lips, and his moving legs, bound up in sausage-skin pants. And he was outrageous: he spun himself blind, he smashed himself and he'd turn his back on the audience, jack-knife from the waist, so that his arse stuck straight up in the air, and then he'd shake himself, he'd vibrate like a motor, and he'd reach the hand mike through his legs at you, he'd push it right in your face. Well, he was obscene, he was excessive. Of course, he was beautiful.

The weird thing was, Jagger on-stage wasn't like Jagger off-stage but he was very much like Andrew Oldham. Andrew Loog Oldham. I mean, he was more a projection of Oldham than of himself. (This happens often. For various obvious physical reasons, most managers aren't capable of getting out and being stars themselves. So they use the singers they handle as transmitters, as dream machines. Possibly, that's the way it was with Jagger and Oldham.)

That time in Liverpool, the night I mentioned before, the Stones put on maybe the best pop show I ever saw: final bonanza, hysterical and violent and sick but always stylized, always full of hype, and Jagger shaped up genuinely as a second Elvis, as heroic and impossible as that.

After the show, I hung around in the dressing rooms. The Stones were being ritually vicious to everyone, fans and journalists and hangers-on regardless, and I got bored. So I went down into the auditorium and it was empty, quite deserted, but there was this weird smell. Piss: the small girls had screamed too hard and wet themselves. Not just one or two of them but many, so that the floor was sodden and the stench was overwhelming. Well, it was disgusting. No, it wasn't disgusting but it was strange, the empty cinema (chocolate boxes, cigarette packs, ice-lolly sticks) and this sad, sour smell.

Throughout this chapter, I've kept on saying how great the Stones were but all I've shown is evil and the question finally needs to be asked: what's so good about bad?

No question, of course, the Stones were more loutish than they had to be but then, after all, each Pop generation must go further than the one before, must feel as if it's doing everything for the first time. Always, it must be arrogant and vain and boorish. Otherwise, it's not being healthy and the whole essential teen revolt gets dammed up, that whole bit of breaking away and making it by oneself, and then it's stored up in frustration, it twists itself and, most likely, it comes out ugly later on.

The best thing about the Stones, the most important, was their huge sense of independence, uncompromised.

In the first chapter, I said that Pop had originally been just that, a movement towards teen independence, and that Elvis was its first great leader. Well, compared to Elvis, the Stones were an entirely different class: they were as far ahead of him as Elvis himself had been ahead of the young Sinatra.

No mashed banana sandwiches, middle-aged managers, GI blues, teddy bears, Gods or obediences – the Stones were a teenage industry all by themselves, self-contained, and the adult world simply wasn't relevant. That's why they were so loathed inside the business, because they threatened the structure, because they threatened the way in which Pop was controlled by old men, by men over thirty.

That's also why they mattered, that's why Andrew Oldham mattered in particular, because they meant that you didn't need to soften up to make it any more. You didn't need to be pretty, you didn't need to simper or drool or suck up – the old men might hate you in every way possible and you could still make yourself a million dollars.

Really, the Stones were major liberators: they stirred up a whole new mood of teen arrogance here and the change was reflected in the rise of Mod, in Carnaby Street and Radio Caroline, in Cathy McGowan and the Who and, later, in Twiggy. These weren't purely teenage happenings, of course, but most everyone involved in them was under thirty and none of them could possibly have happened in the '50s. For the first time, England had something like a private teen society going and, myself, I think it was the Stones rather than the Beatles who led it.

Certainly, the Beatles were the bigger group but, until they turned to Love in 1967, they never greatly changed the way that anyone thought. They were self-assured, cocky, and they took no shit but they were always full of compromise and they appealed as much to adults as to kids. They weren't committed. The Stones were.

In this way, then, the Stones were the final group of the '60s and their image was the final image, Jagger was the final face and their records were the final records. More than anyone, more even than Bob Dylan, they became their time.

Apart from anything else, they made marvellous music.

In the early R & B phase, they were wildly exciting but also crude, derivative, very limited, and they shaped up only as a short-term craze. But then, just as things were wearing thin, Jagger and Keith Richards suddenly upped and exploded as writers. Out of nowhere, they started churning out monsters: 'The Last Time', 'Satisfaction', 'Get Off Of My Cloud', 'Mother's Little Helper', 'Under My Thumb', 'Paint It Black'.

They weren't much on melody, their words were mostly slogans, and a lot of their songs were non-music. None of that mattered. All that counted was sound – and adapted Spector-sound but less symphonic, less inflated – and the murderous mood it made. All din and mad atmosphere. Really, it was nothing but beat, smashed and crunched and hammered home like some amazing stampede. The words were lost and the song was lost. You were only left with chaos, beautiful anarchy. You drowned in noise.

Their best record was probably 'Satisfaction'. Their most archetypal was 'Get Off Of My Cloud', which sloganized the sixties just as 'Blue Suede Shoes' had the fifties.

According to the story line, Jagger lives in an apartment on the ninety-ninth floor of his block and sits alone by the window, imagining the world has stopped. He plays records incredibly loud, makes holocausts of noise, and nobody can reach him, nobody can turn his volume down. People from below try to shut him up but he takes no notice. He sits and plays records and watches and floats. He can't be touched.

P. J. Proby

THE FIRST TIME I MET P. J. PROBY, HE WAS AT HIS PEAK. HE HAD BEEN IN England for about a year and, immediately, he had cleaned up, he'd established himself as the most mesmeric solo act we'd got. So he was the biggest new star around then but he was also one long streak of trouble and he was always neck deep in hassles. He was intuitive, fast, hysterical, paranoid, generous, very funny, hugely imaginative, original, self-obsessed, self-destructive, often impossible, just about irresistible and much more besides. Truly, he was complicated.

I went to see him and he was sitting in a darkened hotel room, downing bourbon and Coke by the tumblerful. He was wearing a grubby string vest, old white socks and navy-blue knickers. And he was tired, his hair hung all unkempt around his shoulders and his eyes were red, his face was swollen with lost sleep. He looked quite defeated.

When I first came in, he said nothing but only handed me a scrap of paper, covered in ragged, semi-illegible handwriting. 'That's my testament,' said Proby. 'Read it.'

On inspection, it turned out to be something like a petition. Crudely paraphrased, it said that, ever since Proby had been in this country, he had been systematically hounded by enemies and fools. His name had been blackened, his life made not worth living, his career half-wrecked. Promoters, record companies and agents had conspired together to bring him down and break him. Until he had finally had enough and now he'd decided to expose them all. Near the end, in a crucial phrase, he said: 'I am an artist and should be exempt from shit.'

All the curtains were drawn tight and the hotel room was full of people: Proby's hairdresser and assistant and publicists, his friends. Great image: Proby himself just brooded, said nothing, and everyone else watched him.

Very suddenly, Proby began to talk to me and then didn't stop for maybe two hours. He told me many things, all about his life and his soul and his many agonies, and he made everything epic, everything wild and somehow magnificent. The way he told it, his life was a composite of Jesus Christ, Judy Garland and Errol Flynn.

According to the saga, he was born in Texas, real name James Marcus Smith, and his father had been a very rich man, a much respected citizen. And his earliest years were filled with happiness, but it didn't last; he was sent away to military college, which trained and disciplined him to be a man, and then he changed his name to Jet Powers, became a singer and went west to Hollywood. He wrote songs and hustled. Waited for breaks to happen and, around this time, he got married. So he and his young bride used to sit in their window when the evening came, looking down into the street below, and they'd dream about the way it'd be when he finally made it, when his name was big in lights. That's exactly the way that Proby told it: young love, first love, filled with deep devotion.

Later, some of his songs were made into hits and he moved up. He was a Hollywood face. And Jack Good planned to stage a musical of *Othello*, Proby playing Iago to Muhammad Ali's Moor. That was really something.

But then, just as the time of his ultimate triumph was approaching, he quarrelled with his true love, and he was all capsized again. He came to England and, of course, he became a superstar but he wasn't happy, he never could be. He was hollow inside.

Picture him: a man crucified, a genius destroyed, a beautiful animal caged – he told me all of that, and, when he was finished, he lapsed into silence and stared at the floor, drank more bourbon. Finally, he raised his head, looked at me, and he flashed me his first smile. Pure malice. 'How's that?' he said. 'Did I break your fucking heart?'

(Being half way honest for once, I have to say that there are many people around who'll tell you entirely different versions of the Proby trauma and they'll all swear blind that theirs is the only right one. Myself, I'd say that mine is as possible as any other and I stick by it.)

At any rate, I was just eighteen when Proby hit me with this and I was never so impressed by anything in my life. The darkened room, the bourbon, the knickers, the fat Texan drawl – this was true heroism and it made me shake. I never grew out of it either.

On stage, he was magnificent.

He'd stand behind a curtain and extend one toe and all his little girls screamed. Then he'd draw it back again, then he'd extend it again, then he'd draw it back again. This might continue for five full minutes, getting slightly bolder, even flashing his ankle, and then he'd suddenly bound out like some puppy St Bernard. He wore blue velvet all over, loose jerkin to hide his paunch and skintight pants, and he had his hair tied back in a bow, and he wore buckled shoes, and he was camp as hell. Simply, he was outrageous.

He'd stand quite still and then he'd turn around, he'd mince across the stage like some impossible drag-queen and then he'd stop dead again, he'd grind his groin like a really filthy burlesque stripper, and then he'd flounce across to the wings like an overweight ballet dancer, and then he'd come back all coy and demure like a small ribboned girl, and then he'd snarl, and then he'd pout, and then he'd start the whole thing over again. He'd sing a ballad and he'd agonize, he'd raise one hand, he'd let fall an invisible rose. Or he'd sing soul and he'd scream, grind, go berserk. Then he'd make a monologue and he'd explain how he was mistreated, conspired against, and how his only friends in the world were his fans, his little girls. Then he'd be camp again and he'd flaunt one hand on his hip and his lashes fluttered like fans. Well, it could all have been horribly embarrassing, it very nearly was, but he had a great voice, he owned real presence and somehow he brazened it out. The way he explained it, he'd taken all his movements, all his faces from different girls. You could well believe it. Whatever, he kept going for a full hour and he screamed himself voiceless, he sweated till he was slimy all over like a toad, till he was quite hideous, and still he piled on intensity, agony, outrage. 'Am I clean?' he'd squeal. 'Am I clean? Am I spotless? Am I pure?'

When he was done, when he'd quite destroyed himself, he'd stagger off blindly into the wings and collapse, semi-conscious, in his dressing room. He'd just lie there for maybe twenty minutes without moving. Then Proby would rise up refreshed and he'd bound out through the stagedoor and into his waiting limousine, surrounded and protected at all times by his entourage, and then the whole circus would roll back to London.

Wild camp, marvellous image: P. J. Proby lay back exhausted in his cushions, the Sun King, his hair like drenched rope, his mouth full of bourbon, and everyone entertained him. No medieval warlord ever had it better.

With all this, he was talented. Specifically, he had giant range, perfect control and he was a flawless mimic, he could turn himself into anyone from Billy Eckstine to Frankie Valli, Gene Pitney to James Brown. And such a voice. As a straight ballad singer, he was on a par with Sinatra or Tony Bennett or any of them, but he'd distort his diction, exaggerate, melodramatize until the whole thing turned into a subtle burlesque of the original slop.

On songs like 'My Prayer' or 'When I Fall In love', he'd be so almost straight that you'd really be fooled and then, just when you'd be nicely lulled, he'd slip in something sneaky and capsize you. Always it was neatly done, never crude. So his version of 'Somewhere' and 'I Apologize' and 'If I Loved You' were strange little classics, almost surreal, and their great flavour was that you never knew just how you were meant to take them.

Anyhow, soon after that first time I met him, things started going very wrong indeed. 'Somewhere' made number three and he landed his first headlining cinema tour, always a major milestone but, on the first night, he split his velvet trousers from knee to crotch. On the second night, he did exactly the same. On the third night, he did it one time too often, and the curtain came down and he was flung off the tour, widely banned, hammered by the press, much insulted by the industry and enthusiastically kicked in the teeth by almost everyone.

This was disaster: he did have other hits, he did hang on but he was cut off from the most crucial outlets and he got progressively cornered.

Even then he never walked small.

The thinking was always simple – Proby was a face, a Hollywood star, and he lived like one. He owed it, not only to himself, but to his fans and, most vital, to his image. At any rate, that's the way he figured it and, accordingly, he kept up a large house in Chelsea and supported an entourage and spent fortunes in discotheques and hired twenty-piece P. J. Proby Orchestras to back him.

He went to America for a year, tried raising horses, failed, and came back to London. This was early 1968 and, by now, he was officially bankrupt but he still smiled smiles, looked angelic and said most solemnly that he was an entirely reformed character. On his first comeback gig, he was heckled. Immediately, he exploded in a rash of four-letter words and the curtain came down. And everyone was happy – nothing had changed.

Whatever else, he has proved himself resilient. His greatest gift has been that he's always been able to convince those around him, myself included, that he was a genius. And just so long as that gift survives, he can't ever be written off and he can't ever starve. He can always find someone to pay his bills and love him and launch him one more time.

Well, I suppose I've given him more space than he deserves and, really, I have no justifications except that I dig him so much. Along with Muhammad Ali, he is the great doomed romantic showman of our time, the Rasputin or Hearst or Jelly Roll Morton, and I'm left with two central images of him.

The first is an outsize portrait in oils (the work, he once told me, of 'an Italian old master') and it shows him all in velvet, angelic-faced, walking on the clouds.

The second is his recording his entry for a San Remo festival and the Italian composer has flown over to supervise. The Italian is a caricature composer, all twirled moustachios and rapturous eyes, and Proby, who isn't entirely sober, is a classic Proby figure, all stubble and blear. And they're standing alone in the middle of a vast studio floor and Proby is singing. He doesn't know a word of Italian, he has no idea what he's saying, and still he spreads his arms, throws his head way back and soars. He'd break your heart. Such pain, such yearning, such terrible passion – the composer has never heard anything like it and he's drooling.

At the end of the take, the Italian flings his arms full round Proby's neck and hugs him. Proby beams. 'Mr Proby,' says the composer. 'How do you do it?'

'Maestro,' says Proby. 'I don't do. I am.'

The End

PROBABLY IT'S NOT BEEN A BAD TIME TO WRITE THIS BOOK: ROCK IS AT ITS most important junction yet, it's in the gap between two major phases, and this has been quite a clean moment to make some interval notes on it.

What I've written about has been the rise and fall of Superpop, the noise machine, and the image, hype, and beautiful flash of rock 'n' roll music. Elvis riding on his golden Cadillac, James Brown throwing off his robes in a fit, Pete Townshend slaughtering his audience with his machine-gun guitar, Mick Jagger hanging off his mike like Tarzan Weismuller in the jungle, P. J. Proby – all the heroic acts of pulp.

Superpop? It hasn't been much, it's been simple always, silly and vulgar and fake, and it has been a noise, that's all. In the end, specific records and singers have hardly mattered. Instead, it's been Pop itself, just the existence of it, the drone and bleat of it running through everything.

I was ten when it started; I'm twenty-two now, and it has bossed my life. It has surrounded me always, cut me off, and it has given me my heroes, it has made my myths. Almost, it has done my living for me. Six hours of trash every day, and it's meant more to me than anything else.

Superpop – it's been like a continuing Western; it's had that same classic simplicity, the same power to turn cliché into myth. It's had no mind of its own. All it's ever done has been to catch currents, moods, teen obsessions, and freeze them in images. It has made giant caricatures of lust, violence, romance and revolt, and they've been the most powerful, most accurate fictions of this time.

And then, beyond the heroes, beyond anything, there's been the noise, the endless and perfect and changeless beat. Noise has been everything.

Anyhow, it's finished now, the first mindless explosion, and the second stage has begun. Pop has got complicated. That was inevitable: everything ends, nothing remains simple. Pop has split itself into factions and turned sophisticate. Part of it has a mind now, makes fine music. The other part is purely industrial, a bored and boring business like any other. Either way, there are no more heroes and no more Superpop. It has all been reduced to human beings.

What's left? In England, the industry is split roughly eighty per cent ugly and twenty per cent idealist.

The ugly eighty are mainline Pop, computerized, and they hit a largely teenybop or pre-teen market, ages six to sixteen, plus a big pocket of middle-aged parents. They have a function, and they sell records. They make money.

The blue-eyed twenty are hardly even Pop any more. With very few exceptions, notably the Beatles and the Stones, they don't sell records, and after all, what's Pop about unpopularity? In ten years, they'll probably be called by another name entirely, electric music or something, and they'll relate to Pop the way that art movies relate to Hollywood. Very soon, you'll have Pop composers writing formal works for Pop choirs, Pop orchestras; you'll have Pop concerts held in halls and the audience all seated in rows, not screaming or stamping but applauding politely with their hands; you'll have sounds and visuals combined, records that are played on something like a stereo system and TV set knocked into one, the music creating pictures and patterns. You'll have cleverness of every kind imaginable, and out of all this you'll get a lot of pretension and bullshit, but you may also get masterworks.

It doesn't really matter to me. Not that I have anything much against masterworks in principle, but I'm hooked on image, on heroics. It's like films – the best in art movies have no doubt been most sensitive, brilliant, and meaningful works of art, and where have I been? In the back row of the Roxy, of course, gawking at Hollywood.

THREE

Arfur

1970

1: Moriarty

THIS IS THE STORY OF ARFUR, THE TEENAGE PIN-BALL QUEEN.

When I was ten years old, I visited the Moriarty funfair and it was a very hot day, an August afternoon, and there were fat people on every side of me and I walked along with my roller-skates slung on my shoulder.

Sweating, I hid inside a house of glass but I didn't like it: there were distorting mirrors everywhere, I was hemmed in by my own freaked images and I got frightened, I couldn't find the exit. Trapped, I began to weep and I tried to break out by force, I blundered into a full-length mirror and smashed it.

I wasn't hurt.

Instead I slid through the glass as soft and smooth as butter and fell down in a heap on the other side, my skates still on my shoulder. And when I opened my eyes, I was in a public park and the funfair was behind me, there was a wooden bench in front of me, and seated on this bench was a Chinaman.

This Chinaman, he had yellow flesh and slit eyes and wispy moustaches, and he smiled at me. 'Little girl,' he said, 'you're welcome here.'

'I was hidden in the glasshouse,' I said. 'I got lost and broke a mirror and fell out on the ground.'

'My name is Lim Fan, I am a barman,' said the Chinaman.

'I'm Arfur,' I said. 'I'm clean.'

It was hot here; there was a crawling heat all around us, and Lim Fan was wearing a white shirt with a polka-dot bow tie, baggy brown trousers with yellow braces, and he seemed scrubbed, he smelled soapy like avocado pear. In the public park he touched me gently, and took me to his room. We walked out in the streets of Moriarty, while my skates jarred on my shoulder with every step I took.

Lim Fan's room was situated at the top of four flights of stairs and there were damp walls all around us as we climbed, decaying boards and the smell of stale cabbage on the landings, and the room itself was small and darkened and disconsolate but filled with maps and diagrams, complex calculations.

Lim Fan smelled like soapy avocado and he washed my legs with a loofah, very grave in all his motions, and my thighs were tickled by the wisps of his moustaches.

Speaking, his voice held no inflection and he was calm. When he moved, his bow tie caught the light and I twanged his braces, I made them snap like bowstrings. 'I work in the tenderloin,' he said. 'Bad men come in most every night and, if they don't feel happy, they turn the bar-room on its head. They pick up bottles and smash them over human heads, they loot and plunder, they cause destruction without purpose. Even me, if I turn my back to sneeze, they stab me in the back and rob me as I bleed.'

'You must be wise,' I said. 'Are you very old?'

'In this room, I sit and study without pause,' said Lim Fan, not hearing my question. 'If you want, I'll teach you, too, and give you knowledge of every kind.'

'Thank you,' I said. 'I'd like that.' And he spoke with me and I was held. I was caught by his yellow flesh and his smell like soap, by his bow tie and his braces, by the way his voice never changed but unfurled like a recorded message. It was hot outside but cool inside this room. Lim Fan whispered, I listened carefully and, at the age of ten, Arfur began.

'In the beginning,' he said, 'the supreme master laboured six days to create the world, and on the seventh day he rested. And by his plan, the earth was made full of lakes, oceans, mountains, verdant valleys and swift-flowing rivers, and Adam lived with Eve in the Garden of Eden, a paradise of all delights, including apricots and pineapples and ripe yams, black grapes and guavas, and no such thing as strife existed, no pain nor evil, only elegance, and the supreme master looked down on his creation and stroked his beard and gladness filled his heart.

'Later on, however, Eve ate an apple, which was temptation, and this was the beginning of discord, which has lasted ever since, and the earth was taken over by wars, riots, plagues and revolutions. As a result of these disasters, we have the world that exists right now, an orb of many contradictions and catastrophes, but life goes on regardless. When we are born we live and, when we die, we don't: this is the full equation.'

Lim Fan sat across the room from me, smoking jasmine cigarettes, and his voice droned on through the afternoon. Lying on the floor, Arfur smiled and fell asleep. Just as I drifted away, however, he came close to me and kissed me softly on my forehead; his moustaches ran like flies on my flesh.

When I woke up again it was night and Lim Fan wasn't there. The tenement was stilled, there were cats fighting in the alley below. All over the walls, there were graphs and pictures of the sky by night. And I was left alone, so I washed my face, combed my hair and I went downtown to find Lim Fan.

Moriarty, I must explain, is the foremost city of the nation, a compound of refinement and squalor, grace and depravity, a resting place for maybe every race of people beneath the sun, a cauldron of the cultures, and it is split into many districts, such as Jitney and Chinatown and Lincoln County, Cicero and Savoy, the Frenchmans and the Puerto Ricos, the wealthy St Jude, the shanty Canrush, the white and the black ghettos, the docklands and, most famous of all, the tenderloin.

The Moriarty tenderloin, in fact, is by common consent the finest sporting district in creation, a nonpareil, being fitted out with every last amenity that anyone could hope for, and it was here that Lim Fan worked.

Eight blocks by five, it was one continuing carnival and I passed through it slowly. I was bustled and blinded by the brightness and, every door I passed, I could see inside to a mansion full of mirrors.

Ladies sat lazy in their windows, draped in silks, and from within there came the sounds of the dirty blues, where the professors were playing boogie and the girls were dancing naked in the halls. And everywhere there was red plush, there were brass fittings and polished pinewood tables, tapestries and giant candelabra. Opulence ran wild and the sports all drank champagne.

In the Moriarty tenderloin, what's more, nobody walked the pavements, they spilled all over the streets instead, winners intermingling with losers, the rich with the poor regardless, the millionaires and the madams and the big-time gamblers, the cheapies and hucksters, punks and palookas, the third-class chippies at their cribs, the dope fiends of the orient, the greaseball Mexicanos and the turbaned Sikhs, the Italian pimps with luminous socks, the gigolos and fancy dans, the professors and the lawmen and the faggots, the entire span of humanity at one time and place, all intermingled in one rich stew, and there was no distinction made, all men were equal.

Lim Fan worked at the Penguin Orlando, a honky tonk of low description, a dive where everything was ugliness.

By the time I found it, past midnight, this place was half-way empty and the only clients that remained were a selection of maybe the ugliest women I ever witnessed in my life, Negresses with box-car bumper lips, plus two tables of card-sharps, both shooting Cotch, a three-card Spanish poker, ideal for the purpose of cheating.

In the Penguin Orlando nobody spoke, everyone watched and the only sounds were the slap of cards on the tables, steady as a metronome, and the thin asthmatic coughing that the women made in boredom. Behind the bar itself there was a big embossed mirror with a crack running diagonally from top to bottom. This was the style here, and Lim Fan was polishing glasses.

Seeing me, he didn't smile but made me a small bow instead and poured me a glass of orange juice. Even across the bar I could smell soap on him and wanted to touch him. 'I'm ten years old and I'm bored,' I said. 'I'd like to stay with you always.'

'This much is understood,' he said. 'I am your protector.'

Reaching out my hand I touched him, and his yellow fingers

twitched inside my palm. In this way I settled and I didn't leave again till I was almost twelve, during which time I explored the city from every angle and witnessed life of every kind.

On this first night, for instance, I saw the attempted murder of Billy Joe Ross by Sheep Eye Jackson.

This is the way it happened: after one o'clock the bar was almost deserted, even the ugly women had departed and the only clients that remained were Ross and Jackson themselves, two cut-price hustlers, who played Cotch through the night and the cards slapped remorselessly on the table.

Billy Joe was a young boy still but very sharp and he wore a hundred-dollar suit with fancy underwear, diamonds all pinned to his garters, and he played good Cotch. Maybe he cheated, maybe he didn't. Either way, he kept on winning and Sheep Eye got mad.

Sheep Eye was hot-tempered and he had big fat eyes without expression. Whenever he was angry, he lost his mind entirely and killed without blinking, he'd cut a man to pieces for a dollar, then turn away and never think of it again. And playing Cotch in the small hours, no hassles involved, he suddenly pulled out a bowie-knife and stuck Billy Joe in the chest.

Straightaway, Billy Joe fell under the table and Sheep Eye followed him down, blood oozed out on the floor, the table was overturned, cards fluttered all across the bar, Billy Joe was squealing like a sow being slaughtered and Sheep Eye made no sound. Meanwhile, Lim Fan stood back and watched and me, I did the same. Then Billy Joe broke free and ran off in the street, bad blood all on his beautiful clothes, still squealing low, while Sheep Eye sat down on the bar-room floor, his knife hanging loose in his hand, and his big fat eyes were bored.

This wasn't violence. Instead, it was something acted out, a ritual, and carried no reality: Lim Fan polished dirty glasses with a dishrag, Arfur kept quiet, Sheep Eye wiped his knife on the back of his hand, blood slipping through his fingers, and everything remained the same. 'I'm a heartless sonofabitch,' said Sheep Eye. 'I am the baddest man that ever lived.'

'You're a monster,' said Lim Fan.

'The very worst,' said Sheep Eye, and he went out in the tenderloin, his knife still in his hand.

The Penguin Orlando was empty and we closed the shutters, locked the door, turned the chairs upside down on the tables. Then we took brooms and it was strange, almost spooky, the two of us in the half-dark, me on my knees scrubbing bloodstains and Lim Fan shuffling in the shadows, such deep silence after such commotion and, sweeping the floor with long brooms, we made the dust rise up and hang and hesitate, then drop back slowly on the floor.

When we went out into the streets of the tenderloin, however, the night was still at its peak and, every corner we turned, there was laughter and movement and colour, pianos playing ragtime in upstairs' windows and pin-ball lights flashing replays in all the bars, neon everywhere. Down here, nothing shut, nothing ever ended.

On the corner of Argus and Melpomene, we waited for a tram and rode it back to Jitney, where Lim Fan lived in his tenement room.

It was three o'clock in the morning and I'd never been up this late in my life before, I was exhausted. When we came inside the tenement, for instance, I could hardly negotiate the stairways, I kept stumbling and my hand scrabbled at the walls, and when we were inside the room itself, I didn't see the maps and diagrams but fell down on the bed and slept. Lim Fan, meanwhile, he stood above me as I drifted and exposed his yellow braces.

This was the end of the first day of Arfur.

By nature, I watched things. At the age of ten, I wore braces like Lim Fan, lace-up shoes and baggy pants and a trilby, my hair fell down in my eyes and I carried a rabbit's foot at my hip. From a distance, it was almost impossible to guess if I was male or female.

Always, I watched whatever happened. I kept my distance and took no part.

Inside the Jitney tenement, every afternoon, I sat on the bed and Lim Fan stood in front of his many charts, a yellow man with skinny eyes, and he gave me knowledge. Tapping out his messages with a busted chairleg, he was a true scholar and had access to secrets of all descriptions.

In turn, he taught me the past and present and future; alchemy and algebra and anatomy; the religions of the world, melodious discourse and the symptoms of insanity, astrology and incantations, the instruments of torture, the patterns of genius. More especially, he told me of heroes through the ages: Genghis Khan, Cuchulainn, the mad monk Rasputin, Marco Polo and the prophet Confucius, Namor the Sub-Mariner and Citizen Kane and Houdini, Sugar Ray Robinson and Sweeny, the bird-king of Dal Araidhe, and the Baron von Richtofen, Dracula, Gottlieb of Chicago and Dixie Dean. And these were peaceful moments in my life, Lim Fan tapping his charts with the chairleg and the drone of his voice winding through the afternoon, the sweet smell of soap and distant clamour of the funfair. Inside this room, nothing moved, nothing changed: Lim Fan unspooled like tape and myself, I sat on the bed and didn't take in details but only the outlines, all these images of style, these manifold heroics, and I was drowsy, time passed, and Lim Fan hooked his thumbs through his braces, telling truths.

One time, for instance, I was told of Gilles de Rais, constable of France, a nobleman and scholar of the middle ages, who used to kidnap small children and slaughtered them inside his castle, utilizing their blood to make an elixir of eternal life, but things didn't work out for him and he was captured, tortured and killed, a tragic end for one of the world's most famous eccentrics.

Lim Fan told me all about him, the original bluebeard, and then he took me by my hand, led me up two further flights of stairs, through the damp and the stale cabbage smells and verminous refuse that surrounded us, and he brought me inside the room of Kristoff, a very old man.

This room was almost entirely filled by one gigantic bed, a mountain plateau, an ocean liner, eight foot long, seven foot wide and five foot high and, deep inside it, there lay Kristoff himself.

He was on his back, his eyes were opened and he watched the ceiling. From the doorway, he looked like some prehistoric dog, a wolfhound, and his skull was all angles, his face was covered by white hair, his eyeballs glowed crimson, his mouth was full of yellow teeth like fangs. Also, he wasn't clean, his hair hung matted to his shoulders and, all over him, there hung the smell of death.

Lim Fan took me close to him and Kristoff turned his eyes on me, saw through me and, when I touched him, his flesh was cold and clammy. 'This man is ninety-one years old,' said Lim Fan. 'For fourteen years, he has lain in this bed without moving. Still, he remains a servant of evil.'

Seen close, Kristoff had blood clotted in his hair, caked beneath his fingernails, even scabbed on the points of his yellow teeth. And he gave no sign, spoke no word but only smelled of death. 'When he was young, he was a preacher of the blood sacrament,' said Lim Fan. 'A vampire by profession, he ranged the streets of Moriarty in a black cloak with scarlet lining, the alleys of the shanty Canrush and the bright-lit boulevards of sumptuous St Jude, the carnivals of the tenderloin and, wherever he met a young girl whose blood was pure, he sank his fangs inside her throat and sucked.'

'Did it hurt?' said Arfur. 'Was it fun?'

'In his prime, he was a terror throughout the city, a health hazard to everyone, and all doors were locked against him, garlic was hung in the windows and there was a silver crucifix at every bedhead. As he grew older, however, his powers waned and he retired to his deathbed, where you see him now.'

'In this bed, in this room, in this tenement, where no one knows his name,' I said. 'What does he do?'

'He waits for death.'

In this style, he had already passed fourteen years but nothing had happened yet. His brain was gone, his gifts of speech and movement, and his bodily functions had all collapsed but his life stayed with him still and refused to quit.

When I loomed above him, for instance, he looked through my face but he didn't register. His eyeballs glowed crimson, his teeth were yellow, his face was covered by hair and he was mindless. 'When he flew, he swooped across the city like a bat,' Lim Fan said. 'When his face appeared in any window, everyone screamed. But when he stared into their faces, they froze and fell down on their knees, their flesh was rotted and he ate them. His cloak came down like a great black tent about their heads and they made no sound.'

Kristoff was sunk in private pictures, visions of castles and candelabra and spiral stairways, earth-filled coffins and running water, the crucifix that stuns, the sunray that destroys, the stave that is driven through the heart. 'Flying, his eyes glowed red and could be seen for miles. Flying through opened windows, he stood at the head of the stairs and he was elegant, dignified, deeply melancholic,' said the Chinaman, 'a thing of beauty, his cloak and his cane and his saddened smile.'

Watching, I was trapped and I touched him with my fingertips. The only thing was, he smelled so strong of death and oppressed us, so that we were finally forced to go away.

Nevertheless, he troubled me, he squirmed inside my mind and I came back to him. Later I got into the habit of visiting almost every day and I sat by his bed, watching him, keeping him company, just in case his death should arrive. It never did.

At night, I had dreams in which I saw a buffalo caught and slaughtered in the middle of a desert and its blood spurted from its cut throat in a fountain. Very slowly, it fell down on its kees, bowed its head one time in reverence and died, while its blood spread in a slow tide across the sands of the desert and sparkled in the sun.

When I went inside Kristoff's room, his eyes glowed in the dark and I thought that his death would never come. One day, though, a new family moved into the room across the landing and they were Irish Catholics. They covered their walls with holy paintings and crosses, statuettes and rosaries and pious proverbs.

Right then, Kristoff began to sink.

At ten o'clock each night, the believers knelt down to say their prayers and Kristoff ran cold sweat. Not moving, he writhed inside himself, choking on sanctity, and he suffered, his smell of death grew stronger all the time.

Hail Marys flailed around his head like shrapnel, battered and smashed him until his mouth hung open in defeat and his breathing rattled in his throat, his teeth fell out. Cold sweat oozed from him continually and the evil that sustained him escaped, all badness driven out by the works of the Lord. And

Satan deserted him, his flesh dissolved into dust and he perished at last, he was dead inside a fortnight.

On the night of his death, I dreamed again of the buffalo, I saw it bow its head in reverence, its blood spread across the desert, and then I put these things aside.

All of these things Arfur witnessed in person and everything was education: standing in an eleventh-floor Jitney window I looked down and there was a very large hole beneath me, as roadworks stretching almost half a block.

It was a very hot day, the street was like a cauldron and, as I watched this hole, two men climbed out of it. One of them crouched down out of the sun and the other stood over him, produced a piece of oil-stained rag and began to wipe the sweat from the crouching man's back.

The rag moved slowly across the man's flesh and there were cars crawling round the edge of the roadworks, their metalwork was melting and everything was uproar, horns blared and people screamed and there was the constant explosion of the power-drill, the day was murderous, but the two men stood right in the middle of it, one squatting and the other standing, and they didn't hear anything, they were conscious of nothing but themselves.

So the rag kept moving in its private rhythm, picking up dirt as it went, and the crouching man wriggled his shoulders in pleasure, and the standing man bent low over him, concentrating, protecting him, and Arfur watched the whole performance from an eleventh-floor window. I was very far away.

Afternoons, I sat in a soda fountain on Central and counted the movie stars as they passed, stuffed myself full of banana splits and read chewymags and acted like a child. Swivelling in my chair, I was still a small girl and had a fondness for bubble gum.

Any chance I got, I hung out in the tenderloin and watched what happened, the ladies standing in their lighted doorways at any time of the day or night, singing songs to any man that passed them by, the dirty blues or dance or even opera, and some of them were happy, some indifferent, some with the desire to end it all by suicide, and some were real ladies in spite of their downfall but some were habitual drunkards and some were dope fiends, as follows, cocaine or heroin or yellow dolls. However they were desperadoes, all of them without exception, and throughout the tenderloin, amidst all the plumes and candelabra and mirrors, fine silks and velvets, the credo remained the same: live for today, tomorrow may never come, the refuge lies in fun.

And Lim Fan was my protector but, in all the time I knew him, he showed me neither love nor even friendship, he never made a single gesture of approval, because that's the way he was, a scholar who smelled of soap, he wasn't capable of demonstrations.

More than anything, he was expert in the fields of prophecy, in clairvoyance and palmistry and astrology, and he owned skills by which he laid bare the fates of everyone, so that many people from the neighbourhood were helped by him; they came to our room and paid a token fee, in return for which Lim Fan fed them on raw turtle hearts, known as cowein, and they enjoyed great good luck.

Lim Fan, he dressed up in the ceremonial silk robes of China, a red dragon emblazoned on his back, and he'd sit very still, staring into infinity, while Arfur waited just inside the door and collected quarters from everyone that passed.

In front of him, on an old table with one leg too short, Lim Fan used a single glass of water, nothing else and, when everyone was duly assembled, I switched off the lights, we sat in the dark and, after a few minutes, while Lim Fan intoned slogans in his native Chinese, the glass began to tremble and a small high voice emerged from inside the water, giving out items of advice and/or prophecy to each client in turn, telling Elsa Zbigniew to cut out adultery, for instance, or Clyde Anson to beware of smooth-talking strangers or young Joey Ramirez not to play with himself, such sly stuff as this, because it was only a glass of water, but, still, it knew no fear.

When it was finished, even when I'd switched the lights back on again, and all the clients had gone away, Lim Fan didn't move but sat tranced and didn't blink for half an hour.

Later, we caught a cab downtown and put our profits towards two monstrous Châteaubriand steaks, deep inside the

Frenchmans, where the meat ran wild with juice and garlic, where it was slavered all over with red wine sauce and mustard, melted butters and spices of all descriptions, and when we cut it fresh blood flowed and spread out in a lake.

Still, Lim Fan didn't smile or act amused. Instead, he tugged softly at the tips of his moustaches and was surrounded by stillness, slowness. 'Bad men are everywhere,' he said. 'Life is a painful path to one and all.'

In times of leisure, we went walking in the public park and watched what happened.

Lim Fan walked in front, his hands folded snugly across his paunch, which made him slow, and I trailed maybe five foot behind him, scuffling my heels in the dirt. Sitting on a bench, we got rained on and fouled by pigeons. Even then, Lim Fan gave no signs but brooded, waited, sank himself in visions.

Solitary by nature, he had no friends, he used no women and he eschewed alcohol, amphetamines, stimulants of any kind. When he walked out in the street, he looked neither to left nor right. Still, he was respected in the neighbourhood and people made way for him, took their hats off as he passed, because he was a scholar, a healer, a man of tongues and there were things he performed that couldn't be explained.

When children were taken sick, for instance, and doctors couldn't ease them, Lim Fan was called to their bedside instead. For only a small fee, he fed them cowein. And if that didn't work, he hung his hands like claws above their eyes and tensed himself, put his whammy on them and drew out their fever through his fingertips. Then he spoke in Chinese, made a secret sign and went away. When I touched his hands, they were burning hot.

Or whenever any argument broke out in the neighbourhood bars, the disputants would bring it back inside our room for judgement and Lim Fan put on his silken robes, sat at his table and consulted the water-glass, and any decision that was given, it was accepted without question, the case was closed.

Barman and philosopher, visionary and loner and chronicler, these were Lim Fan's components and, riding home from the tenderloin in the early dawning, he told me stories of Finn MacCool, a hero of old Ireland, whose thighs were each the thickness of a horse's belly, whose chest was wider than the poles of a chariot and whose backside was big enough to halt the march of any army through a mountain-pass; of Pigeye Pete, a half-hand bigshot from Pensacola, who was once set upon by the Fat Daddy gang of Tucson but defended himself with a cue, braining two of his assailants and maiming three others, before leaping out of a window, tumbling twenty foot to safety and, ultimately, making off with no more than one sprained ankle; of Sam Langford, the Boston Tar Baby, a black prize-fighter who went blind but still refused to quit and fought on sightless, finding his opponents by instinct alone and felling them with a single left hook, then fumbling his way back to his corner and rejoining his guide dog; of Roland, warlord of France, who held off a horde of Saracens single-handed, one man against ten thousand, and then he blew his horn of polished ivory, summoning help, and he blew it three times, so long and loud that he burst his lungs and his blood gushed forth in a fountain; of these and many more besides, heroes all, he spoke with reverence.

In particular, there was a certain story that summarized his nature and, also, the relation between the two of us, Lim Fan and Arfur, as follows: Once upon a time there was an old man with a big red beard, who sat in the middle of the desert and spooned delicious junket from a bottomless bowl and, as he spooned, he thought.

One day the old man decided to award a prize to anyone that could come to him and tell him what he thought as he spooned, and so people came from all across the nation and formed themselves into a long line like a crocodile. One by one, they approached the old man with the big red beard and told him what he thought as he spooned. One by one, they were all wrong.

In this way, the old man sat in the desert and ate delicious junket, while the people of the nation filed sadly past him, until there was no one left but a single small boy, who wore his left sock pulled up to his knee and his right sock hanging at his ankle.

At last the small boy approached the old man, the old man ate junket and the small boy said: 'I know what your thought is.'

'What is my thought?'

'Your thought is as follows: Junket Is Good,' said the small boy, and this was the right answer, and the old man gave him his prize, a bottomless bowl of junket, and everyone gave a hearty cheer and went back home to tea. And the old man and the small boy sat side by side in the desert, spooning junket, and they stayed there ever after, sitting still and thinking their thought, which was

JUNKET IS GOOD.

The Moriarty Chinatown was built of wood. About once every three years fire broke out and everything was razed to the ground, the streets were filled with the smell of frying flesh, shacks flared up and burst like paper bags, ten-floor tenements collapsed like a house of cards, and all the other inhabitants of Moriarty stood in their windows, watching from a distance, feasting on the way that the flames licked red against the sky.

Beautiful it was, and everyone headed for Chinatown, waited until it was safe and then ran riot in the streets, looting and raping and laying waste, rekindling the fires wherever possible and, in a good year, the holocaust was sustained over several days.

Physically, Chinatown was shaped like a sugar bowl, sunk deep inside a valley; its narrow streets were filled with coloured signs, its shops spilled out across the pavements. Exotic foods were displayed at every corner and the houses themselves were all painted bright, sky-blue or blood-red or gold, tenements and one-room shacks jumbled together without any logic, the whole neighbourhood a labyrinth, and the inhabitants wore robes of many hues. The shopkeepers stood out in their doorways, the alleyways were lit by Chinese neon and everything was permeated by the scent of burning incense, while me and Lim Fan, we walked together to his father's barber shop.

Teatimes were strange: Lim Fan wore his smartest clothes, a pin-stripe suit and braces and polka-dot bow tie, and he combed his moustaches, he scrubbed himself until he gleamed. Then we sat on a wooden bench, right outside the barber shop, and the striped sign twirled red and white above our heads.

On every corner, there were certain men who wore suits

instead of robes, double-breasted jackets and high-buttoned boots and fedoras, holsters beneath their armpits, and these were the hoodlums of Chinatown, the gunmen of the Tongs, thin-lipped and slit-eyed, who ruled the neighbourhood by terror alone.

Because of the Tongs, most of the residents went underfed and shoeless, scuffling to survive in rat-infested huts, while the big-time hoods were transported everywhere by litter, potentates with droopy moustaches and French perfumes and, as such, they hid themselves in marbled mansions where they partied until the dawn, champagne flowed free and beautiful women of all descriptions sported nude in the pool.

Mr Robinson, Lim Fan's father, for instance, laboured seven days a week, supporting a family that was almost numberless, and he had half of his earnings taken by the Tongs, who claimed it as their rightful due, so that he worked away his life for nothing. Still, he made no fuss, knowing well that he'd only get his throat slit with a rusty razor if he did.

Nevertheless, Thursday teatimes were calm: we sat on the bench and, all around us, there were orientals, who brought us jasmine tea and sesame seedcake, Chinese delicacies, and we ate them on the sidewalk, watching whoever passed us by.

Many people bowed to Lim Fan as they shuffled on, Lim Fan bowed back and everything was dignified. The warlords were carried past in their litters, the gunmen stood out on the corners in their fedoras and this was very nice, the two of us in the sun, scissors snipping steadily behind my head, seedcake crumbs all around my lips and the sign twirling slowly above me, the smell of incense everywhere and all these strange Chinese, their blanked-out faces and their robes, their words that made no sense.

Myself, I wore a black corduroy cap and black lace-up shoes, a black jacket and white shirt, and I was ten, almost eleven. I'd been with Lim Fan for many months and anything that had happened before I fell through the funfair mirror no longer existed.

The thing I liked best, the district was filled with fine hotels, the Excelsior and the Negresco and the Grand, large wooden structures with fire escapes of rusted iron and, inside, they weren't modern but they were magnificent just the same.

They sported palm trees in the lobbies and red velvet fittings, paintings in oils and alabaster cupids and gilded mirrors, cut-glass flowers in the rooms and the bellhops all arrayed in scarlet uniforms with gold epaulettes and, without exception, the very best in Chinatown society assembled here, the pashas and the potentates, so that I'd hang around outside and watch the celebrities being carried past inside their litters.

It was from the fire escape of the Negresco, for instance, that I caught my glimpse of Little Pete.

At this time, Little Pete was the undisputed overlord of Chinatown, having vanquished all of his rivals in open warfare, and he was a hoodlum but he was also a man of cultivation, he had style.

During his reign, furthermore, he had brought great benefits to the neighbourhood, he'd centralized all its industries under his own leadership, the laundries and the barber shops and the brothels, the yen trade and all the Tongs, so that carnage was largely cut out and the hatchets of the warring gangs grew rusty on their walls.

For all these reasons, Little Pete was a hero and, the first time I saw him, he was still only thirty-three years old but right at his peak, a ruthless operator, of course, but suave, swift-witted and subtle, a fluent linguist, a connoisseur of fine red wines, a mathematician and deep-sea diver and part-time poet, and one afternoon he was carried to the Negresco in a pearl-encrusted Egyptian litter.

When the door was opened and he stepped out on the sidewalk, he was seen to be wearing a suit of white silk, a white felt hat pulled far forward across his eyes, a camel-hair coat, a diamond tie-pin and big black shades. Then he was smoking a cigar and, on his fingers, there were many rings of emerald and ruby and solid gold, and he had a thin white scar on his left cheek.

Five full seconds, he was framed and I trapped him, his image caught for always, this small oriental playing hoodlum on the sidewalks, the uniformed flunkeys that surrounded him, the white-robed heavies that protected him and Little Pete himself, the white silk suit and the camel-hair coat, the hat pulled low across his face and the shades, the many rings, the fat cigar.

On the edge of Jitney, there was a small Germanic quarter, in which I frequented a neighbourhood bar, the Alexander Casino.

Descending four steps from street level, I'd push aside the heavy leather curtain that kept out the draught and the room that I entered was long, low and dingy, lit by Chinese lanterns and festooned with dusty streamers. Also, round the walls, there were wicker tables and big shabby sofas and trellis-work alcoves, arboured over with plastic cherry-blossom, and the whole place smelled damply of beer.

Inside the Alexander Casino, everyone was permanently depressed: the proprietor, an ex-boxer, rested his paunch on the bar and one hangdog waiter shuffled round the tables in a soiled white coat, two fat girls danced together in front of the jukebox, five men played Cotch without talking, an elderly man held hands with a boy inside an alcove and myself, I sat by the stove and read *True Romance*, I kept my mouth shut and everyone ignored me.

One night, though, a man came in called Otto Schultz, an operator with wet lips and puppydog eyes, very sentimental, and he sat down at my table. Straightaway, my eyes filled up with tears and I began to ooze. 'Why do I weep?' I said. 'I've never even met you before.'

'I'm a tearjerker, that's my vocation,' said Otto, and he looked smug, he was carrying a satchel filled with small black canisters. 'Everywhere I go, the people cry,' he said. 'According to their temperaments, they whimper or scream, snivel or tear their hair but the end result is always the same, they wind up shedding tears.'

'Please,' said Arfur. 'I don't understand.'

'In these canisters, I carry tear-gas and this is my profession, I sell it off at fifty cents a time. Going from door to door, I offer it as a cure-all and there's hardly anyone so serene that they go without. As soon as I've gone, they lock themselves in their bedrooms and fling the canister against the wall, breathe in deeply and cry their eyes out. All over the neighbourhood, they roll on the floor and I am their salvation.'

Sipping orange soda, I dripped tears steadily from my chin and Otto Schultz dangled one of the canisters beneath his nostrils, he smirked, he savoured the subtlety of its bouquet and then his face collapsed. Right then, he let out a high-pitched whine like an electric saw and buried his head in his hands.

Within seconds, all the other customers had joined the act – the canisters were passed from hand to hand, the gas was used like yen and the whole of the Alexander Casino was wiped out by grief.

Standing on the bank of a canal, I threw a stone up in the air and watched it fly, curve and drop back towards the water.

On the far side of the canal, there were many dark factory chimneys and I had toothache, it was drizzling, there was a dog behind my back and the stone was spinning, it fell, it didn't move.

My tooth howled, the chimneys were black, the dog was lame. The rain got in my eyes, made my nose drip, the stone kept dropping towards the water, it didn't move, my tooth said one word, the sky was grey, my hand was white, the chimneys were very black. The dog was ugly, the rain was wet, my tooth hurt, the stone fell for ever, it never moved.

2: Willie the Pleaser

WHEN I WOKE UP AGAIN, I FOUND MYSELF IN A SMALL CAVERN, LIT BY scarlet lanterns and hung with tapestries of exotic design, and on a gilded couch, there reclined a very fat man, Willie the Pleaser, a notoriety sport of the Moriarty tenderloin.

Three hundred pounds, he was wearing a double-breasted suit, a red carnation in his buttonhole, rings all on his fingers, and his fat hands were folded on his paunch, he smiled benignly. Straightaway, I liked him: when he saw my eyelids flutter, for instance, he reached down and tousled my hair. 'Arfur,' he said. 'You're welcome here.'

By reputation, the Pleaser was a card-sharp without equal, flash and fly without limitation, and lying on his couch, he ate juicy black grapes from the vineyards of the south, his chins were shaking with enjoyment and he was tended by a lady called Bessie Lou, a fox, shiny and sinuous, who soothed his brow with a scented cloth.

Rubbing her eyes, yawning and stretching like a cat, Arfur was much refreshed and Willie the Pleaser touched her with his fingertips, hugged her to his belly, and she ate his grapes: 'Little girl,' he said. 'Let me show you a trick.'

'Willie,' I said. 'I'd like that.'

Holding out a pack of cards, he asked me to select one and I did, it was the jack of spades but I didn't reveal it, I hid it against my chest instead. And the Pleaser looked in my eyes and concentrated, he pressured me until my mouth twitched and then he smiled, he showed me a mouth full of diamonds. 'You hold the jack of spades,' he said.

'I do,' I said, and this was the moment when the Pleaser became my new teacher.

Down in the labyrinth, therefore, I sat on his lap and he spent hours showing me many tricks, spraying cards like confetti and chortling, all his chins shaking with merriment and Arfur thought he was sweet.

Sucking fat, black grapes, I spat out the pips and the Pleaser performed. Bessie Lou had smooth, brown flesh that shimmered like foil and, the three of us, we got along very nice. When we were tired, we slept all in a heap, and when we woke up again, we studied amusements of every kind. In this style, we passed twenty hours, at the end of which we left the Moriarty labyrinth, emerging through an iron grating, never again to return within.

On the corner of Albuquerque and Vine, blinking in the strangeness of the afternoon light, Willie the Pleaser beamed on me and touched me with his fingertips: 'Arfur,' he said, 'I like you.'

'Willie,' I said. 'I like you, too.'

'More precisely, you hit me where I live: you speak my language, you're fun and I want for you to travel by our side.'

I didn't even have to think it over – it was time for me to make a change, I knew that, and I went back inside the Jitney tenement one last time, I packed my grip.

Lim Fan was seated at the table, staring into a crystal ball, and there was the smell of stale cabbage all on the landing, the walls were wet.

Leaving, I shook him by his hand and my eyes brimmed with tears but Lim Fan gave no sign, he smelled soapy and watched me without expression. 'Live clean,' he said, his voice uninflected. 'Think clean as well.'

Two years solid, I had lived in this cockroach room and Lim Fan had filled my life but, when I quit, he couldn't even smile, he didn't say goodbye and I went away unwarmed.

This was the Moriarty style: out in the street, it was dark and

I was alone, there was no flash of yellow inside the tenement window and Lim Fan was gone for good.

In conjunction with Willie the Pleaser and Bessie Lou, his concubine, I travelled the nation from end to end, touring without a pause until the time of Willie's untimely death.

The way that his life was structured, the Pleaser would stay in each town for about a week, he'd line up every sucker available and then he'd move out fast, outstripping his fate, his winnings hidden in his shaving stick. In this style, his existence was perpetual motion and everything that he did, it was performed with flash.

Hitting a new town, for instance, he'd retire straightaway to his bedroom and groom himself, dress himself in white silk and pamper himself with cologne, sprinkling l'Amour behind both his ears, and then he'd emerge very slow and walk down the most major thoroughfare, a perfect vision, while all the ladies squealed low behind their curtains.

Right then, he'd double back down an alley and sneak inside his hotel again, drive his fat up the stairs two at a time and into his room, where he stripped off his white silk and climbed into mohair instead, or black barathea, or lightweight pin-stripe flannel, and then he'd repeat the whole performance, he'd motivate back into the street, a turnip watch peeping out from his fob, a fat cigar clamped in his teeth, and this time the ladies were entirely fractured, they fell down on their knees.

Four times he'd repeat this manoeuvre in its entirety, emerging each time in an outfit more stylish than the one before. Then he retired inside his hotel room one last time, locked the door and didn't mess with the ladies any more because, truthfully, he loved Bessie Lou and had no eyes for anyone else.

Travelling, Arfur was content: I kept company with Bessie Lou, a slow brown with flesh that rippled like tinfoil, and she spent her days lying naked on her couch, eating ripe plums and reading magazines.

Her favourite reading was *True Romance*, a chewymag, and many times big tears escaped her eyes, coursed down her cheeks and dripped on her breasts. At such times, I gave her a handkerchief and she ate another plum, all pain was forgotten.

Bessie Lou, she didn't say much, she only smiled and rolled her eyes. But she had an interesting scar that ran diagonally across her belly and it was her diversion to flex it in front of the mirror, watching it grow and squirm and pucker. Then she'd smile and fall asleep on her couch.

In the evenings, she'd dress herself in red velvet, a costume that revealed her bosom, and she walked out on the Pleaser's arm.

Together they went inside the gaming rooms and Willie got rich. At the tables, he flashed his cuffs, he beamed, he exchanged pleasantries with his opponents and he was an image of true urbanity. Bessie Lou stood right behind him and ran her shiny fingers in his hair, and the suckers swarmed round, and the Pleaser's mouth was full of diamonds, and Bessie Lou yawned, and Arfur waited in the background, Arfur watched.

Willie the Pleaser, he was a cheat without equal and he taught me many strokes, how to flare, how to float, how to flick from the elbow, so that I became expert in all the paths of subterfuge. A fat man with love to spare for everyone, he wasn't removed like Lim Fan, he laughed all over his face and his teachings were all contained in a single word: fun.

'When I was young, I was sad and skinny,' he said, 'I wore shades, I was moody, I kept getting into bar-room brawls, I was a fool to myself and I walked alone in avenues of melancholia.

'One day, however, I met a man called JoJo Smith and he changed my life by his laugh alone, which was the loudest in creation.

'The way it was, JoJo was a large man of Irish extraction but he didn't like to work, he preferred to sit in the sun and drink beer from a big tin pitcher. In this style, he was lazy and he loved to laugh.

'For example, when someone made a joke, JoJo would flare his nostrils, whinny like a horse, snort one time inside his nose and then he'd rise up from where he sat, he'd stagger out in the open street, purple-faced and breathless, tears running down his cheeks, and he'd roar like a lion, he'd bellow like a bull, reeling blindly in the neighbourhood, clutching at lampposts to stop from falling, drunk on mirth alone, and the city was filled with nothing but the sound of his laughter, windows were shattered, tall tenements were shaken to their foundations and, three hours solid, he laughed without a pause until, quite suddenly, he stopped dead and the silence then was strange.

'Because of this laugh, JoJo was most unpopular with his neighbours and they showered him with filth, they emptied buckets of cold water over his head and abused him with many obscenities but JoJo, he took no notice, he only laughed.

'Concerning my friendship with him, I met him in East Caboose, when he was thirty-eight and I was twenty-four.

'Being very green at this time, I got caught sharping in the local casino and the neighbourhood sports took me out in the alley, held me up against a wall and hit me until I became unconscious. Then they left me and I lay down in the dirt.

'A few minutes later I went out in the street and my clothes were all besmirched, my face was covered in blood and JoJo witnessed this. He was sitting in a doorway, relaxing in a rocking chair and drinking beer from a pitcher and, seeing me, his laughter was loud.

'Clutching at his guts with one hand, he pounded the boards with the other, he howled and my first reaction was one of rage, I wanted to smash his purple face in but then I understood his meaning, I suddenly saw myself straight and I began to laugh as well, so that we put arms around each other, held each other tight, rocked on our heels and finally collapsed all in a heap.

'From then on, we became constant companions and my whole life was altered, I cast aside solemnity and filled my heart with fun. And me and JoJo, we spent that whole summer sitting in the shade, our hats over our eyes, drinking beer and dozing. Or we lay in hammocks and read the funnies. Or we laid down banana skins on the sidewalks and hid, waiting for disaster, or we sprinkled tintacks on cinema seats, or we wore water-squirting carnations in our buttonholes. This was juvenile, of course, but we didn't care: we fell down in the street and grovelled, whispering puns in the dirt, and nothing bothered us, we laughed and we laughed and we laughed.'

*

Everywhere that the Pleaser went, times were fat and in particular Arfur learned to understand the pleasures of elegant discourse and the soft feel of silk against her flesh, the textures of quail and artichoke, the subtle spices of the orient, the sweetness of flinging dimes to bellhops, the glint of well-turned epigrams, the clean smack of cards on baize and, also, the many nuances of Willie himself, the scent of his cigars and the diamonds that shone in his mouth, his beneficence and humility, and the glittering company that surrounded him, the ladies in velvet and the men like penguins, the things of terrific gaiety that he said.

All of this I came to take for granted, not to mention Bessie Lou and her smell like sweet earth, her soulful stride and her scar that twitched so saucy in her guts. And me myself, how my lace-up shoes gleamed like ice and how I held up cutlery that was greasy, dangling it in my fingertips, and how I ever laughed. At the age of almost twelve, Arfur was cute.

Truthfully, I overdid it and I came on snob but the Pleaser was wise to all these pitfalls and he punctured me fast but softly, teaching me mottoes that kept me clean. 'In all things, be humble,' he told me. 'Beneath our clothes we have no clothes, not one of us is excepted.'

A fat man with many chins, the Pleaser took me in his arms, I smelled L'Amour behind his ears and he laughed very soft, he kissed me on my mouth. Right then, I knew that I'd gone wrong and was ashamed. I hung my head but Willie only smiled and bought me a knickerbocker glory de luxe in the corner drugstore, a confection consisting of tastifreez ice-cream with canned peaches and fresh whipped cream, melba and chocolate sauces, pistachio nut flakes and caramel crackling and raspberry flavouring, plus other treats too numerous to mention, and it took me fully fifteen minutes to eat it all. 'This much is important,' said the Pleaser. 'To live with style, to die with dignity. At all times, to know repose.'

In one month alone we began in Bayard and we were trapped in a greaseball hotel where the hot water ran cold, where the Pleaser's champagne was flat and the mattresses were filled with fleas,and the suckers wouldn't bite, the bell-hops gave us sauce and, finally, Bessie Lou was forced to get down in the streets and wriggle her scar, just enough to put us on the bus to Scorn, and we rode eighteen hours unbroken, all through the night and half-way through the following day, winding up in a roadside café where the cruets were chained to the tables, the tea tasted of vinegar, the jukebox played Perry Como records and the Pleaser's silk suit was hassled by truck drivers, who wanted to punch him in the face, and Arfur sucked her thumb but, when we got to Scorn, we booked into the Excelsior regardless, twenty dollars each a night, and Willie ordered oysters and Bessie Lou ate plums, the walls were covered with art works and, that very night, the Pleaser took two thousand dollars from the ageing juvenile Valentino Frost at Cotch, and we slept through till after lunch time the next day, when the Pleaser bought his concubine a new pearl necklace and Arfur herself was treated to a pair of lace-up shoes in zebra skin, and everything was cool, except that Willie then got rash, was almost thrown in jail and, running hard, we stole a car off the first corner we came to, a cherry-red Jitney '53, and we rode it fourteen hours flat-out across the Magdalena desert towards Pontiac.

Half-way across, however, we ran out of gas and were forced to camp out in the open, surrounded by wild animals, the buzzard and coyote and rattlesnake, but we cooked up ham and beans. We showed fortitude and in the middle of the night, without any warning, the Pleaser woke up laughing. Then Bessie Lou caught the fever, so did I, and our shrieks echoed far across the night, my mouth was filled with sand.

With JoJo in mind, we hitched a lift and made Pontiac by noon, a fine wide-open city with many amusements, bars and brothels and lush casinos, and we were broke again but, what odds, we took a suite at the Sands and gorged ourselves on roast suckling pig with an apple in its mouth, pigeon breasts and crayfish, boars' tongues in aspic and raspberry syllabubs, and we stayed in this place for nine whole days, during which the Pleaser racked up many thousands of dollars and cast it all to the winds.

Bored, we moved on, riding the pullman through Orangeburg and Dylan, Paducah and Lake Cadiz, stopping off for a couple of days at random while Willie earned some trash and then setting out once more, grinding on through all the steppes and mountains and mighty rivers of this nation, which is a universe in itself, and we covered around four thousand miles in one week, flying loose, until the Pleaser got mugged in some downtown Orly alley and his wallet was stolen, every last cent he possessed, so he came home bleeding, disconsolate, and Bessie Lou laughed out loud at him. This was our style and Willie laughed right back.

Once in Macon, we holed up inside the Hotel Mordo, a structure that was strange and sinister, filled with the smells of dust and dark and death. The foyer itself was dominated by three stuffed parrots and in this hotel there were bald-headed salesmen, dope fiends, dying women, midget wrestlers, felons and busted cardsharps.

At the far end of long deserted corridors and sweeping stairways, overhung by candelabra, we were given a room with curtains of faded red velvet, collapsing sofas and, in the closet, a long black overcoat, nobody inside.

For two full days, we locked ourselves inside and skulked. Willie sat by the window, laying out patience, and the corridors creaked beyond our door, the curtains rustled in the night, many shadows raced on the ceiling.

Bessie Lou lay naked on her bed, her scar didn't move and Arfur slumped in a deep armchair. Sometimes she was asleep, sometimes she wasn't. In the end she lost track of herself, she forgot which was which and she existed in a blur.

On the night of the third day, however, Willie the Pleaser rose up at last and put on a dark-blue pin-stripe, placed a pink carnation in his buttonhole, sprinkled l'Amour behind his ears and disappeared downtown, hot for action.

During his absence, Bessie Lou lay on her bed and scratched herself. Meanwhile, I wandered the passages of this hotel, I passed through many halls and balconies and vistas, spiral stairways and cloisters, until I came at last to a certain room on the seventh floor in which lay Arnold Jackson, a fighter.

The first moment I saw him, Arnold was sitting on his bed, drinking beer out of a can, and the carpet was scuffed, the light bulb swung nude above his head. And he himself was a man shaped like a bullet, bald-headed, with swollen ears and his nose smeared across his face.

In earlier days, Arnold Kid Jackson had been a left-hook artist from Pearson County, a craftsman and punchbag who had met the very best in rings around the world, but now he was retired and he was employed by Stillman's Macon gym, corner of Aitchison and Swift, where he ran messages and swept the floors and locked up when everyone else was gone.

At midnight, I stood in his doorway and coughed into my hand: 'I'm new in town,' I said. 'I travel with the Pleaser.'

Arnold Jackson didn't react: he was a silent man, whose eyes didn't focus right and, when he drank beer, it frothed in the corners of his mouth and dribbled on his vest and, when he moved, he shuffled, he ducked his head in behind his shoulders, taking no chances. He was amiable by nature, however, and I stayed with him all night long, leafing through his scrapbooks, watching him bleed in many nations, eyes half-shut and his mouth gasping like a fish, while Arnold himself shadow-boxed against the walls of his hotel room, dressed only in his vest and socks and flannel underpants, shuffling and shambling, his feet stuttering on the carpet. Even now, though, he could hook: he'd suddenly throw his left out of nowhere and it was a thing of beauty, it flew, and for one moment only he wasn't old at all, he wasn't bald or punchy, he was an assassin again.

At three in the morning, I fell asleep in his crimson dressing gown, *Kid Jackson* emblazoned in big gold letters on the back, and I dreamed of uppercuts.

As for Sasparillo, it turned out to be a resort of true distinction, complete with palm trees and fountains and swimming pools, marble columns and boulevards and, living lush, the Pleaser eased himself into ten thousand dollars within a single week.

On the terrace of the Pompadour, high above the camargue, I drank lemon juice with Bessie Lou and sheltered from the sun, while Willie sat in the casino, ten hours each day, and accumulated.

Whole days, we sat still without speaking. Bessie Lou passed her tongue all pink across her lips, this was the only thing that happened, but I wasn't bored. Instead, I lapsed into a dream and my mind was filled with the manifold styles of Lim Fan and Little Pete and Otto Schultz, and Doctor Sax, the spook of St Jude, and Clarence Troy passing among his people like a pasha, all of these things in my past, and I played bassoon, I was soothed.

Out in the camargue, wild white horses ran loose in tribes and the sand rose up in clouds beneath their thundering hooves, and herons stood on one leg, not moving. Cowboys rode alone in the burning sun, their water canteens hung empty at their sides. Hiding under stones, fast alseep, there were many rattlesnakes.

Willie the Pleaser got rich: by temperament, he wasn't a madcap, he took no risks but was rather a veteran in his trade, calm and competent in everything that he did. For this reason, he was greatly respected inside his profession and apprentices swarmed to watch whenever he appeared. But Willie only smiled, shot his cuffs and gathered the chips in his two fat hands, swallowing them like a python.

Sweet Mister Willie, he owned thirty suits and forty-five silk shirts, twenty-six ties and eleven hats, twenty-six pairs of shoes. His favourite food was oysters, his favourite drink was dry champagne. His favourite colour was blue and his favourite town was Moriarty and his favourite book was the Bible.

The biggest break in his career was when he broke the bank at Lake Cadiz. His sign was Taurus, his best friend was Bessie Lou. His likes were silk underwear and aces and jollity. His dislikes were messy eaters, unhappy endings, smog and lawmen. His professional ambition was simply to travel. His personal ambition was happiness.

Fat daddy, he was nothing but jive, and down in Sasparillo where flamingoes fly, he triumphed.

Nights, Bessie Lou put on her velvet gown and we sported in the gaming rooms, where all the cavalry officers were resplendent in their scarlet uniforms and gold braiding, silver spurs and waxed moustachios, and the young ladies of the southlands bared their silken shoulders and flashed their teeth in smiles of fearful gaiety, yearning for a husband. The orchestra played slow waltzes, Nigras served iced fruit punch and the phaetons waited outside in the gaslight. Meanwhile, in the upper room, the Sasparillo sports played baccarat, chemmy and poker for stakes that knew no limit.

Nevertheless, at the end of nine days, we packed our bags yet again and headed for bedrock Gladstone, because the Pleaser didn't believe in stability no matter how tempting the circumstances and, from Gladstone, we proceeded all through the south, to Pavane and New Paul and Sparta, Collard and Sprat Bushes, winding up in Grand Coyote, famed for the beauty of its sunsets.

By this time, we'd hit nineteen towns in fifty days, and covered twelve thousand miles, and won thirty thousand dollars, give or take a few, and blown it all, thrown away four thousand on champagne alone, fifteen hundred on caviare, and the Pleaser was bloated like a bladder.

For ten months in all, we didn't stop travelling and I learned many things, I was toughened and aged, made wise. But, now, I sensed that this phase of my education was drawing to its close, something new was coming and I was right, of course, because Willie got shot in Open Door.

A gold-rush settlement that was rough in the extreme, Open Door had no more than five hundred inhabitants but seven saloons were required to cater for them, three morticians and a graveyard filled to overflowing with new-mown corpses.

Most every night, there were gunfights and any man that walked the streets without a holster, he was guaranteed dead. In this place, for a fistful of dollars you could buy death. For a few dollars more, you could buy genocide.

The way things worked out, the Pleaser hadn't originally meant to stay here at all, he'd only wanted to stop off overnight but then, three o'clock in the morning, somebody stole our stagecoach and left us stranded.

Accordingly, the next morning, Willie went down inside a saloon to play some Cotch and raise enough capital to take us into Monroe, the next town down the line. Being smart, he laid aside the apparatus of cheating and played it straight, knowing well that he'd get his brains blown out if he was caught in any misdeed.

When darkness fell, the saloon filled up with prospectors, big black-bearded men with hands like hams, and the atmosphere was hectic. The pianist played ragtime, the chorus girls kicked their legs up in the air and the prospectors soused themselves in rot-gut whisky. Inevitably, as the night wore on, fights broke out and knives appeared. Glasses were smashed, the language was foul. Silently, a man fell dying on the floor, a knife between his shoulder blades.

All this time, the Pleaser went on playing Cotch, he took no notice of anything but the cards in his hand and Bessie Lou stood right behind him, very lovely in her velvet gown.

As for Arfur, she watched and drunken men surrounded her, black beards and yellow teeth, many scars and blood-encrusted fingernails but she wasn't scared of anything, she twanged her yellow braces.

The Pleaser was smooth. Anarchy raged about his head but Willie was calm and, around midnight, having racked up five hundred dollars, he rose up from his table, bowed to each of his opponents in turn and walked towards the door.

This is what happened next: a prospector called Jake drew a gun and shot the Pleaser through the heart, killing him instantly.

Willie fell face downwards on the floor and didn't move. Nobody cared, nobody even noticed, only Bessie Lou, who dropped to her knees and cradled the fat head of her lover against her breast, weeping bitterly.

Then I turned around, walked out of the saloon and stood alone in the darkened street. On the corner, I thumbed a ride into Monroe and this was the sour ending of Willie the Pleaser.

3: Pin-ball Travels

AT THE AGE OF ALMOST FOURTEEN, I SHOT PIN-BALL.

Down in the docklands of Chester, I spent my time inside a sawdust bar and many men gave me dimes to pay for my games. When I put my money in the slot and pulled the handle, the ball ran up fast and sheer inside its socket and exploded all over the table. When it dripped down slow towards my flippers, I hit it back up again.

In the mornings, I lay inside my bed and hid my head under the blankets. Many people from my block came and knocked upon my door, asking me to play songs on my second-hand bassoon, but I didn't answer and I didn't move, I gave no sign.

The cats cried on my window sill, the tallymen went by in the street below and I turned my face against the wall. Around noon, I rose up in my room and put my clothes on, my hat and my braces and my baggy woollen trousers, and I combed my hair in front of the mirror, I flexed my fingers.

In the docklands, where the wind blew bitter and everyone knew me by my name, I went inside a certain bar, which was known as Happy Haven, and I played clean pin-ball, which is known in the trade as Shooting the Straights. When I put my money in the slot, the ball flew free and lights flashed, bumpers buzzed, numbers reeled off constantly on the backboard. In due course, there came a moment when I was joined with the table by mystic connections, we formed a oneness and it wasn't possible for us to fall. At this time, Arfur was fulfilled and knew that pin-ball was her life. Accordingly, she set her sights on perfection, nothing less would do.

Four hours each day, I learned my trade and, when the ball dropped down towards my flippers, I hit it back up again. And when it dropped back down again, I hit it back up again.

On a certain morning, at seven o'clock sharp, I left my room with my suitcase under my arm and I journeyed through the empty streets until I reached the central bus station, where I boarded a Greyhound and, once more, faced the open road.

My friend Porky LaMotta sat beside me and my bassoon was wrapped in greaseproof foil, stashed away beneath our feet. Outside, a group of gypsies were huddled tight against a wall, hiding from the rain and, somewhere behind us, there was a baby crying. Without exception, Chester was the most godforsaken city in the nation.

When the Greyhound began to roll, Porky turned away and made the sign of the cross three times above his heart.

The first place we headed for was the mountain El Gris, a small village several days distant by road, a citadel for fugitives and a noted meeting-place for pin-ball artists of every description, and we travelled towards it for a hundred hours without stopping. Five times we changed buses and the roads grew ever rougher, the motors older, the countryside more barren. We slept upright and we woke with aches all over us. We moved all the time, we never paused and we spent whole days staring out across vistas of sky and rock and burned earth, the heat was ferocious and we had no water.

Finally, we crouched in the back of an army truck, curled up in the dark with homecoming peasants and their possessions, their suitcases tied with string and their dogs and their goats and we couldn't breathe, we couldn't see. It was one hundred degrees of heat; I played bassoon in the darkness and Porky was asleep. Every so often the truck stopped, and someone got out, someone else got in. Everything proceeded in a dream and, close beside me, a young girl sat without talking as she fed her baby at her breast.

When we came at last to El Gris itself, it was six o'clock in the morning and the square was deserted, the sun was just rising and the village was painted white, everything was clean.

El Gris, for almost two centuries, had been famous as a hiding place for running men of all kinds, whether bank robbers or bandits or defeated armies, whores or adulterous husbands, pin-ball artists or dope fiends or revolutionaries. Situated at twelve thousand feet above sea-level, it was hidden on a small plateau between many mountains and could only be reached by the single dirt-track that we'd used ourselves, so that it was foolproof against sudden attack or siege, no matter what. Inviolate, it stood remote from the world at large and was known as an earthly paradise.

Me and Porky LaMotta, we stood in the square and blinked, our eyes were hurt by the light. A dog sniffed at our ankles, a dead bird lay in the road. Across the square, beyond a small cluster of trees, there was a cantina and from deep inside it there came a sound that no one could mistake, the noise of pin-ball being played, the buzz of bumpers and the flutter of passing numbers.

Under the fig trees in the middle of the square, there were two wooden benches and, exhausted, we lay down on them, shut our eyes and we fell fast asleep. Just before he started to snore, Porky touched my hand.

By the time we woke up again, it was already noon and the square was full of children, who circled us and watched us without blinking. My skin crawled and my mouth was caked. I sat up and rubbed my eyes, discovered Porky beside me and he had a face like a pig. He made me feel safe, I touched him. Meanwhile, the children stared without expression.

I walked across the square and into the cantina, which was small and dark and cool, and a man with a moustache was asleep behind the bar, and an Armenian was shooting pin-ball in the back room.

This was the beginning of something new: Arfur took up her position on a high stool, she crossed her legs and the Armenian was playing Gottlieb's Ship Ahoy. Truly, he was a gifted performer. Just the same, I stepped up smart behind him and showed him five dollars tucked tight in my fist: 'Mister,' I said. 'You shoot elegant.'

The Armenian was a large man with bad teeth and yellow eyes. Behind him, there was a marmalade cat, sitting on a shelf, and the cantina smelled of cold earth, the room was still and the Armenian looked at me without curiosity. 'I'm Arfur,' I said. 'Here's five dollars says I can beat you easy, a thousand clear a game.'

The Armenian looked down at me, very patronizing, and he didn't speak, he simply ran off three fast games, not messing, not falling short of brilliance at any point. Then I smiled, a small girl aged thirteen, and I beat him easy, a thousand clear a game, shooting the straights in this empty cantina in the mountain El Gris, where fugitives converged from all across the nation, the Armenian among them, no doubt, and the sun beat down on the square outside.

Porky LaMotta was still snoring on the bench. When I stuck five dollars in his open mouth, however, he woke up with a jerk and he smiled. A man with his nose smeared half-way across his face, he took my winnings and kept them safe for me. And in that moment, I became a pin-ball hustler by profession, a winner by my nature.

El Gris was filled with silence, nothing moved and a small boy led us through a labyrinth, through alleys and archways and tunnels, until we came at last to a large house set apart, a mansion almost, surrounded by lush-scented gardens and protected by high fencing.

As soon as the small boy had knocked at the gate, he ran away into the night and many watchdogs snarled and strained at their leashes but me and Porky, we stood our ground and, in due course, the gate was opened by a Negro in the uniform of a butler, who ushered us onwards into the mansion itself.

Straightaway we found ourselves in a large area exactly like an amusement arcade, a hallway that seemed to extend into infinity, filled with pin-ball tables in rows of dozens, all of them occupied.

Nobody spoke, nobody even looked at us. Without exception, the artists were conscious only of their machines and they shot the straights as if nothing else existed.

Myself, I came upon a Gottlieb Royal Guard, two-flipper, four-bumper and eight-target, and I began to spar with it, gently at first, then with concentration, until I was playing to my fullest capacity, and I went through twenty games without a pause, I flew and was fulfilled.

At the end of ninety minutes, however, I was interrupted by a hand upon my shoulder and, turning, I found myself confronted by a man of middle age, a grandee of great distinction, who wore boots of red morocco and an elegant goatee beard. And this man was smiling but his eyes were sad, he was the most melancholy person I'd ever met. 'Little girl,' he said. 'I like your style.'

'I'm Arfur,' I replied. 'And this here is Porky LaMotta, my partner.'

'My name is Don Pedro Sanchez,' said the man. 'I own this mansion, which is the finest home of pin-ball in creation, and these are the maestros who entertain me, these are the machines that surround me, all of this is mine.'

So saying, he turned on his heel and led us slowly through the aisles of players, pointing out a few of his favourites along the way. 'This is Samson Denver, the Eastern ace,' he'd say. 'And this here is Dumb Crambo, a behemoth from Decatur, who is the stupidest man that ever lived but shoots the pin-ball of a genius; and this is Claw Petrie, a veteran from Corinth, and this is Hassan Ali, an infidel, and this here is Sam Sloop from Clemence, and this is Billy John Hard.'

In this style, we walked for maybe half a mile up and down the arcade and the only sounds were the buzz of bumpers, the flurry of numbers, the deep-down explosion of replays. Don Pedro escorted us throughout with grace and *savoir faire*, he was truly a gentleman but always a sense of tragedy showed through his elegance.

At the furthest end of the pin-ball arena, there was a doorway and we passed on through, we came into a large and luxurious study, where the walls were covered by paintings in oils, leather-bound volumes filled the bookshelves and there was a blazing log fire, with two gundogs asleep on the hearth. Lighting a cigar, Don Pedro then settled himself in an armchair and he stroked his beard, his head was ringed with smoke: 'In this room, we are alone,' he said. 'We can speak as we choose.'

'My message is simple,' I said. 'Pin-ball is my life.'

*

When I reached the bottom of the embankment, I lay quite still and Porky came down on top of me, he squashed me flat. In this way, I returned at last to Moriarty, my place of origin.

It was still daylight and, rubbing our abrasions, we shuffled off towards the centre of the city, us and the hoboes together, derelicts of every description, and Porky himself was no better, he was unwashed and unshaven, his mouth hung open. I felt ashamed to be with him.'

As soon as we came into the streets of the tenderloin, however, we were surrounded by sports and the pavements were flooded with light, ladies leaned out of their windows and music was everywhere. 'This is where I began,' said Arfur. 'Lim Fan raised me here, he taught me the basics.'

'It's pretty,' said Porky.

'In these few blocks, the whole of existence is contained and nothing is missing. Within a few hundred yards, there is a cosmos.'

But when I looked more closely, I found that things were changed. Seen in detail, the mansions seemed less splendiferous than before, the velvet drapes less opulent, the dresses of the ladies less dazzling. When I went into Penguin Orlando and inquired after Lim Fan, no one had ever heard of him. When I looked into the faces of the sports, they were men like any others. Many of the ladies were downright ugly. Much of the neon was broken. When I drank champagne at the Maison Lafitte, it was flat and sweet, it made me think of Cydrax. Nobody wore lightbulbs in their toes, nobody had diamonds in their teeth. The walls were damp, the plaster was peeling. Inside their cribs, the ladies had dirty fingernails.

In the Dopey Duck arcade, shooting the straights, I found myself caught with a bent machine and the replays didn't register. When I twanged the handle, the ball ran crooked in its socket and fell into the table with a plop, making me ashamed. 'Everything is busted,' I said. 'Nothing remains the same.'

'I'm sleepy,' said Porky.

'You have a face like a pig.'

I went inside a bar and it was full of mirrors. All along the counter there were women with pink shoes and orange lipstick, who were watching their reflections without blinking. Everything was bright, everything was made of neon or plastic or aluminium. In the far corner, I caught a glimpse of William's Apollo.

Everywhere, there were these smells of cheap scent and sweetness and rotten fruit. Still, I played pin-ball and my touch returned, I started to fly. When I racked my first replay, I laughed out loud and everyone turned to stare.

Soon, a small man approached me and stood close behind my shoulder. After a time I turned to face him and he was retarded.

He was my own height, five foot three, and he was as round as anyone could reasonably be. He had flesh like puff pastry, his face was like a sack. He was albino and he had a crewcut, his eyes were pink. He kept blinking, he kept grinning. Nevertheless, I was polite: 'I'm Arfur,' I said. 'Can I help you?'

'I've been waiting,' he said. 'My name is Catsmeat.'

Nodding, I turned back to the table and twanged the handle. Right then, the ball ran fast inside its socket and exploded all over the surface, there was magic in my fingertips. Meanwhile, Catsmeat kept on blinking and he had little fat hands, he was grinning. 'I've come to fetch you,' he said. 'It's time for us to leave.'

'I can't,' said Arfur. 'I have a friend called Porky LaMotta, he's still asleep, he needs me. Together, we have travelled all across the nation and we have lived a lifetime in a single year. We have battled with the federals, we have ridden with los Santos, we have starved in mountain caves. We have burned and looted and plundered. We have sampled the luxury of El Gris, the splendour of the steppes, the icy winds of Chester, the degradation of the freights. Many times, we have almost been killed.'

'I brought you this,' said Catsmeat, unmoved, and he reached inside his pocket, produced a hundred-dollar bill and placed it in my fist. All the time, he was grinning and blinking, an albino with pink eyes, all fat and soggy: 'All of this is yours,' he said. 'One hundred dollars.'

'I'm Arfur,' I said. 'Who needs it?'

Seven o'clock in the morning, the first light, I kept playing pin-ball and the ladies went home, leaving behind them glasses smeared with green and orange lipstick. But the brightness didn't quit, the neon glare, it hurt my eyes and Catsmeat stood behind my back, my money in his hand. 'It's getting late,' he said. 'We'll get into trouble.'

I ignored him, I racked more replays. When I was satiated, only then, I straightened up and looked into his face: 'One hundred dollars,' I said. 'Who wants me?'

Catsmeat didn't answer but gave me the money, which I pocketed, and we went into the market. Many trains passed above our heads, each one exploding like the end of the world. And Catsmeat put his hands in his pockets, slouched his shoulders and, quite deliberately, he dragged his feet in puddles of juice, splashing me as we walked.

Out in the streets of Moriarty, we wandered from Lincoln County to Little Savoy, from Jitney to St Jude and on, beyond, passing through Caldonia, the shanty Canrush, the strangeness of Chinatown.

Outside the Hotel Negresco, where once I had caught a glimpse of Little Pete in his white silk suit, we were picked up by a long black limousine with darkened windows, in which there was a uniformed chauffeur, a man with purple epaulettes and gilded buttons.

Driving away, I saw that the barber shop of Lim Fan's father had been changed into a supermart. Nothing remained the same, all my life was transient and we passed from Chinatown into the open countryside. 'What place are we headed for?' said Arfur. But the chauffeur didn't answer and Catsmeat only picked his nose, dangled his heels in idleness. He was a very small man. Leaning back in his cushions, his feet didn't reach the floor.

For fully an hour, we drove in silence and then we stopped outside a large white house, a residence in the Southern style, complete with pillars and bougainvillaea and peacocks strutting on the lawn.

This is what happened: the door was opened by a Nigra. The house was filled with the smell of home-made lemonade. The hallway was decorated with tigers' heads and buffaloes, bearskin rugs and antlers. Out on the veranda, there was a scent of jasmine and everything was elegant.

When I went inside the library, however, I wasn't met by an aristocrat but by a young man in an Elvis Presley T-shirt, his long hair tied back in a scarlet bow. He was six foot tall, twenty-four years old, and his flesh gleamed like gold. Simply, he was the most beautiful person that Arfur had ever seen and, straightaway, she loved him.

As soon as I entered, he rose up and clasped my hand. Smiling, his teeth were perfect and he gazed into my eyes, he breathed on me softly. 'My name is Johnny Angelo,' he said. 'I am still the greatest.'

We were partners. More exactly, Johnny Angelo was the Lone Ranger and I was Tonto, he gleamed like gold and I clung on tight behind. Every door that we passed through, we smiled and many flashbulbs exploded in our faces.

Each night, after Johnny Angelo had left the stage, I went down in the alley and shot straight pin-ball at the neighbourhood arcade. Running loose, I hustled anyone that I met and my pockets were filled to overflowing with nickels, dimes and quarters. Then I was satisfied and I went back inside Johnny Angelo's suite, I scattered my winnings at his feet.

This was the time when Johnny Angelo kissed my magic fingertips and wrote a song, as follows:

> Down in bullshit alley,
> I believe that we are clean.
> Me and my friend Arfur,
> Teenage pin-ball queen.

At last I wound up in Cancre, a small-time pin-ball centre in the northern steppes, where down-at-heel sports retired to recuperate and plan a fresh campaign.

The standards in Cancre were low indeed and Arfur cleaned up. Within a single week, she had filled her pockets with almost a thousand bucks and the living was lush.

Rescued so suddenly from the breadline, I put up at the Hotel Nonpareil and existed in the style of the Pleaser, namely champagne and quail and oysters, silken sheets and satin underwear, chamois pin-ball gloves and a black velour hat, perfection in every detail. And this was the beginning of yet another phase, almost the last one, because for the first time I now became a full-time artist, completely self-supporting, and nobody protected me.

It is truly said that when one door shuts a new one opens and I came now into the lushest segment of my life to date, during which I toured the nation all alone, shooting the straights from town to town, and my success was terrific, my reputation spread wherever pin-ball reigned.

At the age of fifteen, I wore the same uniform that I had employed since the very beginning, baggy pants and lace-up shoes, braces and hats and good luck charms, and this appearance became my trademark, so that everywhere I went, I was a noted rider and the people knew me by my name.

Furthermore, I was rich: I carried a billfold in my belt, a wad that was maybe five hundred dollars thick, maybe more, and I handed out tips like confetti. The times in which I had struggled to place fifty dollars in Johnny Angelo's hand were now long gone and it was nothing unusual for me to stake a monkey on a single play.

I was mean, I was fast, I was flash. Shooting evil pin-ball, I showed no mercy and my challengers were stripped to the bone.

Everyone stood and watched me burn. My challengers formed queues and I beat them without sweating, my cap pulled low across my eyes, my mind in tune with nothing but the table. When the winning score was made, the sports applauded and brought me orange sodas, complete with caramel sauce, and they carried me on their shoulders, the arcades were filled to overflowing and, everywhere that she went, Arfur was a heroine.

Nevertheless, I was lonesome: at the age of fifteen, I had no home, no friends, nothing to depend upon and, no fixed point in my life of change. I was loveless, I lived for no one but myself. I travelled without pause and knew no rest. Many times, I felt abandoned and wanted to stop. Nevertheless, I went on travelling.

Pin-ball was all that sustained me.

Six hours a day I stood upright and shot the straights without blinking. If I put in a single nickel, it usually lasted the whole day through, I was that efficient and, when I twanged the handle, the ball ran up fast and sheer inside its socket, it exploded all over the table. And when it dropped down towards my flipper, I hit it back up again. And when it dropped back down again, I hit it back up again.

Walking in the streets or looking through my window or sipping sodas through a straw, my head was crowded with the noises of the tables, their buzzings and flashings and hissings, their whisperings and explosions and, also, the patterns traced by the balls themselves, the ways in which these patterns made sense and the ways in which they didn't, the eternal mystery of the machines which had no beginning or end. This was all that moved me, nothing else existed.

All I wanted was to be a legend in my lifetime and, in Sasparillo, where flamingos flew I caught up with Eddie Schmidt, Fast Hand Eddie, an all-time immortal of the circuits, and I beat him eight games in ten. From that time on, I was established as a major contender and only Goldstuds Johnny Ace, the Ransome renegade, was rated above me.

As I travelled, I kept hearing stories of the Pin-ball Phantom, a legend in every place that pin-ball ruled and, even though he'd disappeared more than ten years previous, he remained a hero without equal, his exploits were relived endlessly and none of the sports ever tired of them, they were definitive pin-ball sagas.

Many times, drinking my champagne, Porky told me stories and Arfur shut her eyes, drifting in a dream: 'When the Phantom appeared in Corinth, he dropped in through the roof. One moment, Fast Hand Eddie was shooting with Mister Dante, alias the Spider, and the atmosphere was tense. The next, a rope ladder had been dropped from the ceiling to the floor and the Phantom had materialized. A man of medium height, wearing an overcoat, he beat them both, Fast Hand Eddie and the Spider, wiped out in a single play and then he disappeared again. Simply, he ascended the rope ladder and was gone.'

'He rode the wind,' I said. 'He vanished without trace.'

'And headed for Pocatello,' said Porky. 'Where he flew in the window of the Coney Coliseum, swooping like a bat, and he shut down the assembled artists without a word, fourteen hustlers eliminated in an hour before he turned around and was gone again.'

The Pin-ball Phantom, he haunted me and, nights, I'd wake up with a start thinking that he was hiding in my room. His shadow lurked behind my shoulder, he hung in the closet like an overcoat. When I played the arcades, I'd sense him watching and I'd whirl to catch him but he wasn't ever there. Walking in the street, I'd become aware of him floating just above my head, but when I reached up to touch him, the air was empty, the Phantom rode the wind.

Shooting pin-ball in shadowy arcades, while Porky kept me plied with ice-cold orange sodas and the dust rose heavy in the street outside, I was still invincible and the living was lush. Trundling across the desert in the painted caravan, I saw a single hawk circle high above us in the heat and Porky lay sleeping in my arms.

Continually Miss Faye told stories of her fame, her spangled youth, while Klaus Antonio threw knives and his partner, the glamorous Patricia, received them without blinking. At last, down in the Ransome boondocks, I caught up with Goldstuds Johnny Ace.

Goldstuds, he had a thin face like a weasel and his hair was swept high in a ducktail, he used brass knuckles and the way he got his alias, he wore a black leather jacket with many gold studs all down the back. Yes indeed, he rode a Harley Davidson and kept a picture of Eddie Cochran pinned close against his heart. Truly, he was a renegade and, in his style at the tables, he was a killer, he rode them like his motorbike, brutalizing them without mercy until they fell apart in his hands, a method that was much frowned upon by purists, but Johnny Ace didn't care, he shot the straights regardless.

On the day that I found him he was slumped in a bar by the railway tracks and he had a four-day beard, his teeth were bad, he smelled. Still, I touched him on his shoulder and Porky LaMotta stood close behind me, then Miss Faye in fine black lace, then Klaus Antonio and Patricia: 'My name is Arfur,' I said. 'I've come to shut you down.'

Goldstuds Johnny Ace made no answer, he simply twanged

the handle and, shooting, he was a hurricane, he rode the tilt like a tightwire, storming and smashing until the table was like to snap in two. But Arfur, she wasn't impressed, and when her own turn came she shot with her usual reverence, she cut him down like chaff. And the more Johnny Ace bulldozed, the more Arfur was clean. Seventeen games in twenty-one, she broke his back.

At the end of ninety minutes, the renegade cracked and Arfur scooped her winnings off the table, led her entourage back into the sunshine. Down in the boondocks, trains were shunting in the yard, kids were playing baseball, dogs were fast asleep. Squinting in the brightness, Arfur twanged her braces and, at the age of almost sixteen, she was a champion, a legend in her lifetime.

So she was satisfied, she had achieved what she'd worked for and, wherever she went, she was now a celebrity, she was asked for her autograph. Furthermore, she was paid hard cash to stand in certain arcades and smile, she appeared in advertisements and she was interviewed by journalists. Every week that passed, her wealth and fame increased.

At the same time, she sensed that her life was ended. In her triumph, she had made herself redundant, there were no further targets to be aimed at and she had a persistent feeling of anti-climax. Passive, she continued to tour the nation, shooting pin-ball and making money but she wasn't involved. Nights, she dreamed only of the Phantom.

Truthfully, I was feeling old and I was sated with colour, with change, with elegance and barbarity, philosophies and deaths and French champagne, until the only things that worked on me were the tables themselves. Pin-ball remained, and the way it looked and the way it sounded and the way it felt, its speed and its slowness, its simplicity and its strangeness, its patterns that never ended and, most of all, its moments of mystic connection – clean pin-ball, it filled my head, it made me breathe and, in arcades all across the nation, I waited for the Phantom.

In cowboy Shane, for instance, I met with Bat Holt, an easy rider; and in Sweet Spring it was Abdul, a eunuch; and in Monroe it was Fuzzy Cupid, a midget wrestler; and in Great

Lamont it was the desperado Kid Melba; and in nightclub Palooka it was the diseuse Avril Orchid who sang of death as follows:

> You looked so clean,
> You were a cheater,
> Electric Man,
> You read my meter.

And all of them, they were elegant, they really were but Arfur was jaded, nothing could arouse her and, in each case, she passed quickly on until she came at last to a small prairie town called Jasper and she stood alone in Rubin's Pin-ball Palais one becalmed Sunday afternoon in early autumn, shooting the straights in her best felt braces, her new zebra-skin boots and her trilby hat pulled low across her eyes.

Outside, nothing moved. Inside, dust rose up off the floor and hung without moving, while Rubin himself studied form and Arfur racked replays. Every noise the table made, it echoed in the empty arcade and there was a dog asleep in the doorway, there were smells of flour and grain and cinnamon, there was a silence so deep that not even pin-ball disturbed it.

At four o'clock I bought an orange soda sprinkled with pistachio and I drank it slowly in a corner, I was listless, I was calm. Sucking through a straw, I didn't think of anything, I only floated, but when I turned my head I was no longer alone, there was a man just inside the doorway.

This man was wearing an overcoat, I couldn't see his face. 'Good afternoon,' he said. 'I am the Pin-ball Phantom.'

FOUR

True Stories

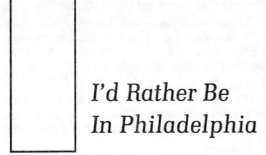

I'd Rather Be
In Philadelphia

I n Los Angeles I wore a white silk suit and stayed at the
Château Marmont, high above Sunset Strip. There was a
grand piano and candelabra in the lobby: within an hour of
my arrival, persons unknown had sent me a Mexican hooker,
name of Angel, who scrubbed my back and cooked me scrambled
eggs.

For three days I sat in my room and waited for Phil Spector to
contact me. Greta Garbo had once lived in this suite, Myra
Breckenridge had looked out through these windows, so I sat and
watched the sunsets, working my way through packet after
packet of Lemon Jumble cookies, while the phone didn't ring.

Here was my Hollywood dream – I went to bed at dawn, rose
in time for lunch and changed my underwear three times a day.
On the third afternoon the phone rang at last. An unidentified
voice asked me if I wished to speak with Mister Spector. I said
that I did. There was a silence. Then the line went dead.

The Château was full of corridors and dark corners. Filipino
bellhops, aged courtesans, ghost-white junkies. Soon I reached
down behind the cooker and came up with a bloodstained silk
kimono. I hid it in the air-vent and went out to cruise the Strip.
When I got back Angel poured me tequila and painted her
toenails scarlet. Afterwards she called her mother, and her
brother, and her best girlfriend in Tijuana. So she said, at any

189

rate, but when I looked down from my window, there was a man with a black moustache, just standing there, motionless.

The phone rang again. This time it was George, Mister Spector's prime bodyguard. Twenty minutes later he arrived in a black Cadillac: three hundred pounds of ex-cop, bearded, beringed and heavily holstered. Together we drove off down the Strip past all the great landmarks, the sacred shrines. Past Dinos and Schwabs and Cyranos, past the Whiskey, past Phil Spector Productions, and on up the hill to El Dorado.

Or perhaps it wasn't El Dorado, after all. At this distance, I can't be sure that it wasn't called Sierra Madre instead, or maybe Besame Mucho or even, who knows, La Paloma. In any case, what matter? It was a mock Spanish mansion in the classic Hollywood style, all balconies and latticed windows, guard dogs and electronic gates.

Originally, like any other palace, north of Beverly Hills, it had been built for Barbara Hutton; twenty or thirty rooms, with circular beds and polar-bear rugs, infinities of stucco and gilt, the works, all paid for in nickels and dimes. The only stroke that she'd missed was the heart-shaped pool.

My own role was Philip Marlowe. As I stepped from the Cadillac, blundering in the dark, I looked up by chance and caught a sudden movement, something shifting behind a curtain. A flurry of pink; perhaps a face; nothing more. Wolfhounds snapped and snarled behind their fence. George pushed a sequence of buttons and buzzers, spoke into a mouthpiece, moved me through an electric eye. First one door, then another opened before us. At last we penetrated the mansion.

I was left alone in a very long and high, very cold and empty reception room. Overhead I could hear footsteps, moving relentlessly back and forth. Coloured lights flashed in the darkness; a door slammed far away.

Everywhere that I turned there were pictures of Phil Spector. On coffee tables, around the pool table, stretched across the mantelpiece – Spector with the Teddy Bears, with the Righteous Brothers, with Ike & Tina Turner, with basketball players and karate champions, with Minnesota Fats, with Herb Alpert, with businessmen, with his mother. In profile, full face, formal or at ease. With companions or, most often, alone.

By the sofa there were three copies of *Tangerine Flake Stream-line Baby*, each with a marker at the chapter on Phil Spector. Underneath there were cuttings from *Time*, *Life*, *Rolling Stone*, each with a marker at the section on Phil Spector. So I sat on the sofa and was idly browsing, when I paused to scratch myself and suddenly there he was, Spector himself, at the far end of the room, on top of a flight of three small stairs, watching me.

At first he did not move. Then I stood up and he came towards me. In close-up, he hardly reached past my shoulder and, even with his gold-rimmed shades, steel-studded wristband and wispy beard, he seemed like a child, maybe ten years old. As unformed and as vulnerable as that – he looked past my left ear, not quite smiling, and bit his lip. 'Pleased to meet you', he said and, finally, shook my hand.

Clearly this wasn't enough. For a very first meeting, something stronger, something altogether more dramatic was called for. So he waited a moment, undecided, and then he gestured round the room, a random sweep that took in the walls, the mansion, the whole of Los Angeles. 'Welcome,' said Spector, 'to Hollywood.'

A routine took shape: I sat in my hotel room and every couple of days the phone would ring. Then George picked me up, took me to El Dorado and Spector talked at me. After some hours, George drove me back to the Château and I settled down to wait for the next time.

The idea was that I would eventually write a book. Therefore I crouched over a tape recorder, looking earnest, and Spector kept up a flow of monologue. Footsteps echoed interminably above us, the wolfhounds howled outside the windows and George sat polishing his guns, peaceful in the kitchen. Once I heard a woman singing in another room. Presumably she was Veronica, originally lead singer with the Ronettes, – now Spector's second wife – she hummed a few bars of 'Black Pearl', then cut off dead, halfway through a line, and I never heard her again, nor saw the least sign of her existence. A shadow behind a curtain, a voice in another room and footsteps overhead – she might have been a wronged Victorian-gothic heroine, imprisoned in the attic.

Phil Spector, meanwhile, was all benevolence. Although we were entombed in this mausoleum, he could hardly have been more genial and he told me jokes, showed me snapshots, kept me plied with drinks. One afternoon he even fixed me a plate of lox and cream cheese on rye, prepared with his own hands, complete with pickles and side salad (blue-cheese dressing). Then he sang me old songs, showed me trick shots at pool and almost beat me at pin-ball. I walked on my hands, he did impressions of Lenny Bruce. Everything was spiffy.

Nonetheless I was spooked. Something in Spector remained shadowy, remote, beyond reaching. Hunched beside me, with his shades and small child's face, he made me think of a boy – his bones were so bird-like, his voice so shrill and he carried such an air of fragility that often I was tempted to lift him up bodily and bounce him on my knee, one hand up his back, like some freaked-out ventriloquist's dummy.

This sense of puppeteering survived in his talk. Time and again, I'd catch a whiff of something mechanical, rehearsed. He'd rap for hours, sometimes quite torrentially, and jump up and down, wave his arms, flash his hands all over the place. In anecdotes his voice would swoop and cackle and shriek in wildest hilarities. He gasped for breath, he clutched his sides. But all of it was performance. Suddenly, without any warning, he'd freeze, in an instant the show was shut down. His limbs set, his eyes went dead. Precisely, the effect was like putting money in a seaside peep-show – pull the lever and he jerked into action, went through his charades. Let it go, and immediately he stopped.

When he spoke of the past, it was different. Turn him loose in New York or Philadelphia, in his golden age, and he flamed. Right away he took on true intensity, outrage and obscenity, wild invention. Labyrinthine sagas came unstoppable, and then he seemed special – obsessive, original, full of overwhelming energies. Here you could see exactly how he'd come to be Spector. But bring him back to the present, even for an instant, and he died.

On paper it was hard to explain, this congealment. He was now in his late twenties, with money, prestige and great talent, adored and protected at every turn, and he lived exactly as he chose. His future was full of new plans and projects; his freedoms, within the limits of human capacity, were absolute. He had a family, he was healthy, he was safe. So he might have been expansive. Instead, he was catatonic.

His life was a blank. He seemed to have no great pleasures, passions, or even hatreds, and no great desires. Sometimes he said he was happy, other times he shook his head and looked sad; but most often he simply sat and let time pass.

What was wrong? At sixteen, at twenty, at twenty-four, his drives had been phenomenal. His rage and speed, his sweep of vision, his will – no one in rock had ever moved faster, or been more gifted, or had a more ferocious sense of his own potential. Once he had dared everything, now he seemed to dare nothing. Only the trappings were left – the mansion and the bodyguards, the gold-rimmed shades, a few gestures and throwaways. Cadillacs and wolfhounds and distant footsteps, the motions of mystique. Beyond all that, nothing.

So one night, when conversation had ground to a halt and it seemed there was nothing to be lost, I asked him if he felt finished. Was he exhausted? Was there anything ahead? Or was his life, in essence, already over?

For a moment he prepared to lose his temper. His face scrunched up tight and his mouth opened wide. But then he paused, right on the brink, and drew back. With the first volley of abuse already half-way up his gullet, he teetered. Let a few seconds pass. Then drew his head in, like a hedgehog taking refuge.

'How,' he asked, with utmost caution, 'exactly do you mean?'

'Finished,' I said. 'Done with. Complete.'

He looked surprised, a bit baffled. With fine drama, he removed his shades and peered past my ear again, off into infinity, as if to signal deep thought. He pondered, reconsidered, took his time. In the end, however, he must have given up, for he only shrugged his shoulders and put his shades back on. 'I guess it is', he said, off-hand, and we talked about something else.

In the first place, more than anything, Spector was a saga of self-invention: a demonstration, on heroic scale, of the possible.

Conceive, as a basis, that every life is shaped by two crucial inventions. The first is imposed from outside, at birth, by environment, family, genes, God; the second is projected from within, as the life picks up momentum, by force of will and imagination. So we begin by being invented and progress, if we can, to inventing ourselves.

193

The decisive element is nerve – how much do we *dare*? If we have been invented as plain, dumb, insignificant, will we dare to re-invent ourselves as glamorous, brilliant, heroic? If we are meant to obey, will we dare to command? And if we are doomed in any case, will we dare to be blown sky-high, in magnificent technorama wipe-out, rather than drain away slowly, on our knees?

In ninety-nine cases from a hundred, of course, we dare almost nothing. We exist as we've been packaged and if we make even minor adjustments – change professions or lovers or countries, say, or wave a few protesting banners – we think that we're being enormous. But who goes to the limit? Who scraps his first self totally and starts again from scratch, rejecting all guide lines? Who runs riot? Phil Spector did.

In his first invention, he could hardly have been less promising. He started in the Bronx, Jewish and undersized, twitchy, panic-stricken. His mother overpowered him, his father died when he was nine. Rootless, he was brought out west, to Los Angeles, and that isolated him even more. He was close to nobody, belonged nowhere, was good at nothing. By his teens, he was completely withdrawn – girls terrified him, and he dreamed he was being strangled.

At Hollywood High he sat apart, stuck away in corners, and festered. Once he showed me a snapshot taken in his mid-teens, surrounded by a group of class-mates, smiling in sunlight. Half a dozen kids in a loose semi-circle, crewcut, golden-fleshed, archetypal Californians: they slouch and chew gum, take their ease, while Phil peeks out, half-hidden, from behind a silver surfer.

It is an image of absolute security. Everyone here has cars, pretty girlfriends, the simplest and safest of futures. But then you glance at Spector and immediately he belongs to a different universe. Bad hair, bad skin, bad posture. Focus on the eyes and all you can see is evasion. White flesh in a world of tan, mess in a world of smooth – everything about him is alien, awkward, discomforting, and the others are all looking elsewhere.

That was the platform he worked off. In the first invention, he had been inadequate, terrified, doomed; in the second, his own, he took revenge. Just like Tommy's campers, he wouldn't take it, no way, and he cast off the imposition. All his pent-up energy and rage, all his caged intensity broke surface. Deliberately, he obliterated the past, wiped out memory, began again from nothing. It was rather like one of those magic drawing pads, where you can draw and erase and draw again as often as you want. At a stroke, Spector rubbed out the accummulated doodlings of seventeen years. Then he drew for himself.

Rock 'n' Roll, in the late fifties, was the obvious testing ground: new and virgin territory, ripe for raiding. The first wild burst of euphoria had just begun to dampen down, there was a temporary hiatus. The natural force of the early rockers had been harnessed and contained by the industry, so that while the young made the music, it was the middle-aged who made the money. What was needed was a champion, someone to take on the massed ranks of baldies and cigar-chewing fatties, wrest away or at least intrude on their control. Someone with so much force and hunger that he would recreate the whole context in which Rock functioned. Release, both creatively and commercially, a true Teen music. And that, more or less, is what Spector achieved.

The actual process by which he did so hardly matters here. Once you accept the basic concept of his re-invention, the rest becomes inevitable. Only invent and the future is inescapable, as irrevocable as past or present – the inventor is controlled by the force of his own invention.

So with Spector: he was a Rock 'n' Roll fan, had a good ear, could play guitar. Soon he started writing songs and his first was 'To Know Him Is To Love Him', the title inspired by his father's epitaph. He took a boy and girl from Hollywood High, called them the Teddy Bears, put them into a neighbourhood studio, sold the product to a local label and waited. When it became a hit, he went to Philadelphia and immersed himself in the industry, blew all his royalties and moved on to New York, where the Brill Building, stuffed to overflowing with Jewish songwriters, was just becoming the new centre of American Teen.

It was now 1960. Spector made tea, ran errands and slept on desks, until Atlantic gave in to him and let him produce some sessions. He had hits with Curtiss Lee and Ray Peterson, and wrote 'Spanish Harlem' for Ben E. King. Next he found partners and backers to set him up with his own label, Philles, and flew to Los Angeles, where he cut 'He's A Rebel' on one Friday,

'Zip-A-Dee Doo Dah' on the next. Both were million sellers.

He set up New York offices and surrounded himself with assistants, flunkeys, bodyguards. He got married, divorced and married again, and he had maybe twenty hit records in two or three years. Not long after his twenty-first birthday, he became a paid-up millionaire and moved west to Hollywood. His wig-hair was long, his clothes outrageous and he wore his shades all the time. He bought El Dorado, an office block on the Strip, a fleet of cars with smoked-glass windows, impenetrable, behind which he could hide, and he trapped the moment absolutely. The industry called him a genius.

The instant passed. After the Beatles, he ceased to be the newest and hottest sensation of all. He still made hit records, still got his picture in the papers but his impetus slackened when he drew back into shadow. When he released 'River Deep, Mountain High' and it wasn't a hit, his very greatest record and his first important failure, he retired.

He was then almost twenty-five. Within five years, he had exhausted the fullest potentials of Pop, as artist, businessman and image, as hustler and myth. Truthfully, what more was left? Nothing, except to lock the gates of El Dorado and disappear. His journey was completed; all that remained was time to kill.

I don't mean, of course, that he managed all this by invention alone, without intellect, gifts, tremendous resources of energy and vision. On the contrary, it was precisely because he had such reserves, unrecognized, that the invention was possible in the first place. With the single exception of Elvis, he was the sharpest and most original talent that Teen produced, and on three levels at least – industrial, artistic and style – his effect was quite enormous.

As a businessman, first of all, it was Spector who created the concept of independence. Before him, rock was controlled by a few major companies – an individual might start his own label and do well enough locally, or within a specific market, but if he wanted to be national, he either had to tag on to one of the majors or pass half his life in slow and squalid escalation.

Spector ripped right through this. Straightaway he was universal, autonomous, insatiable. After the first few months, he controlled every detail of his enterprise – production, publicity and distribution, hiring and firing, dealing and scamming, art work, letterheads, even the colour of the toilet paper. No one had ever moved so fast, hustled remotely so hard and, by all logic, he should have fallen flat on his face. The industry wasn't constructed for this, it should have squelched him.

How did he escape? He made good records, of course, and he understood money, but that was hardly enough to faze a whole entrenched establishment. In the end, one can only explain it by personal force: face to face, he must have carried such impact, such obsessive certainty in his own rightness that custom, prejudice, pettiness, indifference simply crumpled before his onslaught. Hunger, fury and flat-out insanity must have dragged him through where reason would have taken him nowhere.

Afterwards, everything was simpler. Once Spector had made the first breach, it was possible for others to slip through behind him and the whole of Rock become looser, less restrictive. Independents took root, began to dictate their own terms. Lou Adler and Andrew Oldham, Shadow Morton and Kit Lambert – indirectly, all of them were created by his precedent. At one remove he was responsible for founding every breakaway in Rock and even now, each time that some new hustler emerges to prate about doing his thing, being free and letting it all hang out, Spector should cop a percentage.

That was finance. At the same time he was also Rock's first flirtation with Art. Previously there had been great performers and there had also been a handful of artists by intuition – Chuck Berry, certainly, and Jerry Lee Lewis, Roy Orbison, maybe Don Everly. But Spector was the first to rationalize; the first to comprehend precisely what he was up to. With him, there was a totally different level of sophistication, complexity, musical range.

This could have been tricky. Rock 'n' Roll, like all mass media, works best off trivia, ephemera and general game-playing, and the moment that anyone starts to take it more solemnly, he's treading on minefields. As performance, it has been magnificent. Nothing has been better at catching moments, and nothing has carried more impact, more evocative energy. While it lives off flash and outrage, impulse, excess and sweet teen romance, it's perfect. But dabble in Art and immediately it gets overloaded.

Somehow Spector got away with it. On one hand, he created a

total imaginative universe, which I take to be the test of any true artist; on the other, he never let go of foolishness. So he was subtle and raucous, bizarre and familiar, emotional and strictly commercial, all at once; he stole from every source he could – Wagner, Leonard Bernstein, dashes of early Stravinsky, a thousand or a million hit singles, Rogers & Hammerstein – and was still completely original. Simultaneously, he was pretentious and funky. Very clever indeed and most beautifully dumb.

What he did, basically, was to combine the two great romances of Rock – rebellion and the teendream – into one. The first meant wild greasy rockers, the second pretty boys. The first was noise and fury and filth, orgy, musical assassination; the second was sweetest, most perfect innocence. No way for the two to intertwine, or so it seemed, until Spector upped and did it. Using the massed songwriting duos of the Brill Building – Goffin/King, Mann/Weill, Barry/Greenwich – he churned out the purest, the most aching and idyllic of all teen ballads.

Into his sound, meanwhile, he poured his rage and revenge. Three pianos, half a dozen drummers, rattlers and assorted thumpers, whole battalions of brass and strings, all crashing and smashing away as hard as they could go, in torrential, deafening, murderous release. His songs might be pure romance, his sound was pure slaughter. Together, they meshed into purest energy.

Finally, after money and music, there was 'Spector' as image, where his influence was greatest of all. Right from the outset he'd been a guerrilla, plunging headlong into riot. When rock was still stuffed full of crewcuts and natty Italian suits, he grew his wig to his shoulders, draped himself in frills and satins, perched on top of six-inch Cuban heels, affected a high-pitched lisp, jangled and shimmered from a dozen gold rings, bracelets, baubles.

Then there was his bodyguards and limos and mansions. His tantrums and his unmitigated gall, for his invention didn't mean that he wiped out his neuroses and terrors, merely that he turned them to his own use. He was as isolated and odd, as screwed up as ever, but now he flaunted it. If he didn't like the plane he was flying, he grounded it; if he didn't like a face, he had it pushed in. So he wasn't precisely a gentleman but he was unquenchable, he was indulgent, hysteric, downright nasty, but he enlarged the possible.

It wasn't that any one of his numbers was unique in itself. Other Americans had grown their hair, dressed in drag, been naughty before. Beats had been more extreme, faggots more decadent, film directors more tantrummed, bike gangs funkier, Trotskyites more radical, assassins more psychotic, gangsters more ostentatious and whores more pious. What was special in Spector was that he combined so many different provocations and dissents at once and still managed to make them work for him, in mass commercial terms. He was a walking, talking V-sign millionaire: for the first time, odium equalled money.

If Lenny Bruce had been John the Baptist in this, Spector was the Messiah and, from him, the word passed first to Andrew Oldham and the Stones, then into the general currency of Rock. Gradually weirdery became the norm. Rock 'n' roll became the new home of the professional freak, medium of the malcontent – Leon Russell and Alice Cooper, Zappa, David Bowie, the Fugs or, at other levels, Dylan, Jimi Hendrix, the Who – soon gesture and offence were commonplace. A whole new middle class was spawned off them, the Woodstock generation, so smug and so secure that it was hard to imagine a time, just six or seven years earlier, when outrage had taken balls.

Money, music, style: in each of them his breakthrough was absolutely basic. At the time, in the early '60s, he seemed phenomenal; in retrospect, he's more impressive than ever. To come out of such a vacuum and wreak such changes, at such speed, with such totality – even now, it's hard to conceive the force and self-belief it must have taken. 'Philip Spector,' as Bert Berns said, 'is a holocaust.'

After 'River Deep, Mountain High', when Spector retired in his huff and went up the hill, the idea was not that he would stagnate but that he'd develop into all kinds of new and most scintillating areas. Perhaps he would produce movies, perhaps he'd set up projects with Lenny Bruce, perhaps he'd invade Wall Street. He would relax and read and finish his education; he would travel and shoot pool and train the American karate team. He would go through psychoanalysis, above all, which would release him from all his traumas and set him up for anything and everything. Soon he would be healthier and happier than he'd ever been, and he could make a fresh beginning.

It didn't work; it scarcely could. The best of Rock is that it traps the instant. The corollary, almost inevitably, is that it misses out on permanence – it's totally unequipped for abstraction, for any profundities or second thoughts. While he had existed in continuous motion, Spector had been invincible. The moment he slowed down, he was stranded. Take away his speed and you took away everything.

He went through the motions. He made long and complex journeys with himself, his analyst, his family, his bodyguards, his environment, his soul, his past, his possible future. He watched basketball and might have produced *Easy Rider*. He contemplated and rejected a dozen new departures, and he spawned a son. At the end of it all, after thirty months, he was bored stiff.

One of the worst things in boredom is the panic it causes. People who stay quite calm through riot, tragedy, even death go berserk in tedium. So Spector, who had thrived under pressure, now cracked on ease. Simply, he lost his nerve, made a fatal surrender, which was to retrace his steps.

One of his favourite dictums, which he told me several times, always in alien contexts, was *never repeat*. 'You can always come back,' he used to say, 'but you've got to come back better. If you come back worse, or even the same, you're dead.' And promptly he came back worse, or the same.

Instead of using Philles, which was at least his badge of independence, he made a deal with A & M. Perhaps he needed the money, perhaps he only needed emotional support. Whichever, it meant that, for the first time since his teens, he became an employee, a hired gun.

Next he signed a group called Checkmates Ltd, a supper-soul act from Las Vegas, and cut a single called 'Love Is All I Have To Give'. By his own highest standards, it was average. That put it at least a class above any other single of its year (1969). The only trouble was that it wasn't new – it was archetypal Phil Spector, technically and musically magnificent, but it broke no fresh ground. Therefore, it wasn't a hit.

The follow-up, 'Black Pearl', was less imposing but more commercial and contained at least one classic teendream couplet: 'You'll never win a beauty prize, no, they won't pick you/but you're my Miss America, and I love you.' As it turned out, that was the last great touch that Spector managed.

When 'Black Pearl' made the American top twenty, he went back into the studios, to cut the obligatory album. Around the same time I arrived at the Château and Angel began to scrub my back.

Thus far it wasn't yet clear what direction Spector's comeback would ultimately take. Perhaps the Checkmates were only a dummy run; perhaps he was biding time. At the proper moment, no doubt, he would leap forth from concealment and launch himself on something completely new, startling, overwhelming.

Admittedly, after I met him, I was bothered by his indifference and seeming exhaustion. Still, I tried not to jump ahead – Spector, after all, was famous for shifts and surprises. 'You can't never tell with Phil,' said George. 'The man is a mystery. The man is a bottomless pit.'

This was the summer of 1969. At the Aquarius, down the far end of Sunset Boulevard, the producers of *Hair* threw a party in the parking lot, late one hot afternoon, for all the rich and/or beautiful freaks of Los Angeles.

We were still in the Love Age then, and the lot was full of baubles, bangles, beads. Paraphernalia by numbers – robes and Indian silks, joints in American flag papers, zodiac jackets, patchouli and joss sticks, Soul handshakes, hand drums and unwashed feet. Kaftaned musicians tootled away on Arabic flutes and pipes, and girls with long, blonde hair kept falling over and giggling. So we milled and mumbled in circles, all smiling beautifully, and I was introduced to Scott McKenzie, who wore an embroidered bedsheet and asked me what sign I was. 'A whole new generation with a new explanation,' he said, several times, and I nodded sagely.

The city was full of Icepack. By the end of an hour the air was thick with smoke, half the guests were horizontal and the hired guards, too stoned to focus, were goosing each other with their nightsticks. The pipes droned on interminably and Graham Nash embraced Cass Elliott, Mike Love embraced David Crosby, Eric Burdon embraced anyone who would let him. Silver spoons appeared. Grotesquerie commenced.

It was then that Phil Spector arrived from El Dorado, immured behind his smoked windows and thickest, most ornate shades. Cruising by, he told George to drive him very slow, rolled his window down six inches and, with most extreme caution, he peeked out through the gap, took in the tableau.

What he saw was girls in semi-undress, doing belly dances on a table full of health foods, cross-legged meditators in a circle, tootlers and thumpers leading an impromptu dance in a procession around the lot, a kind of hip Bunny Hop; a couple fucking in a giant bowl of brown rice; acid freaks shrieking or laughing uncontrollably, clawing at their eyes, flapping their arms in attempted flight, expiring; the guards collapsed in a heap; and John Sebastian, standing on one foot, improvising a psalm for all humanity.

Spector did not run away. Instead, as though unable to trust his senses, he rolled down his window a couple of inches further and put his eye still closer to the gap. And this was his undoing, because he was recognized and everyone came towards him.

Here was a major Hollywood event. Since his retirement, Spector had scarcely ever appeared in public, had cloaked himself in the greatest secrecy, thus acquiring an almost mythic stature. Elsewhere he might be forgotten but Los Angeles was still his town – he remained the biggest, hottest, most mysterious number of all and the moment he was spotted he was surrounded.

Jiggling their beads, jangling their bells, the guests all waved and salaamed, brought him their flowers and their joints. Some of them stripped their clothes off and did a dance of celebration. In a sense, after all, he was their creator and was entitled to every mark of obeisance.

Spector himself, meanwhile, seemed paralysed; gazed out at these hordes in a stupor, both motionless and expressionless, while they swarmed fingers all over the paintwork. It was only when some Laurel Canyon speedfreak in a loincloth actually put his hand through the lowered window and tried to touch him that he suddenly came alive and flung himself backwards across the seat, shaken by spasms. Frantically he tried to wind up the window again, trapping the speedoo's fingers as he did so.

The crowd began to shuffle and look uneasy. Hare Krishna chanting was heard. 'George, get me out of here', shrieked Spector, in utter panic, and so they departed, dragging the wretched freak a few feet by his fingertips.

Spector collapsed in a corner, trembling, green-faced. Outside a funeral parlour, a couple of blocks downtown, George gave him a big red pill and gradually he began to subside, was still. In the distance the guests continued to caper and flaunt but he didn't look back. Eyes half-shut, he seemed drained; absolutely exhausted. 'Who were they?' he asked at last, and shook his head slowly, as though shell-shocked. 'I mean, who were those *animals*?'

Sessions were like old-boy reunions. For his return Spector had reassembled the same technicians, musicians, arrangers and even, in a couple of cases, the same songs that he'd used in his days of glory and the atmosphere was heavy with nostalgia. In between takes, the rhythm section would burst into impromptu jams on old Philadelphian hits; on the playback of 'Spanish Harlem', the whole studio seemed to sing along. Many of these men were middle-aged, essentially jaded and disillusioned, but somehow reverence for Spector had managed to fire them up and there was a sense of mild jollification. Gags and catch-phrases from ten years ago were brought out of storage and dusted down. Backs were slapped, wrists pulled, cigars handed round. One of the trumpet section produced a yellow balloon. 'Party time,' said Larry Levine, the engineer. 'I'd forgotten that sessions could be such fun.'

And Spector himself? He was the centre, naturally, and for most of the time seemed jubilant. His lines were the fastest, his put-downs the most outrageous of all and I could hear his squeaks and yells from right down the hall.

On good takes, when things began to cook, he was marvellous: first he shuffled and sang along in an undertone, then escalated gradually, through whoops and shimmies and little leaps, until in the end he'd be falling about in delirium, arms flying, head flung back, shrieking with all his lungs. His shades fell off; his tiny feet flew out sideways, like sparks off an anvil. Ecstatic, he burned.

Not that such high jinks were continuous – every so often, without warning, his head went down and he sagged. Then he'd slump in a corner or lock himself in another room and nothing could make him react. Ten minutes would pass, fifteen, twenty, and all action was suspended. No more gags, no more old routines – everything hung fire until his return.

Sometimes the silence would be broken by a furious tirade,

offstage. Torrential outpourings of abuse, uncontrollable, incomprehensible; one pictured him, like Rumpelstiltskin, growing more and more frenzied, until at last he screwed himself into the ground. At last his passion would exhaust itself. Then there would be another long silence. Everyone waited patiently. Most of them had been through all this before, countless times, no doubt, and they played cards or smoked in corners.

Finally Spector would reappear, smiling, refreshed, with a new one-liner already on his lips. Right on cue, someone would answer back and Phil would top them, and the tension fell away. The rhythm section remembered some more old riffs, the horns remembered some more old anecdotes. Time restarted.

The music itself was problematic. Technically, there was no question that Spector was still absolutely brilliant. His sharpness of ear, speed of reaction and precision were all astonishing, and so was his certainty. Each track was packed with ideas, fire, real beauty.

Still there was something missing. For all the fine moments, there was an absence of surprise, a lack of real creative need. Just like the singles, Spector had been here before, many times.

Possibly he knew it. At any rate, after sessions, he tended to go a bit glum. He left the studio quickly, got into his limo and George drove him straight back home. Most nights he kept silence all the way, hunched in a ball. But once, just down the block from his office, we passed some cops beating up on hippies and Spector was enraged. For some minutes he lost himself in one of his harangues, a wild and hilarious Bruceian satire. Then he fell quiet and looked prophetic. Obviously he was preparing a final pronouncement, a clincher, but in the end he only sighed and shook his head. 'This city sucks', he said, and pretended to fall asleep.

Perhaps this wasn't the most sparkling of all his epigrams. Still it triggered me. For no obvious reason, I was suddenly reminded of W.C. Fields and his deathbed. Feeling the end come upon him, the comedian turned his face to the wall and said: 'I'd rather be in Philadelphia.'

Our book came to nothing. After each meeting, I'd take the tapes back to the Château and painfully transpose them, while Angel sucked lollipops, but the results were uniformly dispiriting. Like the Checkmates' album, they were full of fine touches – perfect little phrases or tales, sudden flashes, razor-sharp punchlines – but when you added them up, somehow they were barren.

The moment had passed, that's all. Philadelphia would have been perfect, New York or even early Hollywood, any time up until his retirement. Then a book might have been alive and bizarre. To write it now, however, was simply to act as obituarist.

Already it was impossible to mistake his future. Having once let go of Philles and let himself be hired, he must automatically lose his uniqueness. As an employee, he ceased to be his own creation and acquired a context, a limitation. Abdicating control, he began a third invention; a second imposition.

Naturally his new self would be coloured by his past, his track record. He would not now be seen as runtish or insignificant; he would become a man of talent and substance, revered as a producer, celebrated as a story. He would be courted and flattered, he would make money and would influence, and he would still be a focus for gossip, emulation. What he wouldn't be, though, was omnipotent. He wouldn't transcend all categories, and he would no longer dictate. When he made a record, it would belong less to him than to the artist or the company. It would still be a hit, no doubt, but it wouldn't be Phil Spector's.

In spite of this, or because of it, he still seemed the definitive Rock 'n' Roll saga. No one else had so perfectly caught its potentials, and also its limitations. He'd been everything that was best – fast, funny and a bit heroic, full of style and marvellous follies; he'd also proved just how fast the medium went sour. It made for marvellous flashes, it never sustained: get into it two-handed, stampede right through it and then quit dead, without a backwards glance. Don't cruise and don't admire the view. Above all, don't ever stop.

The melancholy truth was that Spector understood this, had understood it from the start. Much of his fiercest contempt, in fact, was reserved for the men who hung about and got old. That was why he retired so fast in the first place, more or less, and that was what made his return so grey.

I packed away my white silk suit and prepared to go home. Angel went away, so did the man with the black moustache and, the day before my departure, the candelabra came crashing down

205

in the lobby, to shatter in a thousand meaningless splinters.

I went to say goodbye. In his office, Spector sat surrounded by numberless gold records and told me, for perhaps the third time, how he'd found the title for 'To Know Him Is To Love Him'. 'I took it,' he said, 'from the words on my tombstone.'

He was standing at the window, looking down into the Strip. For a few seconds he noticed nothing. Then he heard what it was he'd said and he turned round to face me, distinctly flustered. 'My father's grave, I mean. My father,' he said, and shook his head, bothered. By the door I shook his hand and he shook mine. 'Weird. Very weird,' he said.

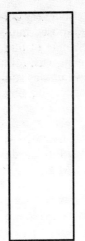

Come Alive With Pepsi

S eventeen floors above Central Park South, I stood out on the balcony and, behind my back, inside the apartment, half the heads in New York were having a party.

There were more than a hundred of them, spread through three rooms, and they wore caftans, see-through blouses, Ethiopian sandals, Indian silk scarves, Mexican charms, Red Indian fringes, smocks emblazoned with appropriate signs of the zodiac, Russian peasant-girl maxi-skirts, Turkish trousers, army greatcoats, sharkskin waistcoats, and they were not drinking but they were smoking grass and popping pills and, huddled over the kitchen table, they were sniffing cocaine.

Abbey Road was playing very loud and the walls were covered with large nude photographs of an elderly adolescent, the hostess perhaps, except that nobody knew who the hostess was and, all over the floors, there were large embroidered cushions, on which bodies were scattered at random. In other words, it was just like a stoned scene on the movies and everyone was smiling, everyone was murmuring, everyone was sighing.

Who were they? They were faces, that's all, and they were the children of rich men, the sons of politicians and the daughters of tycoons, and also their friends, who were hair stylists and photographers and designers, hip lawyers and TV actors and speed-freak faggots, coke contacts with golden spoons, several black girls but no black men, since token Negroes are out, and also a very tall model who might have been Verushka, and a broken-nosed midget who was nearly Michael J. Pollard, and a wide range of film makers, currently in search of a sponsor, and rock guitarists, folk guitarists and jazz guitarists, and groupies of all sexes, junkies and electric poets, pimps and wasn't that Michael Brody, the boy millionaire, who wishes to give away his fortune? No, it wasn't. But it wasn't far off.

In fact, this was just the new American upper class, second grade. Not quite the élite, the real oligarchy, but solid. Inside these rooms, there was money and sex and status. Almost certainly, someone here had touched a Beatle.

Standing out on the balcony, I looked down. Below, there was a constant stream of cars and taxis, dumping extra guests outside the door. The pavement was full of beautiful persons.

And somewhere around midnight, a very large limousine drew up and out stepped an egg, about six foot high by three foot in diameter, made of thin cardboard, painted speckled brown and tied around its middle with a satin bow.

This egg was then borne across the pavement by two friends who carried it chest-high. They got it through the doorway and disappeared from my view, across the hall, into the elevator and up seventeen floors. Arriving at last outside the door, they rang the bell and, when the door was opened, they brought in the giant egg.

Dumped on the floor, the egg didn't move at first, just vibrated slightly and then, when the most cool of all the cool faces had been forced to watch, it hatched. The cardboard burst out sideways, crumpled on the floor and, out of the wreckage, there stepped a man of medium height, about thirty years old, who wore yellow crushed-velvet trousers, two sizes too small, and a big black leather belt with a golden buckle, a white voile bodyshirt, an orange silk scarf. He was short-sighted. He was going bald.

And nothing happened: no one fainted and no one screamed. Sprawled out on their cushions, the faces smiled just like before, nodding and mumbling. 'Abbey Road' had been replaced by 'Let It Bleed', fresh joints were rolled and the eggman was left stranded, with his shell around his ankles and his paunch slurping over his belt.

Down on the avenue, there was a siren passing by and I peered over the balcony. By the time that I turned back into the room, the eggman had gone away.

Close beside me, though, there was a girl with black hair almost to her waist, Rita Hayworth lips, and she gave me pills: 'Tell me,' I said. 'Who's the egg?'

'Oh,' said the girl. 'That's Mike.'

She was very stoned. After each phrase, she stopped and sank into a dream, staring off into space and then, maybe a minute later, she'd say something new. 'He's a head,' she said. 'He does this every week,' she said. 'He works for Pepsi.'

'He what?'

'He sells Pepsi-Cola.'

Right then, on Central Park South, I was granted revelation and my eyes opened wide. *He does this every week. He works for Pepsi.* And looking through the room, I saw them all afresh, the faces and the freaks, and then I had them covered, I knew them by their name: the Pepsi Generation.

Quite simply, Pepsi is the compromise version of Hippie, the style in which you can enjoy all the pleasures of the drop-out revolution without actually having to drop out yourself.

In the Pepsi Generation, you get it both ways: you smoke the joints and use the language and listen to the music, draw on all the fringe benefits and yet you don't need to go the whole way, you don't leave home or get arrested or give away all your money.

In the beginning, it wasn't so cosy. Around 1965, when the first Hippies emerged in Haight Ashbury, there were kids who truly believed that a whole new age was dawning, that all Hate would cease forthwith and that Universal Love would reign ever after and, in this cause, they were even prepared to suffer, to be jeered at and beaten up and busted, to go hungry and sleep on floors, to share out everything that they owned.

Once they had been discovered by media and Hippie began to be fashionable, however, things changed fast. Reading about Haight in glossy magazines or watching it on TV, all kinds of latecomers jumped on the bandwagon, just to be hip. In particular, with 'Revolver' and 'Sgt Pepper', the Beatles changed everything. Even though they belonged in the movement, what with dropping acid and meditating and so forth, they also commanded the mass public and, through songs like 'Eleanor Rigby' and 'She's Leaving Home' and 'A Day In The Life', they recruited a whole second wave, middle-class and only half-way committed, the Pepsi Generation.

Even apart from the vision on Central Park itself, Pepsi makes a suitable symbol. After all, in the history of colas, Coke came first, the original, and Pepsi arrived as a latecomer, a sweeter, lighter and fizzier alternative.

From the start, Pepsi has been based on a single age-old precept: it's fun to be a freak. And it is, of course. It's fun to get stoned and float on giant cushions, to stay up past your bedtime. And it's fun to visit *Hair*, to go up on stage and dance with the kids, belonging, and believe that you've had access to secret knowledge, revelations that the straight world doesn't even suspect.

It is even fun to be misunderstood, to feel yourself martyred, a rebel and outsider. What isn't much fun, though, is to be punched in the face and thrown into jail. Not at all, it isn't and, therefore, the political and philosophical basis of the movement has been more or less forgotten. Officially, Pepsi still stands for all the old slogans, Love and Peace and Flowers, the downfall of the WASP and the rescue of the Oppressed but, in practice, nothing gets done: the revolution has become a game.

And this is the whole trick with Pepsi, in fact, that you take it just as far and no further than the point at which things begin to get unpleasant. You speak the lines, play out the rituals but, in the end, you take no risks. In New York, you run with the game but, when you visit Houston, you wear a conventional dark business suit.

Pepsi comes in four main classes. The first is Park Avenue or Scene Pepsi, which is where the eggman appeared and which is just a gathering together of the élite, an extension of the Beautiful People. The three lower castes are: Rock Pepsi, Pink-shirt Pepsi and Village Pepsi.

Ever since Bob Dylan and Paul Simon and the Beatles, ever since it became fashionable to think of Pop as Art, it's been almost impossible to make it in Rock without pretending profundity. Accordingly, the business now consists of hundreds and thousands of Old Testament prophets.

As it happens, in the fifteen years of its existence, Rock has produced maybe six, maybe ten, major figures, which is very good going. However, by the nature of the industry, which is essentially ephemeral, no less than fifty-two major figures are required per year and these days, every time that you open up *Cashbox* or *Billboard* or *Rolling Stone*, there he is, this week's all-time genius: a toothless black guitarist; a blind folksinger with a flowing white beard; an albino blues singer from Texas.

The name of this game is Hype, which means to hustle. From Bill Haley on, this has always been the basis of the whole Rock process, and the coming of Pepsi has not lessened its power, not a bit. The style has changed, that's all.

In the fifties and early sixties, when Pop was run by middle-aged businessmen, Hype was simply a more polite word for Payola and, whenever you launched a new record, you bought it straight up the charts, no messing. But in the mid-sixties, as Hippie emerged, many of the businessmen were toppled and their places were taken by earnest young men, Pepsi to the heel, who wished to purge the industry of all corruption.

On its own terms, though, the Pepsi Generation is just as gullible as any of its predecessors. Instead of falling for stunts and toothpaste smiles, it gets suckered by pomposity. Despite its essential fakery, it takes itself with deadly solemnity and anyone who can work on its pretensions, flatter its perception and twist its fear of being unfashionable, has got it made.

And so instead of Money Hype, Rock now works through Concept Hype and the rules are very clear. As soon as you've found an act, you start by finding a label for them: Supergroup, Kharma-Rock, Midget Athethoid Bard. Then you lard in a few favourite adjectives, add a couple of nude photographs and top off with sample lyrics, printed as poems. Finally, if all else fails, you ask the one crucial question: *Are you ready for this*? Since to be unready for anything is the ultimate Pepsi sin, you can hardly miss.

Right now, the two biggest Pepsi groups in America are Blood, Sweat & Tears and Crosby, Stills & Nash. Both of them in slightly different ways, sum up the system.

Blood, Sweat & Tears play a mixture of white modern jazz and white commercial R & B, highly thought out and arranged, and their gimmick is just that they're musicians. Right here in rock and roll, real musicians who play trumpets and saxophones, who can change tempo in the middle of a number and who use terms like harmony, chord sequence and interval. Straightaway, that makes them superstars.

In the heart of the Pepsi Rock fan, there lurks a secret shame at the blatancy and vulgarity of the music's past, Elvis in his gold lamé suit, Little Richard jumping on the piano and Jerry Lee Lewis so greasy, all those wild and orgiastic exhibitions. Just like the jazz fans of 1960, who preferred Dave Brubeck to John Coltrane, they want it both ways: they want to be hip, to be in the game and yet, in the end, they don't want to get their feet wet.

For these purposes, Blood, Sweat & Tears are perfect. They may look like a Rock group, they may dress and talk and smell like a Rock group but then, when they start to play, their music is strictly polite, very smooth and entirely safe. The fact that they're also derivative and limp, thoroughly third-rate both as jazz and as Pop, hardly comes into it. If anything, in fact, it's an advantage.

Crosby, Stills & Nash lean more towards folk and country than jazz but, this apart, they offer the same equation. They are slick, soft and intricate, much given to wistful melancholy. In addition, they have been the biggest success yet in that most favourite of all Pepsi Hype – the Supergroup.

The theory behind the Supergroup is that you take the star members out of three or four established groups, throw them together and come up with a fusion of souls. In this way, Dave Crosby of the Byrds joined up with Steve Stills of the Buffalo Springfield and Graham Nash of the Hollies, and they then spent a few months rehearsing before bringing out an album. An album that sounded like Pepsi Semprini, sickly sweet and boneless, full of fake sensitivity. Altogether, an exquisite drooling nothingness – and now Crosby, Stills & Nash make up to £10,000 per concert.

More than any group, however, Rock Pepsi has been summed up by *Hair*. Right there, you have the full production, the whole thing epitomized: the surface rebellion, the noise and the flashing lights, the movement and freshness and energy and, underneath all that, what else? Fifties' showtunes dressed up as Rock; Ragni, Rado and McDermot, three middle-aged hepcats; a compendium of Hippie clichés, Our Hundred Favourite Platitudes – *do your own thing* and *tell it like it is, get it together* and *groovy, far out* and *beautiful, man, you're beautiful*; and then, of course, the climactic moment, the most exact expression of Pepsi so far, when all the cast take their clothes off and face the audience. Naked in the nude, frank and unashamed. With all the lights turned out.

Pink-shirt Pepsi is centred in New York, although London runs a close-up second, and involves career men and women, mostly between the ages of twenty-five and forty, people like publishers, academics, admen and lawyers, journalists and publicists and analysts.

Basically, they are people who feel embarrassed by the straightness in their lives, people who are scared of middle age, who are worn down by their commitments and duties, by the fact that they're mortgaged and contracted and insured, when they'd like to believe that they're still running free. On Saturday nights, therefore, they smoke grass and around Christmas, they may wear a silk scarf to the office.

As I've mentioned already, they first got involved with the Beatles. Before that, they'd never taken Rock seriously at all, they'd much preferred Miles Davis and Dave Brubeck and the Modern Jazz Quartet. Once the first breach had been made, though, the rest was inevitable. From 'Sgt Pepper', they moved on to Joan Baez and Bob Dylan, and then further on still, right into the jungle, as far as the Rolling Stones. And soon they'd bought their first pink shirt, their bedroom walls were covered with personality posters and, in no time, someone passed them a joint and they thought, *Wow, that's the real thing* and yes, they plunged.

Accordingly, in Tarreytown, in Westchester County, on a September evening, four young married couples sat around a scrubbed pinewood table and ate soul food with their fingers, just like the black folks in Harlem. Bar-B-Q Spareribs, Candied Yams, Sweet Potatoes and Stringbeans, Grits and Cole Slaw, and they washed it all down with Miller's Hi-Life, the Champagne of Beers.

Of the four men, two were publishers, one was an adman and the last was a journalist, all of them between the ages of thirty and thirty-five, and as they ate, they discussed Paul McCartney, was he really dead and, if so, had John Lennon had him murdered?

When that was exhausted, they spoke of various Pepsi cults of that moment, notably Johnny Cash, the great Country 'n' Western singer, who had been making records for fifteen years but had just recently become fashionable, due to his friendship with Bob Dylan; and also Mae West, Aleister Crowley and Louis L'Amour, an old-time writer of Westerns.

After dinner, everyone moved through into the living-room, where there were large pictures of Che Guevara, Humphrey Bogart and Jean-Luc Godard, and the metal sign: *Don't Walk On the Grass*. And they sat on sofas and in armchairs, while 'Nashville Skyline' played in the background, and a joint was passed from hand to hand, through the first publisher, the second publisher and the adman, and through their wives, until it came at last to the journalist and then to his wife, a small brunette named Sheila, who had hardly spoken all evening.

Very tense, she sat up straight and she squeezed the joint between her thumb and forefinger, stuck it in her mouth, sucked in quietly and breathed out again, much too fast, so that the smoke didn't reach her lungs but came straight out through her nostrils, wasted.

Never mind, it didn't make much odds, the joint was very weak. Still, it passed on down the line and the music went on playing and everyone got stoned regardless. Slouching in the cushions, they composed their bodies into all the time-honoured movie junkie poses, nodding to the beat, giggling or staring smokily into space, and none more dramatically than Sheila, who coiled and uncoiled like a cobra. Quite suddenly, without warning, she squeaked and put her hand up to her mouth, her eyes wide with revelation: 'Oh,' she said. 'Oh, such colours, such beautiful colours and shapes, such beautiful . . . oh, wow . . . such beautiful, beautiful shapes.'

For a moment, no one said anything and she was lost in visions, gazing up through the ceiling with all-seeing eyes. Then her husband reached over, tight-lipped, and touched her: 'Wrong drug,' he said. 'That's acid.'

Village Pepsi, finally, is simply the newest form of that time-honoured ritual by which middle-class kids leave home, dress up as freaks, spend a couple of years in Greenwich Village finding themselves, and then, somewhat disillusioned but also vaguely relieved, they head back where they came from.

Over on the East Side, around St Mark's Place, there are the young kids from Montana, Ohio and Idaho, who sleep in crash pads and panhandle for dimes and sit out on the fire escapes, not moving for hours at a time; back on the West Side, there is the hip bourgeoisie, musicians and writers and so forth, Arts graduates all; on Christopher Street, there are the new homosexuals, the Gay Power militants, screaming at every cop that passes: 'Look at me, man, I'm bent'; and branching out from Washington Square, there are the weekend trippers.

In each case, it's still the same old village style, the same pattern that has existed here for the last twenty years or more. Bohemian or Beat or Hippie, the names may keep changing but the symbols are eternal: cheap wine and French bread and cheese, the smells of old socks and sex, the unfinished novel in the typewriter, the cockroaches in the bath, the friend who is a junkie, the friend who is Black, the friend who is queer.

To this, Pepsi has added very little. Rock instead of jazz, of course, and even more emphasis on drugs. That apart, it has managed only a series of cults: meditation and UFOs and black magic, Wilhelm Reich and his Orgone Box, J. R. Tolkien and Kahlil Gibran, Pueblo Indians, Country 'n' Western and, above all, astrology.

Since the eclipse of the Maharishi, astrology has been the stock Pepsi religion, though challenged lately by a growing fad for Satanism, and any room that you enter, it's odds on that someone will approach you, look deep and soulfully into your eyes, smile wisely and guess your sign. Guess it wrong, what's more.

On Sunset Strip in Los Angeles, I walked past the Whisky A GoGo and was picked up by a nymphette groupie, who asked me for a dime. I gave her a quarter. 'Far out,' she said, very coyly: 'Are you Aquarius?' and that's when I understood Pepsi astrology, not as a science but just as a come-on, a hip replacement for *Hi there, Big Boy, wanna buy a girl a drink?*

Oddly enough, as the chances of any real youth revolution have disappeared, Pepsi has been getting more and more powerful. Not in politics, perhaps, although it will be twenty years before one can be sure even of that, but certainly in media, which are almost as important these days. Already, it has gained control of large segments of the music business and has gained very real footholds in TV, publishing, the theatre and journalism. Above all, it has turned Hollywood upside down.

Within the last year, almost every film that's been made has been affected by it. Apart from the obvious examples, like *Easy Rider* (runner-up to *Hair* as the most comprehensive collection of Pepsi clichés yet), *Alice's Restaurant* and *Zabriskie Point*, little snippets keep sneaking into essentially non-Pepsi movies – the bicycle ride in *Butch Cassidy*, for one, or the party scene in *Midnight Cowboy*, and Dustin Hoffman driving across the bridge in *The Graduate*, with Scarborough Fair on the sound-track.

The point is only that Pepsi films are cheap to make and that their potential profits are immense. In an age when the studios can no longer afford to chance twenty million dollars on a single blockbuster musical, Pepsi is a godsend. For a million dollars, the basic salary of Julie Andrews or Elizabeth Taylor, you can now turn out an entire movie. A movie without stars, style or brains, but no less likely to score for that. As Kit Lambert has said, in a pop context: 'Underground is just the new word for Money.'

This is the guts of the whole situation, in fact, the reason why Pepsi, unlike all previous such youth movements, may sustain and expand: it pays. In this generation, for the first time, there's a mass audience ready and panting for any kind of freakiness that may get thrown at them and, since all American media are run on a strictly commercial basis, freakiness is exactly what they'll get.

After a couple of years, of course, the novelty will probably wear off, and we'll all get back to *Mary Poppins* and *South Pacific*. If it doesn't work out that way, though, there's a very grim prospect ahead because, in America, Pepsi has already begun to build up its own back-handed censorship.

Because it takes itself with such great solemnity, it can't bear that anyone should fail to share its values. Out of its very rejection of conformity, it has constructed a conformity of its own, just as crippling as the WASP brand. Merle Haggard, probably the most talented Country 'n' Western artist since Hank Williams but also resolutely redneck, has been blacklisted by Pepsi radio stations everywhere. So, for that matter have Elvis Presley, Billie Holliday and Beethoven, the Monotones and almost all jazz.

At this rate, it won't be long before nothing un-Pepsi can get through, in which case the writers who would be out of print would include Dickens, Nabakov, Evelyn Waugh, Flann O'Brien and Marcel Proust. Just possibly, they might be turned into a fast camp cult. Failing that, they'd be out.

All right, I'm melodramatizing. But out in San Francisco, I remember doing a radio interview with some local Pepsi DJ and, when I said that I hadn't enjoyed 'Abbey Road' the lines were jammed with abusive phone calls. As I walked out from the radio station, I was heckled, hissed and, all the way down the block, I was pursued by a troupe of beards, headbands and fringes. Finally, I took refuge in a drugstore, and, while the love generation pulled faces through the windows, I lurked behind the bookstand. There, shaking, I sipped Coke.

Jesus Christ Superham

Thirty miles outside Jerusalem I was taken into a labyrinth of underground caves, where the apostles and their women were performing a dance routine. The atmosphere inside was rank and airless, the heat was murderous. After half an hour, half-choked by dust, I came stumbling out into the sunlight and fell asleep beneath an olive tree, dreaming of Gadarene swine. When I awoke I saw a figure perched motionless on a rock above me, a small man in a coarse white robe, with a cassette recorder pressed against his ear. For some moments he gazed blankly at the horizon, lost in the music, and then he came down slowly towards me, to crouch beside me in the dirt. His beard was silky, his eyes full of light. 'You must be Jesus,' I said.

'Sure am,' he replied, and I shook his hand. We ate shrivelled olives and he nodded his head in time with the songs, sandals tapping. When the Stones became suggestive in their lyrics, he turned the volume down.

'What does it feel like?' I asked him. 'I mean, to be the Son of God?'

The small man considered carefully. Lizards scurried by his feet and he stared into infinity. 'Outasight,' he said at last. 'It's really a far-out trip.'

When John Lennon said in 1966 that the Beatles were more popular than Jesus Christ, one could hardly have conceived how soon and how directly he'd be given the lie. Yet *Jesus Christ Superstar*, in three years, has grossed somewhere between £50,000,000 and £80,000,000 and is currently hotter than the Beatles, The Rolling Stones and any half dozen other rock groups put together. *Variety* calls it 'the biggest all-media parlay in show-business history'; *Time* simply calls it 'Gold Rush to Golgotha.'

A movie – *a major motion picture* – was inevitable. Yet, Hollywood's enthusiasm has been tempered by considerable caution. Film executives still look on Rock (and on youth) with deepest distrust. Occasionally, it has made their fortune; much more often, it has showered them with offal. So these days they tend to hover desperately on the fringes, like so many dirty raincoats lurking outside a clip joint. They know, of course, that they're bound to get sucked in sooner or later, yet they can't stop wheedling for discounts and guarantees, in case the bar girls turn sour on them.

Universal Pictures, having bought the rights to *Superstar*, promptly began to do the crab walk. It restricted the budget to $3,000,000, which for a Hollywood musical is peanuts, and it stocked the cast with virtual unknowns. Originally, Mick Jagger had been proposed as a possible Jesus. So had Lennon, Elvis Presley, and unimaginably, David Cassidy. But the part went to Teddy Neeley from Ranger, Texas, 'for an undisclosed fee,' as one apostle put it, 'rumoured to run into three figures.'

The producer and director was Norman Jewison, whose last picture had been *Fiddler on the Roof*. That probably made him the most reliable profit maker in Hollywood. He had made *In the Heat of the Night*, *The Cincinnati Kid*, *The Thomas Crown Affair* and *The Russians Are Coming, The Russians Are Coming*.

His interest in *Superstar* went back almost to its inception. Long before it became successful, someone had sent him the original album. Straightaway, he was hooked: 'Without doubt a unique statement for our age,' he said, with reflex overkill. 'Possibly not a masterpiece. At certain moments pretentious, at others naïve and superficial. Nevertheless, a major breakthrough, an original and unforgettable vision.'

Reverence ran deep. No true child of Hollywood can ever resist the lure of the *religioso*. So Jewison filled his script with symbolism, spoke with awe of *The Greatest Story Ever Told* and, inevitably, chose to film in Israel – or rather, as he never failed to call it, the Holy Land.

'Piety,' Orson Welles once said, 'is a showbiz term of unknown origin, meaning money.' In Jewison's case, however, the common rule came unstuck. He meant to make enormous profits, of course, and was prepared to be ruthless in pursuit of them. But there was no mistaking the missionary glint in his eye. He clearly had his sights set on Art: 'A total experience,' he said. 'Truth, meaning and beauty.'

Most of the cast were *Superstar* veterans, selected from various American stage versions. Judas was a big black stud named Carl Anderson from Washington; Mary Magdalene, played by Yvonne Elliman, was a surfer's dream from Hawaii; Herod was Joshua Mostel, Zero's son. As for the others – apostles, Romans, whores – one half looked like refugees from *Hair* and the rest like dropouts from *The Boys in the Band*.

On the whole, they were not respectful. *Superstar* was an experience that they'd already been through and, frankly, they were bored. Sated with solemnity, they wanted to get back to good hard Rock and goof off again, get stoned onstage, boogie. So they went into the film for the exposure and the bread, but they groused behind their hands: 'The vehicle,' said the incarnation of Saint James the Elder, 'is bullshit.'

Israel changed that. On the road in America they had merely been performers. But the moment they arrived in the actual setting, they began to mesh with their roles. Bypassing the opera, they went directly back to the source, to the original Gospels. *Superstar* became irrelevant. Now it was Christ himself who concerned them.

Thus, a couple of days before filming began, Saint Bartholomew and Saint James walked out together into the desert and sat down on a rock. All afternoon they squatted crosslegged and did not move or speak. For hour after hour they watched the shepherds tending their flocks, the olive trees, the scrub, the ageless stone. Nothing had changed here for 2000 years; possibly nothing ever would. Time was meaningless: afternoon moved slowly into twilight and on into night, heat faded into cool, and still they didn't stir.

When at last they returned to themselves, they found their faces wet with tears.

Jewison, is a stocky, sun-browned Canadian in his middle forties. He has been making films, first for TV and then for Hollywood, for twenty years and therefore is rarely to be seen without a fat cigar, which he smokes in the style of Ed Begley, all puff and no drag.

On the set he invariably wore shorts and a battered old bush hat, so that he looked like a reject from a B-feature thriller, set in the Australian outback, who had wandered into *Superstar* by accident. A grizzled, nuggety gold prospector, perhaps, or a cranky mule driver. A character role, at any rate, with plenty of scope for excess: 'I'm a ham,' he said. 'I can't help it – audiences are my lifeblood.'

He can sniff out a journalist or a prospective Boswell at fifty yards and immediately, in the very instant of recognition, is overwhelmed by rhetoric. Ask him a question and his eye becomes a beacon, his cigar begins to belch forth smoke like a factory chimney and out gush anecdotes in a torrent. Reminiscences, parables, apocryphal fables of vintage Hollywood, all as dazzling and as dubious as the sequins on a Bluebell girl.

Even more than yarn spinning, however, he is addicted to profundity. Touch on any of the great flowerpots at random – art, religion, love, life or death – and you are immediately engulfed in proverb and portent. Thus, when Barry Dennen, alias Pontius Pilate, came to Jewison between takes and asked his advice on some small point of interpretation, he did not reply at once but creased his face like an accordian, puffed three mighty puffs on his cigar and, finally, raised a solemn forefinger. 'Just remember this,' he said. 'Whatever you do, however you play it: Unto thine own self be true.'

Now Jewison stood framed in left profile. Silhouetted against the first glow of sunset, he crinkled his eyes and flung his arm out across the valley below. 'There are kids down there in tears,' he said. 'Why? There are grown men breaking down and bawling, there are cameramen and grips and hard-boiled pros who've been in this business for twenty years and don't give a fuck for anyone or anything and all of them are crying. Why? Jesus is crying. Judas is crying, all the apostles are just wiped out. Why? They didn't cry in London. They didn't cry in New York or Los Angeles; they didn't cry in Hoboken. So tell me, why are they crying now? Why?'

Everyone looked blank. The assistant director, the production supervisor and the unit publicist crowded in close, like Los Angeles Rams in a huddle, waiting to be instructed, but Jewison took his time. 'Why?' he asked again and, noticing that his cigar had gone out, paused until the assistant director relit it. Fat Israelis were swilling out latrines in the background. Extras straggled past, holding hands and snuffling. The valley turned purple. 'Because we're here,' said Jewison suddenly. 'That's why.'

'Because we're here,' echoed the production supervisor, and he looked profound. Clearly, he was troubled. So were the others.

But Jewison was triumphant. 'Right,' he roared. 'Because we're here. Because it's the Holy Land. Because we're all in this simple valley, just us and the olive trees, the mules, the mountains above. Because it's real.'

His cohorts began to catch the drift. 'Because it's real,' intoned the assistant director and he beamed at the unit publicist, who beamed right back and said, 'Because we're here.'

Soon the mood became frankly celebratory. 'Reality,' declared Jewison. 'No studios, no faking, no bullshit. Only the rock and the sand and the sky. Only the truth.'

Inspired, he half-turned and looked directly down into the valley at a small patch of vivid green grass, especially flown in from England, because there isn't much green grass in this part of Israel. Saint Peter sat cross-legged beneath a tree, reading *The Autobiography of a Yogi*; Saint John was writing home to his mother; Saint Bartholomew was busily goosing Saint Thaddeus with an olive branch. 'Reality,' said Jewison one last time, and, clambering into his Jaguar, he was driven off into the sunset.

The crying, once launched, did not easily let up. The apostles and most of the cast cried when Jesus got the shits and had to rush for the sanctuary of the honey wagon; they cried when Judas turned nasty and raised his voice to them; most of all, they cried when they saw themselves on the rushes. 'Very emotional boyos, these,' said the Irish chief caterer. 'Thank the Lord I've got plenty of spare buckets.' Several times, at the end of a take, Jesus and Judas capsized sobbing in each other's arms. Then Jewison joined them for a choked embrace. Within seconds, the set was awash. Gradually, even the technicians and the extras were snared. By the end of the third week, the unit nurse was so deeply moved by the sight of a young Arab boy picking flowers that she fell over a small stone wall and sprained her wrist.

Along with the general gushing, meanwhile, a macabre little charade began to unfold. The apostles had apparently identified themselves so utterly with their roles that they began to look on Teddy Neeley as though he were, indeed, the Messiah. They followed him everywhere, took him food and drink, massaged his neck when he was weary, carried his burdens when he felt depressed and, of course, bathed him with their tears whenever the script made him suffer.

Undoubtedly, he was a gentle and sympathetic spirit, a very nice man. Still, to the outsider, such worship was startling. No matter, worship him they did: 'Would I give up my life for him?' asked Saint James rhetorically. 'Who can know such things? But I would fight for him, I'd even put up with loss and abuse for him. Why? Because he is warm and tender and good. Because, if Christ were alive today, he would be someone like Teddy Neeley.'

Teddy, it must be said, neither encouraged nor discouraged all this. He was altogether too polite ever to propose himself as the Godhead. On the other hand, the journey from Ranger to Calvary *had* taken him fifteen scuffling years and he wasn't about to blow his ticket. He had spent three years playing Saturday-night dances in Palo Pinto County, six more on the road to Los Angeles and whole eternities in Vegas, or in warm-up bands for Opry tours, or singing suppertime schlurp at the Cocoanut Grove. He had cracked up in Hollywood, broken down in Hawaii and his first gig in *Superstar*, on Broadway, had been as an understudy. Now he was Jesus Christ: 'the big cheese himself,' as Jewison put it, and who could blame him if he wore his robes in the shower or made a few ambiguous passes with his fingertips? 'I *know* what I am,' he said. 'Others can see what they choose.'

Big black Judas, inevitably, caught the backlash. Jesus liked him fine, but the apostles ran away every time he approached. 'Rough, tough and baad,' squealed Saint Bartholomew. 'Just looking at him is enough to make you cream. Now you tell me, honey, who wants to cream at a time like this?'

Judas was not unduly distressed – isolation suited him. Intensely competitive, implausibly handsome, he had brisk contempt for mass opinion and locked himself up every night in his hotel bedroom. 'People are a pain in the ass,' he said. 'and nice, well-meaning people are the biggest pain of all.'

Nonetheless, like Jewison, he was a compulsive performer and, while on the set, he played at Captain Superspade, all soul handshakes and funky little finger pops, eye rollings, mouth gapings and splutters of dirty laughter. He had enormous presence and, undoubtedly, was going to be a star. Kids adored him, so did the Israelis and so, of course, did women. Soon he built up a following all his own, a group of antidisciples, who idolized him as much as the apostles idolized Jesus.

Every day, in the luncheon tent, the two factions would mumble in corners and watch, waiting for a showdown. Their leaders, however, let them down completely. Obstinate, not to say unsporting, they insisted on remaining good friends and swapped cassettes, shared salads, embraced in the sunshine: 'Rip-off!' squawked Saint Thaddeus. 'It wasn't like that in the script.'

Still, away from the set, Judas started showing signs of strain. There was a series of explosions – blazing rows with hotel managers, semibrawls by swimming pools, tales of unpaid bills and overturned tables. In between outbursts, he withdrew entirely, immersing himself in solitude and silence. Having sent for his girlfriend from Los Angeles, he found he couldn't even speak to her and had to parcel her off forthwith. All human contact, all sentiment irked him unbearably. 'Judas means distance and coldness,' he said. Then he suddenly laughed. 'Loneliness, bad vibes, being mean,' he chortled, 'and man, I really dig it. A few times I think I'd really like to be close to someone, but then, as soon as I am, I start feeling trapped and have to run away. Anyone I care about, I destroy them, try to drive them off. I hate responsibility, dependence, need, any kind of closeness. Deep down, I just don't give a fuck.'

Jesus, when told of this, was saddened but not shocked. Spreading his robe serenely about his feet, he squatted in the shade and heaved a deep sigh. 'Whether you're Judas or Jesus or even Mary Magdalene," he said, 'this gig can be a killer.'

What was all the fuss about *Superstar* in the first place? Certainly it was amiable and energetic, full of bounce and good intentions, all the things that musicals are meant to have. Then, of course, the Messiah has always been box-office boffo and the notion of rocking the Gospels was predictably good for a storm of controversy. In its field, it was a thoroughly skilled and entertaining night out and one could easily see why it was a hit. But the biggest all-media parlay in showbiz history? Even allowing for the hyperbole, that was a dream coat of quite another colour.

Larry Marshall as Saint Simon the Zealot, a marvellous skin-and-bone streak of a New York speedoo, alone among the apostles had failed to weep. He explained the bonanza in terms of the perfect compromise. 'All the trappings of rock, none of the reality,' he said. 'Colour, noise, brashness, a little outrageousness – people feel groovy and adventurous because they go to see it and yet, at the same time, it keeps them safe as milk.'

It was true that *Superstar*'s public was essentially half-way house – middle-aged, middle-class, middle-brow, demihep – and that, even when it reached the young, it missed the hardcore rock fan. What it marked, in fact, was the final integration of Pop into the mainstream of Western culture. Here at last was a kids' show for all the family. Electric guitars no longer meant orgy, anarchy, imminent holocaust – in *Superstar*, din was mere high spirits, anger only a gesture. 'Sit back and enjoy it,' Saint Simon said, 'and remember it's only a story.'

As such, it became, a rallying point. There were millions, after all, who had grown weary of Herb Alpert but couldn't yet stretch to Frank Zappa: who liked to smoke three joints a month, taken after dinner, but went cold at the very thought of needles; who deplored the Vietnam war and were civil to all ethnics on principle without remotely wishing for revolution. A massed liberal bourgeoisie, oozing with cash and changed aspirations.

Somehow, before *Superstar*, they had been overlooked. No one had quite perceived their growing friskiness, their enormous willingness to flirt. Even *Superstar* had originally been aimed at the kids – Jesus freaks, lapsed hippies, just plain fans. Thus, the initial combustion, as with all the greatest successes, was largely unexpected.

As soon as it had happened, however, and the smoke had cleared, it was obvious that the pickings, both short- and long-term, were stupendous. A whole new market, almost a whole new class, turned *Superstar* into a celebration.

The same valley, a different sunset: 'We could have been vulgar,' said Jewison. 'We could have played this for cheap. Nothing simpler. Guaranteed socko at the box office. We could have been really filthy. But we weren't.'

Right on cue, the chorus took up the refrain.

'We could have been,' said the assistant director.

'But we weren't,' said the unit publicist.

'For instance,' Jewison continued, 'we could have had Mary going down on Jesus, right there on the cross. Can you imagine that? And half the apostles are gay, right, and what about Jesus and Judas? I mean, would you just look at those guys? A big wet smackeroo, right on the lips? How about that? Oh, yeah,' and here he went hushed, 'we could have been vulgar, all right. We could have milked it for every grab in the book.'

'Sensationalism,' said the unit publicist.

'Cheap thrills,' said the production supervisor.

'But we didn't,' said Jewison firmly. 'Instead, we decided to make it beautiful. We came here to the Holy Land and we played it straight, we gave it faith. We made it into a spiritual experience and it's beautiful, and Jesus is beautiful, the kids are beautiful, it's going to be a beautiful film. People are going to see it in drive-ins and neighbourhood nowhere theatres and they're going to be moved by it. People who were never moved by this story before. People who always thought that Jesus Christ was some kind of schmuck. They're going to see something beautiful and they're going to cry. They won't be able to help themselves.'

There was an awe-struck silence. The last of the sunlight disappeared behind the mountaintops. Everyone gazed into the darkening valley. 'When you really come to think of it,' said Jewison, in a sudden flash of self-mockery, 'we're doing Him a favour.'

Possibly He did not fully understand this. At any rate, half-way through the filming of the Crucifixion, quite without warning, there came an apocalyptic thunderstorm. Jesus bled and twisted in his agony, lightning flashed, the rain beat down torrentially, the music swelled, the very heavens trembled. And then, inevitably, everyone began to cry. Jewison and the apostles, of course; then the secretaries, the stand-ins, the caterers, the latrine attendants, the money men and the Arab peasants watching from afar. Only Jesus himself was stoic and serene, as the elements smashed and exploded about his head. Afterwards, some of the spectators said they had felt his soul ascending.

When the shooting was over, as soon as Jesus was brought down from the cross and had gone home to tea, the storm suddenly died down and everything was calm again. The unit hairdresser called it a miracle.

That was the climax. The anticlimax came one hot morning, while they were setting up the Last Supper. Growing bored, I began to climb up a goat track, rocky and precipitous, and headed for a tiny Arab village on a mountaintop.

My hands were scraped and torn. I sweated like a hog and once I was almost swept away by a minor avalanche. Still I persevered and, at the end of an hour, I stood at the summit.

In the village street, there were perhaps a dozen bronze tables, set in open doorways, and around them sat the elders, complete with robes and headdresses, puffing peaceably on their hash pipes. They didn't look at me and they did not speak. Every now and then, one of them would slowly keel over and topple into the dust. After a pause he would be picked up and dusted off.

I got a contact high from the fumes alone and sat down in the shade to steady myself. Forty or fifty children clustered around me, laughing and pointing, and fat ripe figs hung thickly above my head. So I ate myself sick and played with the kids and soon I grew sentimental.

Gazing out across the valley, in great stoned solemnity, I thought about timelessness and balance. Then I turned my head and was confronted by a face in a doorway, surmounted by a baseball cap. 'I'm from Orlando, Florida,' said the face. 'How about you?'

I was taken indoors. A young girl brought me olives and iced Coca-Cola. There was a TV in the corner and the man from Orlando couldn't stop laughing. Ten years before, he said, he'd won a trip to Florida in a competition. Once there, he got a job in plastics, bought a home, started a family, changed his name. Now he was home on a three-week vacation.

He was very inquisitive. He asked me if I were married, and did I like the Miami Dolphins, and who was the greatest man in the world? Where had I bought my shirt? What did I think of Raquel Welch's thighs? What, above all, were all those people doing down below, milling about in the valley and shouting?

I answered as best I could, curled up with my Coke, and the young girl took out her dentures, to show me how they worked. The man from Orlando, for the most part, seemed satisfied by my responses and we got along just fine. But in the last analysis, one point still troubled him: What, who and why was a superstar?

Not easy to convey. A superstar, I attempted to explain, was a star who transcended performance. When you felt his full impact, he took you over, possessed you absolutely; became, for the moment, godlike. 'Hence,' I said, 'Jesus Christ, Superstar.'

For a moment he still looked uncertain. Then his face cleared, light flooded his soul. Jubilant, he jumped to his feet and, handing me a second Coke, he gave me the sweetest, most radiant smile.

'Like Perry Como,' he said.

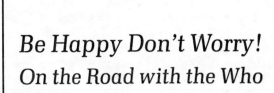

Be Happy Don't Worry!
On the Road with the Who

T he first thing is the unreality. On the road you live in a capsule, a time machine, completely insulated against all normality or balance. You exist entirely in interiors – hotels and airports, limousines, dressing rooms – and everything that you see has been filtered through glass. Night and day become meaningless, and cities are interchangeable. There are no restrictions or rules, and so you pass directly into fiction.

Each day presents a different gig, therefore a different landscape, therefore a different movie. There is no continuity, which means that you can do precisely as you choose, you can sink yourself and wallow in every possible and impossible outrage, excess, invention, since tomorrow you will be in a different script and everything will start afresh. You can't be reached and you can't be tied. Locked up safely inside your capsule, you skim above all retributions; can pretend to be infinite.

At first this feels quite marvellous – total release, speed, abandon. In the first week alone, I was P. J. Proby, Proust and Randolph Hearst in turn, before settling for Akim Tamiroff.

Why stop there? In New Orleans, I looked into the dressing room and glimpsed the most beautiful girl, absolutely, that I had ever seen in my life. Ultimate teen angel – golden flesh, long blonde hair, big blue eyes and kisses, no doubt, much sweeter than wine.

At any other time, in real life, I would have dithered, fainted, let her slip away. But here, from within the capsule, it was the simplest thing in the world. Just walk up to her directly, look deep into her eyes and unleash the line of lines 'Young lady,' I said, 'I believe I could make you a star.'

She did not scream, she did not strike me. On the road she merely flapped her eyelashes and, the very next morning, flew with me to Hollywood, where I did not make her a star and she ripped me off in handfuls.

Or again. In Tuscaloosa, Keith Moon drank a bottle of brandy and began to feel quite frisky. So he destroyed his hotel bedroom. First he ripped down the curtains, smashed the mirrors, overturned the bed, slashed the mattress, fouled the sheets, put his fist through the bathroom wall. Then he kicked the TV until it expired, wrestled it through the door, heaved it over the balcony and watched it drop into the swimming pool below. The splash was spiffing – groupies of every sex stood by the water and applauded. With the utmost dignity, Keith took a bow and went back into his room, where he lay down in the debris and straightaway passed into deep and righteous slumber.

Next morning, when the management presented him with their bill for fifteen hundred dollars, he remembered nothing and felt no pain. No remorse, no trace of embarrassment, not even a hangover. And why should he? The limousines were waiting at the door, after all, and he was already in the next reel.

That's the benefit; the major drawback is psychosis. In a world without restrictions, there are also no guidelines, nothing left to cling to. You drift in weightlessness and, unless you have real resources of strength and imagination, this drives you into delirium.

No patterns are definite. Time and place evaporate, all norms are obsolete. You sleep in sunlight and soak in brandy for breakfast, Bloody Marys for elevenses, tequila for lunch; swallow uppers by the handful, downers by the tub, smoke and suck and sniff on whatever comes to hand, until you spin too fast to hold and fall down in a heap.

Minutes or hours or several days later, you come round and sit up. Immediately you start to whirl again, shuttling back and forth in time and space. You pass out in Dallas, which is 1964, and wake up in Los Angeles, 1980; expire in Phoenix, 1953, and are reincarnated in San Francisco, 1966. You go to bed with Lolita in Miami Beach and wake up next to her mother in Newark, New Jersey. Or you lay back on velvet cushions, you float in indoor swimming pools, sleek and serene in Malibu, and the next thing you know you're destitute, besmirched and in jail, forty miles from Poplar Bluff.

If you can ride such games, you may fly faster, float freer than ever before; if you can't, you perish most horribly. Thus the tour is littered with numberless corpses. Roadies fall down elevator shafts, groupies suffocate in the shower. Promoters go bankrupt, security guards run amok with their nightsticks, the warm-up group blow themselves up. Journalists, almost always, are shipped home under sedation.

As for the Who themselves, their crises are now quite traditional, an integral part of the package. They have toured America fourteen or fifteen times and never once escaped without a major holocaust, so that they've learned to traipse through their traumas almost automatically, in a kind of formalized gavotte. So they break up, reform and break up again; threaten suicide, speak of murder; suffer, bleed, disintegrate and, in the epilogue, come home with a million dollars, more or less, for five weeks' work.

Even for such veterans, however, the tortures can sometimes be extreme. Early in the tour, Pete Townsend spent a couple of days at the ex-headquarters of Meher Baba, his avatar. The residents showed him the house where Baba had slept and left him alone in the avatar's bedroom. It was a stark little cell, like a third-rate hotel room, with only a bed and chair in it, and Pete could think of nothing to do but go on his knees, try to pray, meditate, whatever he could manage.

Straightaway he could sense that Baba was present and waited to be blessed. But the avatar was not so benevolent – instead he took his disciple to pieces; poured, in Pete's own phrase, all the shit of the world on him; ravaged him, obliterated him, left him so smashed that, when the other followers opened the door again, they found him prostrate, unable to speak or move, scarcely able to breathe.

For the next few days, back on tour, he locked himself in his hotel rooms and talked to no one. On stage he moved and played like a zombie; in dressing rooms he crouched in corners, dead-eyed, drained, and twitched whenever anybody came close or touched him.

The rest of the group enjoyed this immensely. Baba has always made them sick and now was their chance of sweet revenge. So they took up the avatar's basic slogan – 'Be Happy, Don't Worry' – and rubbed Pete's nose in it. A shattered shambling wreckage, he tried to back off but they pursued him, harried him relentlessly: 'Be happy', Keith kept chanting, exultant, flinging it out like a scarlet rag. 'Don't worry, be happy, don't worry, be happy.' Pete made no response. Just sat there and continued to suffer.

One of the basic Who patterns is that their (very real) love for each other can only be released by extreme cruelty. They goad and downgrade each other continually, taking it in turns to play victim, until they reach breaking point and almost pass it. Half-way over the brink of total destruction, they suddenly relent and fall into each other's arms. For a moment they are satiated, and everyone embraces everyone. Soon enough, however, serenity begins to pall. Constant sweetness and light grow tiresome. Tempers fray, bickering begins again. A new victim presents himself and the cycle is launched once more.

At last, in Miami Beach, Pete broke surface. Somewhere out among the swamps, a fat rich freak had layed on a house for us, complete with saunas and swimming pools, unlimited alcohol and chemicals, and possibly thirty young ladies, of every colour, size and proclivity. Bad music played very loud and I lay down in a sandpit, where I soon passed into a stupor. Minutes or days elapsed: 'You are floating on the astral plane', someone kept telling me, not unkindly, and perhaps I was. But then I opened my eyes and there was Pete, half-naked, extremely drunken, forcing his face into mine and demanding that I go swimming with him – skinny-dipping, he called it.

I refused but he insisted; I refused again, and he grew abusive. 'Chicken', he screeched. 'You're ashamed to show me your dick. All Jews are ashamed to show their dicks. You probably haven't even got one.'

When I still refused, he changed tacks and grew maudlin. 'Aren't you human at all?' he said, softly pleading (but of course I wasn't). 'When I wrote "Pin-ball Wizard" for you specially. My best song and I wrote it for you and now you won't even skinny dip with me. One small favour and you turn me down.'

For a few moments he thought about weeping but decided not to and trailed off down the stairs instead, to frolic with large blonde nymphs beneath. Salvation through degradation, I suppose, and it must have worked, because next morning he fairly bounced, chipper as a chipmunk. From then on, right through the tour, he went from strength to strength – a still centre at the heart of chaos, while all around him capsized.

The next to crumble was me. On the seventeenth floor of the Playboy Plaza, looking out across the lake and its lurid technorama sunset, I was having my shoulders rubbed by a half-Mexican, half-Cherokee stripper named Shanda Lear, when there was a sudden flash of light and both of us felt an angel fly over our heads. Shanda Lear fell backwards on the bed, screaming and clutching her hands to her belly. Next morning her fingers, where they had been touching my flesh, were covered in festering blisters.

As for myself, I felt stunned but ecstatic. Since I had never had any mystic tremors before, and did not believe in such stuff anyhow, I made the very most of this and drifted through Memphis in a trance, borne up on waves of bliss. I was sanctified, my spirit had been saved. Then came the kickback. In New Orleans, I got staggering drunk and, hot to transmit my new condition, I jumped up in a nightclub, grabbed the microphone and broke into an impassioned, strangulated version of 'My Prayer'.

I must have made a truly horrendous figure: my voice was a croak, I couldn't stand straight and tears coursed down my cheeks in rivulets, plopping one by one on my shirtfront. I rambled and gurgled, dropped the mike and nobody reacted, nobody made a sound. All I could see were beady eyes in the dark, watching me without expression. I tried to run away but couldn't. My hands were shaking uncontrollably. Angels laughed in my face and I sank to my knees.

It was then that Keith rescued me from total and final decimation, jumping up on stage, commandeering the drums and playing along behind me, projecting such zest and conviction as he did so that fiasco was turned into high-camp vaudeville. People began to laugh and jeer, and I was released. Stumbling off into the night,

I fell fast alseep and woke up next morning, purged and clean, ripe for a new beginning.

By nightfall I was already superseded. In my place one of the roadies, lost in acid, attempted self-crucifixion on a surfboard and all but succeded. This game try made him the undisputed lion of the moment and, when he appeared backstage before the show, blushing but unbandaged, shyly triumphant, he received a massed ovation.

Glasses and silver spoons were hoisted in salute, the stigmata inspected with awe: 'Is this a Who tour?' cried Keith Moon, exulting, 'or is this a fuckin' tour?'

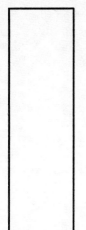

Pop Goes Othello

In a Manchester Methodist mission called the Albert Hall, P. J. Proby is rehearsing.

Outside, it is raining steadily and there are placards saying DISCOVER GOD'S LOVE AND GOD'S PURPOSE; inside, there is Proby, lying full-length on top of a sideboard in the basement, drinking tea out of a cracked mission mug, while a man in a khaki coat sweeps the floor around his feet.

Proby is thirty-one now and looks like a heavy in a low-budget Western, a bandido, marauder and layer-waste of homesteads. He has lost weight and his hands don't shake. His hair is kempt and falls sleekly about his shoulders, and he is wearing high-heeled boots, white denims, a cowboy hat and a crocodile coat.

This basement is desolate. Altogether, the mission is an outsize nineteenth-century public lavatory, full of green and white and orange tiles, and it smells of damp and desertion.

In another room, there are sounds of rehearsal – muffled shouts, a few random thumps on a piano – and it is freezing cold in here. But Proby seems content. He stretches, props himself up on his elbow and begins to drink from a bottle of Merrydown wine.

In *Catch My Soul*, he plays Cassio and means to become a second Edmund Kean, with whom he sees close parallels: 'When Kean first came to Drury Lane, it was just like when I first came to England. The scene was dead. It needed a boost, an inspiration.

237

Then Kean arrived and, the very first night he walked on stage, he tore the place apart. He was a madman. He broke all the rules, turned everything on its head. Nobody could believe him. All the chicks went wild. As for the critics they went away and wrote "We can't describe him, we don't know what happened, we can't say a word, except it was FANTASTIC".

'He was a very great man,' says Proby, drinking deeply. 'He was an actor at five, a drunkard at eighteen, and he was dead at forty-five, from a mixture of alcohol and genius, which go hand in hand.'

Catch My Soul was thought up by Jack Good. He, too, is a very great man. He began in the mid-fifties, when he came down from Oxford, where he had read philology and been president of OUDS, and first he became an actor and then, almost by accident, he became director of 'Six-Five Special', the first rock 'n' roll TV show.

After that, he did 'Oh Boy!', which was better still, and then he moved to America, where he directed *Shindig*. In 1964, he came across Proby, who was a moderately successful songwriter in Hollywood, and brought him to England and produced his first hit record, 'Hold Me'.

Since then, Good had spent his time mostly in America, making occasional TV specials and acting in a sequence of impressively obscure B-films and, through all this time, he has remained by far the best of all Pop directors, the fastest and tightest and most raunchy, the most impervious to bullshit.

He is a round man with a round face and round glasses, very short hair and pink cheeks like a doll. In fact, he looks like an undergraduate, rehearsing a rag-week review, but his energy and involvement are limitless, and he is also tough. With Proby in his cast, he should be.

Catch My Soul goes back ten years. Since Good was a Shakespearean actor by training, a Rocker by profession, and equally obsessed by both, it was inevitable that he should combine them, and his original conception was of Little Richard as Othello, Elvis Presley as Iago. Not amazingly, this proved impracticable.

Now he's in Manchester, with Proby as Cassio, a Louisiana rocker called Lance LeGault as Iago and Good himself as Othello, and they are coming to London early in November.

*

'It seems I cannot win,' says Proby, fondling a different bottle and resettling himself on his sideboard. 'I have tried being a nice guy but it does no good, they will never let me return.'

It is now five years since Proby split his pants on stage and was banned from TV and the cinema circuit. For a time, he went on touring and having hits but his spending was phenomenal and he ran out of money. He went back to America but that didn't work either. He got married and it lasted just one week. He managed one American hit, 'Niki Hoeky', but couldn't find a follow-up.

By 1968, his debts had caught up with him and he went bankrupt for £185,000. Then, back over here, he began to work the northern clubs, six days a week and fifty-two weeks a year, and pay his earnings direct to the taxman. He has kept this up non-stop for two years, until he says that he owes only £44,000 and has had enough: 'I have issued an ultimatum. I will pay them £10,000 and not a dime more. Either they can take it or they can go frig themselves – I will be crucified no further.'

Down in the mission basement, slouched on the sideboard, he still smells of Bel Air, of circular beds and tiger-skin rugs and plum-coloured velours slippers with P.J.P. monogrammed in gold.

For the moment, however, he drinks and belches. 'The Grades are conducting a vendetta against me, they just won't quit,' he says. 'They can't afford to. The moment they let me back, all their biggest stars would be stone cold dead – Tom Jones, Engelbert Humperdinck, all of those bums. Because I started it. Before me, none of them were anything and now they're getting all this publicity and making it big but it makes no difference, not a bit: there is still only one, and that one is . . .' he covers his heart with his hand '. . . Proby.

'But I will fight them. Oh yes, I will smash the Grades and I won't let up until I am chairman of their board and they are in the gutter, or otherwise I will not rest until my ass is six feet underground. I will restore non-monopolism to England. I will commence total revolution.'

Sometimes he is shouting but he also laughs a lot, piratical, and he does not seem discouraged. Simultaneously, he is quite serious and quite camp: 'Some of the things I say, you understand, I mean them but my tongue is in my cheek.

'Everyone says I'm making a comeback but I haven't ever been gone, I have always been number one. I made two million pounds in a year. I had ships, yachts and eight Rolls-Royces at once and houses all over the world. Now I'm almost out of debt and this time I won't blow it, I will put all my money in my father's hands – he is president of the Angelo Crocker Citizens' Bank.'

This is a surprise. In the past, Proby's father has been a subject to avoid – Proby was wont to break out in bloodcurdling obscenity at the very mention of him, or else extravagant maudlinity, and one suspected that his father's lifelong disapproval and neglect of him was a major source of Proby's problems. But now, apparently, all that is past. 'I never got together with him until I was twenty-nine,' Proby says. 'Then I went to his house one day, while he was out at the bank, and I started looking through my yearbooks, all through my childhood and my days at military school.

'Suddenly, I realized that they went on past my childhood, all through my career, with every cutting and review and interview I'd ever had, all stuck there by my father. So then I knew. Then I understood at last and I went downstairs, I sat and I waited for him to come home.

'When he came through the door, I did nothing, I just looked at him. Then I said: "You big bag of bullshit". Just like that, with no warning, and he stared at me, I believe that he was frightened. "Oh, you big bunch of bullshit," I said, "all these years you let me believe that you didn't dig me, you were ashamed of me and now I find that you loved me, yes you did, you were a proud daddy to me all along."

'He didn't move. He just stared at me and then he laughed, and I went across the room to him. Maybe he thought I would hit him. But instead I reached out and shook his hand. "Thanks, buddy," I said, and my daddy cried.'

Now Proby intends a fresh beginning. He says that he has finished with nightclubs, possibly even with making records, and his future lies in acting. He wishes to be calm. He has acquired a daughter, aged ten, and he wants to buy a farmhouse. 'As the public sees him, Proby needs just one thing – the big M, Maturity – and the only way I can find that is to have an anchor, someone to love, and all that I love is my daughter,' he says. 'Without her, I am wild; with her, I rest in peace.'

In his plans, *Catch My Soul* is crucial and he's determined to make it work: 'Cassio has never been played right. He has always been underrated, because he is a lieutenant, and lieutenants are boring assholes. Now I'm going to revolutionize him.

'I'm going to play him with a mixture of Leslie Howard and Trevor Howard. When he is sober, Cassio is upstanding and dashing, beloved by everyone, and he has good looks, charm and he's dynamite with women, and I will play him with all the grace of Leslie Howard in *Gone With The Wind*. But when he gets drunk, he is a pig and I will inject Trevor instead.

'People may be offended because I bastardize the classics but the world is full of revolution now and it can't be stopped. Anyhow, I won't be disrespectful – I will ad lib and be sensational but I won't detract from William's words.

'The critics will not affect me. The only critic I will recognize is Sir Laurence Olivier. If he digs me, I will be enthralled; if he doesn't, I will ask him why; and if he lies to me, I will walk right out on him. Any time that he speaks to me, he'd better choose his words real careful.'

Another bottle is empty. Proby is due back in rehearsal. Concentrating, he wipes his mouth on the back of his hand. 'This is the truth,' he says. 'I am schizoid. I am a Jekyll and Hyde, different all the time. One day I will do the world for you; the next I will break your jaw. But nobody understands – because I hit you, it doesn't mean I don't love you.'

'This guy is a nut,' says Lance LeGault, speaking of Iago. 'Still, I have a lot of respect for him. He's sick but he is clever. One by one, he eliminates them all because he is an animal. He is wild. Oh yes, he is a rock 'n' roller all right but he never loses control. He will take on two women, three women at a time and orgy all night long but he never stops thinking, scheming.' LeGault chews at his lips, tugs at his beard. 'Oh, yes,' he says. 'I'm only the sergeant-major but I will take them all apart.'

LeGault is thirty years old, a tight-knit man with buckskin boots and a big blond beard, and he talks in a bearlike rumble, very stagey. He comes from New Orleans and has been on the road since he was thirteen, without having hits or ever making it big. Still, he has worked consistently, year after year, and now he is not unwealthy. Apart from his singing, he is a stuntman and choreographer in films, and that's how he first met Jack Good, when they were both working on *Clambake*, an Elvis Presley film.

Good liked him and brought him to England to star in a TV special 'The Three Ages Of Rock'. But *Catch My Soul* is his best chance yet: 'Seventeen years of paying my dues – now I can get up at last and go like hell.'

His father was a Cajun and, as Cajuns often are, LeGault is both extrovert and extremely watchful. Down in the mission hall, he struts and swaggers, out-talks everyone but his eyes are careful all the time. He has been touring a long time, he knows showmanship backwards but he doesn't lose himself. In fact, he's very much like his own image of Iago: a trouper, wild but canny, always controlled.

For the moment, he wishes very much to be a Thespian, a full-blown Shakespearean actor, and he comes on like a nineteenth-century Shylock, all winks and nods and flourishes, sly fingerings of his beard and rollings of his eyes, stabbings and waggings of his forefinger. Even his small talk has a double ring – he cannot pour a cup of tea now or scratch himself, not without some apposite quote from the Bard, a little gem. He no longer speaks but quoths, hollas or whispers, aside: I have been a tradesman. Now I may be an artist.'

As for *Catch My Soul*, he sees it essentially as the Lance Le-Gault Show, plus full supporting cast. 'In this production, Iago is everything,' he says. 'Not that he can carry the show alone, not by any means. He needs great help and understanding, or else the play will crumble around him.'

He muses. Reflective, he waggles his eyebrows, scratches his ear, raises one finger in admonishment. 'It is a challenge, yes, and a very great responsibility,' he says. 'I am humble. Yet I am also confident.'

In the evening, there is a lecture at the mission and the basement is filled with Ena Sharples and Minnie Caldwell, listening to an account of missionary work in Bechuanaland.

Catch My Soul, meanwhile, goes on in a small side room, obviously used for Sunday school, because there are children's drawings all around the walls, with mottoes saying *God knows* and *God needs us* and *God is clever*.

Proby is not sober. He sits slumped in a chair, strumming idly at a guitar, and his face is white and clammy, and his eyes are gone. 'I was given a year to live,' he confides. 'I was drinking brandy, six bottles a day. I had so much sadness, the troubles of my life, I'm sure you understand . . .' He shakes his head, smiling wistfully, and his hair is stuck with sweat to his temples and cheeks. 'Then the doctors told me to quit and I did. Now I drink only wine and I feel so good. Oh, I feel terrific.'

There is a stand-up piano against one wall, a true school rattler, with a tone like falling slates, and LeGault bombasts all up and down the floor, alaruming. Obviously, he's going to be splendid but, even so, Good is looking harassed and Proby sits with his head down, strumming and sipping, and seems quite oblivious of everything that surrounds him.

When his own turn comes, he does a song called 'Drunk'. He stands close to the piano, peering over the pianist's shoulder at the score and, at first, he gets nowhere. He cannot read the lyrics, he has trouble with the key changes. Then he has drunk too much, his voice is shot and, every time he goes up high, he rasps and cracks and collapses, has to start all over.

But then, without warning, he suddenly comes good. He turns half aside and his mouth flags wide open, his jaws begin to quiver and, when he comes to the high bit, he flies.

He looks as though he may pass out. His face is drained, his eyes blanked out, his hair all straggled and raddled with sweat. His voice keeps trying to fail, give way beneath him but he clenches his fist, he throws his head far back and, way up high and over, he soars:

> Save me,
> Oh God, save me
> From the devil in the wine.

He does it once more. Again, he stumbles and stops; again, he restarts; again, he comes to the high bit and gathers together and launches himself. And he reaches it, he meets it perfectly. He holds it a long time. He does not move. Then he ducks his head, hides his face and he sings, quite softly:

> Save me,
> God save me,
> Oh save me from the wine.

The Return of the Gentleman?

I first heard of the Baron Lambert shortly after Christmas, in the course of a country-house weekend. At the time I was feeling stranded: I had been away from England for the best part of two years, off and on, and had drifted out of touch, especially when it came to modishness. The last sensations I could remember were Mr Freedom and the Great American Disaster. What, I asked, had happened since? Who was new, and where, and why?

Simple answer: Gentleman were new.

Gentlemen?

Taste and manners, style, decorum, grandeur.

Decorum? Grandeur?

The Baron Lambert.

Apparently the movement was back towards formality. True, the Fulham Road was still a nightly orgy of Mickey Mouse T-shirts, tap dancing and transport-caff camperies; true, the smart Sundays still drooled over hot-dog sofas and gold lamé underwear. But that was strictly for the stragglers – the insiders had long since departed. Among the avant-garde, Pop was a back-number now, and so were its attendants: kitsch, outrage, calculated excess. In their place was a resurrection of correctness.

Correctness like what? Well, like the opposite of incorrectness.

It was, for instance, incorrect to be seen in boutiques or trattorias, to drop the names of Rock stars, to own a motorbike, to speak of dope or astrology or alternative societies. It was also incorrect to be very young or beautiful. It was unforgivable to be classless.

On the other hand, it was not incorrect to be élitist; quite the opposite. Marks were to be gained by joining clubs, by wearing a bowler hat, by employing a valet, by holding up one's socks with suspenders. Once again it was permissible to hold oneself aloof from the mass, even to be disdainful, and it was daring but dazzling to speak of discipline.

As yet, of course, all this was restricted to a cabal – freedom fighters of the underground. But the counter-revolution was on its way, make no mistake, and the Baron Lambert was to be its rallying point. Pop would be destroyed, its crassnesses and follies put to flight and, on that day, the Baron would emerge as the arbiter, the absolute of new rectitude. 'Terrifying,' I was told. 'This man is a fanatic.'

Yes, but who exactly was he, and where had he come from? Everyone I talked to had a different story.

What was certain? He was a gentleman, was a gentleman, was a gentleman. This much was agreed.

But that, for the moment, was all. A few nights later, however, over dinner, the name cropped up again; and then a week after that, over lunch at the Grand Véfour; and then in a sudden flood, at bars, on balconies, in the back of taxis. By the end of a month, the Baron had grown to mythic proportion.

Briefly, the saga was as follows: he was an Englishman, of Russian descent, of a line of Prussian military, of a clutch of French surrealists. He was a real baron, that much was certain, and a fake, that much was also certain, and he was connected to a merchant bank, or he had production money in movies, or he was something to do with uranium (or was it cobalt?). He was in his late twenties, mid-thirties and early forties, an enigmatic presence in white silk suits, or frock-coats and ascots, or antique Turkish dressing-gowns. He was a Jew and a Jesuit. He had been a gun-runner in the Persian Gulf, and a mercenary in the Congo, and a chess Grand Master, and a lost explorer. He had never done anything.

Facts! He owned a town house in Campden Hill (or was it

Regents Park?), and an estate somewhere in Suffolk, but he lived alone. He had menials, acquaintances and almost-friends but no true intimates and he dined by himself, at one end of a long table, in full evening dress, beneath a candelabra. He collected butterflies. He wrote *pensées*. He played the bassoon. More than anything, he sounded like a reincarnated William Beckford.

The bizarre thing was, few of these reports were presented as hearsay. Almost all of my informants claimed to have met the Baron in person; some to know him quite well; and yet each of them had come away with directly conflicting impressions.

For a time I thought I was being hoaxed, victim of a mammoth exercise in myth-making. But hardly. My material had come from too diffuse and too strait-laced sources, and besides, Patrick Procktor had shown me a sketch, doodled on the back of a menu: the Baron caught for posterity.

He looked just as ambiguous as his publicity – manic and melancholic at once, with messianic eyes and despairing, twisted mouth. Spiritual, satanic. 'I found him most odd,' said Patrick.

By now I was absolutely hooked; I also had a theory. Given two basic premises, that the Baron was a gentleman and that he appeared in different form to everyone who met him, it seemed that he might be something most powerful: a human blackboard (*tabula rasa*, as they say in *Pseuds' Corner*), on which each individual might scrawl their personal fantasy. Whatever their vision of the gentleman, he became it on the instant.

True chameleons are very great rarities. Each phase produces one prime example. Mick Jagger had been the last – was the Baron Lambert the next? I sent him urgent messages, requesting a meeting.

For two weeks I had no response whatever. Then my telephone rang and it was the Baron's social secretary, a Mr Crimp, to inform me that my application had been duly noted. As yet no date could be fixed for a confrontation, nor any promises made, but at least I was on some list. Meanwhile, wait until contacted.

So I waited. And I waited. A month passed, and in the interim I did some considering, both about the Baron Lambert and about the concept of gentlemen in general. All this talk of a revival, what exactly did it entail? In 1972, what *was* a gentleman, and what was his function?

For myself, I had no ideas, so I went and talked to a cross-section of gents and bounders, and a few unbiased onlookers, to see what the consensus was.

Not simple. The gentleman has always been a complex and slippery ideal, of different connotation to each generation and class, and long decline had left it more elusive than ever. A dozen conversations produced at least a dozen different visions: clearly, the gentleman had no single meaning, could be judged by no single standard. In fact, it was easier to say what he wasn't, or what he had ceased to be.

What he wasn't, principally, was anything to do with his dictionary definition: a man entitled to bear arms but not of the nobility. In all my conversations, only Lord Sudeley mentioned heredity at all.

Lord Sudeley is a young man of exquisite bone-structure, with a baggy tweed suit and silver watch chain. His Christian name is Merlin, his recreations are ancestor worship and cultivating his sensibility. The English gentleman is his special study, and his erudition is dazzling, his own lineage quite impeccable.

Sipping Madeira, he said he thought that gentlemanly behaviour was probably gone for good, but that in three or four generations, as national chaos grew worse and worse confounded, sanity might prevail at last and breeding would again become a right to leadership: 'The point is, it works.' For the moment, however, it was hardly possible even to speak of gentlemen. Beneath a certain age, they simply didn't exist.

'Perhaps an exaggeration,' James Laver thought. 'Ladies are extinct, yes, but the gentleman hangs on precariously.' Not for long, though – he had belonged to a patriarchy, in which young women had searched for men from the same mould as their fathers, to be protectors. Now women didn't care about reliability; they wanted fun in bed. Birth and code meant nothing, and gallantry less than nothing.

'I'm afraid that Laver is right,' said Hugh Fraser. 'It isn't a word I use much any more, gentleman, or even think of. I suppose it's rather wrong of me.' What did it denote? Courtesy, integrity and thinking of others. Breeding and background were not important, not any more – some of the greatest gentlemen in the House of Commons had been dockers or miners.

Cecil Beaton took the same line. 'A good family helps, perhaps, and a certain amount of education but I don't think there are any hard-and-fast rules. A gentleman is simply someone who behaves himself. Tact is very important, and so is consideration. I mean, I don't want to be stuffy but I do find it most offensive when somebody shakes hands with his other hand still stuck in his pocket. How rude! A gentleman has style and intuition, and just a hint of witty insolence. He is the opposite of a shit.'

'Quite right,' said Simon Raven. 'The trouble is, it pays better to be a shit these days. If you behave like a gentleman, you either make yourself a laughing-stock or you find yourself stabbed in the back. Usually both.' Was there any solution? 'Well, if the gentleman is to have a future of any sort, he must first recover a position of power. Not via money, I think, but through influence – politics or the Civil Service, as a man of good will, a sort of do-gooding, administrator. Perhaps, if he managed that, people might respect him again. I must say, though, it seems a slim chance. Deference is dead.'

'And just as well,' Cyril Ray said. 'It's all very well being sentimental about lost graciousness, I sometimes am myself, but most of it was guff. *Noblesse oblige*, my foot – when I think of the times that I've been really badly let down in life, I've usually had a gentleman to thank for it.

'The point about gentlemen at their best,' Kenneth Rose thought, 'is that they did give existence a certain stature. Lord Salisbury was the most perfect gentleman and enhanced everything that he came in contact with. Even when he was crippled with arthritis, he never failed to rise when someone entered the room, even a twelve-year-old boy or inferior. He was incapable of discourtesy or casualness, unless he felt it was merited.'

'Lord Salisbury, of course, epitomized the ideal,' said Cecil Beaton. ' "A gentleman is never unintentionally rude," he said – I think that's probably the best definition I can think of.'

'Lord Salisbury?' said Cyril Ray. 'He could have shat for Britain in the Olympic Games.'

'Actually,' said Anthony Powell, 'I don't think that they mean anything specific any more; they're a state of mind. I mean to say, if one feels that one is a gentleman, then I suppose one is.'

'A gentleman is simply a gentleman,' said Lindy Guinness. 'Either you are or you aren't, and that's all there is to it. These definitions and sub-divisions get you nowhere. A gentleman is someone you meet and you know at once that he's a gentleman and nothing he can do will make him anything else. Poor thing, he's stuck with it.'

That seemed as close as anyone was likely to get. 'Gentlemen? Of course, you can never tell for sure,' said Patrick Procktor, musingly. 'They can be very funny things at times.'

A few notes. Gentlemen are almost impossible to pin down. Like anything else that belongs to the English class system, there are so many ramifications and sub-clauses that definitive statements never work. The gentleman changes with time and milieu, and elusiveness is part of the mystique. Whatever rules one makes for them, the opposite tends to be true as well.

Still, some generalizations: historically, gentlemen have been judged by two main criteria – heredity and behaviour.

Originally they were country squires, lowest rank among armigers, but privileged, and they lived by a code of obligation. Obligation towards their feudal lords, as providers of horse and arms, and obligation towards their peasants, as protectors. They *served*.

In this role, the ideal was straightforwardness. To be trustworthy, considerate, fair-minded – a man of honour. High intelligence or wit, over-sophistication or creativity were superfluous; probably rather suspect.

Over the centuries the squirearchy lost most of their money. Gentlemen tended to leave the countryside and come to London, to enter the city or the Civil Service, or to go into politics. Inevitably, their standards declined but the ideal survived: to do one's duty, fulfil one's public obligations. Guy Crouchback in Waugh's *Men at Arms* trilogy is a perfect example.

Inevitably, a certain ambiguity was involved. Gentlemen of this type were conscientious but not without arrogance. They toiled for the public good and, in return, they expected deference. The benificiaries must toe the line and not ask questions, create no awkwardness. Gents were not to be argued with.

Then there was the second concept of the gentleman, based on manners. This derived from the medieval ideal of courtliness. Gallantry and selflessness: the perfect gentle knight. In this context, gentlemanly behaviour applied not only to squires but upwards, throughout the aristocracy. Sir Philip Sidney giving his dying drink of water to a fellow-sufferer, Raleigh and his cloak, even Charles I.

With time the aim became less romantic, more rule-bound. A gentleman was meant to set an example, and there was a passion for pedantry. This is where gentlemen became a list of observances – Lord Chesterfield's letters or Lord Curzon's dictums. 'A gentleman does not wear brown suits', 'a gentleman does not take soup at luncheon' and so on. Even 'a gentleman does not look out of windows' – Evelyn Waugh, according to Cecil Beaton.

The crucial word was *tone*, I suppose, and tone is ephemeral. Moralities change quite slowly but manners evolve continually. What is perfect etiquette in one generation is obsolete in the next. So the gentleman as country squire, as servitor, could continue more or less unchanged for a century but the gentleman as social arbiter was never still. No matter. Out of all of the separate strands, what, if anything, is common to each? Only the ideal of courtesy, and of not making gaffes. Whatever his context, a gentleman was always expected to show consideration. He was gracious, honourable, unselfish; above malice or prejudice; God's servant.

At the same time, he was allowed an aloofness. Lord Salisbury's *a gentleman is never unintentionally rude* caught the note exactly – a surface *politesse*, an underlying arrogance.

Beneath this, there was a belief more basic, that man must live by a code. If he trusted to instinct, he would plunge into anarchy. That, above all, was the function of the gentleman's obligations, rituals, rules: to keep the beast at bay. Take away structure and everything collapsed.

Of course, this was not a notion confined to England or gentlemen; most of Western civilization, from the Dark Ages on, has been controlled by the same belief. But the gentleman was England's most major contribution, its greatest attempt at self-restraint. Refine, channel and sublimate. Up and out of the alley, away from the swamp.

One value lay in comfort. 'Rules are very useful,' said Anthony Powell. 'That is my personal view, naturally, but it seems to me that conventions make life so much simpler. Impulse is romantic but messy. To behave like a gentleman saved an awful lot of time and confusion.'

After 1945, that view became sacrilegious. The post-war movement was all away from compromise and containment, back towards the blood. Sweep away the rigidities, let loose instinct. That was what Pop sprang from.

By all logic, the decline must be permanent. Gentlemen – middle-class values joined to upper-class style, as Simon Raven described them – were simply too leisurely, too cumbersome to compete. As society grew increasingly fluid, and bloody-minded, they were left stranded. Raven was absolutely right: 'When people cease to respect him, the gentleman is impotent.'

So how come this talk of a revival? Essentially, it was frivolity. There was no suggestion of a real return to codes of obligation or honour, or to lost structures in society. In those senses, the gentleman was done for. All that was possible was an exercise in nostalgia and fancy dress. What was proposed, in essence, was a fashionable game.

People had grown bored with sloppiness, that was all. Pop had run its course. In the first place, in the '50s, it had real function – England was grey, mean and pompous and needed an explosion, the ruder, more radical and more outrageous the better. A declaration of independence, celebration of youth and style. Hence Teddy boys, hence Chelsea, hence the Beatles and the Rolling Stones.

But the battle was won, no further gestures were necessary. All the urgency had drained away, and what was left was rehashing. Long after the barricades had been deserted, Pop still flounced and flittered, with its tongue stuck out and hair in its eyes. Frozen yobbery, computerized abuse and mindlessness. 'Jolly boring, I call it,' said Anthony Powell, and it was.

Thus the gentleman's revival is only fashion recovering its balance. It is time now to be washed and trimmed again, to use whatever brain one has, to reinstate grace; simply to be comfortable and civilized again. Just the same, certain relics of Pop survive. The concept of image, meaning flash and camp and outrage, has penetrated too deeply to be cast aside so fast. The new gentlemen are rock stars in a different shape. Forget about armigers and their burdens – the qualification now is purely surface style: 'Pseudo-aristocratic flaunting,' said Simon Raven.

Heredity and public schools are useful; failing them, make do with will-power. Once you decide to be a gent, all you really need is brazenness. First you go shopping and stock up on waistcoats, bowler hats, silver-topped canes and ascots. Then you bone up a bit on etiquette and try to join a club, upgrade your vowel sounds, throw out your Bob Dylan albums and Free Angela Davis buttons, stop taking soup at luncheon. If you can stretch to it, you also acquire a place in the country, a gun and a couple of dogs. Given all that, you can scarcely miss.

There aren't even any sacrifices involved. The props of Pop must go but the real treats survive. All possible decadences of sex and dope are still allowed. Gambling debts are dashing, scandal is spiffing. 'New-fangled gentlemen,' says William Curbishly, a leading young blood of the moment, 'are simply old-fangled bounders.'

And the Baron Lambert? At long last, towards the end of my fifth week in waiting, I had a message from Mr Crimp, granting me an audience for the following morning.

At the appointed hour, I was collected by a Bentley. The chauffeur said not a word and drove me, neither to Campden Hill nor Regents Park, but to somewhere at the back of the Harrow Road. We stopped outside a run-down terraced house, indistinguishable from any other in the street, with hardboard covering the ground-floor windows and cracked front steps. Then the door was opened by Mr Crimp, a smooth and shiny man with a smile like a knife in the shoulder-blades, and he led me upstairs. The floorboards were rotten, the plaster crumbling and everything smelled of decay.

But when Mr Crimp opened a door and I stepped in, I was suddenly sunk in pure whiteness – a long, high room with white walls, white curtains, white carpet; camellias and great mirrors; a sense of infinite space. Across the floor, by the window, the Baron Lambert was sitting in an armchair and he was wearing white as well: suit, shirt and palest green tie.

He was a small man, dark and elusive, probably in his mid-thirties, and wholly unnatural. When he rose and shook my hand, he was smiling but his eyes couldn't be still and he had the most painful mouth I had ever seen, even more distorted and despairing than Patrick Procktor had made it. More decadent than gentlemanly: 'Please be seated,' he said. 'You are a young man of whom I have heard most favourable reports.'

I was flattered, I simpered. For perhaps the third time in my life, I was overawed. Champagne was brought to us and we sat together by the window, twitching, the Baron caught by a shaft of sunlight, myself in shadow.

For ten minutes, we made conversation, or conducted an interrogation, in which the Baron offered no opinions but kept me plied with questions that had no answers: Did I find London amusing? Was I fond of the cinema? What was my view of Mallarmé?

He sat very stiff and straight, and his eyes were everywhere. His manners were impeccable, the champagne continuous, but he was stretched taut as high-tension wire and, as for myself, I was panic-stricken. My voice sounded shrill and false, and my sentences all came out scrambled. Was I comfortable? the Baron asked. Would I care for some marzipan? Had I ever been to Smyrna?

In the end, I could only plunge in headlong. I'm sorry, I said, this must sound most clumsy, but what about gentlemen? Would he care to attempt a definition?

Then he smiled. For the first time, he looked in my eyes and his expression was one of softest, most tender regret. He was silent a moment; his smile was unbearable. 'A gentleman,' said the Baron Lambert, 'is someone who does not talk to magazines about gentlemen.' And with that he called for more champagne.

FIVE

Today There Are No Gentlemen

Pre-History

MODERN ENGLISH MENSWEAR BEGAN WITH BEAU BRUMMELL. THAT'S a most sweeping generalization, of course, but essentially true just the same and, if one is going to understand what has happened to men's clothes since, one must understand first what Brummell really meant.

His image has always been one of wild flamboyance, all frills and fripperies – the archetypal peacock, in fact, forever preening. But he wasn't really like that, not at all. Instead, he was a sartorial puritan, who believed that the elegant man should be virtually invisible: 'If John Bull turns round to look after you, you are not well dressed,' he said, 'but either too stiff, too tight or too fashionable.'

Brummell has been misunderstood, basically, because the word *dandyism*, with which he is associated, has taken on a totally false meaning. Popularly, it is supposed to mean display, exhibitionism; but, in fact, it only means perfectionism. Dandies take care – they do not make gestures.

It's an understandable confusion. When one looks now at a picture of Brummell, he looks extremely flash. But in his own time, his dandyism was a stern reaction against the *beaux* and macaronis of the eighteenth century, who had been foppish beyond all bounds. By their standards, Brummell produced a style of such severity as to amount almost to renunciation and, during his years of pre-eminence (1799–1810) he set standards that remained unchallenged for almost a hundred and fifty years. These standards were neatness, simplicity and, at all times, correctness.

But there was one great difference between Brummell and the generations that followed him – Brummell himself was obsessive. He may have believed in discretion; he also believed, most passionately, in taking pains, in working on each and every detail until it was faultless, even if that meant trying and discarding twenty cravats each morning.

In this, his successors abandoned him – they kept his taste for reticence but lost his love for dress itself. Over the years, they became not merely diffident but actively hostile, until the tradition was established that it was undignified to care for clothes and downright caddish to innovate.

The central reason for this was that, in all the years of Brummell's dominance, male dress was ruled by what James Laver has called the patriarchal principle. In other words, young men copied their fathers. They did not rebel, or create fresh standards for themselves. As far as possible they preserved their fathers' values, both morally and in their tastes, and this meant, right up until 1939, that they tried to be gentlemen.

Throughout the Victorian age, and for several decades after, this counted above all – not to be beautiful or funny or bright, original or sexual, but simply to play by the rules. Just so long as you behaved yourself, you passed.

Naturally, this expressed itself in clothes. Unlike almost every other period of history, dress was not used to attract or intrigue, it did not say *I am a man*; it said *I am a gentleman*.

In such an atmosphere, it was obvious that deviations must be frowned upon and, from generation to generation, respectable male costume became more and more restricted in scope.

Victorian men were still permitted a certain range. Figures like Joseph Chamberlain and Lord Randolph Churchill were genuine dandies, formal but given to elaborate footwear and cravats, and there was a distinct resurgence in the 1880s, with brighter colours and loud-patterned tweeds. However, these were reserved for country wear; in town, gentlemen remained cautious though spruce.

After the turn of the century, even mild experiment became

taboo. Victorian elegance, expressed in frockcoats, cravats and buttoned boots, gave way to shapelessness. Style, cut and fabric became standardized, all clothes swallowed up in a blanketing greyness and, by the thirties, the slightest hint of dressiness was enough to make one suspect.

Winston Churchill was a good example of this. In his youth, he'd been distinctly dandified and, though he lost this early dedication, he remained original all his life, what with his siren suits and his Pickwick hats, his fur-trimmed duffel coats. He was scarcely an exquisite but he was odd and, until 1940, he was much disliked for it. Of course, he was disliked and distrusted for other reasons as well, but still, in Chips Channon's diaries, his sartorial aberrations are brought up among the clinching points against him.

Behind all this, there lay fear of the flesh, and that is where the greatest difference lay between Brummell and his descendants: his own style had been based on narcissism; the Victorians thought the body shameful. More and more, clothes were used for disguise, to camouflage whatever shape or sexuality one might possess. In particular, they were made baggy. Jackets hung off one in drapes, trousers formed elephant folds underneath the arse.

This doesn't mean, however, that clothes were unimportant. On the contrary, they meant a very great deal, probably more than they do today. Exactly because the scope for self-expression was so small, every detail became all-revealing.

In the '70s, so many people dress up that the signals have been blurred. When someone makes his entrance in a frilly shirt or tight pants, it may mean almost anything. But in the decades of the purge, you could tell a man precisely by the style of his boots, the collar of his shirt – his social background, his temperament, his ambitions. If you asked him the name of his tailor, it was just about the furthest-reaching compliment you could pay him.

Perhaps that sounds like exaggeration. But one need only read Anthony Powell's *Music of Time* novels to see how crucial clothes were. Apart from their qualities as fiction, these books are definitive accounts of middle-class, upper-class and bohemian life between the wars and, in them, description of dress is one of the main ways of conveying character.

The severity is frightening. Personality hangs on the pattern of a tie or width of a trouser-leg and Peter Templer, one of the central protagonists, is damned repeatedly because 'there was always a slight impression that he was too well dressed.'

Too well dressed, that catches it exactly. One must be correct, yes, but the correctness must be instinctive, inbred. One must not try, because effort was common. In fact, one must go to the other extreme, make efforts to be anti-effort. If one bought a new suit it must not look new: if its creases hung sharp as a knife, one must scruff them up a bit, or else be thought a parvenu: 'Very spruce,' said *The Times* of Rex Harrison, and meant it as a put-down.

First Stirrings

BY NOW, IT HAS BECOME ALMOST IMPOSSIBLE TO WRITE ABOUT THE War and its effects without sinking neck-deep in platitudes. The ground has been covered so often and so thoroughly already, and the conclusions to be drawn are so clear-cut – I can see no way in which to be original.

Crudely, the point is this, that the revival in menswear sprang out of the War and that it happened because the War had given society a whole new mobility. Once and for all, it had smashed the assumption that a man must stay forever in the class to which he was born; from now on, there was flexibility.

I'm not saying that the class system was killed off completely, or even that it ceased to matter. But it was at least loosened, especially among the young and, out of this relaxation, there came in time a series of explosions, in music, in language and in dress – Pop culture.

Naturally, all this was not obvious straightaway. Immediately after the war, the feeling was not so much of revolution as of frustration, a hopeless rage at the way things were. Young men were getting demobbed and resuming their former lives and hating them. They had wasted six years, a great chunk of their lives. Now they were freed, and what happened? They were given the same old deal, expected to scuffle and survive in perfect meekness, as though the war had been nothing.

The majority grumbled but took it; a minority refused. They wanted more. They tried to make up for lost time, immerse themselves in treats. Anything would do, really anything, just so long as it made a diversion.

The trouble was, there wasn't much available. There was no money about, no new careers. As long as rationing lasted, rebellion had to work to a very small scale.

Therefore, there was a terrific boom in frivolity. All the pent-up energy, the sense of waste and being cheated, went into leisure. Football and cricket crowds reached new levels, dance halls were packed, and so were theatres and cinemas. There was much drinking and gambling, and very much whoring and, as far as rationing allowed, these were fat years for menswear.

The opportunities were limited. Throughout the late forties and early fifties, clothing was brought by coupon, which meant that, unless you used the black market, your chances of dandyism were nil.

At the same time, manufacturers were kept under tight restrictions as well, both in the quantities they could turn out and in the range of materials they could use. Many factories were idle altogether; others worked at half-steam; and the net result was that many men owned only their demob suits, grey and shapeless.

Within these limits, though, there was a distinct upsurge of interest, most of it concentrated on the Charing Cross Road. In those days, this was distinctly racy, a haven of song pluggers and dirty book stalls, caffs and surgical trusses and, also, menswear retailers. Of these last, some were proper shops, famous for their brashness; and others were army surplus stores.

Army surplus played a crucial part in this period. It was cheap and it lasted and, if it wasn't elegant, it could at least be tarted up and made bearable. So duffel coats became popular, and also battle dress, which was then dyed black or dark green, and they became the standard uniforms of the revivalist jazz fans, around the Soho clubs.

The real crux of Charing Cross Road, however, was Cecil Gee's store, which sold the flashiest, most glamorous suits in England: 'after the blitz, here comes the ritz'.

Gee was a small man in his early forties, the son of a Hatton Garden jeweller, and he had a little moustache, a bald patch and spectacles. In many ways, he was an archetypal Jewish shop-keeper, shy but shrewd, with a great and equal respect for both quality and profit.

Before the war, he'd owned several shops in the East End and belonged, as George Melly has written, in 'the East End Jewish tradition of good tailoring, as exclusive in its way as Savile Row, if based on a different premise: the necessity to reveal conspicuous expenditure rather than to conceal it.'

In line with this, he'd always been more vivid and adventurous than the menswear trade in general. In the early thirties, he had sold striped shirts, and coat-shirts, and coloured shirts with collars attached, all of which were startling at the time, and his main shop, in the Whitechapel Road, attracted pilgrims from all over London and from the provinces too.

'Sunday was the great day in the East End,' he says. 'The shops stayed open late and everyone came down for the day, from Leeds and Sheffield and everywhere. It cost nine shillings for a day return from Leeds and business was fantastic.'

The Sunday Closing Act finished that and destroyed the East End as a shopping centre. But by then Gee had moved up West. In 1936, he opened in Charing Cross Road and, straightaway, he annexed most of the musicians' trade. By the war, he was dressing Jack Hylton, and called himself 'The Swish Tailor', aka Mister Swish.

Just the same, it was only after the war that he really took flight. In 1946, he introduced his American Look and, within weeks, there were queues all along his block, and half-way along the next.

The American Look was based on double-breasted, wide-shouldered jackets, rather like the ones Cary Grant and Clark Gable had worn in thirties' films. They were often pin-striped, with wide lapels and big drapes, and they looked very much like the gangster suits that came in with the Bonnie and Clyde cult, twenty years later. (During the later craze, in fact, it became a favourite gambit for boutique owners to go down to the second-hand markets, buy up old Cecil Gee suits, clean them and tighten their fit, and then resell them. In the markets, they cost £4; in the boutiques, they fetched £20 or £25).

Along with the jackets, Gee also sold imported American shirts, with long pointed collars (the 'Spearpoint'), and hand-painted ties, with pictures of cowboys and Indians or aeroplanes on them, and wide-brimmed American hats. The total effect was masculine, very confident, a bit rakish. In retrospect, they look a bit hoodlum; but at the time, they only seemed flash. Coming after the seediness of demob suits, they felt like luxury.

Teds

IN TERMS OF ENGLISH TEENAGERS, TEDDY BOYS WERE THE START OF everything: rock 'n' roll and coffee bars, clothes and bikes and language, jukeboxes and coffee with froth on it – the whole concept of a private teen life style, separate from the adult world.

Before the war, working-class and most middle-class kids had shared everything with their parents. They had danced to the same music, sat through the same films, worn the same clothes. 'In the thirties, being a teenager meant a pound a week and acne,' says John Taylor, who edits *Style Weekly*. 'They tried to dress like their fathers, they wore tweeds and smoked pipes. It was like lamb dressed as mutton and, even if they tried to be different, all they could get was a sixpenny tie from Woolworth's.

The reason for this lack of identity was simple: they had no money to spend. They were apprenticed or they were on the dole or they gave their wages to their mothers. In any case, they had no means of rising up and running amok.

Even after the war, things stayed tight. But by the early fifties, the austerity was ending and it was possible to experiment. For the first time, teenagers found themselves making proper money, anything up to £20 a week, and they started looking for things to spend it on.

In the beginning, this wasn't easy. Since the adolescent market had always been minimal, there were no businessmen aiming for teenage custom. There were no teen clubs and no teen music, no teen foods or clothes. Nothing that didn't apply equally to adults.

By the middle fifties, the gap would be filled. Catching on fast, businessmen began to bombard the market with gimmicks and a whole new industry was launched.

But when the Teds first started, around 1952, they had none of this. They existed in a vacuum, without any kind of sponsorship and/or exploitation. They rode bikes or went to the movies or hung around in arcades. Mostly, they stood on street-corners, watching.

The first Teds emerged in the East End and in North London, around Tottenham and Highbury, and from there they spread southwards, to Streatham and Battersea and Purley, and westwards, to Shepherds Bush and Fulham, and then down to the seaside towns, and up into the Midlands until, by 1956, they had taken root all over Britian.

Essentially, their uniform was a bowdlerization of the Savile Row Edwardian Look, hence the name Teddy Boys, but they also used elements of the zoot suit, with a very long and loose-draped jacket.

Drapes apart, they wore tight drainpipe jeans, tapered to the ankle, and luminous yellow socks; creepers, large crêpe-soled shoes like boats; brass rings on several fingers, worn both for ornament and for destruction; riverboat gamblers' bootlace ties; and often, in the back jeans pocket, a flick-knife.

They also had a standardized face, which was pinched and underfed, a bit ratty, and they tended to pimples and acne. But their greatest glory was their sideburns, which had to spout well past the earlobe, and their hair, which was worn long and swept up in a quiff at the front, then dragged back at the sides and slopped down heavy with hair-oil.

This style was known as the duck's arse and variations were a diamond-shaped crewcut on top, with the rest hanging down from the crown, and the Boston, cut straight across at the back, above a shaved white neck.

That wasn't all. The draped jackets would be black or maroon or sometimes powder blue, and there might be a flash of fancy waistcoat as well. Altogether, the effect was one of heroic excess: garish, greasy and quite magnificent.

None of this was cheap: a proper Ted suit would cost between £15 and £20, hand-made by a back-street tailor, and all the accessories would double that. If you wished to make top Ted, you had to be prepared to stroll into a dance hall with £50 on your back.

This dedication was one of the things that made Teddy Boys so different from all that had preceded them. They had no concern with morals, politics, philosophies of any kind – Style was their only value and, about that, they were fanatic.

It wasn't an easy discipline to survive in. The photographer Don McCullin, for instance, lived in Tottenham and used to hang out with a gang but never got fully involved. 'I was making £3 a week on the railways,' he says. 'How could I keep up?

'The Tottenham Royal was the biggest centre in North London and, the moment you walked in, all the birds would put a price on you. Your jacket, your shoes, even your tieclip – before you'd even noticed them, they'd have you costed down to your socks.

'There was always a greasy comb around. That was a major instrument of attraction. Before you asked a girl to dance, you'd stand in front of her and comb your hair, staring right at her, with sort of hooded eyes.

'Most of the time, we used to hang around the amusement arcade in Seven Sisters Road and play pin-ball, for a cigarette a replay. Right across the road, there was Greys Dance Hall, where the policeman was stabbed. Bert Assirati, the wrestler, used to be on the door and if he caught you with a razor or bicycle chain he'd fling you out in the street. But there were fights just the same, and knifings and slashings – that's where it all really happened.'

Such intensity couldn't last. By 1955, Bill Haley's 'Rock Around The Clock' had been released, and the following year there was Elvis Presley, and Chuck Berry, Little Richard and Jerry Lee Lewis, the whole rock 'n' roll pantheon.

On, the surface, this provided the Teds' finest hour. They rioted and tore up cinema seats, they got headlines in the papers and were turned into TV documentaries and had middle-aged businessmen pursuing them in hordes, as though they were a holy grail. They turned from a minority cult into a mass crusade, and there were months of wild excitement, in which it must have seemed as if they, the teenagers, were going to take over completely.

All of this was idyllic. But in the long run it was also ruinous because, as the message spread, so its style became diluted and it lost its guts and identity.

In this, the Teds provided a blueprint for all future teenage cults. One by one, they would form underground and lay down their basic premises, to be followed with near-millennial fervour by a very small number; then they would emerge into daylight and begin to spread from district to district; then they would catch fire suddenly and produce a national explosion; then they would attract regiments of hangers-on and they would be milked by industry and paraded endlessly by media; and then, robbed of all novelty and impact, they would die.

So it was with the Teds. Although their riotings had been triumphant in themselves and the movement grew beyond recognition, most of the new converts stopped half-way. They didn't bother with the full uniform, down to the bootlace ties and luminous socks, but contented themselves with a pair of tight blue jeans and a duck's arse haircut, just to give the general impression.

After 1956, creepers began to be replaced by black, Italian-style, pointed-toe shoes and this became the basic teenage look of the late fifties and early sixties, especially in the north: blue jeans with turn-ups and, sticking out underneath, winkle-pickers.

Around the same time, the draped Ted jacket also began to fade out, to be replaced by the short, box-like Italian look and, from then on, the signals were plain: by 1958, the full Teddy Boy regalia had become hopelessly outmoded and those that wore it were deliberately archaic.

Most of the original Teds passed twenty and got married and settled down; some turned to leather jackets and motorbikes, and became the first Rockers; and just a few refused to be budged. Mule-headed, they stuck to the old ways and old uniforms, and they remained steadfast for ever.

They are still the same today, middle-aged men with paunches and Skinhead sons but quite unswerving in their loyalty. They are a sect, a secret society. Organized into cabals, like the North Finchley Rock 'n' Roll Preservation Society, they meet in the back rooms of pubs and appear once more in their fineries, the velvet drapes and spangled waistcoats and rings, and their hair, what's left of it, is still thick with grease, and their sideboards are like scimitars.

Then they sit in corners and speak of Eddie Cochran, of James Dean and Mamie van Doren, as though remembering a bygone age, when men were men and died as they lived, and women all had big breasts. It's still only fifteen years ago but they might as well be talking of the Irish Easter Rising or the Boer War, it seems so distant: stiletto heels and beehives, red ruby lips, Vince Taylor, and do you remember Sabrina?

Still, however anachronistic they may have become, the Teds' initial impact was terrific. In particular, they made two break-throughs that have dominated male fashion ever since.

The first was that they made clothes sexual again. After a hundred and fifty years of concealment, it was Teddy Boys who brought back flamboyance and preening. The baroque complexities of their costume, the tightness in the thigh and crotch, and their rituals of attraction, like the hair-combing in front of women – all of this was in the classic peacock tradition: direct sexual display.

Because of this, the post-Brummell conventions became meaningless: there was no more hankering after social status, and no more pretence at anonymity. Clothes became slogans.

The other great breakthrough was in establishing the working class as the new arbiter of style. Before then, fashion had always been created by the upper class and then filtered gradually downwards; but now the old order was turned upside down.

Obviously, these were far-reaching changes and at last, with the Teds, the full effects of the War became apparent. It had destroyed the sense of family and tradition, of one generation handing on to the next. For the first time, kids didn't want to look like their fathers. In fact, whatever their fathers looked like, they wanted to look exactly opposite. James Laver's patriarchal principle had been smashed completely and, since they thought of their fathers as safe and grey and sexless, a bit seedy, the Teds now tried to be desperadoes. Essentially, their clothes said just three things: *I am different; I am tough; I fuck.*

In the place of heritage, the Teddy Boys began a new culture in fact a whole new aristocracy: Pop.

Yellow Socks are Out

THE FIRST TIME THAT I CAME TO LONDON, IN 1956, I USED TO SPEND ALL my afternoons in the Charing Cross Road, with my nose pressed up tight against the musicians' window at Cecil Gee. Inside, there was a Vathek-like magnificence, the most splendorous sights that I'd seen in my life: danceband uniforms of lamé or silk or satin, all tinselled and starred, a shimmering mass of maroons and golds and purples, silvers and pure sky-blues, like fireworks.

It was one of London's great landmarks and, to me, the finest of all Gee's creations. For Mister Swish himself, however, it must have been a backwater, one tiny facet of an empire that had grown to fourteen shops by 1959 and had reached a yearly turnover of almost £2 million.

Right up to 1957, he remained unchallenged, both in theatricality and value. Whatever the fashion, he did it first and did it brashest and, when rock 'n' roll came in, he dressed Tommy Steele and Marty Wilde, just as he had once dressed Jack Hylton.

He also had a near-monopoly of modern jazzmen, who wished to look American. By the fifties, the transatlantic style no longer meant zoot suits or hand-painted ties. Instead, this was the age of Cool, of Gerry Mulligan and Chet Baker, and drummers with hooded eyes and a cigarette hanging off their lower lips, short-cropped Nero haircuts, hypodermics and shades. Everything was saturnine, understated, and the suits were dark and conservative, but cut bigger and more butch than most English suits, with lots of chest and shoulder.

If you wanted to get it exactly right, you had to go to Ben Harris, a Soho tailor, who cut the most advanced and authentic-looking American suits in London ('Almost a genius,' says Eric Joy, who worked for him, 'and the best, most honest man I've met'); but if you were poor and impatient, which most musicians were, you made a compromise with Cecil Gee and consoled your-self with Old Spice aftershave, which was then unavailable in England and had to be brought back from New York by Geraldo's navy.*

The modernist look was used not only by musicians themselves but by the whole Bop scene, semi-pros and fans and hangers-on, and by many of the younger West End hustlers.

Still, this was all on a very small scale compared to the Italian Look, which Gee launched in 1956.

'After I opened up in Shaftesbury Avenue, I knew there had to be a return to neatness, after the razzle-dazzle American styles,' he says. 'Then I went to Italy for my holidays. There were all these marvellous fabrics and colours, and the manufacturers would give you anything you asked for, and I thought *This is for me.* So I put on a whole Italian season and that was the first time that elegance came to England.'

Actually, there was less divine inspiration involved than this might suggest. The San Remo festivals, and the work of designers like Brioni, had already made Italian styles known over here, at least within the trade, and fashion journalists had been predicting a boom for months. Cecil Gee did not discover the look; he was merely the first with courage and energy enough to get behind it and shove.

Brioni, of Rome, was the leading Italian stylist at the time and Gee's look was a variation and tarting-up of his basic shape: a short, box-like jacket, with narrow trousers, in a lightweight fabric like mohair.

Even in Brioni's version, this produced an effect of squatness and constriction; but when Gee took it up and exaggerated it, one

---

*Geraldo, the band leader, supplied musicians to the transatlantic liners and, throughout the fifties, they provided an invaluable source of supply for all things American.

came to look like a man in his kid brother's clothes. The jacket would ride up at the back, thereby giving the style its nickname, the 'bum-freezer', and the pants were too short in the ankle, and the buttons too tight across the chest. Worn with pointed-toe shoes, which pinched the feet, the result was one of agonized, bottled-up confinement and, every time one sneezed, a button popped.

The look had many refinements. As well as its shortness, the jacket had narrow lapels and a rounded, scooped-out hem. The shirts were small-collared and, by the late fifties, button-down. The ties were skinny. Hair was worn short. Everything was skimped – narrow legs, pointed feet, no shoulders.

It was not elegant, no matter what Gee had intended. Aesthetically, it was no great improvement on the High Street, the dark grey undead. But at least it was action – it was new, and a bit flashy, and it became the basic young man's suit of the late '50s, especially in London and the south.

In fact, it was an even greater success than the Teddy Boy look. It wasn't exclusively working-class; it had no delinquent undertones; it was almost respectable. Hard-line Teds would have nothing to do with it, thinking it soft.

More than any previous style, it was classless, not worn by extremists but by jog-along youths in the span from working to middle class, boys with jobs and families and fiancées, boys who carried no razors and didn't swear in front of ladies.

Furthermore, it lasted. Over the next eight years there was a whole sequence of similar styles, all based on short jackets and narrow pants: first the Italian Look itself; then the round-collared Cardin suit, later revived as the Beatle suit; and finally the Mod suit, the first standby of Carnaby Street. Elsewhere, it survived even longer. In black Africa, bum-freezers and pointed-toe shoes are still going strong today. 'You'd be surprised,' says Don McCullin, who has photographed innumerable African wars. 'The number of times I've come up over a sandhill and seen a pair of winklepickers, pointing up at the sky.'

Only two minorities refused to tag along: ton-up boys, later to be Rockers, and Beatniks.

Ton-up boys were the natural successors to Teds, in attitude, language and values. Only their uniform was changed. Instead of mock-Edwardiana, they took their style from Marlon Brando's film *The Wild Ones*, and from the Hell's Angels who lay behind it, and they wore black leather jackets, with studding on the back, and high black boots. They rode on motorbikes and travelled in packs, and lived off greasy eggs and chips, and hung out in transport cafes, and liked blondes with big breasts, and still worshipped Elvis Presley.

In the late fifties, a firm called Anello & Davide, who made theatrical boots in the Charing Cross Road, began to promote the Cuban-heeled, or Chelsea boot and that became part of the uniform as well.

It was a beautiful, ornate and decadent object, elastic-sided with built-up heels, maybe two inches high, which gave it a deeply hollowed instep. It spoke of heroics, of gunfights in the noonday sun, of violence and sex together – and ton-up boys, who saw themselves as desperadoes, loved it. Not only ton-up boys, either – less stylized groups took it up as well, kids without motorbikes. Soon it had spread throughout the whole spectrum of teenage hooliganism and flash. Then the multiple shoestores adopted it and made it amost respectable. They gave it a winklepicker toe and lost the depth of the instep, which was its great splendour, and the Chelsea boot became part of the standard blue jeans and hair-oil uniform, specially in the North.

At the same time, the first Beats were emerging. They were purely an American imitation, gleaned from Jack Kerouac and Allen Ginsberg, and most of them were concentrated in London, although each provincial town would have its own cell, maybe twenty beards strong, huddled together in basements, where they listened to poetry and jazz and looked solemn.

In the bohemian tradition, they wore anti-dress: long hair, rancid old sweaters and paint-stained jeans, bare feet or sandals, and Ban the Bomb badges. They wished for profundity and originality and sometimes, rather nervously, because they weren't used to it, they would pass a joint around.

For themselves, they didn't matter much. In America, the movement grew quite large and meant something, paved the way for real changes; but in England, there were never more than a couple of thousand full-timers and they were always a bit of a joke, tame fall-guys for cartoonists.

Their influence, however, was considerable. In the long term they proved to be forerunners, advance warnings of the Hippies to come, in their long hair and beards, their total contempt for straight society, their conformity within anarchy.

In the short term, they also provided a base for hordes of part-timers, who took the high seriousness of the Beat stance and turned it into games. A generation of art students, and those who hoped to be taken for art students, and rebellious sixth-formers, and Aldermaston marchers in general joined in the pretence. They grew their hair a bit long and produced paint-stains for their jeans and mouthed a few slogans about squares and warmongers. But instead of studying Zen Buddhism and immersing themselves in Thelonious Monk, they settled for getting drunk and jumping up and down to Trad.

They wore impossibly baggy sweaters and, often, battered bowler hats with Acker written on them, after Acker Bilk, the clarinet-tist. They went on marches, as much for the sex as the politics and, altogether, had a jolly good time.

University students, meanwhile, tended more towards the duffel coat, which was also anti-dress, but tacitly so. It had first become popular in the army surplus days after the war and then, in 1951, had been brought out commerically, for the use of 'gentlemen, gentleman farmers, mariners, men of leisure and intellectuals'.

At first, they lived up to this and Winston Churchill bought one for his birthday, complete with fur collar. But gradually they became a uniform for students and readers of *The Outsider*. With their hoods and toggles and utter shapelessness, they were at least defiant in their ugliness. They weren't a gesture like bohemian anti-dress, aimed at whipping up rage and horror; rather they were a quittance, a denial of all interest, to be worn with curry stains down the front and the poems of Rimbaud in the pocket, so saying *I am above vanity, above flesh; I move in higher regions*.

All the time, however, so gradually that you couldn't really put your finger on what was happening, the level of general male interest in clothes was rising. There might be nothing as radical as the Teds; but the industry as a whole was beginning to stir.

Everything was loosening. As sexual and social standards became more flexible, and England settled into Wondermac cosiness, it was inevitable that dress became more permissive as well.

The old strictures hardly applied any more. It wasn't necessary for clothes to announce one's parentage, nor that they should stay the same for ever.

This last was the biggest shift – the speed with which styles changed. Before the war, any new fashion had been good for a decade at least; now it might disappear within months.

So it was, when George Melly went to Cecil Gee and asked for a pair of yellow socks, that the salesman stared at him and smirked. 'Oh no, sir,' he said. 'Yellow socks are out,' and Melly went away blushing.

In and Out: it was a new concept, and fascinating. From then on, Carnaby Street was inevitable.

Chelsea

IN THE YEARS AFTER THE WAR, AS IN THE THIRTIES, SOHO REMAINED the undisputed centre of London bohemia. Its heroes were Dylan Thomas, Francis Bacon and Johnny Minton; its citadels the York Minster (the French pub) and Muriels; its fulcrum alchohol; and its uniform consisted of baggy sweaters, baggy corduroy trousers and sandals, the classic arty costume.

Towards the mid-fifties, however, the balance began to shift from Soho to Chelsea and then clothes began to matter much more. Basically, the reason was that the whole bohemian vision was changing, under the influence of the Teds and the new-wave American movies, especially those starring James Dean and Marlon Brando. To a large extent, the Artist was being replaced by the Hustler as the central fantasy, and the Soho romance was starting to lose its attractions. Starving in garrets, pouring out one's soul through a pen or paint brush and drinking oneself to an early death – such picturesque squalors seemed somehow less heroic and, in their place, there sprang up a vogue of toughness.

In the style of Mailer and Jackson Pollock, artists began to come on like heavyweight boxers. It became chic to cut corners, to gamble and dabble in illegalities and carry an air of mystery, to know gangsters by their first names. The crucial new word was Cool, which was interchangeable with Hip, and they involved charm and style and self-sufficiency, which in turn involved money and status symbols. In other words, image, and with image, there came clothes.

I don't mean that the older style died out, or that it doesn't survive even now. The veterans carried on very much as before, trundling from the French to Muriels, and from Muriels to Wheelers, and from Wheelers back to the French again, and there were the same discussions and arguments, the same drunken scenes, the same baggy pants. From time to time a new stirrer would be added, like Brendan Behan or Frank Norman, and they were always well surrounded.

Just the same, it had lost conviction. These were tired old rituals now and, more and more, Soho turned into middle-aged territory.

Chelsea, by contrast, was very young. Until the fifties the district had been nothing very special, just a fairly smart middle-class retreat. No doubt that helped to make it attractive, the fact that it was uncharted territory. At any rate, a migration began to the Kings Road and, by 1955, a new circuit was established, based upon a pub called the Markham Arms and a coffee bar called the Fantasy, and combining elements of traditional Soho bohemia with romanticized crime and *Vile Bodies* slumming.

At first, the game was distinctly upper class, made up of a few discontented debs, notably Suna Portman and Lady Jane Vane-Tempest-Stewart, and a gaggle of public schoolboys, in search of riot. Together, they threw a lot of parties, at which criminals and jazz musicians and black men would be present, and they had love affairs, listened to Elvis Presley. Some of them dabbled in chicanery, some made exotic marriages, some turned homosexual. The ambience, altogether, was more evocative of Montparnasse than of Soho's Greenwich Village and it all made marvellous copy for the gossip columns, who reported each fresh extravagance and invented something called the Chelsea Set, who were the Bright Young Things of their time.

At the centre, there was the aforesaid Suna Portman and Mark Sykes and for years, they were a fifties equivalent to Mick Jagger and Marianne Faithfull.

Sykes was an ex-Etonian, with not much capital but a great deal of charm and nerve, and was the leader of a definite group: himself, Simon Hodgson, Robert Jacobs and Christopher Gibbs. Together, they went into business, officially described as property redevelopment, and they made enough money to live roughly as they wished, which meant wide. They took a lot of holidays, gambled and drank, and spent a lot on clothes.

Simon Hodgson is good about the period, and about Sykes in particular: 'He needed to be young, poor thing. He was frightfully funny and used to do absolutely anything he could get away with, marvellous trips abroad and cars and clothes. He got away with murder for years.

'He adored getting his name in the papers, which one rather disapproved of. He was always giving interviews, saying that he was going to buy an old dinghy, moor it in the middle of the Thames and write his memoirs on it. He was going to call them "Lilies That Fester".

'We were all very spoiled and very tiresome. Most of us were subsidized by our families and our lives were built around going to parties, and getting drunk, and meeting gangsters. Nobody had ever spoken to gangsters before – they seemed rather chic. But we were really frightfully snobbish. Everyone had to be rich, funny or famous, or at least notorious.'

There were japes. On one occasion, Sykes and Hodgson fell on their knees in front of a parson, outside Sloane Square tube station. He blessed them and moved on without a word, and the Markham was electrified. Or again, they waltzed together twice round the floor at a pompous debs' party and then dashed straight out the door: 'That sort of thing,' says Hodgson. 'People used to think it frightfully amusing but it wasn't, of course. It was just rude.'

Put like that, it all sounds an embarrassment, and it was, but there was also energy in it, and real celebration: 'The war took so long to die. Even ten years later, one was still caught up in the aftermath. Then people suddenly said "Gosh, we're safe at last" and began to splash out.'

So there were follies, and extravagant balls, like the one at Petworth, when the whole house was lit by the spotlights on the Turners, and a series of fancy-dress parties, which dragged on till dawn and only ended when the booze ran out: *The Sun Also Rises*.

And there were clothes, lots of them, split into two distinct types. 'There was a terrifically strict line drawn between formal and casual clothes,' Hodgson says. 'One used to go to one's father's tailor for suits and then buy outrageous fun clothes as well.'

Fun clothes, for the most part, meant Ted-inspired. 'For the first time, poor people's clothes were imitated by the rich. We all had long hair, or longer than anyone's else's at the time, and very tight trousers that showed our cocks. That was the focal point, the crotch; and then, if we wanted to pile outrage upon outrage, we wore blue suede shoes as well.'

Among the Sykes gang, the best-dressed was Christopher Gibbs, who was a few years younger than the rest and who, over the next fifteen years, remained consistently the most innovatory and wide-ranging dresser of all.

Like Mark Sykes, he had been to Eton, where he had been tremendously dandified and had sported a monocle, and a silver-topped cane with blue tassels, and had handed out visiting cards. Expelled in the same term as Sykes, he went to the Sorbonne and then arrived back in London in 1956. He was eighteen.

He was very flash. Sometimes he just wore tight jeans or fancy dress, like the others; but mostly his tastes were more elaborate: suits with double-breasted waistcoats and cloth-covered buttons, and velvet ties, and striped Turkish shirts with stiff white collars, and cravats. Above all, he had a passion for carnations and was forever buying new strains, pink-and-yellow, or green-ink, or purple with red flecks. 'I must have thought I was an aesthete,' he says. 'A *gentleman* aesthete. But I was a bit grubby as well; a dandy with bitten fingernails.'

Carnaby Street

IN THE BEGINNING, BILL GREEN WAS A PHOTOGRAPHER, SPECIALIZING in stage portraiture. Then, during the war, he got involved in weight lifting and, after he'd been demobbed, he began to photograph muscle boys and wrestlers, doing figure studies for the male magazines. For this, he called himself Vince.

At first, he had problems: 'In those days, it was all very perilous, shooting the male nude. Several photographers had got into serious trouble that way. So I reached a compromise – I made my models wear briefs, and I had them specially made up from cut-down Marks & Spencer roll-ons. They were skimpy but ever so comfy and they caused a terrific reaction among my models and my readers. Everyone was thrilled.

'After a time, I began to make the briefs myself and I thought perhaps I should sell them commercially. So, in 1950, I took out an advert in the *Daily Mirror*. It came out on Saturday and on the Monday morning, I took £200 worth of orders.'

Very quickly, selling briefs was taking so much of his time that his photography was swamped. In 1951, he started a mail-order business, working from a studio in Manchester Street, then he went to France: 'This was during the existential phase. All the boys were wearing black sweaters and black jeans, which were unheard of in England. Over here, everyone still dreamed of imported Levis, so I could see a potential and I brought out a catalogue of sweaters and pants.'

These were also successful and, in 1954, Green opened a shop in Newburgh Street, which was just round the corner from Carnaby Street, which in turn was just behind Regent Street. He called the shop Vince.

It was a pretty shabby district. Technically, it may have belonged in Soho but it had nothing colourful or sinful, nothing remotely exotic. It was full of attics and small workshops, scuffling tailors and locksmiths.

From Bill Green's angle, its attractions were simple: the rents were cheap and Newburgh Street was just next to Marshall Street baths, where all the muscle boys and butch trade trained. As they came out, they were confronted by a dazzle of hipster pants, expensive tight sweaters (about £7), briefs and shirts in bright reds, yellows and purples.

This was the start of Drag, not in the transvestite sense, but as used by the menswear trade, to mean fashionable fancy dress. For the period, it was all quite outrageous and, straightaway, Vince became the butt of much music-hall hilarity: 'The only shop where they measure your inside leg each time you buy a tie', said George Melly and, ten years later, David Frost was saying it still.

The camp element was undeniable, but Vince had other qualities. At a time when men's shops were almost all pompous, it was fun, and so were its clothes: lurid and sometimes badly made but, at least, never boring. 'I always put the emphasis on impact, not make,' says Green. 'I used materials that had never been used before – lots of velvets and silks, trousers made of bed-ticking, and I was the first with pre-faded denims – and I made everything as colourful and bold as I could.

'You'd be surprised by our customers, too. Everyone thought we only sold to Chelsea homosexuals but, in actual fact, we catered to a very wide public, within an age range of about twenty-five to forty. They weren't teenagers, because teenagers couldn't meet our prices, but artists and theatricals, muscle boys, and celebrities of every kind.

'I don't like to name-drop but my customers included Peter Sellers, John Gielgud and Lionel Bart. The King of Denmark brought swimming trunks from me; Picasso ordered a pair of suede trousers; Lord Snowdon used me for most of his trousseau.'

Green is quite right – not all his custom *was* queer. But if he'd been in business before the war, it would have been, and that's what made Vince new and important: it sold stuff that could once have been worn by no one but queers, and extremely blatant ones at that; now the same things were bought by heteros as well.

Behind this, obviously, there was a major shift in male identity. 'One of the things about us,' says Simon Hodgson, speaking of Chelsea, 'nobody gave a damn what sex you were. Everyone realized that we're all a bit of everything.'

In other words, men were coming to terms with the feminine sides of themselves. They were beginning not to be afraid. Narcissism and flirtation and cattiness – all these things had become acceptable as male components, in a way that the Victorian age would have found horrific; and skin-tight pants expressed the change.

This was yet another facet in the same central break-up, the crumbling of the English structure. Nothing seemed fixed any more – all the roles were blurring, and there was an evolving of the whole concept of what makes men attractive. It seemed much less important, suddenly, to look like a he-man, to have biceps like grapefruit and hairs on your chest; if you were good in bed that was all that counted and there, clearly, a certain ambiguity was no bad thing.

Of course, as yet, this was on a very small scale. Soho and Chelsea, and Vince's celebrities 'of every kind', were hardly typical of the country as a whole and the new expansiveness was unthought of outside London.

Still, once the first breach has been made, the cracks are bound to get wider and, within a few years, the same sexual relaxation was to form the basis for Carnaby Street and all its triumphs. Drag was worn by teenagers, suburban swingers, middle-aged tourists from Idaho.

To an extent, in fact, all male fashion of the sixties was homosexual-derived. In that, the retired Indian Army majors and lorry drivers were quite correct, yelling 'Fairies' and 'Poofs'. They remembered the signals of their youth and now that the message had altered and complexified, it was natural that they should be confused.

In that sense, Bill Green was a seminal figure. He was not a great designer, aesthetically, nor a great theorist and he probably had no clear idea of what he represented. Nevertheless, his was a vital breakthrough: 'I invented a long-felt need,' he says and, despite the *non sequitur*, it's true.

Vince was also a major force towards informality, as well as ambivalence. For the first time, leisure wear became high fashion. Sweaters and jeans began to be chic, not yet worn for business, perhaps, but quite all right for evenings-out or parties. 'Male costume evolves by adopting a sports costume for ordinary wear,' as James Laver has written, and that's exactly what was happening in Newburgh Street.

On paper, Bill Green should have made his fortune. Apart from his shop, his mail-order business was flourishing, too, and he started a wholesale business, with contracts at Marshall & Snelgrove and Macys in New York. When the Carnaby Street boom came in, one would have thought, he should have been made.

It didn't happen like that. 'I understand promotion,' he says. 'I could photograph something dull and make it look glamorous and sell it. But I never learned business. I didn't know how to set things up so that I'd receive the proper benefit. I needed some tough Jewish pusher behind me, to cash in, but I never found him.'

He did all right until the early sixties but then, when Carnaby Street took flight, he began to flag. He was in his fifties and, where once he had led, he could hardly keep up. Teenagers swarmed all over him and drove away his own clientele, now middle-aged; his styles looked oddly old-fashioned. Quite simply, he had lost the knack and, in 1967, he moved out to Thayer Street in Marylebone. Finally, in 1969 he went out of business altogether.

Now he runs a restaurant called Aunties, near Warren Street. He is sixty-one, with short grey hair brushed up in a semi-quiff and a somewhat melancholic smile. He is likeable; not at all embittered. 'If I was in menswear today, I wouldn't even know where to begin,' he says. 'I wouldn't understand what was happening.'

When I ate there, his restaurant was almost empty. For dessert, there was chocolate mousse or strawberry tart or fresh oranges, and he ate the lot, everything that was left over, mixed together in a single bowl. 'I only hope that when you write your book, the Jewish pusher who missed me in 1955 will realize at last and be sorry,' he said, and he began to clear away the plates, a dignified man.

In a way, he cuts a parallel figure to Bill Haley, the first rock 'n' roll star. Just as Haley, a fat man with a kiss curl and five children, laid down the groundwork and was then blasted out by Elvis Presley, so Green was replaced by John Stephen.

Stephen was a Glaswegian, whose father owned a confectionery business, and he came to London when he was nineteen, to work in the military department of Moss Bros. After that, he became a salesman at Vince ('Not much good,' says Green. 'Always dreaming of bigger things'), and he managed a shop in Notting Hill Gate and then, in 1957, he started his own company, working out of a second-floor room in Back Street, and called it His Clothes.

At the beginning, his styles weren't unlike Vince – the same rainbow colours, the same tightness and the same camp outrage: pink denim jeans, lilac shirts, striped matelot T-shirts.

What was different, straightaway, was the scale. Bill Green, basically, had thought in terms of a single successful, gossip-column boutique; John Stephen intended a holocaust. From the word go, he meant to turn menswear upside down, change everything. 'My ambition is simple,' he told *Men's Wear*, when he was just beginning to expand. 'I want to own more shops than anybody else.'

It was strange. In his business dealings he was said to be sharp and decisive but, when you met him, he seemed paralysed with shyness. He had a most beautiful face, in the James Dean manner, with curly hair and hollowed cheeks, and solitary eyes, and he spoke in a curious, high-pitched key. When he shook your hand, he couldn't look at you.

Yet his ambitions were infinite. When he had worked in Notting Hill Gate, he had doubled as a night-waiter in Fortes, saving up to start on his own and, once he'd achieved that much, he used to put in a hundred hours a week. 'That's why he was a genius, because he followed his obsessions,' says Michael Fish, who once worked for him. 'He was like Picasso or Michelangelo or Adolf Hitler.'

Today, looking back, he can give no explanation of what drove him, or why he cared so passionately. 'It was something I believed in,' he says and that, more or less, is as verbal as he gets.

My own guess, however, is that his hunger was for success in general, rather than for recognition as a designer or for anything specifically to do with clothes. As I see him, he had a built-in restlessness and couldn't ever have settled for orthodoxy – a steady job and a semi-detached. Somehow or other, he had to find an escape route and menswear provided it. No doubt he also liked clothes, enjoyed selling and designing them but, if circumstances had been different, he might equally well have been a Pop manager, or an adman, or a property developer.

Still, having made his choice, he immersed himself totally. Because he was young himself, he perceived that basic changes could only come through teenagers. Adults were too scared ever to take a lead; kids had no such inhibitions and Stephen set out to get them.

He was not successful immediately. Holed up in Beak Street he struggled for a time and then, just as he was getting himself established, he went to lunch and left the electric fire on. By the time he got back, his entire stock was in flames.

He wasn't sidetracked for long. Within a few months, he had moved round the corner into Carnaby Street and reopened. This time he was in direct competition with Vince and he won. Everything that he did, he did it faster and cheaper. At first, his trade was largely camp but soon pop stars like Cliff Richard and Billy Fury came to him, bringing their fans behind them.

To reach the teenage market, Stephen turned His Clothes into something equivalent to rock 'n' roll. All the traditional standards – wear, finish, craftsmanship – were made secondary to the instant, and he changed styles monthly, weekly, even daily.

He also cut his prices. On an average, he charged £7 to £10 for jackets, £3 to £5 for trousers and about the same for shirts, and compared to John Michael or Vince, this worked out at around half as cheap again.

Above all, he made his shops like amusement arcades. He had records blaring as loud as they would go, kaleidoscopic window displays, garments hung around the open doorways and spilling out across the pavements, in imitation of St Tropez. For the first time shopping ceased to be a chore. Instead of ducking in and out quickly, kids would go along especially, as a treat, and trail slowly along the parade, fingering the clothes in the doorways, dazzled by colours and deafened by Pop. Inside, there was more, infinite brightness and newness and glamour, and they would be drawn in helplessly. Clothes had become an adventure.

There were other ploys, lots of gimmicks and publicity stunts. But this was all embellishment. Underneath, the central equation was that, every time you walked past a John Stephen window, there was something new and loud in it, and when you counted out your money, you found you could afford it.

Very quickly he had opened a second branch, also in Carnaby Street and, seeing the signals, other boutiques like Donis and Domino Male moved in alongside him. By the end of 1961, Stephen had four shops, and had expanded on to Regent Street, and Carnaby Street had turned into a definite menswear colony.

Somewhere along the line, the word *boutique* had come in, although no one now seems sure who used it first. Partly, it was used because a lot of early Carnaby Street styles were French-inspired; partly out of camp; but in any case, it caught on immensely and, by the early sixties, even the multiple stores were calling departments boutiques.

In 1962, a range of His Clothes was modelled by Billy Walker, the heavyweight, and this was also important. Walker, at the time, was still in his Golden Boy phase, the great hope of British boxing, and he was worshipped so much that not even pink denims could sully his manhood. Huge blow-ups of him in drag appeared in all Stephen's windows, and in the press, and they worked wonders. From then on, Carnaby Street seemed almost respectable.

But the floodgates didn't open fully until after the Beatles. In 1962, they cut 'Love Me Do'. By the following summer, Beatlemania was raging at full force and the great teenage boom was under way, a cult that turned Carnaby Street from a backwater into a massive worldwide madness.

I can't overpitch this – the Beatles changed everything. Before them, all teenage life and, therefore, fashion, existed in spasms; after them, it was an entity, a separate society. Therefore, the Beatles were more important in the rise of Carnaby Street than Stephen himself. They were the deep-down force, the release; Stephen was merely the medium by which it was transmitted, a middleman of the right talents, in the right place, at the right time.

The Beatles' actual clothes were influential as well – round-necked jackets dominated teenage fashion for over a year and they made Chelsea boots more popular than ever. But that was secondary. Their true power went much deeper.

Nor was this power confined to adolescents. The hysteria might be teenage but they caught the attention of everyone, in every class and age-group, and it was they who raised up the godhead Youth.

Suddenly, kids were the focus. From being completely ignored, except as slogans in sermons, political speeches and sociological treatises, they became the centre of rapt attention, to be studied and analysed and aped.

Media tried frantically to court them. New TV shows were created, like 'Ready, Steady, Go!'; pimpled youths, myself included, were signed up by the hundredweight to be journalists; politicians queued up to be photographed with Ringo Starr, or just to get his autograph. Out of nowhere, the word Young had become the highest praise possible. Young novelists, young film-makers, young businessmen – they all cleaned up and, on their thirtieth birthdays, men went out alone and got very drunk indeed.

As far as teenagers themselves were concerned, such adulation was no doubt very flattering. More to the point, however, was the fact that business had finally woken up to them and was making real attempts to get through to them.

Already in the '50s, as I've said before, this had been tried. But then the businessmen had worked by their own values. They had produced what they thought kids *ought* to like and left it at that. Hence the inanities of Casualwear, or '50s English Pop: products were spewed forth endlessly, more or less at random, in the knowledge that eventually, by the law of averages, something was bound to catch on.

Now all that was changed. The teenage market was analysed carefully, and its attitudes observed, and kids were finally given things they might actually want. A new generation of entre-preneurs arose, people like Brian Epstein, manager of the Beatles, and Andrew Loog Oldham, first manager and record producer of the Rolling Stones, and Ronan O'Rahilly, organizer of Radio Caroline. Like John Stephen, they were younger, brighter and altogether more involved than their predecessors.

This didn't mean that teenagers weren't exploited any more. Very likely they were hustled worse than ever; but at least the exploitation was less crude, a bit less irrelevant, and didn't come from contempt. Epstein and Oldham and Stephen might get rich but they weren't cigar-smoking baldies, simpering and smirking, with one hand in the till.

At first, therefore, Carnaby Street was not a clip joint, or not excessively; in fact, it was very exciting. Just to be able to turn off Regent Street and plunge oneself into so much colour and dazzle and commotion, such a carnival – after a hundred and fifty years of greyness, it was too new and had too much energy not to be attractive.

Soon enough, the euphoria was gone. Within a couple of years, all the freshness would disappear and Carnaby Street would become a tourist trap, a joke in bad taste. But that belongs in a later chapter. For the moment it was enough that it existed, a teenage street at last.

Mods

OF ALL TEENAGE MOVEMENTS, MOD IS THE BEST EXAMPLE OF THE process I spoke of earlier, by which Pop cults rise up out of the undergrowth and spread and escalate into mass-media terms, and are softened up, and then disintegrate.

It had its roots around 1960, when a few teenagers emerged as utter clothes fanatics, obsessive to a degree that had been unknown before, and that has remained unequalled since.

There were not many of them, just a few dozens scattered around the countryside. They did not run in groups, or stem from any earlier teenage style, and they were not upper-class, as almost all original dressers had been in the past. If they followed any patterns at all, they tended to come from the middle, sons of clerks and small businessmen, and a lot of them were Jewish. They were not rich but they did have enough money and security, enough remoteness from wars and depressions, to dare almost anything.

They were purists. Every penny that they had went straightaway on clothes and each detail was conceived in passion. They spent hours each morning in front of the glass, changed their underwear three times a day. In Newcastle-upon-Tyne, I knew a boy called Thomas Baines, who refused to have sex at parties unless there was a shoe-tree available and a press for his trousers.

Such figures did not become famous, simply because they called themselves by no brand-name the media could catch hold of. They weren't tangible, fell into no easy patterns and, since none of them has made a mark in other spheres and their styles never caught on generally, it is hard to choose an example. That was the point of them, in fact, that they weren't examples but existed, each of them, as individual stylists.

Nevertheless, Bernard Coutts was fairly typical. He was Jewish and middle-class by background and grew up in Southgate. When he was fifteen he left school to become a hairdresser and met a girl called Maria, who lived in Highgate: 'She was fantastic. She was so advanced and her ideas were incredible. She wore maxicoats with a fur collar, and she had dark red lips and dark eyes. She taught me everything and I woke up to clothes.'

Inspired, he went along to the offices of the *Tailor & Cutter*, the trade magazine, and thumbed through their nineteenth-century back-numbers, until he came across a Victorian frock coat, which he then had made up for himself. It was of dark grey worsted, with a double-breasted waistcoat, high buttons and flared trousers, and he wore it with a turquoise tiepin, a cravat, a stand-up Victorian collar and a gold watch, complete with chain.

At the time, he was making three pounds ten a week and this one suit alone cost £35: 'But I felt like a totally new person. When I put it on, I felt as though I was starting my life all over again.'

He progressed. Soon he was having shirts hand-made in Jermyn Street, white lawn with lace ruffles at the wrist, for ten guineas a time, and he grew his hair long in a fringe, and he haunted jumble sales, picking up tiepins, detachable shirt-collars, anything that he could find. Then he ordered a second suit, in Harris tweed, a green and brown check, made up as a hacking jacket and, when he went out with Maria and they stood together in the tube, everyone else would look amazed and move away.

'I always believed in certain values,' he says. 'Everything that I wore had to be exclusive and I could only wear a shirt once. I couldn't put on a soiled shirt and say "that's good enough", because it wasn't good enough, not for me.

'I bathed as often as I could, twice a day if possible, and I used to wash in cologne, Vent Vert by Carvin. I was never casual. Even in summer, I'd look just as good, in tweeds and waistcoats. No matter what the heat, I'd suffer, because I wanted to be perfect.

'I would have been lost without a mirror. It was my life.'

In its single-mindedness, shamelessness and snobbery, this was in the true Brummell tradition, although there was a desire to be stared at, of which Brummell would not have approved. But, in essence, Bernard Coutts and his contemporaries were genuine dandies, the first teenage exquisites. Unlike Teds or any other forerunners, they didn't wear uniforms and they didn't use their clothes for aggression, as weapons in a running battle with grown-ups. First and last, their involvement was with themselves – a true dandies' narcissism.

Because they didn't get in the papers or on TV, their influence was only local. But other kids would see them on the street, admire them and spread their message, carrying it and filtering it from neighbourhood to neighbourhood. Gradually the new attitude caught on, the notion of dressing out of self-love rather than rebellion and, by 1962, there were enough converts to make a sect, which was called Mod.

Inevitably, with the emergence of a formalized movement, the original perfectionism became a bit diluted, and most of the individualism disappeared as well. To Bernard Coutts, Mods were downright shoddy – they did not buy each item hand-made, didn't bathe in cologne. 'It wasn't what I was used to,' says Coutts. 'People used to call me Mod but I thought I was more mature. I wanted to improve myself. I couldn't just drift with the crowd.'

However, if Mods fell short of Bernard Coutts' criteria, they went far beyond anybody else's. At first they were concentrated in a few London suburbs – Stamford Hill, most notably – and they were very young, anything from fourteen upwards. Mark Feld, the infant prodigy, later Marc Bolan, Pop singer, currently successful with T-Rex, started at twelve.

'There were about seven guys living in Stamford Hill who were among the first Mods,' he says. 'They were about twenty and most of them were Jewish and none of them worked. They just ponced about and lived off their parents. All they cared about was their clothes and they had new things all the time.

'I thought they were fantastic and I used to go home and literally pray to become a Mod. I really did that. Then I started and gradually I came to have about six suits. Suddenly people started to look at me and come up to me and then I was accepted as a Mod.

'At this time, clothes were all that Mod was about. The music and dancing and scooters and pills came later. I'd say that Mod was mentally a very homosexual thing, though not in any physical sense. I was too hung up on myself to be interested in anyone else and, besides, I was still very young.

'I didn't think at all. The only thought I ever had was "Oh, I just bought one suit this week and I should have bought three." That was all. I was completely knocked out by my own image, by the idea of Mark Feld.'

As for the actual clothes, they changed with each neighbourhood, so that it wasn't yet possible to talk about an over-all Mod Look. Many of the jackets were updatings of the Italian style short and boxy, and there were very tiny, elfin shoes, and Levis were more prestigious than ever. But there weren't any rules. In 1962, Mark Feld appeared in *Town* magazine, wearing a long and beautifully cut jacket, and a black leather waistcoat, a pocket handkerchief, a round-collared shirt. The effect was immaculate but unclassifiable.

Such ornateness was only possible because teenagers, during the early '60s, were in a position of unparalleled affluence. Mods could not remember the war, nor, except as a shadow, the austerity, and they were not threatened by any real poverty. When they worked, they were wealthy; even when they didn't, they collected unemployment benefit, and this cushioning produced in them smugness, a sense of power and, yes, decadence.

I do not mean that poverty disappeared. Where it survived, however, where teenagers were trapped in slums and scuffled to survive, they did not become Mods. They were ton-up boys or just plain hooligans; but Mod was a product of safety.

From the suburbs, it spread all over London, and established a new mecca in Shepherds Bush, and then swept on the south coast, and up as far as Nottingham, although it never amounted to much above the Trent; and, as it expanded, so its style diversified. Instead of existing purely for clothes, Mods became involved in music and possessions. The Rolling Stones emerged from Richmond and became the first Mod group (they were not Mods themselves but Mods adopted them and supported them) and, when they moved on to a national scale, they were replaced by the Yardbirds; 'Ready Steady, Go!' was basically a Mod TV show; Carnaby Street, very briefly, was also Mod.

This was the Shepherds Bush era and, just as Bernard Coutts had disapproved of the first Mods, so Mark Feld now disapproved in turn. 'It began to get out of hand,' he says. 'The Mods were uncool and I wouldn't speak to them. I took it all incredibly seriously and they seemed like a travesty.'

It is true that the Shepherds Bush Mod was made of coarser stuff. Instead of creating his own look, he began to huddle in packs and he was louder, less fastidious, more physical; but scarcely less involved.

He was usually very small and solemn-looking, and about seventeen years old. He rode on a scooter and travelled in a gaggle. In every district, there would be a top Mod and, depending on how he dressed himself, that's how the whole district would dress.

In this way, Mod style varied around the country; but there were certain basic looks: little mohair suits with narrow trousers, which were pressed every day and carried around in a bowling bag, to be put on fresh before entering a party or dance hall; Ivy League jackets, in white-and-blue-striped cotton or seersucker, with long side vents; maroon or mustard-coloured suede shoes, or desert boots; army surplus anoraks, known as Parkas with bits of fox-fur sewn around the collar; knitted ties; short-legged, ankle-swinger trousers; and clip-on braces, worn beneath a jacket.

With the exception of the Parkas, which were only meant for scooter-wear, all of this was aimed at neatness and precision, because Mods were not flamboyants. They had short hair and avoided fancy dress – when Carnaby Street went riotous and tried to trap tourists with jokes, they abandoned it fast. In their tastes, they were puritan.

They were curiously self-contained. They tended not to be interested in girls, nor in anyone else. In clubs, they danced by themselves, lost in narcissistic dreams and, wherever there was a mirror, they formed queues. Often, they would wear make-up – eye-liner and mascara – but that didn't mean they were queer, or not necessarily; it was just a symbol of strangeness.

Their girls, meanwhile, camp followers, wore long fake-leather coats, suede shoes and had cropped hair and, traipsing around the boys, were ignored. They looked extremely miserable.

At weekends, the Mods came up into the West End and stayed awake for thirty-six hours. They hung around in clubs, in coffee bars and on Soho street corners and when they got tired they took pills to keep going, great handfuls of purple hearts. Apart from that, they did nothing. They seemed sexless and emotionless, passive in everything. They were not happy and not unhappy and, to the outsider, they were scary: a race of undead.

The high point of Mod undoubtedly came with the emergence of The Who, halfway through 1964, when they began to play Tuesday nights at the Marquee Club. They came from Shepherds Bush and were Mod, or semi-Mod themselves. They were clothes-obsessives, with Union Jack jackets and Pop Art T-shirts, and a totally new outfit each for every performance, and Pete Townshend alone, their lead guitarist and songwriter, used to spend upwards of £100 a week on his clothes. He also wrote 'My Generation', which became the Mod anthem:

> People try to put us down,
> Just because we get around . . .
> Things they do look awful cold –
> Hope I die before I get old.

By this time, Mod had been discovered by media and, from here on, the movement began to go backwards. Up till now, Mods had been something quite specific, a distinct style and approach; but now the press and TV began to use the word indiscriminately. Because Mods had once shopped in Carnaby Street, the whole Carnaby Street ballyhoo was now called Mod. After that, it was only a matter of time before anything young, anything remotely new or fashionable, was pigeon-holed Mod and, therefore, made instantly comprehensible to the general public. The Beatles were Mod; Mary Quant was Mod, and so were Mario & Franco's restaurants, and David Bailey; Anthony Armstrong-Jones was very Mod indeed. In the hands of admen, it became an all-purpose instant adjective, like Fab or Gear, to be used for Pop groups or cornflakes, or dog biscuits alike. By 1965, it had lost all meaning.

Pressured and confused by all this, thousands and tens of thousands of teenagers decided to be Mod, without ever knowing what it implied. They were just ordinary kids, a bit restless and a bit loutish, a bit bored and hot for novelty; dandyism and exquisiteness meant nothing to them whatever. 'False Mods,' says Chris Covill, a top Mod of the Shepherds Bush age. 'Just nowhere-kids who weren't dedicated. They wanted to be cool but there was violence in them and they couldn't change.'

They had none of that generic Mod self-absorption. They didn't carry their suits in bowling bags, or preen, or sit for hours in front of mirrors. Instead, they hung out in dance halls and got into fights and had sex, and they screamed into Carnaby Street, buying everything that was gaudy and cheap, while the original Mods looked on in disgust.

In reaction against Mod, meanwhile, a counter-movement had sprung up: the Rockers.

These were ton-up boys by another name and, before Mod had come along, they had been flagging. In London, ton-up boys had declined into near-extinction and, even in the provinces, they survived only in patches, last-ditch guerrillas on motorbikes, mooching about in transport caffs.

When Mod caught on, however, there were many teenagers who refused to go along with it. Especially in the north, and in rural districts, they found it soft and creepy, and they went to the opposite extreme, butched themselves up in drainpipes and winkle-pickers. From the ashes of Ton-up, there rose like a phoenix the Rocker.

Most Rockers, it has to be said, were short on vocation. They were involved as a reaction against Mod, rather than out of any inner compulsion, and when Mod went kaput, so did they.

Even so, for the moment, they stuck to the rules and greased their hair, wore black leather jackets with studding and tigers embossed on the back, worshipped Jerry Lee Lewis, and battle was joined: false Mod against false Rocker.

Through 1964 and 1965, at bank holidays, they converged on towns along the south coast and clashed head-on. For forty-eight hours, there would be continuous mayhem. Then everyone turned round and went home again. While it lasted, it felt exciting, and media loved it, and it provided tailor-made material for leader writers, politicals and preachers, so that everyone was satisfied. Like the Isle of Wight pop festivals, five years later, they were perfect hype occasions – twentieth-century pantomimes, with fun for all the family.

But after the sixth or seventh successive holocaust, all roughly identical, the craze began to lose its magic. Media were losing interest, and so were the participants, particularly the Mods. The riots themselves were all right but the bits in between, all the cruising about on scooters and popping pills and the word Mod itself, seemed used up.

New styles were coming in. Marijuana was offered instead of pills, long hair instead of short, revolt instead of passivity. The ground was being cleared for Hippie and, by 1966, Mod was virtually done for. From Stamford Hill to the last seaside scufflings, it has lasted less than five years, and Mark Feld was now eighteen. 'Sometimes I looked back,' he says. 'It made me feel very tired.'

Dandies

BAUDELAIRE, WRITING IN 1836, PRODUCED A BLUEPRINT:

Dandyism appears especially in the transitory periods when democracy is not yet all-powerful, and when aristocracy is only partially unsettled and depreciated. In the confusion of such periods, some few men who are out of their sphere, disgusted and unoccupied, but are all rich in natural force, may conceive the project of founding a new kind of aristocracy . . .
Dandyism is the last splendour of heroism in decadence.

So it was, more or less, in the early '60s. Public schoolboys, arriving in London, were no longer faced by clearcut alternatives – politics, the army, the city. They were no longer born to govern, had no inbred function. On the other hand, they had not yet been assimilated into the mainstream. For the moment, they fitted nowhere.

Stranded, the brighter and more unconventional ones looked around for diversions. Where once they would have been busy building empires, now they gambled and smoked hash, and immersed themselves in Pop. From time to time, they would acquire new toys, like a boutique or an antique shop or a photographer's studio, to give the illusion of purpose.

That was the secret, to keep always on the move, so that tedium and the sense of futility could never catch up. There were nightclubs and journeys, constant treats, novelties of every kind. Above all, there were clothes.

In this, Christopher Gibbs provided a base. He wasn't dominant emotionally, not being a guru by temperament, but he was a bit older than the others, a bit wiser and better dressed than anyone, except perhaps for Michael Rainey: 'Christopher Gibbs,' says Eric Joy, exaggerating only slightly, 'is the most avant-garde dresser that this country has ever had. He had more effect on fashion in the '60s than half the designers put together.'

In 1961, he was wearing flared trousers, probably the first Englishman to do so, and waistcoats with frogging from Beirut and, during one brief phase filled with pink champagne, apricot silk pyjamas. Through it all, however, there ran a certain amount of humour and Gibbs was less fanatic than others in his set. Mark Palmer, for instance, an old Etonian who had served three years in the hulks as pageboy to HM The Queen, would ring up Gibbs and talk for forty minutes about what tie he was going to wear.

As with the middle-class dressers of the same period, like Bernard Coutts, this was not quite dandyism as laid down by Beau Brummell, because it begged for attention. Still, forty minutes spent on a tie – even Brummell could not have called it sloppiness.

Nor was the obsession with clothes confined to Gibbs and a handful of his friends. In a milder form, it was manifesting itself among young aristos all over the country and, by 1962, the movement had grown large enough to support its own tailor – Blades, of Dover Street.

This was not a phenomenon to be confused with Carnaby Street, or with Mod. To a large extent, it sprang from the same sources – ignorance of the war and its aftermath, increased leisure time, sense of safety, the rise of Pop – but it had a very different atmosphere. Although they may have rejected pre-war moral values and lifestyles, they remained traditionalist in that they cared very much about quality, and style. They were Pop, certainly; but they weren't popular, meaning common, and they had nothing but scorn for Carnaby Street in its tattiness. 'Trash,' says David Mlinaric. 'Always was, and it still is.'

In theory, the dandies were both liberal and liberated. They bought Beatle records and spoke of their Generation, as though the young formed a single brotherhood. But in practice, the generation they meant lived entirely in Chelsea and Kensington, and was rich and civilized. They did not count the spotted millions, swarming about in dance halls, factories and football grounds. 'Everyone now goes round loving each other,' Mark Palmer said but, by everyone, he meant only himself and his friends.

They were, in fact, an élite. But it was not an élitism based on breeding or manners, as it would have been in the thirties, and they were no longer Gentlemen, despite their background. If they were anything in particular, they were Stars, and they made their valuations by Hollywood criteria: good looks, charm, sexuality, success.

This then was Baudelaire's new aristocracy, and the inheritors, like Palmer and Michael Rainey, were only half of it. The other, more famous and more powerful half were newcomers, heroes of the media.

Just as Beau Brummell, whose father had been secretary to Lord North, had started out a nonentity and finished up more influential than even the Prince of Wales, so the real leaders now were Pop stars – the Beatles, above all, and Mick Jagger – and the aristocrats by birth became peripheral, often outright sycophantic.

The centre of the circuit was the Adlib, a discotheque just back off Leicester Square and, throughout 1964 and 1965, it was a nightly carnival, where the Beatles held court, and the Pop Establishment surrounded them – rock groups and their managers, models and their photographers, groupies, note-takers and dealers, and the dandies as well – and everyone stared at everyone else, and at their own reflections.

For over a year, the regulars virtually lived there and, for every visit, they would prepare themselves with as much anguish as a schoolgirl on her first date. 'One spent a lot of time preening and had a good few tries before one was satisfied. One was very narcissistic indeed. If anyone else wore the same outfit, one was furious,' says David Mlinaric. 'Or pretty cross, at least.'

There was also a great deal of paint. Christopher Gibbs, for example, used to lard himself with cosmetics, even more so than a Mod – Floris and Guerlain colognes, Man Tan and Kohl. But at the Adlib, as with the Mods, such stuff didn't mean you were queer, not by definition. You might or might not be and, in any case, nobody thought that it mattered. Whatever stunts you pulled, they were seen only as gambits, one more stroke by which passers-by might be made to gasp and start back afrighted.

Objectively, the Adlib may be hard to justify, in its self-love and exclusiveness and indulgence, and soon enough, it was soured. But for the moment, just as with Carnaby Street, distaste was swept aside by the sheer euphoria of the instant, the sense of unleashing.

Everything was new. Pop and drugs and clothes, discotheques and trattorias – with every month and every week, there would be some fresh treat. 'One had waited so long,' says Christopher Gibbs. 'All one's life, it seemed, and now it was actually happening. Suddenly, everyone seemed to be dressing up and rushing around; having fun, at last.'

If it was indulgent, therefore, at least it was impelled by pleasure. 'It wasn't boring,' says Mlinaric. 'It was all a great joke, it was shameless. It was marvellous just to show off and be stared at. One enjoyed amazing people.'

Of all the fashion innovations of this period, the most satisfying, aesthetically, were the hats of Herbert Johnson in Bond Street.

The original Johnson had made hats for Edward VII, in partnership with a man called Glazier, and the firm had stayed in the Glazier family ever since. Perhaps because of this, it had grown into a refuge, an atmosphere so calm and cosseted that entering it was like stepping back into the womb. Salesmen approached you like father confessors, bringing out hats, dimpling them softly, placing them with reverence on your brow. Every gesture was performed in gravity and repose and just as long as you stayed inside, you felt safe from all catastrophe.

Until the sixties, Herbert Johnson churned out roughly the same hats as anyone else, trilbys and Homburgs and so forth and, as such, they were going through a very harsh time. Since the war, hat sales had been plummenting. More or less, they seemed redundant, one more casualty in the destruction of the Gentleman.

In the past, hats had had a real social function. Probably more than any other garment, they had been symbolic of status and class. The topper and the bowler, the trilby and cap – each placed its wearer precisely. But now all that was dying – hats were no longer required for respectability and, in their present form, they had nothing else to recommend them. They were unwieldy, sweaty, and, nine times out of ten, ugly as well. They kept the rain off, but that wasn't enough and most of the big stores were forced to shut down their hat departments totally, or at least to shrink them.

At this moment of maximum gloom, Tim Glazier began to design for Herbert Johnson. He was thirtyish, a grandson of the first hatting Glazier and, like all his family, hats dominated his life.

He was realistic. He understood that the trilby and bowler were done for, and so were hats in general, as everyday wear. Even so, he loved them and was loyal. He believed them to be potentially the most dramatic and expressive of all male garments, and so he set out to revive them, not to be functional but as fashion, as 'instruments of amusement'.

First, he began to make caps, which before had always been confined to the working class, and he started the student-cap fashion, which led to other styles, corduroy and leather caps, mock-yachting caps, caps like small helmets.

Then, in 1965, he turned his attention to the hat proper and produced what he called 'the Big Hat', wide-brimmed and high-crowned, so that it felt like a sail on the skull and made one float down the street like Cleopatra's barge.

Writing in *Style Weekly*; Glazier described them perfectly: 'What is the magic of the Big Hat? To discover one has only to put one on. Immediately the back straightens, the chest swells, the shoulders square. One is looking down on the world from an unfamiliar height. A new grace and dignity enters one's movements: manners and chivalry return . . .'

He was right, they were quite magnificent. Alone of all English designs in this decade, they were worthy to be put beside the best styles of any age: white felt, with a thick black band, or furl-brimmed velours, of bottle green or cream, deep purple or chocolate, to be stroked and tilted and preened in for ever: 'High and noble crowns, wide flowing brims that have life and movement. Hats that are soft and flexible, that can be shaped to the character and mood of the wearer with a flick, a pull and a pinch. this is how hats should be . . .'

Hippie

AS WITH BEAT, ENGLISH HIPPIE WAS TAKEN WORD FOR WORD FROM the American original and, again like Beat, it was essentially middle-class. In essence, it was a continuation of the same old line, from Beat through the art schools and on through long hair, and it didn't change its motivations.

Its novelty lay in its gentleness. Because it was tied up so deeply with drugs, and drugs at first are so calming, it was much softer than its forebears. Instead of sitting through the night in cellars, or churning out poems and pamphlets, one need only be still and smile and say, 'You're beautiful, man, you are beautiful.'

These were very real attractions and, for the next year, euphoria was unconfined. Hippie hadn't yet been taken up by the media, or commercialized. It didn't show up in the hit parade, or in Carnaby Street, or make warm-up laughs for the London Palladium. For the moment, it lurked in the Underground, which was the new name for the Hip élite. It was no more than ten or twenty thousand strong, and everyone involved believed in it with passion.

The heart of it was UFO, a basement club in Tottenham Court Road, and every weekend there would be an all-night session there, at which the new world unfolded.

On these nights, everything that Hippie stood for worked. As there must have been in Haight Ashbury at first, there was a sense of a completely fresh start, all sensation created anew. Underground, there was music and warmth and pleasure, an infinity of marijuana, and everything was shared, everyone thought they they were One.

The Adlib aristocracy took part in it, but this was something different. There were no cliques, no top-team tables. The famous were neither fawned upon nor hassled. They were drawn into the whole, which involved the full range of middle-class dissent – art students, hipsters, bohemia; and would-be disrupters were pacified, just as hysterics were tranquillized, cynics disarmed, observers involved. Even the drug squad, disguised as freaks but detectable by their boots, would be sucked in: 'Every man a Superstar,' said Paul McCartney, and many believed him.

Clothes came from all over the place. If you had money, you shopped at Hung On You, or at the other New Hip boutiques, like Dandy or Granny Takes A Trip; if you hadn't you picked up whatever you could: military uniforms from Portobello Road, imported exotica from the East, bits and pieces from markets, and bells, of course, and beads.

The ideal was excess. Deliberately, everything was overdone and exaggerated, garments thrown together at random, colours clashing wildly. With half a dozen scarves and a few more necklaces, and shoulder-length hair, streaming in the wind, one aspired to magnificent mess.

In the traditional sense, this was anti-taste: 'I think of taste as something very boring and meaningless,' said the singer Donovan. 'It makes me think of grey and tired old men.'

Actually, this was great ignorance on his part: taste is not an absolute but evolves constantly and what is good taste in one age may be rotten in the next. During our time, it has been used as a synonym for orthodoxy and politeness but that's a misuse. Good taste, if it can be defined, means whatever works *in its own moment.*

Nevertheless, misconceived or not, the fashion of anti-taste was very much a part of the Hip culture, in which it meant to break rules, to go free. 'We accept no restrictions,' said Mark Palmer, pat. 'We're blowing our minds.'

If Hippie dress had a centre, it was a stall in the Chelsea Antique Market, owned by Vernon Lambert and Adrian Emmerton.

Emmerton and Lambert had been waiters together at Parkes,

and had been bored and, in 1962, they had opened an Art Nouveau stall at the antique supermarket, in Marylebone. For a time, they chugged along serenely and then they came across a collection of twenties' Chanel dresses, which excited them more than antiques.

They moved to Chelsea and devoted themselves to clothes full-time. They bought up Regency coats and Victorian frock coats, Art Nouveau shawls; found some old sailors' trousers and took them in and dyed them, thereby creating some of the first flared jeans in England; picked up odds and sods in junk shops, like old cravats, and resold them. Soon they were flourishing. Twiggy worked for them in her school holidays, while still Lesley Hornby, and the Pop groups began to gather.

Then Hippie started, and they came fully into their own. In the winter of 1966/67, Vernon Lambert went to India and came back loaded down with silks. They hung two thousand bells from the ceiling and got to work, selling lace shirts with frills, and three-button T-shirts, hand-dyed in washing machines, and demob suits, tightened; and the Indian silks, made into shirts and scarves and dresses; and wide twenties' ties, and more and more frock coats. When these last ran out, they replaced them with military uniforms and, all the time, they were disposing of beads by the hundredweight.

'Fancy dress,' says Lambert. 'Whatever we could find, it sold out straightaway,' and at weekends, there were queues all down the stairs, as though this were the Charing Cross Road reborn. 'Everyone came rushing in and grabbed whatever they could lay their hands on, whether it fitted or not,' and the Beatles shopped there, and the Rolling Stones and the Who, and Brigitte Bardot: 'Even Yves St Laurent dropped in to pat our backs. He told us "Keep up the good work, lads" – that pleased us a lot.'

As the fancy dress boom kept growing, others stepped in to milk it. A whole crop of Hippie shops sprang up and, while they weren't as crude in their exploitation as Carnaby Street, they weren't committed either. They enjoyed the fun and games, no doubt, but profit was important as well.

This was new. In the first flush, when Hippie was still confined to the Underground, it had stuck by the original Haight Ashbury tenets. Believing that a new world had been born, its converts had wanted only to be stoned and ecstatic forever. No one had thought to get rich off it, not straightaway. Now it was spreading and surfacing, and business joined in.

In Portobello Road, Ian Fisk ran I Was Lord Kitchener's Valet and made a killing off military uniforms. At this distance, it isn't possible to say who actually sold them first, but certainly Fisk plugged them hardest and they caught on hugely. They were cheap, bright and extremely insulting to the Establishment, in their mockery of the Empire's lost glory. As such, they were most desirable and they caught on beyond the Underground, turned into full-scale Fab Rave gear for teenagers. Very soon, Lord Kitchener had opened extra branches in Soho and Chelsea, and the news was out: *love equals money*.

As long as the summer lasted everything was fine. Never before had there been a season so jam-packed. Flower Power and meditation, 'Sgt. Pepper', the hounding of the Stones and Legalize Pot, New Mexico and India – the permutations seemed infinite.

But when autumn came, and the rain and cold, the impetus disappeared. Among the Underground, a series of rifts emerged, opposing factions; among the floaters there was simply a staleness. The media had hammered too hard, it had been too shrill and relentless: already, the rituals had been exhausted. Within six months of their greatest splendour, they were boring.

The film *Bonnie and Clyde* came out and started a fashion for gangsters, which replaced bells and beads. At Kleptomania, there were rows of double-breasted suits, and co-respondent shoes, and hand-painted ties, all very much in the style of Charing Cross Road just after the war. They sold but were no substitute for the summer. They weren't a religion or a new beginning; they were fashion, that's all, and anti-climatic. Bit by bit, it became obvious that Flower Power had not worked. While it had lasted, it had felt beatific but, by the summer of 1968, one could not fail to notice that it had been quite ineffectual. Clearly, this business of everyone loving everyone else was going to take longer than one had first supposed.

Disconcerted, the Hip movement split into two distinct approaches: a minority turned into serious political activists; the great majority stopped trying altogether, gave up on spreading Love and got quietly stoned instead.

Most of the politicals were students or, in the case of their leaders, ex-students and they ranged themselves in various warring factions, Maoists bickering with Trotskyites, Yippies with orthodox Marxists. Despite the internal disagreements, however, an overall dress-style emerged and it went back past Flower Power and Psychedelia through the Beats to Bohemia and the thirties. Setting out for the demos of 1968, the New Left looked much like Anthony Powell's Erridge in the *Music of Time* sequence, off to the Spanish Civil War: '. . . a straggling beard and air of utter down-at-heelness.'

The basic uniform restricted itself to anoraks, T-shirts, dirtied-down sneakers or running shoes. Jeans were left unwashed until they could almost stand up unaided, beards and hair grew as tangled as darkest Orinoco. Anything more fancy was seen as a frivolity, effete and improper: a cop-out.

Non-political Hips didn't go quite that far but, even here, the costume had turned scruffy. The flamboyance and elaboration of Flower Power was replaced by a conscious sloppiness. Individual garments might still be wild; there were still lurid velvet trousers, patchwork boots, embroidered skeepskin jackets; but the essential look was now one of worked-at trampishness, as it had been with Beat.

The reason for this was that dressing up, in itself, no longer carried any impact. It was increasingly adopted by the middle-class and middle-aged and, therefore, had become useless as a form of protest. Male fashion was no longer something strange. Admen might wear flower-patterned shirts and tight trousers; shop salesmen had hair all over their collars; Television Centre was filled with extravagances of every kind. Simply outrage had become bourgeois.

What wasn't bourgeois was squalor. As with the Beats, the pretence of poverty became the Hippies' last refuge, the only way left in which they could proclaim their independence and so, as well as being anti-taste, they became anti-fashion. All effort was uncool, a hassle. If one made an attempt to look pretty, one was backsliding, because true beauty was not, could not be in one's trappings but only in oneself. Hence the vogue for walking up to cripples and the variously afflicted, and saying, with sincerity, 'like you're beautiful, man'.

What clothes there were came mostly from the Kensington Market, an offshoot of the Chelsea Antique Market but cheaper and scummier. One or two of the stalls, like Cockell & Johnson, had serious ambitions to style and wanted a future; but the vast majority were passing ships, each run by a couple of Heads, who would chug along for a few months and then get bored or go broke and quit. 'I mean, like we're not a shop, man,' one told me. 'We're just doing our thing, y'know, and like getting our heads together.'

They sold things like pre-faded Levis and tie-dyed T-shirts (the shirts knotted and then dipped in dye, thus producing patterns or, more often, a series of stains and blotches), and ethnicry, like ponchos, suede or buckskin fringes, embroidered handbags and, for women, peasant-girl long dresses. In 1970, inspired by the vogue for Country Rock, there was a move towards Country 'n' Western clothes: cowboy shirts, leather jeans, high boots worn outside the trousers.

As before, the ethnic styles were aimed principally at disguising the wearer's origins, their basic middle-classness, and perhaps that explains why Hippie dress has always seemed so half-baked by comparison with the equivalent working-class cults. The latter, whether Teds or Rockers or Greasers, Mods or Skinheads, have always been an expression of a real situation and identity, while Hippie has been a charade, an imitation of an American imitation. Working-class uniform has said *I am*; Hippie has said *I wish I was*.

Michael Fish

THROUGHOUT ALL THE RAMIFICATIONS OF HIPPIE, THERE WAS A fashionable inner circle, who played out the movement's rituals but took none of its risks. Sunday-supplement Heads, they grew their hair long and wore fancy dress, went to see *Hair* and *Easy Rider*. They smoked joints after dinner and adopted the Hip jargon. But they didn't leave home or get arrested or give all their money away. In short, the trick was to take the game just as far and no further than the point at which things began to get awkward; to strike the stance of revolution while preserving the status quo.

This was the Pepsi generation, the descendants of the Adlib aristocracy – musicians and actors and mediamen, models and photographers, finger-popping businessmen and toe-tapping peerage – and, throughout the late sixties, they were the heart of male high fashion. Wherever they shopped, fashion journalists clustered round and their readers came running behind.

By this time, most of the Adlib originals had dropped away. The Beatles had taken separate paths and retreated into seclusion; other heroes had died, gone to live in Los Angeles or been discredited. As for the dandies, they had become bored.

Michael Rainey shut down Hung On You. Mark Palmer, who had been running a model agency called English Boy, shut down as well and took off for the wilds in a gypsy caravan. Christopher Gibbs and David Mlinaric merely stopped trying.

The reasons were complex. Partly they had grown tired of being aped; partly it was disillusion with the way that the Hippie movement was going; partly it was just growing up and its accoutrements: wives, families, commitments.

Besides, it was logical. If the first effect of Hippie had been to make dress freer, the second was to push the same thought further and reject dress, as a vanity, altogether: 'I finally tumbled that fashion was a fallen angel,' says Gibbs. 'A pernicious force to keep you running from yourself. We're torturing ourselves, aren't we, and what for? Tight pants are sexually damaging; almost everything that looks nice is constricting and unhealthy.'

As early as 1968, those most finely tuned to the waverings of fashion could have picked up the signals: elaborate fancy dress was about to become unchic. Very few did so, however, and, for the moment, the circuit carried on undiminished. In fact, it had a brand new leader, Michael Fish.

Fish was tall and gangling and loquacious, and came from Wood Green, describing his parents as 'very ordinary'. Having made such a splash at Turnbull & Asser, with his technorama shirts and kipper ties, he decided to go it alone and found financial backing from Barry Sainsbury, grandson of the grocer. In 1966, Mr Fish opened in Clifford Street.

On the label of all his garments, he printed the legend PECULIAR TO MR FISH and he took this, in its campness and calculated weirdery, as his text. Simply, he set out to be outrageous.

He succeeded. His shop was a holocaust of see-through voiles, brocades and spangles, and miniskirts for men, blinding silks, flower-printed hats. In fact it was a Pepsi equivalent to Kiss Me Quick. Nevertheless, it went down a storm.

This was Pepsi at its most definitive – all the surface mannerisms and mouthings of Hippie, but none of the intent. 'Oh, no,' says Barry Sainsbury now, a bit appalled at the thought. 'We didn't try to change the world. We just wanted to be chic.'

Like John Stephen, Fish was hardly a designer; he was a moment. He coincided perfectly with the first eruptions, grew up alongside UFO and Flower Power, and he caught the mood. It was a time when the young rich wished, above all, to be wild and exhibitionist and foolish, and he was all of these things in abundance. In no time, his clientele included Terence Stamp and Mick

Jagger, David Frost and Lord Snowdon and David Bailey, the Dukes of Bedford and Ellington.

Socially, he was a great success as well. He had charm, was funny and bitchy and emotional, and his customers took him up as something of a mascot, so that he was forever dining with politicians or Pop millionaires, or indulging in badinage with Princess Margaret. For two years, perhaps more than anyone else in London, he had what Pepsis themselves called Nowness: you could have shut him in a time machine, labelled him 1967 and our descendants would have known all.

In the *London Magazine*, he wrote an explanation and justification of his stance, under the title 'Doing Your Own Thing', and it summed up Pepsi exactly: 'People can be divided into doers of their own thing and non-doers of their own thing.'

At the beginning of this piece, he also wrote: 'I don't accept divisions of society into fashion and non-fashion. The people who come into my shop don't have to dress to conform to any given image. They dress as they do because they're confident in themselves. They're blowing their minds.'

Despite his prices of £100 a suit and up to £20 a shirt, this naïveté was not assumed. Having interviewed him at length, I'm fairly sure that he really believed it and, very likely, it was this innocence, this total unawareness of the motivations that he was dealing with, that let him come on with such brashness and blatancy and, therefore, be successful.

Within eighteen months, his turnover had gone up to £250,000 a year but it wasn't his money-making that was so impressive; it was the way in which, within months, he was accepted as an authority. *Women's Wear Daily* called him 'the arbiter of chic from London'; *Elle* called him, enigmatically, 'Fish-Fash'; and *The Times* called him 'the celebrated outfitter.'

The tabloids, meanwhile, were equally keen on him, because of his flair for gimmickry, the way he could always be relied on for a picture story whenever hard news was short. There was a period when you couldn't wake up with a hang-over without being faced by Mr Fish in a minikilt, or Mr Fish in silver sequins.

Among the follies, he also found time to produce several styles that were fashionable at other levels, and were taken up by Carnaby Street or the Kings Road or even, on occasion, by the High

Street: roll-necked silk shirts, which had a year of vogue at every level from couture to Marks & Spencer; kipper ties, of course; and leather maxicoats, first designed for him by Eric Joy, so Joy says, in November 1966.

Personally he was a mixture of extroversion and insecurity, folly and shrewdness, campery and solemnity. 'I have tried to break down the frontiers of man,' he told me. 'Do I care about the masses? Jesus Christ had only twelve disciples and one of them was doubting Thomas.'

These apparent *non sequiturs* cropped up at regular intervals in his pronouncements, giving conversation a slightly hallucinatory flavour. When I asked him what influence he'd had, for instance, he thought it over and said, cagily: 'What do you call a Negro with a spear? Sir? Of course you do.

'I am a typical Taurean, which means that I'm an ardent lover and firm friend but the deadliest of enemies. I can be very sweet, though, at times.

'I'm very shy. Most extroverts are shy. I would rather have people laugh at me and walk past me than have them confront me seriously. Mind you, if I don't get whistled at and jeered when I pass a New York building site, I feel underdressed. Four years ago, I thought that success was being mentioned in the gossip columns of the *Daily Sketch*. Now I'm much deeper. Every time I get in a plane, I smile and I go on smiling all through the flight and I know that I'll smile even if I crash, because I'm convinced that I'll be able to lift my spirit from my body. I believe that there's a common spirit linking everyone.

'I don't care about taste. I think taste is a word like love; it should be forgotten for fifty years. I don't even know what it means. Actually, I always think I'm very vulgar. Revolutionaries have to be.'

Revolution? One of the truisms of breakthrough, whether in fashion or in general social climate, is that it's almost impossible to move direct from A to B. If the breach is to be made at all, it takes excess to achieve it. It cannot be done by logic, or calm calculation; it can only be done by an advance-guard jumping blind and landing straightaway at C.

Having got that far, there can then be readjustment. Some of those at C may press on still further, to D, but the majority are likely to relax or grow tired and slide back a bit. Meanwhile, many of those who were too nervous to jump in the first place will have been reassured and begun to move forward as well. In the end, there may be a meshing round about B.

Clearly, that is great simplification, a kind of revolution by numbers but, in essence, it seems to me to express what has happened to men's clothes in the '60s and what is happening now. Beyond clothes, it may also express what has happened and is happening to Pop culture as a whole.

By any standards, the last decade has been a period of quite terrific upheaval at every level of the fashion market, and most of the changes that have been made have been basic and irreversible. To make these changes, however, it has been necessary to do a great deal of overblowing of fancy dress. As the '70s have begun, this is starting to seem redundant.

I have already described the signs of surfeit in high fashion, among the Hippies and in Carnaby Street, and the same sense of satisfaction has been emerging throughout fashion. The '60s were great but too much,' says Tom Gilbey. 'Now there's going to be a bit more thought, and standards.'

While I was writing this book, I went to Manchester for a couple of days and stood around on street corners, taking in the clothes of every man as he passed. Being based in London, I'd realized how easy it was to lose proportion, to see menswear purely in terms of Chelsea and the chic magazines, and I wanted to see how much had really changed.

Obviously, there was nothing scientific in this; I was curious, that's all. I ignored all the obvious extremes, of class and age and taste, not being concerned with trendy teenagers or Fab Gear fashion, and I concentrated on the bulk – what one might call the middle Englishman.

And what *had* changed? The short answer is quite a lot. About half the men that passed me were wearing slimmer trousers, rather more fitted suits than they would have done ten years before; about one in four used colour – a patterned tie, a bright shirt; and about one in ten was decidedly dressy, clearly went to trouble.

But actual changes in style interested me only secondarily. What

I was really after was the redevelopment in the Englishman's self-image, his public personality, as expressed through his dress. Before the war, clothes had said *I am English, and a gentleman*: what did they say now?

This answer was quite complex. For a start, it was plain that older men had moved very little. If their taste had been formed by 1939, that is to say if they were now in their mid-forties or over, their message remained essentially the same. They wanted to be respectable, discreet, unseen. If they wore a brighter tie, it was only because brighter ties were now accepted universally, did not disrupt one's anonymity.

Among younger men, however, there had been a shift, although hardly a revolution, in Carnaby Street or high-fashion sense. They still didn't express themselves individually, they were still unsexual and inconspicuous. Their clothes still said, . . .*I am an ordinary man*. They still conformed to an overall pattern.

But the pattern itself was new, and what had happened, crudely, was that clothes had become amoral. They were no longer bothered with standards of behaviour, or with reliability, or with knowing one's place. They didn't say *I can be trusted*, as they used to. Instead, they said simply *I am, or I can be, a success*.

Predictably, the younger the man, the more this showed and it was only fully realized among the twenties and under. Still, weaker or stronger, the same atmosphere seemed to permeate through most men not yet in their forties. In intent at least, their clothes gave off efficiency and push, and allowed for no predestined status. They were not classless in the sense that you couldn't guess where the wearer came from or roughly how much he earned; they were classless in that you couldn't guess where he thought he'd end up. Unless you were truly working-class, meaning that you laboured with your hands and muscles, you no longer wore your job in your uniform.

After three days, I was satisfied. I felt that I'd understood the adjustments tolerably well, and, smug, I prepared to leave. But then, almost as an afterthought, I flashed upon something much more basic: Englishmen no longer dressed as Englishmen.

It wasn't that they looked like anyone else. They did not ape the French or Germans or Americans; if they'd gone abroad, they'd have been instantly recognizable. But it was no longer an issue.

Before the war, it had been the basis of all men's clothes, *I Am English*, and it had produced all the secondary characteristics, like the sense of tradition and attempted dignity. It had been a protection, and now the protection was gone. In present-day uniforms, what had been assertiveness had become mere acceptance, saying *I live in England, therefore I wear its clothes*; no more than that.

This seemed to me the crux, the most basic point of all that had happened to male costume since the war. On the surface, there had been a liberation but that was not so – there had only been a substitution of one discipline for another. Before the war, there had been Englishness, and the securities that Englishness implied. Now Englishness counted much less and the securities were gone. Accordingly, clothes were no longer expressions of stability. Once they had spoken of acceptance, of knowing one's place; in 1970, they spoke mostly of self-improvement.

In Manchester, for instance, I asked questions, wanting to know what men's clothes meant to them, at a conscious level. Predictably, in nine cases out of ten, the answers were scrambled and unhelpful; but just once, I got a response that seemed to sum up all the previous stumblings. In a pub, I met a research chemist, thirty-one-years old, who was married and had two children and earned around £40 a week. He didn't follow fashion but owned seven suits, all bought at Burtons, and chose them with care. He thought that they mattered, not as objects but symbolically, and each purchase was a major event. 'When I buy a new suit,' he said, 'it's almost like getting promotion.'

SIX

In America

King Death

O ne day, towards the end of a long, dry summer, Seaton arrived in Tupelo and stopped at the Playtime Inn. It was a stifling afternoon, the town lay in a stupor and, for lack of anything better, he stood at his bedroom window, half-hidden behind a net curtain, looking out across the street.

From where he was stationed, he could see three shop-fronts: a Chinese laundry, a pool hall and a saloon called The Golden Slipper. Between them, they occupied perhaps a dozen yards of sidewalk. In addition, if Seaton craned his neck, he could just make out the first three letters of a gilded nameplate – WIL, as in WILKES & BARBOUR (Noted Upholsterers).

Within this frame, the action was severely limited. An antique Chevrolet was parked outside the pool hall, a mulatto woman was scrubbing the steps of the saloon and a mongrel lay panting beneath a lamppost. In the doorway of the Chinese laundry, there stood a man in a heavy black overcoat, black gloves and a black slouch hat, and between his legs there was a small black suitcase.

Seaton watched, and time dragged by very slowly. He felt sticky and unclean and, from time to time, to ease his boredom, he would turn away and flop down on his bed, or splash his face with lukewarm water, or help himself to a cigarette. He

317

was an Englishman born and bred, and at the bottom of his suitcase, there was Wisden, the Cricketers' Almanack, for 1921; three old school ties, all different; and a photograph of the Queen Mother.

So the afternoon passed. Propped up behind the glass like a tailor's dummy, Seaton began to nod, and a large blue fly settled on his nose. The Chevrolet drove away, the mulatto maid finished her scrubbing, the mongrel wandered off round the corner. Finally, only the man in black remained, and even he was lost in shadow, all except for his shiny black boots, which protruded an inch into the sunlight, toecaps glinting.

Possibly Seaton drifted off into a doze, perhaps he simply ceased to register. At any rate, when a siren sounded on the corner, it took him by surprise and his head jerked, his eyes opened wide.

It was past five o'clock. The sun had lost its force and his sweat had turned cold on his flesh, a sensation which made him shudder. Wincing, he shook himself and stretched and yawned, and he was just on the point of moving away when a stranger in a blue pin-striped suit emerged from the pool hall, and began to stroll down the block.

He moved with bent head and slouched shoulders, and it was not possible to make out his features. From a distance, however, he seemed roughly the same age and build as Seaton himself – squat and stubby, slack-fleshed – and he did not walk so much as amble, splayfooted.

As he came abreast of the laundry, he produced a cigar and paused for a moment to light it, holding it up to his nostrils, rolling it lovingly between his thumb and forefinger. Immediately, the man in the black overcoat stepped out from the doorway, hand outstretched, as if to proffer a light, and the stranger half turned to meet him, inclining his head.

At this moment, something odd occurred. The two men, as they touched, appeared to mesh. There was no noise, no semblance of a struggle, but the man in black, flowing into the stranger's flesh, seemed to pass straight through him and come out on the other side, all in one smooth motion.

For an instant, as he stepped clear, his face caught the light and his eyes were seen to gleam and sparkle, like tiny mirrors refracting. Before Seaton had time to focus, however, they had dimmed again and he had turned his head. Stepping down from the sidewalk, momentarily eclipsing the WIL of WILKES & BARBOUR, he tucked his black suitcase underneath his arm and, sauntering, he disappeared off the edge of the frame.

The man in the pin-striped suit was left behind. For several seconds, he hung without moving, cigar still half-way to his lips, head still inclined towards the empty doorway, as though he were listening to something very faint and difficult, which required his utmost concentration. Seaton could hear dance music playing on a radio, saw a flutter of pink silk in the depths of The Golden Slipper. Then the stranger gave a sigh and, folding gently at the knees, he slid down on the sidewalk, where he twitched three times and was still.

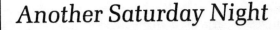

Another Saturday Night

Vincent was the very best dancer in Bay Ridge – the ultimate Face. He owned fourteen floral shirts, five suits, eight pairs of shoes, three overcoats, and had appeared on American Bandstand. Sometimes music people came out from Manhattan to watch him, and one man who owned a club on the East Side had even offered him a contract. A hundred dollars a week. Just to dance.

Everybody knew him. When Saturday night came round and he walked into 2001 Odyssey, all the other Faces automatically fell back before him, cleared a space for him to float in, right at the very centre of the dance floor. Gracious as a medieval seigneur accepting tributes, Vincent waved and nodded at random. Then his face grew stern, his body turned to the music. Solemn, he danced, and all the Faces followed.

In this sphere his rule was absolute. Only one thing bothered him, and that was the passing of time. Already he was eighteen, almost eighteen and a half. Soon enough he would be nineteen, twenty. Then this golden age would pass. By natural law someone new would arise to replace him. Then everything would be over.

The knowledge nagged him, poisoned his pleasure. One night in January, right in the middle of the Bus Stop, he suddenly broke off, stalked from the floor without a word, and went outside into the cold darkness, to be alone.

He slouched against a wall. He stuck his hands deep into his overcoat pockets. He sucked on an unlit cigarette. A few minutes passed. Then he was approached by a man in a tweed suit.

They stood close together, side by side. The man in the tweed suit looked at Vincent, and Vincent stared at the ground or at the tips of his platform shoes. 'What's wrong?' said the man in the suit, at last.

And Vincent said: 'I'm old.'

Before Saturday night began, to clear his brain of cobwebs and get himself sharp, fired up, he liked to think about killing.

During the week Vincent sold paint in a housewares store. All day, every day he stood behind a counter and grinned. He climbed up and down ladders, he made the coffee, he obeyed. Then came the weekend and he was cut loose.

The ritual never varied. Promptly at five the manager reversed the 'Open' sign and Vincent would turn away, take off his grin. When the last of the customers had gone, he went out through the back, down the corridor, directly into the bathroom. He locked the door and took a deep breath. Here he was safe. So he turned toward the mirror and began to study his image.

Black hair and black eyes, olive skin, a slightly crooked mouth, and teeth so white, so dazzling, that they always seemed fake. Third-generation Brooklyn Italian, five-foot-nine in platform shoes. Small purplish birthmark beside the right eye. Thin white scar, about two inches long, underneath the chin, caused by a childhood fall from a bicycle. Otherwise, no distinguishing marks.

That was the flesh; but there was something else, much more important. One night two years before, he had travelled into Queens with some friends and they had ended up in some club, this real cheap scumhole; he couldn't remember the name. But he danced anyhow and did his numbers, all his latest routines, and everyone was just amazed. And then he danced with this girl. He'd never seen her before and he never saw her again. But her name was Petulia, Pet for short, and she was all right, nice hair, a good mover. And she kept staring right into his eyes. Staring and staring, as though she were hypnotized. He asked her why. 'Kiss me,' said the girl. So he kissed her, and she went limp in his arms. 'Oooh,' said the girl, sighing, almost swooning, 'I just kissed Al Pacino.'

In his first surprise, assuming that she must be teasing, Vincent had only laughed and blushed. But later, thinking it over, he knew she had really meant it. Somehow or other she had seen beneath the surface, had cut through to bedrock, to his very soul. That was something incredible. It blew his mind. In fact, if anyone ever asked him and he tried to answer honestly, looking back, he would say that was the happiest, the very best, moment of his life.

Since then, whenever he gazed into the mirror, it was always Pacino who gazed back. A killer, and a star. Heroic in reflection. Then Vincent would take another breath, the deepest he could manage; would make his face, his whole body, go still; would blink three times to free his imagination, and he would start to count.

Silently, as slowly as possible, he would go from one to a hundred. It was only now, while he counted, that he thought about death.

Mostly he thought about guns. On certain occasions, if he felt that he was getting stale, he might also dwell on knives, on karate chops and flying kung fu kicks, even on laser beams. But always, in the last resort, he came back to bullets.

It felt just like a movie. For instance, he would see himself at the top of a high flight of stairs, back against a wall, while a swarm of attackers came surging up towards him to knock him down, destroy him. But Vincent stood his ground. Unflinchingly, he took aim and fired. One by one they went crashing backwards, down into the pit.

When the battle ended and he had won, he stood alone. Far beneath him, he knew, there was blood and smoke, a chaotic heap of bodies, dead and dying. But that did not enter the physical vision. On the screen there was only Vincent, impassive, ice cold in triumph, who put his gun back into its holster, wiped away the sweat that blinded him, straightened his collar, and, finally, in close-up, smiled.

At one hundred, he let out his breath in a rush. The strain of holding back had turned him purple, and veins were popping all over his neck and arms. For some moments all he could do was gasp. But even as he suffered, his body felt weightless, free, almost as if he were floating. And when he got his breath back, and the roaring in his temples went away, it was true that he felt content.

That was the end; the movie was complete. Turning away from the glass, and away from Pacino, he would flush the toilet, wash his hands. He combed his hair. He checked his watch. Then he went out into the corridor, back into the store. The week behind the counter had been obliterated. No drudgery existed. He was released; Saturday night had begun.

Lisa was in love with Billy, and Billy was in love with Lisa. John James was in love with Lorraine. Lorraine loved Gus. Gus loved Donna. And Donna loved Vincent. But Vincent loved only his mother, and the way it felt to dance. When he left the store he went home and prepared for 2001 Odyssey. He bathed, he shaved, he dressed. That took him four hours, and by the time he emerged, shortly after nine, he felt reborn.

He lived on the eleventh floor of a high-rise on Fourth Avenue and 66th Street, close beside the subway tracks, with the remnants of his family. He loved them, was proud that he supported them. But when he tried to describe their existence, he would begin to stammer and stumble, embarrassed, because everything came out so corny: 'Just like soap,' he said, 'only true.'

His father, a thief, was in jail, and his oldest brother had been killed in Vietnam. His second brother was in the hospital, had been there almost a year, recovering from a car crash that had crushed his legs. His third brother had moved away to Manhattan, into the Village, because he said he needed to be free and find himself. So that left only Vincent, his mother, and his two younger sisters, Maria and Bea (short for Beata), who were still in school.

Between them they shared three rooms, high up in a block of buildings like a barracks. His windows looked out on nothing but walls, and there was the strangest, most disturbing smell, which no amount of cleaning could ever quite destroy.

Hard to describe it, this smell; hard to pin it down. Sometimes it seemed like drains, sometimes like a lack of oxygen, and sometimes just like death, the corpse of some decaying animal buried deep in the walls. Whichever, Vincent wanted out. He would have given anything. But there was no chance. How could there be? He could never abandon his mother. 'You must understand,' he said. 'I am the man.'

Here he paused. 'I am her soul,' he said. Then he paused again, pursing his lips, and he cast down his eyes. He looked grave. 'Understand,' he said, 'my mother is me.'

It was the guts of winter, bitter cold. But he would not protect himself. Not on Saturday night, not on display at Odyssey. When he kissed his mother goodbye and came down on to Fourth, strutting loose, he wore an open-necked shirt, ablaze with reds and golds, and he moved through the night with shoulders hunched tight, his neck rammed deep between his shoulder blades in the manner of a miniature bull. A bull in Gucci-style loafers, complete with gilded buckle, and high black pants tight as sausage skins. Shuffling, gliding, stepping out. On the corner, outside Najmy Bros. grocery, he passed a Puerto Rican, some dude in a floppy velour hat, and the dude laughed out loud. So Vincent stopped still, and he stared, a gaze like a harpoon, right between the eyes. 'Later,' he said.

'Later what?' said the dude, lolling slack, sneaking his hand back in his pants, grin slapped clean across his face. 'Later who? Later where? Later how?'

'Hombre,' said Vincent, expressionless, 'you will die.'

It was not quite his own. To be perfectly truthful, he had borrowed the line from Lee Van Cleef, some Spaghetti Western that he'd seen on late-night TV. But he drawled it out just right. A hint of slur, the slightest taste of spit. 'Hombre, you will die.' Just like that. And moved away. So slick and so sly that the dude never knew what hit him.

Two blocks farther on, Joey was waiting in the car. Joey and Gus in the front, Eugene and John James and now Vincent in the back, trundling through the icy streets in a collapsing '65 Dodge. Nobody talked and nobody smiled. Each scrunched into his own private space; they all held their distance, conserved their strength, like prize-fighters before a crucial bout. The

Dodge groaned and rattled. The radio played Harold Melvin and the Blue Notes. Everything else was silence, and waiting.

John James and Eugene worked in a record store; Gus was a house painter. As for Joey, no one could be sure. In any case, it didn't matter. Not now. All that counted was the moment. And for the moment, riding out toward 2001 Odyssey, they existed only as Faces.

Faces. According to Vincent himself, they were simply the élite. All over Brooklyn, Queens and the Bronx, even as far away as New Jersey, spread clear across America, there were millions and millions of kids who were nothing special. Just kids. Zombies. Professional dummies, going through the motions, following like sheep. School, jobs, routines. A vast faceless blob. And then there were the Faces. The Vincents and Eugenes and Joeys. A tiny minority, maybe two in every hundred, who knew how to dress and how to move, how to float, how to fly. Sharpness, grace, a certain distinction in every gesture. And some strange instinct for rightness, beyond words, deep down in the blood: 'The way I feel,' Vincent said, 'its like we have been chosen.'

Odyssey was their home, their haven. It was *the* place, the only disco in all Bay Ridge that truly counted. Months ago there had been Revelation; six weeks, maybe two months on, there would be somewhere else. Right now there was only Odyssey.

It was a true sanctuary. Once inside, the Faces were unreachable. Nothing could molest them. They were no longer the oppressed, wretched teen menials who must take orders, toe the line. Here they took command, they reigned.

The basic commandments were simple. To qualify as an Odyssey Face, an aspirant need only be Italian, between the ages of eighteen and twenty-one, with a minimum stock of six floral shirts, four pairs of tight trousers, two pairs of Gucci-style loafers, two pairs of platforms, either a pendant or a ring, and one item in gold. In addition, he must know how to dance, how to drive, how to handle himself in a fight. He must have respect, even reverence, for Facehood, and contempt for everything else. He must also be fluent in obscenity, offhand in sex. Most important of all, he must play tough.

There was no overlapping. Italians were Italian, Latins were

greaseballs, Jews were different, and Blacks were born to lose.
Each group had its own ideal, its own style of Face. But they
never touched. If one member erred, ventured beyond his own
allotted territory, he was beaten up. That was the law. There
was no alternative.

Then there were girls. But they were not Faces, not truly.
Sometimes, if a girl got lucky, a Face might choose her from the
crowd and raise her to be his steady, whom he might one day
even marry. But that was rare. In general, the female function
was simply to be available. To decorate the doorways and
booths, to fill up the dance floor. Speak when spoken to, put out
as required, and then go away. In short, to obey, and not to fuss.

Fuss, in fact, was the one thing in life that Faces loathed most
of all. Vincent, for example. The moment that anyone started to
argue, to flush and wave his hands, he would simply turn his
back and start walking. No matter what the circumstance, there
could be no excuse for whining. It was not clean. It made him
sick to his stomach.

That was why he loved to dance, not talk. In conversation,
everything always came out wrong, confused. But out on the
floor it all somehow fell into place. There was no muddle,
nothing that could not be conveyed. Just so long as your feet
made the right moves, kept hitting the right angles, you were
foolproof. There were certain rules, watertight. Only obey
them, and nothing could go wrong.

Sometimes, it was true, people did not understand that.
Some outsider would stumble in, blundering. A complete un-
Face, who wore the wrong clothes and made the wrong moves,
who danced last month's routines. And that could be ruinous.
Absolutely disastrous. Because the whole magic of the night,
and of Odyssey, was that everything, everyone, was
immaculate. No detail was botched, not one motion uncon-
sidered.

Purity. A sacrament. In their own style, the Faces were true
ascetics: stern, devoted, incorruptible. 'We may be hard. But
we're fair,' said Vincent. So they gathered in strict formation,
each in his appointed place, his slot upon the floor. And they
danced.

On the first night when the man in the tweed suit arrived

from Manhattan, it was only nine o'clock and Odyssey was still half empty. He had come on the Brooklyn-Queens Expressway and when he descended into Bay Ridge itself, he found himself in a dead land. There were auto shops, locked and barred; transmission specialists, alignment centres. Then the Homestead Bar and Grill, and the Crazy Country Club, advertising 'warm beer and lousy food'. But there were no people. Only railroads and junkyards, abandoned car seats, hubcaps, tyres, scattered by the side of the road. A wasteland.

It was another frozen night and, when he climbed out of the car, the sidewalks were so icy that he slithered at every step. Guard dogs snapped and leaped in the darkness, and sleet whipped at his eyes. So he huddled deeper, tighter, into his overcoat, and set off towards a small red light at the farthest end of the street.

This was 2001 Odyssey. On the step outside, Vincent stood waiting, smoking, and did not seem to feel the cold at all. His hair was blow-waved just so, his toe caps gleaming. *Brut* behind his ears, *Brut* beneath his armpits. And a crucifix at his throat.

Inside, Odyssey was as vast and still as a Saturday-night cathedral. Music blared from the speakers, coloured lights swirled back and forth across the dance floor. But no one answered their call. Perhaps a dozen girls sat waiting, on plastic seats, in scalloped booths. Four Faces in shiny suits stood at the bar, backs turned to the floor. The manager standing by the door scratched himself. That was all.

Then the music changed to 'Baby Face', and a boy in a red-patterned shirt began to dance alone. He came out of nowhere, down from the tiers of seats at the very back of the hall, the bleachers, which were completely shrouded in darkness. Skinny, shrimpish, he stood out in the very centre of the floor, caught by the swirling lights, and did one half of the Rope Hustle. Only half, of course, because the Rope Hustle cannot really be performed without a partner. So he twirled in irregular circles, his arms twining and unfurling about his neck, vaguely as if he were trying to strangle himself. And the Faces at the bar, without even seeming to look, began to snigger.

Hearing mockery, the boy flushed and lowered his eyes, but he did not back down. For twenty minutes, half an hour, he kept on spinning, wheeling, in total isolation. 'Later on, he'll have to leave,' said Vincent. 'Now it doesn't matter. Not yet.'

'Who is he?' asked the man in the suit.

'His born name is Paul. But he calls himself Dean. A very weird guy.'

'How come?'

'He cries.'

When at last the boy came off the floor, he sat down at the bar and stared directly ahead, towards the mirror. His face was pale and pinched, his Adam's apple kept leaping in his throat, and he ordered lemonade. Over his heart there was a small tin button printed with black letters that said: 'I believe.' He drank his lemonade in three clean gulps. Then he wiped his lips and went straight back on the floor, still all alone, as if to resume a vigil.

When the music turned to 'Wake Up Everybody', he spun too fast, lost control, stumbled. Then Vincent sighed and shook his head. 'Funny guy,' he said. 'When I was five, my father broke my arm. Twisted it until it snapped. Because he was drunk, and he hated me. But I didn't cry. Not one tear.'

Gradually, the floor began to fill; the night embarked in earnest. The girls emerged from their booths, formed ranks, and began to do the Bus Stop. A band appeared in blue denim suits embossed with silver studding. Blacks from Crown Heights, who played as loudly and as badly as anyone possibly could, grinning, sweating, stomping, while the dancers paraded beneath them, impassive.

One after another the stock favourites came churning out. 'Bad Luck' and 'Supernatural Thing', 'What a Difference a Day Made', 'Track of the Cat', each reduced to the same automaton chugging, interchangeable. Nobody looked and no one ever applauded. Still, the band kept pounding away, kept right on grinning. 'These guys. Those shines,' said Vincent. 'We wind them up like clockwork. We pay, and they perform.'

Outside, his companions sat in the car, Joey and Gus in the front, Eugene and John James in the back, drinking whisky from a bottle in a paper bag. They still made no conversation, did not relax. But as the alcohol hit, they started to mumble.

'Mother,' said Eugene.

'Fucker,' said Gus.

'Motherfuckin' right,' said Joey.

Sometime after ten, feeling ready, they stepped out on the sidewalk and moved toward Odyssey in a line, shoulder to shoulder, like gunslingers. Heads lowered, hands thrust deep in their pockets, they turned into the doorway. They paused for just an instant, right on the brink. Entered.

Vincent was already at work on the floor. By now the Faces had gathered in force, his troops, and he worked them like a quarterback, calling out plays. He set the formations, dictated every move. If a pattern grew ragged and disorder threatened, it was he who set things straight.

Under his command, they unfurled the Odyssey Walk, their own style of massed Hustle, for which they formed strict ranks. Sweeping back and forth across the floor in perfect unity, fifty bodies made one, while Vincent barked out orders, crying One, and Two, and One, and Tap. And Turn, and One, and Tap. And Turn. And Tap. And One.

They were like so many guardsmen on parade; a small battalion, uniformed in floral shirts and tight flared pants. No one smiled or showed the least expression. Above their heads, the black musicians honked and thrashed. But the Faces never wavered. Number after number, hour after hour, they carried out their routines, their drill. Absolute discipline, the most impeccable balance. On this one night, even Vincent, who was notoriously hard to please, could find no cause for complaint.

At last, content in a job well done, he took a break and went up into the bleachers, where he sat on a small terrace littered with empty tables and studied the scene at leisure, like a general reviewing a battlefield. From this distance, the action on the floor seemed oddly unreal, as though it had been staged. A young girl in green, with ash-blonde hair to her shoulders, stood silhouetted in a half-darkened doorway, posed precisely in left profile, and blew a smoke ring. Two Faces started arguing at the bar, fists raised. The dancers chugged about the floor relentlessly, and the band played 'Philadelphia Freedom'.

'How do you feel?' asked the man in the tweed suit.

'I'm thinking about my mother,' said Vincent.

'What of her?'

'She's getting old. Sometimes she feels so bad. If I was rich, I could buy her a house, somewhere on the Island, and she could take it easy.'

'What kind of house?'

'Big windows. Lots of light,' Vincent said, and he spread his hands, describing a shape like a globe. 'Space. Chickens in the yard. A grand piano. Grass,' he said. 'My mother likes grass. And blue sky.'

Down below, without his presence to keep control, the order was beginning to fall apart. Around the fringes, some of the dancers had broken away from the mainstream and were dabbling in experiments, the Hustle Cha, the Renaissance Bump, even the Merengue. Vincent looked pained. But he did not intervene. 'Chickens,' he said. 'They lay their own eggs.'

A fight broke out. From outside, it was not possible to guess exactly how it started. But suddenly Gus was on his back, bleeding, and a Face in a bright blue polka-dot shirt was banging his head against the floor. So Joey jumped on the Face's back. Then someone else jumped in, and someone else. After that there was no way to make out anything beyond a mass of bodies, littered half-way across the floor.

Vincent made no move; it was all too far away. Remote in his darkness, he sipped at a Coca-Cola and watched. The band played 'You Sexy Thing' and one girl kept screaming, only one.

'Is this the custom?' asked the man in the suit.

'It depends.'

'On what?'

'Sometimes people don't feel in the mood. Sometimes they do,' said Vincent. 'It just depends.'

In time, the commotion subsided, the main participants were ushered outside to complete their negotiations in private. Those left behind went back to dancing as if nothing had happened, and the band played 'Fly, Robin, Fly'.

John James, the Double J, appeared on the terrace, lean and gangling, with a chalky white face and many pimples. There was blood beneath his nose, blood on his purple crêpe shirt.

'Mother,' he said, sitting down at the table. 'Fucker,' said Vincent.

So the night moved on. The Double J talked about basketball, records, dances. Then he talked about other nights, other brawls. The music kept playing and the dancers kept on parading. From time to time a girl would stop and look up at the terrace, hoping to catch Vincent's eye. But he did not respond. He was still thinking about his mother.

Somebody threw a glass which shattered on the floor. But the Faces just went One, and Two, and Tap, and Turn. And Tap, and Turn, and Tap.

'I was in love once. At least I thought I was,' said Vincent. 'I was going to get engaged.'

'What happened?'

'My sister got sick and I had to stay home, waiting for the doctor. So I didn't get to the club until midnight. Bojangles, I think it was. And by then I was too late.'

'How come?'

'She danced with someone else.'

'Only danced?'

'Of course,' said Vincent, 'and after that, I could never feel the same. I couldn't even go near her. I didn't hate her, you understand. Maybe I still loved her. But I couldn't stand to touch her. Not when I knew the truth.'

Around two, the band stopped playing, the Faces grew weary, and the night broke up. Outside the door, as Vincent made his exit, trailed by his lieutenants, a boy and a girl were embracing, framed in the neon glow. And Vincent stopped; he stared. No more than two yards distant, he stood quite still and studied the kiss in closest detail, dispassionate, as though observing guinea pigs.

The couple did not look up and Vincent made no comment. Down the street, Joey was honking the car horn. 'God gave his only son,' said John James.

'What for?' said Vincent, absentmindedly.

'Rent,' replied the Double J.

It was then that something strange occurred. Across the street, in the darkness beyond a steel-mesh gate, the guard dogs still snarled and waited. Gus and Eugene stood on the curb directly outside the gate, laughing, stomping their feet. They were drunk and it was late. They felt flat, somehow dissatisfied. And suddenly they threw themselves at the steel wires, yelling.

The guard dogs went berserk. Howling, they reared back on their hind legs, and then hurled themselves at their assailants, smashing full force into the gate. Gus and Eugene sprang backwards, safely out of reach. So the dogs caught only air. And the Faces hooted, hollered. They made barking noises, they whistled, they beckoned the dogs towards them. 'Here, boys, here,' they said, and the dogs hurled forward again and again, in great surging waves, half maddened with frustration.

Even from across the street, the man in the suit could hear the thud of their bodies, the clash of their teeth on the wires. Gus sat down on the sidewalk, and he laughed so much it hurt. He clasped his sides, he wiped away tears. And Eugene charged once more. He taunted, he leered, he stuck out his tongue. Then he smacked right into the fence itself, and this time the dogs flung back with such frenzy, such total demonic fury, that even the steel bonds were shaken and the whole gate seemed to buckle and give.

That was enough. Somewhat chastened, though they continued to giggle and snicker, the Faces moved on. Behind them, the dogs still howled, still hurled themselves at the wires. But the Faces did not look back.

When they reached the car, they found Vincent already waiting, combing his hair. 'Where were you?' asked Gus.

'Watching,' said Vincent, and he climbed into the back, out of sight. Inside 2001 Odyssey, there was no more music or movement, the dance floor was deserted. Saturday night had ended, and Vincent slouched far back in his corner. His eyes were closed, his hands hung limp. He felt complete.

Another Saturday night. Easing down on Fifth and Ovington, Joey parked the car and went into the pizza parlour, the Elegante. Vincent and Eugene were already waiting. So was Gus. But John James was missing. Two nights before he had been beaten up and knifed, and now he was in the hospital.

It was an old story. When the Double J got home from work on Thursday evening, his mother had sent him out for groceries, down to Marinello's Deli. He had bought pasta and salad, toilet paper, a six-pack of Bud, a package of frozen corn, gum, detergent, tomato sauce, and four TV dinners. Paid up. Combed his hair in the window. Then went out into the street, cradling his purchases in both arms.

As he emerged, three Latins – Puerto Ricans – moved across the sidewalk towards him and one of them walked straight through him. Caught unawares, he lost his balance and his bag was knocked out of his arms, splattering on the curb.

Produce scattered everywhere, rolling in the puddles and filth. The frozen corn spilled into the gutter, straight into some dog mess, and the Latins laughed. 'Greaseballs,' said John James, not thinking. All that was on his mind was his groceries, the need to rescue what he'd lost. So he bent down and began to pick up the remnants. And the moment he did, of course, the Latins jumped all over him.

The rest was hazy. He could remember being beaten around the head, kicked in the sides and stomach, and he remembered a sudden sharp burn in his arm, almost as though he had been stung by an electric wasp. Then lots of shouting and scuffling, bodies tumbling all anyhow, enormous smothering weights on his face, a knee in the teeth. Then nothing.

In the final count, the damage was three cracked ribs, a splintered cheekbone, black eyes, four teeth lost, and a deep knife cut, right in the meat of his arm, just missing his left bicep.

'Three greaseballs at once,' said Gus. 'He could have run. But he wouldn't.'

'He stuck,' said Vincent. 'He hung tight.'

Judgement passed, the Faces finished their pizzas, wiped their lips, departed. Later on, of course, there would have to be vengeance, the Latins must be punished. For the moment, however, the feeling was of excitement, euphoria. As Eugene hit the street, he let out a whoop, one yelp of absolute glee. Saturday night, and everything was beginning, everything lay ahead of them once more.

But Vincent hung back, looked serious. Once again he had remembered a line, another gem from the screen. 'Hung tight,' he said, gazing up along the bleak street. 'He could have got away clean, no sweat. But he had his pride. And his pride was his law.'

Donna loved Vincent, had loved him for almost four months. Week after week she came to Odyssey just for him, to watch him dance, to wait. She sat in a booth by herself and didn't drink, didn't smile, didn't tap her foot or nod her head to the music. Though Vincent never danced with her, she would not dance with anyone else.

Her patience was infinite. Hands folded in her lap, knees pressed together, she watched from outside, and she did not pine. In her own style she was satisfied, for she knew she was in love, really, truly, once and for all, and that was the thing she had always dreamed of.

Donna was nineteen, and she worked as a cashier in a supermarket over towards Flatbush. As a child she had been much too fat. For years she was ashamed. But now she felt much better. If she held her breath, she stood five-foot-six and only weighed 140 pounds.

Secure in her love, she lived in the background. Vincent danced, and she took notes. He laughed, and she was glad. Other girls might chase him, touch him, swarm all over him. Still she endured, and she trusted.

And one Saturday, without any warning, Vincent suddenly turned toward her and beckoned her on to the floor, right in the middle of the Odyssey Walk, where she took her place in the line, three rows behind him, one rank to the left.

She was not a natural dancer, never had been. Big-boned, soft-fleshed, her body just wasn't right. She had good breasts, good hips, the most beautiful grey-green eyes. But her feet, her legs, were hopeless. Movement embarrassed her. There was no flow. Even in the dark, when she made love, or some boy used her for pleasure, she always wanted to hide.

Nonetheless, on this one night she went through the motions and nobody laughed. She kept her eyes on the floor: she hummed along with the songs. Three numbers went by without disaster. Then the dancers changed, moved from the Walk to something else, something she didn't know, and Donna went back to her booth.

335

Obscurity. Safety. She sipped Fresca through a straw and fiddled with her hair. But just as she was feeling stronger, almost calm again, Vincent appeared above her, his shadow fell across her just like in the movies, and he put his hand on her arm.

His shirt was pink and scarlet and yellow; her dress was pastel green. His boots were purple, and so were her painted lips. 'I'm leaving,' Vincent said, and she followed him outside.

His coat was creased at the back. He didn't know that, but Donna did; she could see it clearly as they walked out. And the thought of it, his secret weakness, made her dizzy with tenderness, the strangest sense of ownership.

'What's your name?' Vincent asked.

'Maria,' said Donna, 'Maria Elena.'

They sat in the back of Joey's car and Vincent pulled down her tights. There was no space, everything hurt. But Donna managed to separate her legs, and Vincent almost kissed her. 'Are you all right?' he asked.

'I love you,' said Donna.

'No, not that,' said Vincent. 'I mean, are you fixed?'

She wasn't, of course. She wasn't on the pill, or the coil, or anything. Somehow or other, she'd never got around to it. So Vincent went away. He simply took his body from hers, climbed out of the car. 'Vincent,' said Donna. But he was gone.

She didn't feel much, did not react in any way. For the next few minutes, she sat very still and tried not to breathe. Then she went home and she slept until noon the next day, a sleep of absolute immersion, so deep and so silent, she said later on, it felt like Mass.

Another week went by; another Saturday night arrived. But this time it was different. On Thursday afternoon she had bought her first packet of condoms. Now they nestled in her purse, snug upon her lap. She was prepared.

Everything seemed changed in her, resolved. Tonight she didn't sit alone, felt no need to hide. She danced every number whether anyone asked her or not. She drank Bacardi and Coke, she laughed a lot, she flapped her false eyelashes. She wore a blue crêpe blouse without any bra, and underneath her long black skirt, cut in the style of the '40s, her legs were bare.

Even when Vincent danced near her, she hardly seemed to notice. It was as if she were weightless, floating free. But when the man in the tweed suit sat down beside her in her plastic booth, in between dances, and asked her how she felt, she could not speak, could only place her hand above her heart, to keep it from exploding.

Finally, shortly after one o'clock, Vincent decided to leave. He disappeared towards the cloakroom to retrieve his coat, and while his back was turned, Donna slipped by, out on to the street, where she waited.

It was raining hard, had been raining all night. Turning up her collar, tightening the belt on her coat, which had once belonged to her older sister, Donna pressed back into the angle of the wall, right underneath the neon sign. And she began to talk. Normally she was cautious, very quiet. But now the words came out in a torrent, an uncontrollable flood, as though some dam had burst deep within her.

She talked about dances she had been to, clothes that her friends had bought, boys who had left her, a dog she had once owned. She talked about home and work, and the rain came down in a steady stream. Ten minutes passed. She said she wanted three children.

At last the door opened and Vincent came out, ducking his head against the downpour. The light fell full on Donna's face; she tried to smile. Her hair was slicked flat against her skull and Vincent looked her over with a look of vague surprise, as if he couldn't quite place her. Her make-up was smudged; the tip of her nose was red. She was fat. Vincent walked straight past her.

He went off down the street, moved out of sight, and Donna remained behind, still standing on the sidewalk. 'Oh,' she said, and she brought her hand up out of her left coat pocket, loosely holding the packet of unused condoms.

She opened it. Gently, methodically, she took out the sheaths and dangled them, squeezed between her forefinger and thumb. One by one, not looking, she dropped them in the wet by her feet. Then she went home again, back to sleep.

Another Saturday night. The man in the tweed suit was sitting in the bleachers, around one o'clock, when Eugene approached him and sat down at his table. 'Are you really going to write a story?' Eugene asked.

'I think so,' replied the man.

'There are some things I want you to put in. As a favour,' Eugene said. 'Things I'd like to say.'

He was lean and wiry, vaguely furtive, in the style of a human stoat, and his yellow shirt was emblazoned with scarlet fleurs-de-lis. His voice was high-pitched, squeaky; his left eye was forever squinting, half shut, as if warding off an invisible waft of cigarette smoke. At first glance he might have passed for an overgrown jockey. But his real ambition was to become a disc jockey, or possibly a TV quizmaster: 'Something daring. Anything. It doesn't matter what,' he said.

Now he wanted to declare himself, to make a statement, his testament.

'Go ahead,' the man said. 'Tell me.'

'First,' said Eugene, 'I want to mention my mother and father, my brothers, my uncle Tony, my grandmother. Also, Roy and Butch at Jones Beach, and Charlie D. in Paterson. And Alice, she knows why.'

'Anyone else?'

'And everyone, as well.'

The way he spoke, measured, remote, it was as though he addressed them from a very great distance, an alien world. From prison, perhaps, or an army camp. Or some secret underground, a Saturday-night cabal, known only to initiates. 'Is that all?' asked the man in the suit.

'Just tell them hello,' said Eugene, 'and you can say I get by.'

On Wednesday evening, to help time pass, Vincent went to see *The Man Who Would Be King* and, rather to his surprise, he liked it very much. On his own admission, he did not understand it, not entirely, for India and the Raj were too far away, much too unreal to make any practical sense. Still, he enjoyed the colour and flash, the danger, the sense of everything being possible, all dreams of adventure coming true.

Afterwards, he sat on a low wall outside a basketball court, across the street from the high rise, and considered. The man in the suit was there again, asking more questions. So Vincent talked about living on the eleventh floor, his windows that looked out on nothing, the smell. And working in a housewares store, selling paint and climbing ladders, grinning for his living. 'Sucks,' he said. 'They've got me by the balls.'

'How about the future?' asked the man in the suit.

'What future?' Vincent said, and he looked askance, as though the man must be retarded to ask such a question. This was not the Raj; he was not floating in a film. There were dues to pay, people to support. That took money. And money, in this place, meant imprisonment.

Still the man persisted, asked him to imagine. Just conceive that he was set free, that every obstacle was suddenly removed and he could be whatever he pleased. What would he do then? What would give him the greatest pleasure of all, the ultimate fulfilment?

Vincent took his time. This was another dumb question, he knew that. Yet the vision intrigued him, sucked him in almost despite himself. So he let his mind roam loose. Sitting on the wall, he bent his head, contemplated the cracks in the sidewalk. Pondered. Made up his mind. 'I want to be a star,' he said.

'Such as?' asked the man in the suit.

'Well,' said Vincent, 'someone like a hero.'

Six weeks passed. Six more weeks of drudgery, six more Saturdays. The Odyssey began to wind down, lose its novelty. It was time to move on. But no replacement had been found, not as yet. So there was a hiatus. The Faces kept in training, waiting for the next step. A fresh sensation, another explosion. Meanwhile, they marked time.

Sure enough, their patience paid off. Outside the pizza parlour, on another Saturday night, Joey, Vincent, the Double J, and Eugene sat waiting in the Dodge, raring to go. But Gus did not show up.

Twenty minutes passed, then thirty, forty. They were almost ready to go on without him. Then suddenly he came out of the shadows, running, burning. His face was flushed; he was all out of breath. Too wild to make sense, he could only spew out obscenities, kick at the kerb, pound his fists, impotent, on the body of the car.

At last he simmered down, choked out his explanations. And the news was indeed enormous. That afternoon, just three hours earlier, his younger sister, Gina, had been molested, debauched, as she crossed a children's playground in the park.

Gus poured out the story. After his sister had finished her lunch, she went to the apartment of her best friend Arlene, who lived about ten blocks away. Both of them were eleven years old and together they spent the afternoon nibbling chocolate candies, trying out different make-up, sighing over photographs of Donny Osmond. Then Gina walked home in the dusk, alone, wrapped in her imitation-leather coat, which was short and showed off her legs. Soon she came to McKinley Park. To make a shortcut, she turned off the street and headed across the park playground.

It was getting dark and the playground was empty, spooky. Gina hastened. Halfway across, however, a man appeared, coming from the opposite direction. He had wispy hair and a wispy beard, and he was talking to himself. When Gina came level with him, he stopped and stared. 'Pretty. Pretty. Pretty,' he said. Just like that. And he looked at her legs, straight at her kneecaps, with a strange smile, a smile that made her want to run. So she did. She sped out of the playground, into the street, down the block.

Just as she reached the sanctuary of her own hallway, Gus was coming down the stairs. So she bumped straight into him, jumped into his arms. 'What's wrong?' he said. But she couldn't say. She just dug her nails into his arms, and she sort of sighed. Then she burst into tears.

He carried her upstairs, cradled like an infant. In time, she was comforted, she calmed down. Finally she told her story, was put to bed, and soon fell asleep. Now all that remained was revenge.

Vengeance. When Gus completed his story, he laid his forehead against the roof of the Dodge in order to feel something cold against his skull, which seemed as though it were burning. There he rested for a moment, recovering. Then he straightened up, and he banged his clenched fist into the meat of his left palm, once, twice, three times, just like on TV. 'Mother,' he said. 'I'll kill him.'

'Tear his heart out,' said Joey. 'Fuck him in the place he lives.'

'Cut off both his legs,' said Vincent. 'Kill him. Yes.'

They all knew who it was. They didn't even have to ask. In Vincent's own building there was a man called Benny, a wimp who had wispy hair and a wispy beard, who shuffled, and he was really weird. He had these crazy staring eyes, this horrible fixed stare. Everyone steered clear of him. Nobody would talk to him or go close to him. Children threw stones to make him go away. Still he hung around, staring.

No question, he was diseased. One day a bunch of kids had waited for him in the park, jumped him, and tried to teach him a lesson. But he would not learn. The more they abused him, beat on him, the stranger he became. He talked to himself, he mumbled stuff that no one could understand. And often, late at night, blind drunk, he would stand outside people's windows, yell and carry on and keep them from their sleep.

And now this. The final outrage. So the Faces drove back towards the high-rise, piled out of the car, descended on the building in a wedge.

Enforcers. Vigilantes. In silence, they came to Benny's door and Gus rang the bell, banged on the door. A minute passed and there was no answer. Gus banged again. Still no reply. Inside the apartment, everything seemed quiet, absolutely still. Gus banged a third time, a fourth, and then he lost patience. He started raging, kicking the door, barging into it with his shoulder. But nobody moved inside or made a sound, and the door would not give way.

Defeated, the Faces stood around in the hallway, feeling vaguely foolish. At first their instinct was simply to wait it out, keep a vigil till Benny came home. But within a few minutes, hanging about, doing nothing, that plan lost its attraction. The hall was deserted, there was no sign of action. Just standing there grew boring, and they started to fret.

Loitering outside the front doorway, aimless, it was Eugene who came up with the solution. 'I don't care. No sweat,' he said. 'Somebody's going to pay.'

'Motherfuckin' right,' said Gus, and he slammed his fist into his palm again; he threw a right cross into space. 'Those greaseball bastards.'

'Mothers,' said the Double J.

'Those motherfuckin' freaks,' said Gus. 'We're going to rip them apart.' And the man in the tweed suit, who had been watching, was forgotten. The Faces looked past him, hardly seemed to recognize his shape. 'We're going,' said the Double J.

'Where to? Odyssey?' asked the man.

'Hunting,' said Gus.

They moved back to the car, they clambered inside. Of course, the man in the suit wanted to go along, wanted to watch, but they wouldn't let him. They said that he didn't belong, that this was no night for tourists, spectators. He tried to argue but they would not hear him. So he was left behind on the sidewalk, and they travelled alone.

But just before the Dodge moved off, Vincent rolled down his window, looked out into the dark. His face was immobile, frozen, in the best style of Al Pacino. 'What is it?' asked the man in the suit.

Vincent laughed, exulted. 'Hombre, you will die,' he said, to no one in particular. And the Faces drove away, off into Saturday night. Horsemen. A posse seeking retribution, which was their due, their right.

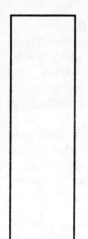

Tu Sweet, No Sweat

U p in Rockland County, they staged the Great American Disco Contest. According to the advertisements, 20,000 feet would engage in the most spectacular Hustle contest ever held, with $1,000 to be won. So I boarded a hired bus and rode interminably through the night, until I arrived at a monstrous concrete fortress, and a sign that read, THIS WAY TO THE HUSTLE OF YOUR DREAMS.

Once inside, the vision was less impressive. The multitude of feet had shrunk to a few hundred; the prize money took five weeks and many dire threats to materialize; and the standard of dancing, by and large, was strictly kindergarten. But there was one blinding exception. Way off to the edge of the stage there was, quite simply, the best street dancer that I'd ever seen.

Physically, he was a most extravagant string bean, manufactured out of black elastic, and his silhouette came straight from a Tenniel cartoon – legs that reached to his armpits, a small head stuck on top, and a wisp of goatee. All around him, the other contestants pounded and whirled and sweated, rubbed raw with effort. But he merely floated, lost in a private time warp.

No heat or fury, no flailing limbs – he worked inside a space about six feet square and, within the basic patterns of the Hustle, created a choreography all his own, filled with loops and dips, double takes, sudden freezes, ebbs and flows, while his partner, a girl called Debbie, cleaved to him like his second self.

Backstage in his trailer, meanwhile, the promoter nibbled morosely at a plate of congealed macaroni and counted his losses, while his subordinates walked on tiptoe and spoke with averted faces, like professional mourners. 'Poor baby. He's really taken a bath,' his publicist said, and the stricken impresario choked. 'A bath?' he groaned. 'I'm stripped to the bone.'

On this note, the competition trailed away, and the string bean was rewarded with a tie for first place. It was an injustice so rank that even his rival competitors jeered. But he only shrugged, walked away without a backward look. 'They call me Tu Sweet,' he said, when I cornered him. 'That means 'right on' in French, and that's the way I am.'

He was stranded, flat broke. So I brought him back to Manhattan and he took me to a disco called Othello, a marvellous place on Eighth Avenue, where he held court. 'I've been around. I have known sadness,' said Tu Sweet, sipping on a Grand Marnier and Coke. 'But this is my time. The cards are stacked, and I can't be denied.'

His saga proved long and labyrinthine. He was a man who liked to talk, no doubt of that, and by the time he paused for breath, it was dawn. I had exhausted two notebooks, and the final chapters lay scattered across the dance floor, scrawled on drink mats, Kleenex and the backs of envelopes.

Apparently, his father had been a celebrated champion of the jitterbug who had won contests through the South, back in the Depression. When Tu Sweet was a small child, his family had broken up, and he was parcelled off to New York. He grew up rootless, running loose. Dropped out of school, decided against work, ran with the gangs. And, as he ran, he danced.

At one point, he revisited his father. The one-time jitterbug, now middle-aged and slow, had become a maintenance man, a jack-of-all-trades, and Tu Sweet was horrified. How could anyone born to dance fall so low, settle for so little? 'Right then, deep down in my blood, I knew I was a star, and that was my true destiny.'

Back in New York he danced the boogaloo, the merengue, and the Funky Broadway, winning contests throughout the five boroughs. But just as his reputation was building, the law came to call, and he spent the next three years in jail.

According to one rumour, he had killed the man who raped his sister, having tracked him non-stop for eighteen months. His own version, however, was less romantic. 'Armed robbery,' he said. 'But I was falsely evicted. I wasn't there; it only look like me; I couldn't afford a proper lawyer. And besides, I never meant no harm.'

When he was released, a year ago, he was twenty-four and his prospects didn't look bright. 'Still, like I always say, comes the hour, comes the man. Before I was hardly out, the Hustle jumped up.'

It started in the Barrio, then worked its way outwards, to Brooklyn, Queens, the Bronx. Along the way it got simplified, cheapened, and soon it was turned into hit records, great fortunes. Now contests sprang up like mushrooms, and Tu Sweet was back in business. In no time, he'd racked up a trip to Atlantic City, a week's free groceries at K-Mart, a fistful of New York City bonds: 'You name it. If I didn't want it, I won it.'

At this point, enter Debbie. She had been studying dance since she was three, had graduated in jazz and rock from the High School of Performing Arts. But she had never found the perfect partner, the mirror image she craved. So, the moment she saw the Tu Sweet shuffle, she grabbed him. 'Almost creased my good new jacket, and I got mad,' he said. 'One thing I can't stand, it's when the young ladies beg me to dance and they can't cut it, they mess up all my moves. But Debbie, she was different. She was so good, she could have been me.'

Since then, contests have kept them alive. Most weeks they entered two or three, and they almost always won. 'Ask anyone. They'll tell you,' he said. So I did, and the answers came in tones of bug-eyed awe. 'This man,' said one bystander sagely, stuffing a note up his left nostril, 'is *the* man. The Master.'

Still, he was not satisfied. Over the months the Hustle had lost its novelty. Now every high school nobody, every pimpled suburban could do it, and the Master was bored. Besides, his style was not truly suited to public competition, which was usually judged by audience applause and, therefore, went to whomever sweated most, indulged in the grossest grandstanding. 'Pigsty stuff,' said Tu Sweet. 'Just a lot of clowning, faking, and kicking up your feet.

That's not the Hustle, and I know for sure it's not Art.'

So now he was looking for fresh pastures. He was giving lessons, working in a dance school, scheming to open his own studio. And, most important, he had devised the moves that I'd seen in Rockland County, his own routine, which lay within the basic Hustle tradition, yet was so personal and complex that it formed a whole new dance. 'I call it the Tu Sweet,' he said, which figured. 'Now all I need is a sponsor, someone with a little bread and faith, and then, no sweat. I know I could sweep the nation, just like they say in the magazines.'

In particular, he saw himself in TV commercials. 'Like they bring out the Rice-A-Roni and its tastes so good, everyone just has to do the Tu Sweet,' he suggested. 'Or how about this? "*Mmmm, I'm in that Tu Sweet mood, and it's all thanks to, aahhh, Brut by Fabergé*." '

For the moment, however, all these dreams hung fire. His rent was overdue, his best costumes were all in hock, and Debbie was about to desert him, zipping off to Puerto Rico with a chorus line. For all his talent and achievements, he owned nothing. And as the night wore on, and the Grand Marnier and Coke took its toll, he began to grieve most sore. 'They call me the black Astaire, the Nureyev of the Hustle,' he said. 'But what good does it do? Like I saw Nureyev on TV, and I thought he was real fine. But how could he work like this? If his partner just walked out the door? And he couldn't get his tights back from the cleaners?'

Ms All-Bare America

T he other week, at the Beacon Theatre, I donned my best
    tuxedo and witnessed the election of the second Ms All-
    Bare America. According to the ads, it was 'the honest
beauty pageant, because the contestants have nothing to hide.'

It proved a most engrossing evening. Rod Swenson, the
organizer, had promised in advance that this was to be no tacky
throwaway, no one-shot peep-show. He intended a fantasia, such
a dazzle that all competitors would be put to shame, and to this
end he had drummed up a covey of fashion sponsors; a panel of
judges that included Jim Rosenquist; Andy Warhol's Tinkerbelle;
and Joe Bonomo, Mr Modern Apollo of 1919, the mythic Her-
cules of the Silver Screen; plus the Dictators, the world's rankest
roll 'n' roll band, to provide appropriate fanfares. He had even
persuaded Don Imus, the NBC DJ, to act as *compère*, resplendent in rented tails and brown suede shoes.

This was only the beginning. Next year, said Swenson, the
pageant would go out on closed-circuit TV, transmitted live to
cinemas all over the country. The whole of America would
watch, transfixed. Giant corporations would struggle to get their
names on the billing, and the girl who won would rise to instant
glory. In the long run, he believed, he was handling a multi-
million-dollar proposition. 'Commercial nudity may be a hype; I
don't deny that,' he said. 'But it's a hype with class, and basic

347

truth. Deep down, we're talking about freedom.'

Twenty-five finalists had been selected, of whom about fifteen turned up on the night. Apparently, most of them were not professional models but secretaries, salesgirls, nurses, lured by the prizes and the vision of instant glory. But the first thing that intrigued me, before the show began, was the audience, who had paid up to $15 a head.

I had expected a sea of men in dirty raincoats: I was entirely wrong. Something like forty per cent of the audience were women, mostly accompanied by husbands or boyfriends, and the general mood was of jovial family entertainment, a night out at the varieties. True, the more popular contestants were greeted with shouts and whistles, but basically, it was a night of utmost decorum. 'A lot of them come from New Jersey. I guess they're a bit overawed,' said the man on my left, who seemed to be an expert. And sure enough, in their sport coats and bright-coloured socks, or in their boufants and frilled blouses, they reminded me of nothing so much as the fans at a Country-and-Western show – genial, gum-chewing, a trifle dazed.

The pageant itself fell into three stages. First, the girls appeared clothed, in their sponsored overalls, Hot Sox and suspenders, while Don Imus read out their ages and measurements, home towns, ambitions, and their reasons for entering the contest. 'Because we are entering very beautifully into the future,' said one. 'Because I want to spread what is inside my body to the general public,' said another. 'My inner glow. My ecology.'

Next, they came out topless, for a 'personality segment', in which Imus asked them how they were, did they feel nervous, and what would they do if they won. And finally, they were completely naked, parading patiently, like race horses in a paddock, while all clapped politely. 'Let's hear a big hand,' said Imus, blowing his nose, 'for these fine, young, *American* women.'

On the whole, as sex goddesses go, they were a mite lacking. 'Canines,' said the sage on my left, succinctly, and I could not argue. On stage, smothered in make-up, they just about passed muster. But upstairs in the dressing rooms, during the interval, the pimple count was prodigious. Queuing up in front of the mirrors, the contestants slapped on the camouflage, in layer upon layer of powder. Even so, the varicose veins, sagging breasts, and cream-bun bellies were inescapable. As one of the girls said herself: 'When you've got stretch marks on your eyelids, it's bad, bad news from the neck down.'

Still, the audience raised no objections. Right from the outset, their predilections were clear. What they cared about were breasts, the more gigantic the better. Shape and condition were irrelevant; all that mattered was volume. In fact, the biggest cheer of the evening went to a lady truckdriver with the shoulders of a George Foreman, the belly of Jackie Gleason, and a chest straight off a men's room wall. 'Why did you enter this contest?' Imus asked, consulting his notes. 'None of your fuckin' business,' came the swift reply.

The winner, Lyn Lindgred from St Louis, was in roughly the same mould: a petite, sturdy blonde with a toothpaste grin that never wavered and breasts that might have daunted Hugh Hefner himself. 'Truly a prodigious development,' pronounced the sage. 'This is a very great honour,' cried Lyn.

Up on stage, after the result had been announced, photographers formed a solid phalanx, clicking away in a frenzy. Lyn had won $2,000, plus a Caribbean vacation: 'We made it! We made it!' she squealed, ecstatic. But already ugly murmurs were afoot. Something was not quite kosher in the voting, apparently. 'An outrage has been committed,' claimed an embittered loser. Voices were raised. Tears flowed. And a few days later, the original verdict was reversed, so that the title was finally shared between Lyn and one Lisa Alligood, a staunch young trouper from Macon, Georgia, who had previously been placed third.

Rod Swenson did not despair. A golden-tanned, balding man with a small satyr's beard, he had known the extremes of triumph and tragedy before. Having studied art at Yale, he'd later turned impresario and been largely responsible for the commercial exploitation of Granola. Not once but repeatedly he had been on the brink of making millions. But somehow he had always contrived to miss out in the final reel, and adversity had taught him philosophy. 'Just a small misunderstanding,' he said, looking back on the débâcle. 'We'll be back again next year, no problem. Nude shows are here to stay. That's the way society is moving, and you can't hold back progress.'

*

In all of these shenanigans, one girl stood quite apart. Her name was Tamara Ward. She was twenty-three and she came from Greensboro, North Carolina. Close on six feet tall, she had long blonde hair, bad skin, and the most extraordinary breasts, which not only drooped downwards but sideways, like the ears of a beagle on the run. 'I am not beautiful, am I?' she asked, eyes downcast. And, objectively, she wasn't. Still, she was hard to forget.

Her teeth were good; she had a nice smile. Clothed, she looked like a majorette or a drugstore waitress, a slightly soiled teen-dream, and every time that anyone spoke to her, she collapsed in giggles, shied away like a startled luncheonette Bambi, because she was uncontrollably bashful.

Before the show, she had been terrified. She sat in a corner, shaking, and thought she couldn't go on. When the moment finally came, however, and she walked out on stage, it felt as though she'd been possessed by somebody else, masquerading in her flesh. Suddenly, she was transformed, released, and she caught fire. While most of her rivals stumbled and lurched, made spastic by embarrassment, she sauntered in perfect ease, loving every moment. Pirouetting, strutting, with her hair swirling free down her back and her mouth half-opened in a pout, she never wanted to stop, and when at last she took her bow, she posed with her hips aslant, brazen, like a lady beneath a lamplight.

Afterwards, she couldn't understand it; this wasn't like her at all. Back home in Greensboro, she worked in an office, tended a terrarium, baked her own bread. She went back-packing on week-ends, she liked to dance and sing along to the Top Forty. 'Nothing special. I could be anyone,' she said.

Her great trouble was that she was too emotional. According to her astrological chart, in which she believed implicitly, she was intuitive, compassionate, idealistic, and intensely sensitive. She tended to lose herself in fantasies and could not cope with real life. As a result, she was not lucky in love because her feelings always ran away with her. Sometimes, especially when she drank vodka, she went a bit crazy and boys thought that she was wanton. That hurt her deeply, she couldn't live with it. So now the truest loves of her life were her dogs, which she called Mamma and Baby. The last time she could remember crying, in fact, was when she'd had to give away some puppies.

As for the contest, she had originally entered as a joke, because a friend had dared her to. So she drove up to New York, presented Rod Swenson with a loaf of her home-baked bread, and was duly selected for the finals. Even then, she didn't take it seriously. 'None of this can be real,' she said, the first time I met her. 'I can't believe it's me.'

This was at a press conference held in a basement discotheque and we stood together in the murk, sipping New York State champagne out of plastic glasses. The music was deafening, the crush unbearable. But Tamara was transported. Nightclubs, champagne, the Big Apple: 'It's like a dream come true,' she said eyes glistening, and she placed her hand gently upon her heart, as though to still its fluttering.

The excitement had just begun. Over the next week, to help with Swenson's promotion campaign, she appeared on radio shows, simpered on daytime TV, was photographed at the Statue of Liberty and on top of the Empire State Building. The thrills seemed never ending.

At the same time, she was terrified. The day of reckoning was approaching fast, and she felt completely paralysed. She couldn't adjust to the strange city, didn't dare go out alone, in case she got lost. She had no friends here, no one she could talk to. At night, she couldn't settle to sleep because she missed her dogs and was worried in case they might pine away without her.

Now all that was over. In the intermission, immediately after her first triumphal unveiling, she was in the communal dressing room and she could hardly speak, she was in such a daze. All around her, there were bored New York girls, powdering and preening. But Tamara sat without moving, hugging her knees, and when I squatted down beside her, I could hear her teeth chattering.

Later, she would be voted second and, presumably, she has since gone back to Greensboro. For a moment, however, none of that mattered. She had performed, and people had cheered for her. For a few seconds, she had not been frightened at all and now she didn't speak, seemed lost in deep meditation.

After a minute, I asked her what she was thinking about that so immersed her. Then she looked up, and she folded her arms across her bare breasts. 'Mamma,' she said, 'and Baby.'

Nowhere
To Run

Friday night, the second weekend in May, the temperature stayed in the eighties. It was the first true night of summer. And the moment the streets turned hot, so did the cars.

All over New York, everywhere but Manhattan, drivers came out from hibernation and went drag racing. They ran in the streets, through traffic, over and under expressways. Anywhere they could find a clean quarter mile.

In Brooklyn, the number-one venue was Fountain Avenue, outside Starrett City. The road ran straight and wide, through the middle of a reconstructed swamp, where nobody lived. During daylight, there was only urban wasteland; storage yards, depots, dumps. But on this Friday night the strip was lined solid, both sides, with hot rods of every style.

At first sight, the congregants seemed a hopeless jumble. Whites, Blacks, Latins clustered at random. Some called themselves Speeds, while others preferred Street Runners. Full-time hustlers mingled with high school punks, jive artists with true mechanics. And they rode in everything from gleaming track cars to scrap-heap wrecks, pick-up trucks and vans, street-legal showboats, resurrected antiques.

They raced for many different reasons. For money, or prestige, or simply for speed, for the act. But all of them, in the end, shared one common cause. They had come here to explode, in the death of the long winter. To rev and roar, and burn in the night heat.

Through the winter, Greg Hansen painted houses with his father, paying off last summer's debts. By the beginning of May, he was finally squared away, and he put aside his brushes, headed back to Tony Gaff's, to cars, and to his other self, the street runner who was called Hawkeye.

Tony Gaff's was a speed shop in Queens, in Richmond Hill. It stood in a giant tin shed off Atlantic Avenue, across from the Long Island Rail Road freight yards. In earlier years, this shed had been a foundry, supplying steel for the Empire State Building, iron girders for the Verrazano-Narrows Bridge. But that was in another time. Now it was half-derelict, with a towing service in the back and the Gaff up front, surrounded by rubble.

Nobody much came around. Apart from Hawkeye himself, there was Big Pete, his right hand, and Don, who was going to be a cop, and Ray Pompano, the owner of the entire shed, and his two sons, Chicken and Pancho, and a Latin who did paint jobs, and a Black who swept up, and sometimes Kevin from the Island, who was also going to be a cop, and maybe one or two others, faces from way back, who still dropped by to relive the past. But hardly any strangers. No one new or moneyed, paying cash on the line.

It wasn't always like this. In the late '60s, when the Gaff first opened up, it was a citadel, a major gathering place, known throughout the boroughs. Street running was in its golden age. Gas was cheap and limitless; cars were built for speed. In Richmond Hill, if you didn't race, you did not belong.

Then the '70s came and things went to pieces. Suddenly the media started harping on pollution, energy crises, the ecology. Cars slowed down and costs went sky-high. On top of which, there was also the recession, making people play safe, close ranks. So the streets emptied out. Runners took shelter in the discos. And Tony Gaff went broke.

Hawkeye took over. He had been hanging around since he was sixteen. At first he did odd jobs. Then he started to race. Within a year, he'd become the best in Queens.

Cars obsessed him: they always had. Not just their speed but everything about them – their stylings, their feel, the way they smelled, the roar when you unleashed their power, the tiniest detail of their mechanisms. From childhood on, all he wanted was to spend his life underneath some machine, getting covered in oil and grease, eternally messing.

Long before he could legally drive, he had picked up his first set of wheels, a '61 Plymouth, which he bought from a woman down the block for $15 cash. It never travelled beyond his backyard, didn't even possess an engine. But he cherished it, kept it gleaming. In his mind he already raced. When he sat behind the steering wheel, motionless, nobody born could out-run him.

This was his escape. Elsewhere in his life, he found himself shackled, held down. He was a high school dropout, caught in living-death jobs. Everything was an ambush. Everything but wheels. In speed alone, he was released.

He was skinny, raw-boned; he did not shave. Everybody treated him like a younger brother. But already he carried visions, an inner compulsion, that would not be crushed. 'I stand up. I don't back down,' he said. 'I believe.'

At fifteen, in 1968, he was working in a local luncheonette when he met a man named Lee, much older than himself. By profession, Lee was a thief; in his spare time, he was also a number-one Speed. Within the neighbourhood, he was a serious star. So Greg became his follower and rode with him everywhere, a hot-rod Sancho Panza.

Travelling with Lee, he received a full street education. He learned how to run and how to hustle. How to hold his cool under pressure. How and when to win. How to stay alive when he lost.

It was Lee who brought him to the Gaff, where he found sanctuary. Here was all the grease, din, mess that he had ever craved. More than a shop, it seemed like a shrine. Straight away, it became his second home.

The Plymouth was replaced by a '64 Chevy and then by a '69 Road Runner, which he made into his first full-fledged racer. It took him six months and cost $5,000, sweated out on construction sites, siphoned off from 'Midnight Auto Supplies'. But when the machine was complete, it was a masterpiece.

He was eighteen years old; he was ready. When Lee got himself arrested, went inside, the apprenticeship was over. Then Greg went hunting in the streets to take his mentor's place, become number one himself. He raced anywhere there was action. On 150th Street, on the Nassau Expressway, on Cross Bay Boulevard. And on the Brooklyn Queens Expressway, right beside Calvary Cemetery.

The BQE, in those years, was a New York institution. Four or five times a week, right through the summer, racers would congregate *en masse*. Crowds of two, three thousand were nothing unusual. Families brought sandwiches and flasks. Old women watched from deck chairs; gamblers descended like locusts. When everyone was assembled, a couple of the runners pulled sideways across the strip, blocking off traffic. Then the shoot-outs commenced.

Faced by such numbers, the police were powerless. All they could do was bide their time until the excitement peaked. Then they'd turn on the fire hydrants, flooding the course, and the crowds dispersed, satisfied, like an audience after a movie.

Mostly, these nights were celebrations, street carnivals on wheels. But sometimes there were misfortunes. Young kids, for a dare, would encroach on the strip, flirt with the approaching cars, then back out of danger at the last possible instant. Not infrequently they jumped too late. Or the drivers swerved, lost control. If they were killed, the other runners called it 'eating a tree.'

For three seasons running, upwards of 500 races, Greg and the Road Runner went unbeaten. He raced for free, for a beer, for $1,000. Challengers came from the Island, the Bronx, from New Jersey and upstate New York. He turned them back, every one.

That's when he began to be known as Hawkeye. Because his instinct was infallible and his concentration never wavered. He could spot a faulty connection at forty paces, diagnose a tune-up in the dark. Anything to do with wheels, he seemed psychic.

His third unbeaten year was '72. Afterwards, things were never so good again. Rising costs were starting to bite, and so was media propaganda. The law toughened up. The runners themselves grew older. One by one, the denizens of the Gaff began to drift away, get married or get a job, go straight.

Hawkeye endured. The following spring, as usual, he started tuning the Road Runner, preparing for the new season. But one day, as he worked, the jack gave way and the car collapsed on his chest. Somehow he got his arms up, managed to hold off the full force, so that he was not totally crushed. Even so, there were three broken ribs and dozens of burst blood vessels.

Even when his body recovered, his morale did not. Instinctively, he believed that the car had turned against him, betrayed him. His own machine. He never drove it again.

This was his first setback; others followed. There were cars that crashed, cars that blew up, and cars that simply ran slow. He began to suffer defeats. For the first time, at twenty-one, he was conscious of passing time. The notion did not thrill him.

Love was another problem. From the age of sixteen he had dated a girl called Charlene. She was cute, she cared. In return Hawkeye said and believed that he loved her, and they planned on getting married.

For Charlene that meant no cars. As a husband, Hawkeye must give up the Gaff, become a regular civilian. 'A married man is a grown man. He lives in the real world,' she said.

'I know it,' Hawkeye replied, and almost meant it. So they kissed, they made love. Afterwards, he spoke of going back to the construction sites, and Charlene was content.

He did his best. For days, weeks, months on end, he'd stop racing. But then some Speed would draw up beside him, without warning, and challenge him. And he could not resist. Automatic, his foot came down, smashed the accelerator to the floorboard, and he was gone. Off running, flying, one more time.

Finally, Charlene had enough. They had been together seven years, which seemed to her like always. After all the promises, the attempted reformations, nothing had changed, and nothing would.

The last straw was her birthday. Hawkeye had meant to take her out, celebrate in style, but when the time came, he was flat broke. So he went out on the Nassau Expressway with his last $4 and turned it into $500. He bought her dresses, baubles, all kinds of stuff. But she sensed how they'd been financed and was incensed. She felt like a kept woman, pimped by a Chevrolet. So she left him, this time for good. She found herself another boyfriend, a cop at Port Authority, who earned a steady dollar and had clean fingernails.

Hawkeye did not complain. He hurt but didn't whine. Deepest down, he understood that Charlene was right. So he let her go, and went back inside the Gaff, where he belonged.

With street action in decline, the shop had turned from a citadel into a foxhole. Its inmates formed a cabal, an underground resistance. Speed might be outlawed now. But someday it would arise, rule again. And when it did, they would be waiting, their engines primed and ready.

Thus it proved. As the '70s ran down, they seemed increasingly barren. On the streets, there was a revulsion against Clean. Once again, kids opted for hot machines, and living in the fast lane.

Down on Fountain Avenue, a new generation appeared. Street-running rookies, they had never raced before, could often barely drive. Enthusiastic, hopeless, they revved loud, talked big. Then Hawkeye came by and picked them clean.

It was easy. But not satisfying. He was used to competition, challenge, and this was automatic. For the first time, the streets began to bore him. Once they had meant release. Now they'd become another trap. Even so, he could not leave them. They were all he understood.

It was 1978 and he was twenty-five. But he looked years older. His beard was grizzled, his long hair receding, and he never looked quite clean, no matter how much he scrubbed. The years of grease and oil had saturated his flesh, stained through to his insides. As for his eyes, deep set, dazed by blowtorches, they were permanently wearied.

Something had to change. And something did. He had a friend called Carson, one of the Gaff originals. Like himself, Carson had outgrown the streets. But now he had found a replacement, which he preached like a new gospel. He had started racing on an authorized stock-car track, Freeport Speedway, out on Long Island. Drivers called it a Rounde-Round; Carson called it salvation. 'Just one lap,' he claimed, 'and a Speed is born again.'

So Hawkeye tried it out. Borrowing Carson's machine, a '73 Mustang, he hit the heater, took off. Everything felt normal. Then he came into the first turn and went into a slide. Instantly, the Mustang went berserk, was transformed into a maddening bronc, bucking, rearing, flinging him every which way. First it charged at the wall, then swerved back inside, then charged again. Using all his force, Hawkeye could only just control it.

He completed the lap. He slowed. Pulling over to the infield, he halted and found that he was shaking, a little bit from shock but mostly from adrenaline, pure blood exultation. 'The greatest lay I ever had,' he said, as soon as he could speak.

Every Saturday night, through the summer of '78, he returned. He competed in the Bomber division, which was legalized kamikaze. And he won. At the end of the season he was voted Rookie of the Year.

The money wasn't much. In the whole summer he earned less than $1,000. But cash was not the point. At Freeport he felt like a professional. His picture appeared in the official programme. Young girls giggled, stared. And this was only the start. Once Freeport had been conquered, he intended to move on and up, go national.

His first need was finance. Lenihan's, a bar on Atlantic, already supplied him with free uniforms. But what he wanted was a full-time sponsor. A bank, perhaps. Or a cigarette company. Someone, anyone, to take care of his expenses, keep him alive and running, until he came into his time.

Such were his dreams. And when next spring came, he couldn't wait to get back to the Gaff. In the summer of '79 he would win the Bomber championship, find himself a backer, then set sail for stardom. Meanwhile, to keep himself in funds, he'd run the streets, one last time.

With all this in mind, he girded himself for one almighty effort: 'Do or die, now or never, back to the wall, take no prisoners, let it all hang out, and devil take the hindmost,' Hawkeye said. 'Here I make my stand.'

<table>
<tr><td>

PART

2

</td><td>

The first Friday night, Hawkeye arrived at Fountain late. The racing had started around ten, but he waited his time, let midnight pass. Then he drove down in a borrowed Chevelle. Don and Big Pete followed in a Ford van.

</td></tr>
</table>

Then came Kevin in another Chevelle, and Carson in a beat-up Camaro. Together, they formed a miniature convoy. Rolling towards the starting line, they travelled abreast, like a posse, like enforcers riding in, and the other runners held back, instinctively gave way.

There was a crowd of maybe 800, but Hawkeye recognized few faces, even fewer machines. There were Superfly Blacks in caps and shoes, Latins in six-inch heels, whites in satin disco shirts. There were motorcycles and blaring radios. There was even one girl Speed, a raunchy brunette with a black Corvette and a customized T-shirt which read; 'If you beat me, you can eat me.'

For a time he was content to watch from the sidelines. The runners rolled two by two, as though on a conveyor belt, without passion or any real sense of combat. Two taxis showed up and raced for loose change. Then two garbage trucks, and they raced as well. When a track car appeared, a '77 Trans Am, it didn't even deign to race but simply stood on display, grandiose, like a public monument.

Finally Hawkeye had seen enough, and he eased up to the start, looking for a challenge. 'Just for the run. No bets,' he said. 'My wheels have been in the shop. The engine's shot to hell.' It was true, the Chevelle had seen sharper days.

Disgruntled, Hawkeye gave the starter one rip and ran alone. But something was not right. Slow off the mark, the Chevelle swerved across its lane, almost stalled, then limped away down the strip, with all the power and grace of a drunken yak.

Crawling back to the parking area, crestfallen, Hawkeye was greeted by a small derisive cheer, and he turned away his head, he mumbled. 'I told you. You wouldn't believe me,' he said. 'It's just a mess of scrap.'

A few feet away there lounged a young Latino, maybe eighteen years old, in a bright-red Firebird, brand-new and gleaming. He had a girl on his arm, a dyed-blond Chihuahua, relentlessly snapping gum; he nestled a fancy tape deck, which screeched 'I Will Survive'. 'OK. Let's go,' the Latino said.

'I told you,' Hawkeye answered. 'I got nothing.'

'Ten bucks.'

Hawkeye could not argue. Street law dictated that he not refuse a challenge, no matter how lop-sided. So he shrugged and moved to the line, where the Latino revved in frenzy, grinning at his girl, who licked her lips in response, ran her tongue all around her mouth.

No contest. At the signal, the Firebird jumped straight out in front. All the way down the strip, the Chevelle lagged hopelessly behind. But then the Latino must have lost concentration, missed a gear. Because, in the last fifty yards, Hawkeye suddenly outran him and finished two feet ahead.

Even before they'd pulled up, the kid was leaning out of his window, the ten bucks in his hand. 'Again,' he said.

'It was a fluke. Next time you'd beat me easy.'

'Twenty bucks. Again.'

So they went again, and Hawkeye won by a yard. And the next time the same. And the time after that. Then he took on the Latino's friends, and somehow he squeaked past them as well. Within an hour he had pocketed $340 and was back in the Gaff, squatting on a discarded tyre, slugging warm beer from the bottle. His face was streaked with grime, his fingernails caked with black. But his tired eyes were satisfied. Thumbing through his winnings, he yawned, and he drank deep. 'Heaven in Brooklyn ain't hard,' he said. 'Hot nights. And hotter cars.'

He lived with his family in a house called Hansen's Noisey Corner. The whole year round, it was hung with Christmas decorations, with twinkling lights and plaster Santas. The house was large and rambling; so was the family. There were three brothers and six sisters, and Hawkeye came somewhere in the middle. With the years, the others had left home. But he stayed on.

Mostly, the reason was his mother. As long as he could

remember, she had been his support, his strength. She believed that he was special. She always had. Out at Freeport, she never missed a night.

Every time that he ran, he carried a slogan on the bodywork, freshly painted, saying HI, MOM! And the moment his race began, she'd be up on her feet and howling, fists pumping the air, shouting down the opposition, refusing to let her son lose. Once, when a stranger blocked her view, she threatened him with her thermos.

Around the Noisey Corner she was quieter, more indulgent, but still a dominant force. On summer nights her home became the hub of the whole block. Racers congregated outside to mess with their machines, swallow a few beers. Hawkeye's father worked out on his archery range, set up in the garage, or tended his goldfish. Younger sisters practised their flirtations, while infants splashed in the pool, out in the backyard. Hot cars roared up and down the street. Neighbours dropped by in a continuous stream. And Mrs Hansen, majestic, presided over all.

Underneath her gaze, Hawkeye felt secure, in control, and everybody listened when he spoke. The following night he was due at Freeport, the first race of the new season, and anticipation made him verbose: 'Over the top,' he said. 'The moment that flag drops, I'm gone, like a bat out of hell. Anyone that stands in my way, he'd better have wings and a harp. Because I'm coming through, regardless. Or I'll perish in the attempt.'

'What if you perish?' a stranger asked.

'I try again next week.'

At capacity, Freeport held around 8,000. On this Saturday night, however, it was half-empty and, with the lone exception of Mrs Hansen, the crowd made little sound. They didn't cheer, did not curse. Even when a crash came, one of the frequent pile-ups, they didn't react much. Instead, drugged by din, they sat passive as garden gnomes and drowned in the roar of engines.

From the stands, the sun died on the right, the moon rose on the left. Out in the pit, which was an outsize parking lot, the cars were penned in like cattle, wedged solid. The cost of one night's racing, in tyres and parts alone, was $250. Among the Bombers, first prize was $100.

Nobody complained. Freeport might not be Daytona, but drivers felt at ease here, there were no hassles. Besides, they raced for the sensation, not cash. Sometimes, when they won, they were interviewed over the microphone. For one minute, maybe two, they became heroic, the focus of all attention. That was sufficient.

The Bombers, officially titled Street Class, were the track mongrels. Any driver who showed up on four wheels, more or less, had permission to compete. Kids showboating, broken-down trundlers, shunt addicts and spoilers. Plus a scattering of true racers.

On an average night there were more than a hundred entrants, split into four heats of ten laps each. The better drivers, like Hawkeye, started at the back. That gave them two and a half miles, or something less than two minutes, to go from last to first.

Each week, before he raced, Hawkeye observed a ritual preparation. All day he kept silence, steered clear of the smallest distractions. In the afternoon he drove to Freeport alone, while Don and Big Pete followed. His family name being Hansen, he liked to see himself as a resurrected Viking, and when he rode out to race, it was as if he were going forth to battle, to vanquish or be destroyed, in the style of a Norse avenger.

In the pit, he stood apart from the crush, he brooded. If strangers spoke, he averted his face, no reply. But if they approached his car, let alone presumed to touch it, he drove them off in a fury, like blasphemers from sacred ground.

Among the Bombers, most of the machines looked like losers in a demolition derby. But Hawkeye's, a '69 Camaro, was immaculate. Freshly painted, a gleaming black, it moved like a swan among geese: 'A car must be like a woman, sleek and glossy, absolutely gorgeous,' Hawkeye said. 'Or else it's diseased to drive.'

Tonight he started twenty-fourth out of twenty-eight in his heat. The only way he could hope to win was to smash straight through the pack, sideswiping and blindsiding, barrelfling into the slowpokes ahead, blocking off the heat behind, until he arrived at daylight. Which was precisely what he did. Place by place, he shot to kill, and succeeded. One lap later, he'd made fourth. Finally, a hundred yards from the finish, he cut sharply in front of his last two rivals, causing them to lose control, collide: 'What did I tell you?' his mother said, subsiding. 'A good boy.'

Unfortunately, the final was not a repeat. This time, starting twenty-third out of twenty-four, he had a whole twenty laps in which to prevail. By the half-way stage, he was lying sixth. Then he was sandbagged from behind coming out of the second turn. The Camaro careened all the way across the track, spinning like a crazed weather vane, before slamming full-force into a concrete wall.

That ended his night. The crippled Camaro was retrieved by the S & M Towing Company, and Hawkeye departed on foot. With the exception of a few bruised ribs, a minor case of whiplash, he was unhurt. But his head was bowed, his shoulders sagged. When he passed his mother, he did not look up.

The Camaro was a wreck. The chassis was bent almost double, the bodywork twisted and crushed. If Hawkeye was going to run next weekend, he would have to start again from scratch, create another machine.

A week was not enough time. Not nearly. But he had no choice. If he missed a night's racing, he lost points for the championship. Unless he could compete, he might as well abandon the season.

Such surrender was unthinkable. On Sunday morning he rose before dawn and went straight to the Gaff. Don and Big Pete were already waiting. 'When the going gets tough, the tough get going,' said Hawkeye. It was a favourite phrase. So the three of them set to work.

They laboured for eighteen hours a day, six days running. First they picked up an abandoned Firebird from the junkyard and salvaged its chassis. Then they blowtorched the Camaro into a dozen fragments, discarded what was ruined, saved what survived. They welded the scraps together and added a 302 Chevy engine. Other parts were borrowed or ripped off. A new transmission appeared, new front and rear ends. The body of another Camaro was fitted over the reconstructed innards. A letterer who signed himself 'Vincent Van Brush' hand-painted the number and a plug for Lenihan's bar. Then Hawkeye sat behind the steering wheel. He triggered the ignition. The engine came alive. And he possessed a whole new car, home-made.

Nobody had been paid a cent. Through the long days, Speeds came by to gossip, to watch. Within minutes they'd be helping, hard at work. They donated spare parts, sandwiches, beer, much sweat. In return, they were allowed to wallow in grease, all the mess they desired, without restriction.

The atmosphere was like a high school locker room's, a non-stop roistering of pranks, braggadocio, mock abuse. For this was a place where adolescence never ended. As long as you remained in the Gaff you could go on playing for ever. But the moment you ventured outside you became an adult, and doomed. Girls turned into wives, work into duty. Realities choked you, remorseless. 'Old Speeds never die. They just get mortgaged,' Hawkeye said.

The best compromise was a badge. By becoming a cop you could prolong pubescence indefinitely. True, you lost auto-nomy. But you could still drive the street, dress up in uniforms, give chase, even carry a gun. 'They pay you to play lawmen,' said Don. 'How bad is that?'

'Like Wyatt Earp. He started out an outlaw, ended up a marshal,' said Big Pete. 'One coin, two sides. That's all it is.'

Hawkeye himself disagreed. Employment in any form, even as an enforcer, meant taking orders, and his blood rebelled at that. 'Only dogs jump through hoops,' he said. 'I don't eat Alpo for no one.'

As it happened, there was a dog out back, a German shepherd named King, who guarded the towing service. But he jumped through no hoops. Instead, he drank beer, had become an alcoholic.

As a pup, the moment he was let off his chain, King would kill anything that moved. So the Speeds threw him cases of beer, to distract him. He bit them open in mid-air, drained them at a gulp. After three, befuddled, he fell asleep.

The only trouble was, when he awoke, he was more foul-tempered than ever. So now he was kept in a continuous stupor. On average he consumed a six-pack a day. He had also become a connoisseur. 'Michelob or Coors. That's all he drinks,' Hawkeye said. 'Once I tried to slip him a Miller Lite and he almost tore my throat out.'

In addition, there was a pet rat. Whenever Hawkeye crawled underneath a machine, the rat would snuggle up, lay its head upon his shoulder. Its whiskers quivered against his neck. Indulgent, Hawkeye called it A.J., after A. J. Foyt, and fed it on Fritos, cigarette butts, the remnants of bologna sandwiches.

He also had a steady girl. Her name was Mary, and the new car was named for her, the *Miss Mary D.* Sometimes Hawkeye referred to her as his wife. Of all the girls he had possessed, she was the first who truly understood, who knew and accepted that his car was his wife as well, and did not force him to choose.

Blonde and smiling, clean-scrubbed, she looked like one of his sisters, a younger version of his mother. And her devotion was absolute. If ever Hawkeye felt discouraged, or mumbled about quitting, it was she who made him press on. Even when she took her vacation, she sandwiched it between two Freeport Saturday nights: 'Say goodbye to the car and you say goodbye to me,' she said.

All through the week he went on toiling, and Mary waited, without complaint. On Tuesday night they had a date to see *Rocky II*, but Hawkeye cancelled out. On Wednesday he was too exhausted to speak to her. Then on Thursday, trying to make amends, he visited her after he'd finished work, around two in the morning. He had not washed or shaved, and his left eye was temporarily blinded, from overexposure to the blowtorch. 'You look as if you've just seen God,' Mary said.

'I have,' Hawkeye replied, and he came into her bed. He turned towards her body, stretched out his hand. Before it touched her, however, he was asleep.

At the Gaff, the regulars viewed their relationship with mixed feelings. As girl friends went, Mary shot straight, knew her place. But she was still female, and that spelled trouble in itself. Every time she phoned, they turned sullen, apprehensive, in case she seduced Hawkeye from his labours. 'Women will do that. All of them,' said Big Pete. 'They start out sugar-sweet. Then they turn. They drink your blood, suck out your spine. Before you know it, you're done for. That's why I don't wash. Always keep a layer of grease. For protection.'

'Like a crucifix drives off Dracula,' said Kevin.

'It's a fact,' said Carson. 'Cleanliness may be next to godliness. But filth is next to free.'

'No sweat,' said Big Pete. 'Anytime I get involved or I might be falling in love, I bring the girl to the shop and introduce her to A.J. It never fails.'

Despite their misgivings, however, Hawkeye held firm. There were times, alone with Mary, when he felt himself waver, and he was filled with yearnings, vague currents which he could not name. But in front of the other Speeds he acted flip, kept his cool. The moment that Mary called too much or made demands he pretended outrage. 'How could she be so selfish? Don't she have no values?' he'd ask. Then he spat on his hands and lost himself in work.

So the circle held. Five o'clock on Saturday morning, the car was finally complete. It was perfect in every detail; even Hawkeye himself could find no flaw. So he went home to the Noisey Corner, to his earned rest.

Sleep was instantaneous. He didn't even undress, just fell face down across his bed and sank fathoms deep. But suddenly, just before he touched bottom, he snapped back awake, aghast.

Vincent Van Brush had forgotten to paint in the HI, MOM!

The trail of disasters continued. Next afternoon, when he was already halfway through to Freeport, it started to rain and the racing was automatically cancelled. 'Hookers and runners can't stand the rain,' Hawkeye said. So he drank beers at Lenihan's instead.

Later on, he took Mary to a motel in Nassau County, just off the Jericho Turnpike, and there was an altercation in the parking lot. For no reason that made sense, some drunk tried to pick a fight. In the end Hawkeye was forced to knock him down, shut him up. Then the law was called. 'My hand slipped,' said

Hawkeye. And the officers did not argue. One of them had raced at the Brooklyn Queens Expressway, remembered Hawkeye well. Though that time had passed, a certain loyalty survived. 'Ride on, cowboy,' the officer said.

So Hawkeye rode. But his losing streak dragged on. The car's name was altered from *Miss Mary D* to *Raquel*, in hopes of better luck. But the following weekend he crashed on the second lap, for no particular cause, except for impatience, a breakdown in discipline.

It was his own fault. The night before, instead of tuning the machine, he had gone out playing with Mary. They had dinner, took in a movie, then made love. When morning came, Hawkeye felt satiated. He thought about getting engaged, being married, and there seemed worse fates, after all. When he remembered Freeport, running seemed like a chore.

The other Speeds were not fooled. The moment they set eyes on him they recognized the symptoms, knew that he'd left his race between the sheets. But they did not accuse him out loud. He had been their leader, their icon, for too many years. Even in this treason, they could not deny him.

They went through the motions, nothing more. When the fiasco was completed, they rode back to Queens in silence. The radio played 'Tragedy', but nobody laughed. In more than ten years' running, tonight was Hawkeye's nadir.

Back at the Gaff he avoided their eyes, and they sat at a distance. Even King didn't bite, could scarcely raise a snarl. When Hawkeye threw him a beer, he let it fall, indifferent.

Then Mary arrived. Remembering the night before, she was nervous, approached with caution. When she entered, nobody said hello, or even looked up. The Gaff felt like a mortuary. 'Who died?' asked Mary.

'*Raquel*,' Hawkeye replied.

Mary was not to blame. He understood that. But humiliation, guilt, unfocused rage rose up in him like pitch, too fierce to be contained. So he pantomimed disgust. Expressionless, he stared straight through her, like a gunslinger in some spaghetti Western. 'What did I do?' Mary asked.

'You made me cheat.'

'I never.'

'On *Raquel*. You caused me to be unfit. So she paid me back and crashed.'

It was a game. But Hawkeye did not smile. Drawing out the charade, he made his eyes burn, his mouth spit flame. The Speeds kept silence and Mary hung back, blushing. 'We could have won, no sweat. But thanks to you, I betrayed her,' Hawkeye said. 'You made me break her heart.'

'I'm sorry.'

'Then say "Forgive me." '

'Forgive me.'

'Now touch her. Touch *Raquel*.'

Mary obeyed without question. Shyly, flushing crimson, she reached out her hand and stroked with her fingertips, caressed the fender. 'Say "Raquel",' Hawkeye said.

'Raquel,' said Mary, and knelt.

Only then did Hawkeye relent. He laughed out loud, cracking up. Then all the other Speeds followed suit. Their brothership was restored, the black mark exorcised. Mary came into Hawkeye's arms and he held her, he hugged her tight. 'Speed lives!' he cried, and all of them rejoiced.

The season was four weeks gone. Unless his luck changed soon, the whole year would be wasted. So Hawkeye set to work on yet another machine. This time around, he called it *Awesome*.

It was his automotive testament. Everything that he'd ever learned or dreamed went into its creation. When it was finished, he believed that he had made himself invincible.

The only trouble was, he was left with $13.45. If he wished to continue running at Freeport, funds were required, and fast. So he went back into the streets and issued a general challenge: a Fountain Avenue shoot-out, single combat, with $5,000 at stake.

On the Friday night appointed, he sat in the Venus Diner on Flatlands, a favourite Speed rendezvous, and sifted through the applicants. Don and Big Pete acted as his seconds. Between them, they carried less than $20.

They drank black coffee; they waited till after two o'clock. Every now and then, prospective challengers showed up, but none could meet the collateral. Invariably, they claimed that they were good for any debts. Hawkeye knew better and dismissed them from his presence.

At last a black man approached. He sported a full-length racoon coat, a Charlie Chan moustache. When he spoke, his language was ornate, most chivalrous and almost entirely in error. 'Gentlemen, good-day. I am in behalf of Flatbush Speed,' he said. 'If a deal should consummate, what apropos do you propose?'

'Best of three. Winner takes all,' said Big Pete.

'And where is your guarantee?'

Silently, Big Pete indicated *Awesome*, shut up in its trailer outside the diner window. The black man pondered a few seconds. Then he nodded and they set forth.

Flatbush Speed, who was also black, was already waiting on Fountain, in a born-again Corvette. He had been a high roller for years, was known throughout the boroughs. A sawed-off torpedo, he was built like a fire hydrant. When Hawkeye and his party appeared, he did not speak one word.

Fountain itself was deserted. All the other runners had long since dispersed, and the swamplands stood silent, stirred only by the night breeze, which made a continuous sound of hissing, hushing, in the long grass. The moon was three parts full. There were no clouds. In the far distance, police sirens wailed.

The showdown was conducted with decorum, the ritual formality of a nineteenth-century duel. Solemnly, with most elaborate care, the two teams of seconds inspected the opposition machinery, in case of violations. Nitrous oxide, laughing gas, was banned. A starter was drawn by lot. Then battle was joined.

First time around, Hawkeye won by a car length. On the second run Flatbush Speed beat him out. So everything, the whole $5,000, hung on the last quarter mile.

At the flag the cars jumped off abreast. All the way down the strip they stayed locked in a dead heat. But inside the last hundred yards, losing nerve, Flatbush Speed suddenly swerved inward, hard into Hawkeye's lane, trying to make him give ground. Hawkeye, however, kept right on coming, refused to yield an inch. The two cars clashed and Flatbush Speed ricocheted, slewed sideways. Out of control, he veered right off the road, then ploughed across the swamp, where he hit a metal barrier and somersaulted, flipping once, flipping twice, before he finally came to rest, upside down, wheels spinning, in a pool of stagnant water.

Hawkeye finished at his leisure. Turning, he cruised back up the strip, in the easy lope of victory. By the time he came abreast of the Corvette, Flatbush Speed had been pulled clear of the wreckage and lay stretched out in the marsh, being tended by his seconds. 'Did he eat a tree?' Hawkeye asked.

'He breathes,' said the man in the racoon coat.

Methodically, the black man counted out the $5,000; equally methodically, Big Pete checked it. Flatbush Speed moaned at their feet, semi-conscious. The moon shone bright. Satisfied, Hawkeye pocketed his spoils. 'Be well,' he said. Then *Awesome* was off, and gone.

From then on, the summer was transformed. At long last Hawkeye possessed both wheels and finance, and he promptly started winning. By July he was running seventh in the championship. By the third weekend in August he was up to third. Two more strong weeks, he calculated, and he would hit the front.

On Friday evening, the night before he raced, he presided outside the Noisey Corner. His father shot arrows in the garage; his mother watched from the sidewalk. On the street, assorted Speeds were clustered around *Awesome*, marvelling. Meanwhile Hawkeye himself stood off to one side, accepting tribute, the picture of proud possession.

It was nine o'clock. Dusk was coming on at the end of a hot and humid day, another ordeal by sweat. The children ate ice-cream, fried chicken. The radio played 'Heart of Glass'. Mrs Hansen mopped her face and strolled towards the garage.

Across the entrance there was a wide patch of grease where Hawkeye had been working on the car. One of his younger sisters had tried to wash it away with a garden hose. But the effect, instead of swabbing it clean, had been to turn it into a skid patch, as slippery as ice. Therefore, the moment that Mrs Hansen set foot on it, her legs flew out from under her and she was swept away, helpless. Skittering, wildly flailing, she headed straight for the garage wall and she cried out for Greg, her son.

Hawkeye's response was instant and spectacular. Whirling across the sidewalk, he launched himself full length, grabbed his mother around the waist, and raised her up. For a moment they moved as one, grotesquely frozen in grace, like a pair of kamikaze skaters. Then Hawkeye hit the wall, feet first.

He made no sound. Very carefully, he lifted his mother's body off his own and set her back on her feet. She straightened her clothes, then tested herself for breakage. All parts were still functional. 'I'm alive,' she said.

Then Hawkeye looked down at himself. Between the ankle and knee of his left leg, the bone stuck naked through the flesh, his pants, everything. It had been shattered in three places.

PART
3

That was the end. For the next ten weeks his leg was encased in plaster. At first he continued to go to Freeport, just to spectate. But that proved more than he could stand. After the second week he stayed home.

Nothing had worked. Of all his targets, not one had been achieved. He had no championship, no sponsor, no real prospect of glory. Truthfully, his whole year had aborted.

Just the same, he did not despair. For all his disappointments, the summer had not weakened him. On the contrary, his resolve now was fiercer than ever. Speed remained his life; it always would. Next year he would return, try again. And the year after that, and all the other years, until he finally triumphed. At root, he had no choice. He had been born to run.

So now, as Fall set in, he sipped beer in Lenihan's and could hardly wait for another Spring. Maybe that would be his time, maybe stardom would touch him at last. Or maybe he'd get himself killed. Whichever, he would take his chance, no complaints. 'Want to know my philosophy?' Hawkeye said. 'I'd rather eat trees than shit.'

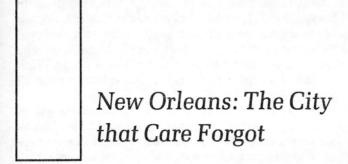

New Orleans: The City
that Care Forgot

I n a cemetery on Basin Street, Tombstone Louie sat beneath
the grave of Marie Laveau, the Voodoo Queen, and studied
the sports section, his eyes set stoic in loss. Tulane had been
thrashed by LSU, and the Saints were 0–11. 'The Sickness,' Louie
said.

'In this city of congeniality, conviviality, historic in tradition, noble
in its innermost spirit and soul, where men intermingle as
brothers, regardless of race, creed or menial distinction, where
prejudice is deemed a lackey and a thief, and the greatness of true
American endeavour shines forth in a beacon, an inspiration of
solicitude to all who garner in its light, one more time I rise from
the ashes of the Phoenix.'

Thus spake Don King. Perhaps he had a point. But for the
skycaps and taxi drivers, registration clerks, bellhops and cham-
bermaids, the Duran–Leonard fight was merely one more in an
endless succession of sporting fiestas, conventions, carnivals that
stretched from Labor to Memorial Day. In another month there
would be the Sugar Bowl. Then the Super Bowl. Then Mardi
Gras, the Jazz and Heritage Festival and the NCAA basketball
regionals. For each, a fresh flood of tourists would descend, run
loose through the City That Care Forgot, gross out on booze, sex,
folly, massed piggery in every form, and then crawl home to

regroup. But when the last horde had departed, by some strange sleight of siphoning and concealment, New Orleans would still be left among the poorest cities in America, a fifth of its households surviving on $6,000 or less.

By the standards of these junkets, this fight was a bagatelle. In 1978, at Super Bowl XII, 60,000 visitors had shed $30 million. For Duran-Leonard, even with ringside seats scaled at a thousand bucks a shot, the plunder would barely reach $5 million. 'Why would anyone blow a grand to see some Nigger hit some spic?' asked my black taxi driver, rhetorically. 'Down here, we get all that at home. For free.'

True enough. In the French Quarter, the main emphasis was on conventions, not pugs – the Equestrian Order of the Holy Sepulchre of Jerusalem, the Clinical Symposium of Gynecological Laparoscopists, Forward with Chevrolet, and California Youth for a Stronger America. Upstairs at the Court of the Two Sisters, on Royal, four middle-aged businessmen sat at a corner table, each wearing a set of plaster antlers, and proclaiming to the world that they were Mooses. A few tables away, one of the Equestrians was singing 'Show Me the Way to Go Home' to a lady not his wife. Across the room, meanwhile, a pair of second honeymooners from Fresno had ordered cherries jubilee.

This proved a major Hollywood production. For almost fifteen minutes, waiters bustled, ingredients were assembled, the tension slowly built. Finally, all was ready, and the *maître d'* commenced to make his magic. Indolently Gallic, he poured, stirred, *frappéed*, pirouetted. Then the house lights were dimmed, the sorcerer struck a match and his creation burst into flame. The couple from Fresno clasped hands, and stared devoutly into the depths of each other's eyes.

'Angel,' said the blonde.

'Sweetness,' said her husband.

'Oh, shit,' said the *maître d'*, and the saucepan swung upside down, its handle suddenly buckled, to deposit the entire contents – syrupy, glutinous, gross – in a heap at the lovers' feet.

Out back at Chris Owens, between the phone and the pissoir, somebody had written on the wall, green ink, in a neat and delicate hand: BOURBON STREET SOKS.

Indeed it did. Canned Dixieland blared from open doorways. Souvenir T-shirts and sex toys filled the windows. A girl with stout ankles swung her legs back and forth through parted curtains.

Duran and Leonard lay three nights ahead. But the girls on Bourbon Street didn't give a dime. Football fans were their game. All fight buffs did was traipse behind their heroes, begging for autographs. A bunch of closets, the pack of them. But football fans were different. Because they were kept apart from the players, could never speak or touch, their deepest hunger was left unfilled. Even after the games, the need of contact nagged. So they came down to Bourbon, and drowned it in working girls.

Super Bowls were best of all. Seventy-five thousand went to watch them, and more than half were tourists. Mardi Gras was well enough, but many of its partisans were young, romantic, broke. With the Super Bowl, the trade was strictly credit card: three-piece suits, high rollers. A cataclysm of media types.

For days before the game, New Orleans became a universal symbol of debauch. Within the Quarter, in particular, excess was *de rigueur*. So Super Bowls here were parties first, contests last. Working girls enjoyed the best week of their year. Likewise ticket sharks, shoeshine boys, taxi drivers, antique shops, barmen, souvenir touts, dope dealers, pickpockets, cops. And even when the game was done, and all the bets paid out, the profits mostly came right back to the streets, to be squandered where they belonged. 'Talk about an industrial boom,' said Shanda Lear, a stripper. 'Blue heaven is beating the Super Bowl spread.'

Growing up black in the 1940s, Tombstone Louie had traded as a streetfighter, bareknuckled in the alleys. When he won, he took home anything between \$20 and \$100 according to the betting action. If he lost, beaten senseless, he worked for free. Now he had a face like sepia scrambled eggs, and he lived in a cemetery. Just a few blocks away, meanwhile, Duran and Leonard, two soft-drink salesmen doubling as welterweights, were being paid fifteen million dollars to dance.

The cemetery was called the City of the Dead, St Louis, No. 1. Surrounded by massive crumbling walls, the tombs rose up like windowless houses or grotesque Piranesi ruins. Because of the swampland below, all corpses rested overground. Some lay in nineteenth-century mansions, others in destitute hovels. Between them, these dwellings formed a brick and marble shantytown, its streets paved with beer cans and empty bottles, broken records, scrap. Even the plastic flowers were wilted.

Mostly Louie haunted the grave of Pierre Derbigny, once governor of Louisiana, 1828–29. But when he read the Sports pages, he moved to Marie Laveau, the Voodoo Queen, for luck. Her tomb was covered with scrawled Xs, beseeching favour. In death, she had become a patron saint of losers; of gamblers, wronged lovers, all forms of derelict.

Louie himself was a true sports fanatic. For almost forty years, he had followed every event in the city. But he could not recall that anyone from New Orleans had ever won much. Willie Pastrano and Ralph Dupas had been world champion fighters, and both had ended up stiffed. Tulane had flirted. Archie Manning had once gone to the Pro Bowl. All the rest had aborted. The NBA Jazz even left town. For Utah, of all places.

He was not crushed, however. Any cash he stumbled on, he still bet on hometown hopes. When you backed New Orleans, you might not win. But the experience was never dull.

On a humid Sunday morning, the air as turgid as gumbo, Louie wore an open raincoat, an undershirt, baggy canvas trousers and one brown shoe, one black. Softly droning, he brooded over the boxscores, saw that all his teams had lost, observed a resigned mourning. Sporting New Orleans was cursed by a malign fate, always had been, and would never be set free. 'Destruction plague. No mortal son escapes.' Louie said. 'Let him start out prancing prideful, no dread upon his soul. Yet in time the Sickness takes him, no matter how hard his fight. It sucks the marrow from his bones, the red blood from his veins. Consumes his very heart, piece by piece. Then all he is, he's dust.'

Over in Algiers, on the other side of the Mississippi, there was trouble. A policeman had been shot and killed. A week later, his colleagues invaded two nearby houses and kicked in the doors. Two suspects were blown away. The neighbours took offence. There were protests, demonstrations. Then the police chief resigned. A fire broke out in an abandoned warehouse. From the top of the Hyatt Regency, one could just make out the glow.

No sanctuary could have felt safer. A hundred yards from the Superdome, impersonal as an airport, the Hyatt was a 32-floor lobotomat, utterly removed from any sense of time, place, passion. Outside on the streets, the city might rumble and stew as it wished. No odour would penetrate here.

Duran and Leonard, plus entourages, plus armies of publicists, camp followers, press, were stuck in this same vacuum. Around the coffee shop and cocktail lounge, overlooked by a monstrous Thanksgiving turkey made out of papier mâché, the sports crowd performed a non-stop cavalcade. On this occasion, they had assembled for a prizefight, and boxing lore held sway. Next time it would be football, basketball; tennis. No matter, one felt, the basic images and gestures would remain interchangeable. Thus, Jim Brown shook hands with Larry Holmes, Angelo Dundee shook hands with Arthur Ashe, Thomas Hearns shook hands with Ken Norton. Emile Bruneau, the chairman of the Louisiana Boxing Commission, referred to Blacks as Nigras. Freddie Brown, one of Duran's aged and battle-scarred trainers, masticated a cigar like a scaled-down torpedo, endlessly retelling the legends of Tony Canzoneri, Kid Chocolate, Hammerin' Hank Armstrong, his voice a death-rattle croak. Superflies hustled up wagers, while groups of Panamanians huddled around their tape machines, warding off demons with Salsa. Christie Brinkley, the swimsuit model, in gold glitter hot pants and matching top, served as official photographer. The flunkies of Leonard stared down the flunkies of Duran, and vice versa. A jazz band played 'When The Saints Go Marching In' for brunch, and the Muzak countered with 'You Light Up My Life'. Don King promoted a miracle water, which he proposed to dispatch in aid of the MGM Grand. A robot in boxing trunks hyped ticket sales. Howard Cosell blew his nose.

According to a story in *The Times-Picayune and The States-Item*, the Mississippi River was trying to alter its course. Weary of New Orleans, it was twisting its banks west, gouging out a whole new route. Unless it could be persuaded to reconsider, it would end up fifty miles away and the city's major industry, its port, would be left high and dry. Then all that would remain would be tourists.

In St Louis, Tombstone Louie took the news philosophically. Tugging at a bottle of Thunderbird, which he suckled like a pacifier, he turned a sour eye upward, towards a marble cross with saint, the Tomb of the Italian Benevolent Society, 1857. 'What use to fuss? A river gets around. She has experience. After all this time, she has to know what's best.'

Along South Rendon, in another part of the forest, the houses were stunted boxes. At Sunday lunchtime, the sidewalks were deserted, and most of the curtains drawn. Sometimes the grass on the front lawns was grey, sometimes a patchy brown. Half-way down the final block, one arrived at the Criminal Sheriff's Boxing Club.

Basically, the building was a half-way house. But one part of the ground floor had been converted into a gym, a high, stark space, with two rings, fight posters and a couple of heavy bags. Inmates and parolees trained here. So did neighbourhood kids.

The main man was Jerry Celestine, a local black light-heavyweight. Now thirty-one, or so he claimed, he'd fought the likes of James Scott, Marvin Johnson and Richie Kates, and had mostly held his own. He hit hard with either hand, a professional tradesman. But promoters said he lacked colour, and *Ring* did not list him among its contenders. He couldn't get enough fights to add much to his non-boxing income. His earnings barely covered his expenses. Running in the dark, sweating stale in this barren room, month after month of sacrifice, self-torture, and never any payoff, not even a guaranteed goal at the end – sometimes he felt it like a living death. As he laboured, he'd relive his victories, running them through in slow-motion replay, time and time again, like talismans. But they brought him no luck. Nothing changed.

Seated on a rickety table, beneath a poster for the Our Lady of Lourdes gym, he could only shake his head. His hairline was receding, and he spoke just above a mumble, with that unblinking gaze, eyes set straight ahead, that so many boxers shared. He was thoughtful, articulate, patient. But he was a fighter. And no one would fight him back.

Against Kates, when a win might have cut him loose, he had been butted in the first round. For three rounds more, he fought half-blind, and almost broke Kates in two. Then his manager stopped it, and he had lost. Afterwards, in his dressing room, he felt a stinging behind his eyes. At first, he wasn't sure what it was.

Then he finally remembered. It was tears inside, pushing to get free.

If he hadn't been a man, he might have broken. But he was. So he endured.

Endurance was his best game. Growing up loose in the city, he'd lived on and by the streets. Even after he started boxing, turned pro, he kept on chasing trouble, couldn't stand to watch it pass by. He was married, had children, separated. Drifted. Ran.

One night, he was cruising the streets with some studs. They were broke, and they needed to get high. So they hit a Pizza Hut.

After he'd been caught, Celestine was sent to Angola, the Louisiana state penitentiary. For six months he could not stop grieving. Something far inside him refused flat out to believe. This had not happened, and he was not here. Nothing around him was fact. So he just sat, stared. As though it was not really him, but somebody else in his flesh. Some other guy, pretending to be him.

By degrees, time and habit calmed him. He submitted and did his time. Finally, he was brought back to New Orleans. Though still incarcerated, he went to school, taking Sociology as his major, Psychology as a minor. He also went back to boxing.

The time came to choose, either to study or fight. He was street black, on his own, in jail. What choice was no choice? He fought.

Eventually he was pardoned. While Celestine was still in prison, a sheriff's deputy named Leslie Bonano became his manager. During this time, one of his daughters came home from school and found her mother dead on the kitchen floors. There had been something wrong in her blood. Sugar could be fatal. But she didn't like doctors. She was frightened. So she stayed on at home. And when the hurting got too bad, she sought consolation inside a box of candies.

That was four years ago. Since then, Celestine had compiled a record of twenty wins, six losses. In his last fight, he had taken vengeance on Kates and knocked him out in the ninth. But his time was running short, he knew that, and still there were no breaks. Even worse, the basic act that he performed, this business of hitting men for money, no longer made him feel good. No pleasure remained, only toil. But he persevered just the same.

His manager played the themes from *Rocky* and *Apocalypse Now* while he trained. A neighbourhood child, maybe ten years old, called him Champ.

Now he had been matched with a prospect called Pablo Ramos, 18–1. If Celestine lost, he was finished. Even if he won, it wouldn't mean much. He understood that stardom, big money, the dream of a title shot were probably mirages. Those things happened up North. In New Orleans, if you were lucky, you made a living. But still he worked. When in doubt, he hit. 'It's what I do,' he said.

Shanda Lear proved right about the fans. While the fight mob remained immured inside the Hyatt Regency, the prospect of *Monday Night Football*, the Saints against the Rams, brought forth Saint supporters like a swarm of Hamelin rats. They descended on the Quarter in a plague, overspilling every bar. Their team might be 0–11. By game time, as they lurched from the last gin palace, they themselves were 11–0.

Throughout the preceding days, the press had spent much ink on a threatened demonstration. Apparently, a group of outraged fans was plotting to run amok on national TV, in protest at the Saints' fatuity. Not wishing to be recognized, they would wear brown bags over their heads, in the style of the Unknown Comic. These disguises had been christened the Aints Bags, and when the cameras came upon them, their inmates planned to jump up and down, wave their arms in the air, shout *Hi, Mom* through the slits.

In other, harsher cities – say, Pittsburgh or Oakland or Cleveland – all this might have been for real, an outlet for anger and hurt. But in New Orleans, it was transparent jive – just one more excuse to dress up, imbibe and stage an exhibition. Milling through the catacombs of the Superdome, the would-be vigilantes reeled and shunted like a gassed conga line. Chants overlapped and jumbled, banners were displayed upside down. Half-blinded behind their slits, the Bagheads couldn't focus on the cameras, and even before they had screened, most had already retreated, back towards the concession stands, in a hopeless ragtag shambles.

They swilled, they gorged, they hollered. The big showdown

over, they raged to their souls' content. But nobody could see them on TV, and after a time they tired, set aside their masks, and trundled back to the Quarter.

Tombstone Louie was nowhere in sight. Having failed to locate him at either Pierre Derbigny or Marie Laveau, I wandered aimless through the aisles, past Blaise Cenas and Bernard de Marigny, Louis Moreau Lislet, the family Montegut, and finally Paul Morphy. 'The Pride and the Sorrow of Chess', who had once destroyed the greatest players in Europe, one by one, in the late 1850s, aged twenty-one. Even in those days, however, New Orleans was ill-starred. His mother ordered him home, and made him abandon the game, which was thought undignified. In submission, he became a lawyer, and then a hermit. In 1884, at the age of forty-seven, a total paranoiac, he died of a stroke.

Towards the rear of the cemetery was a row of small red-brick bunkers, like a series of antiquated bakers' ovens. They had lost their doors, seemed on the verge of collapse. Inside the fourth in line, Louie lay curled up on his side, fast asleep.

Rags lay under him. The sports pages covered his face. Across the entrance to the tomb, he had hung a *Do Not Disturb* sign. On the flip side, it said *Please Make Up My Room*.

Half an hour after crying 'No Mas', Duran sat in a Winnebago, in the bowels of the Superdome, and waited to be removed. The bus was filled with vassals in softball uniforms, PANAMA printed in red on the backs. All kept silence, and Duran ignored them totally. Unseeing, he stared straight ahead, while his right hand dangled from the open window, limp and flopping, a fin.

Panamanian women clustered around him. Some wept, some keened and some clutched at his hand. One, old and bloated in swathes of pink, prostrated herself, face down, on the floor, scouring her temples against the cement till she bled. Others mumbled wordless incantations. As if at the foot of a cross, they raised imploring hands and prayed for signs. But Duran gave them none. Expressionless, he suffered them to touch him, paw at his hand. But he did not move his head, and he would not meet their eyes. ·

I had loved him many years. I loved him now. In some feeble gesture of gratitude or consolation, I came close among the women, and I took his hand myself. Perhaps it was some difference in the way I held him, or in the texture of my flesh. Whatever, something stirred in him and he turned, looked directly in my face.

He did not see me. I am sure of that. His eyes were focused on something far beyond, in a region that I could never enter, or even recognize. But when I moved to slip my hand away, his fingers suddenly tightened, convulsive. For a moment he clung on fiercely, nails biting into my palm. Then his grip relaxed. Then came a sequence of three small spasms, soft, softer, softest. And then again he went limp, as before. His head turned away. Once more, he stared straight ahead, into nothing.

The following morning, Tombstone Louie was back at his post, in the shadow of Marie Laveau. Predictably, the sports pages had torn Duran to shreds. He was a quitter, a dog, a disgrace to the Sweet Science. Even Louie himself was not amused, for he had plunged a dollar fifty, and was now destitute. Nonetheless, he refused to join the lynch mobs. In his view, the loss was not Duran's fault. The whole affair had been beyond his control. 'He never quit,' Louie said. 'He just caught the Sickness is all.'

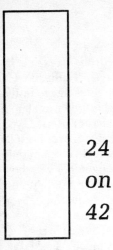

24
on
42

I have a problem,' I said.
    'How's that?' Tu Sweet asked.
    'I'm about to be dead.'

It was early in the morning. Tu Sweet, the self-styled 'Black Fred Astaire and Nureyev of the Hustle', was relaxing in my neighbourhood bar, fresh from a night in the discos. Breakfasting on Grand Marnier and Coca-Cola, he studied his picture in a beat-up magazine, which never left his person. 'How dead is dead?' he asked.

'Severely.'

'What for? Have you committed some rashness?'

'I agreed to write a story on 42nd Street,' I said. 'I didn't want to. Right from the gitgo, I thought it injudicious. But my young lady forced me. When I tried to back out, she called me a mewling, cringing travesty of manhood. She said I had the heart of a flea-ridden cur.'

'So?'

'So I weakened. And now I'm trapped. I must live through twenty-four hours, one full cycle, down on the Strip. What's more, I must go to the limit. No cheating, no ducking or dodging – come what may, I must endure.'

'Twenty-four on 42,' said Tu Sweet. 'So where's your problem?'

'I am a mewling, cringing travesty of manhood. I have the heart of a flea-ridden cur.'

'And you fear that you'll wind up extinct?'

'That is the truth,' I said.

Tu Sweet took his time. Reluctantly laying aside his magazine, he made a series of minute adjustments to his collar, shirt cuffs, tie. He ordered another shot of breakfast, contemplated his image in the backbar mirror. When at last he broke silence, his tone was almost biblical. 'Have no fear,' he said. 'Right here, at your service, you possess the number-one expert on the Street that was ever born or created. For a small consideration, the very merest token, not only will I keep you safe, but I'm willing to act as your guide. I will show you everything you dreamed of and plenty more you didn't. Just stick with me and in twenty-four hours, you have my guarantee, you will know the Ultimate.'

I asked no questions; there was no point. Head bowed in resignation, I stuck my hand in my jacket pocket. 'How much?' I asked.

'For the Ultimate?' said Tu Sweet. 'A fifty would suffice.'

'Thirty-five.'

'Forty.'

'Done,' I said.

And so we set forth.

It was 9 a.m. when we started. Rain was falling steadily; the air was as clammy and chill as an undertaker's handshake. Still, this was Saturday morning, the main day of the week, and the street was buzzing, regardless.

Between 7th and 8th, all along the Strip, the sidewalks were jammed solid. This was the vortex, the central bedlam of cinemas and sex shops, burlesques and discount boutiques, greasy spoons, peep shows, dirty bookstores. Tu Sweet called it Hustle Heaven.

No doorway stood empty. Like an open box, each framed its own performers. Motionless, expressionless, they posed like dummies in a waxworks, eternally frozen in waiting.

Between them, they formed a frieze, a kind of skid-row *tableau vivant*: black hookers in hot pants and lacquered wigs; bodybuilders and midnight cowboys; tattooed sailors in leather; evangelists with pamphlets or sandwich boards; Polaroid photographers, two bucks a shot; pubescent Puerto Ricans; Superflies in fancy hats, murmuring promises of cocaine, mescaline, speed; children who stared without blinking; all-Americans with blue eyes, bulging biceps, and

Man-Tan golden flesh; furtive men in overcoats, growing old; junkies and transvestites, assorted; policemen in twos, idly twirling their nightsticks; young girls from Kansas, their jeans as tight as sausage skins; ex-fighters, lost in fog; pimps and enforcers; defectives; derelicts; and scattered tourists, gawking.

It was a familiar cast. So familiar, in fact, that it almost seemed faked. These faces, all these set poses and pitches – over the years, I'd seen them aped in so many movies and plays, such a multitude of TV potboilers, that even the genuine articles now looked staged. At any moment, as we cruised, I half expected the Strip to fade and be replaced by commercials pushing diapers, paper towels, detergents.

Tu Sweet took charge from the outset. This was his beat, his true homeland. The moment that his feet touched the Strip, he put more jut in his strut, an extra glide in his stride, and he started to dictate. 'First of all, the rules,' he said.

'What rules?'

'The ways to stay alive. Down here, you understand, not everyone is a gentleman, and accidents can happen. That has been known. But I have five golden rules. Just follow them clean, and your ass need fear no evil.'

We stood on the corner of 8th, where we got wet. In a puddle the size of a small pond, printed pamphlets floated at random. Each bore the slogan 'You don't have to be Jewish to love Jesus.' 'Rule 1: Be prepared,' said Tu Sweet. 'Rule 2: Beware of strange bathrooms. Rule 3: When in doubt, don't. Rule 4: Never look back. Something may be gaining. Rule 5: Have a nice day.'

It sounded simple: I felt encouraged. Ambling back and forth along the Strip, three times east, three times west, I raised my eyes from the performers and began to contemplate the cinema awnings. According to my instant spot-check, thirty-eight movies were playing on this one block. In particular, I was tempted by *Master of the Flying Guillotine* or, better yet, by 'Love Slaves Tortured to Blood Dripping Death' in *Sanctuary of Satan*. But Tu Sweet wouldn't let me go in. He said that work came first. After all, we were on a mission. 'So where do we begin?' I asked.

'Sex,' he replied. 'Where else?'

For $3 each, we paid our way into an X-rated movie. The film dealt with dairymaids, farmhands, and high jinks in haylofts. At one point, a man and two women frolicked together in a pigsty. This made me think of my home in England and my prize sow, Gertrude, my favourite Welsh White, who once won third prize in the Hertfordshire County Show, Open Class. Homesickness overwhelmed me.

After the film, there was a live performance. A thin girl with very white skin appeared onstage, accompanied by a boy with long, lank hair and lots of teeth. They took off their clothes, folding them neatly. Then the boy lay down on a mattress, staring at the ceiling, and the girl performed fellatio.

It seemed like hard work. The girl was methodical, earnest, determined, but the boy showed no reaction. The cinema was dark and airless and smelled of disinfectant. From time to time, the girl would draw back and massage her jaws, to ease the cramps, before resuming her labours. The audience kept perfectly still, making no sound. So did the boy onstage.

Warmth and fug made me drowsy. As the performance dragged on, with no apparent end in sight, my eyes grew heavy, and I started drifting. The man beside me was already sleeping, gently snoring. I thought of corned-beef hash and fries, of chocolate-fudge sundaes. On my right, Tu Sweet complained of toothache.

Finally, after eight minutes and fifty-three seconds, the girl achieved success. The boy gave a few feeble twitches and raised one hand, fist clenched in the air. There was a round of polite applause. Rising from the mattress, the boy and girl smiled and waved goodbye.

Afterwards, I saw them in a nearby cafeteria, recharging themselves with beef-filled turnovers. Close up, apart from a few scattered pimples, they looked as clean-cut, as antiseptic, as newlyweds in a TV commercial advertising dandruff shampoo.

They were married and in love. The girl came from Holland, and the boy played rock 'n' roll. Sooner or later, they were sure, he would become a star. But right now money was tight. A few months ago, they had been reduced to living in the back of a van. Then they'd strolled past the X-rated cinema and decided that, in the last analysis, sex was more fun than starvation.

Conditions were not easy. To begin with, they had worked four shows a day, seven days a week. That had been exhausting. But they had stuck it through, they'd won their spurs, and now they reaped the rewards. Their wages had been upped, and their schedule cut in half. Audiences were respectful. So were their fellow professionals. For $40 a day, tax free, they had no complaints.

The only problem was the law. They had already been busted twice. True, the cinema paid their fines. But the experience disturbed them just the same. The day after the last raid, his nerves still on edge, the boy had failed to perform. Still, that was life, he said. You win some, you lose some; *che sarà sarà*. In a few months more, they would have saved enough to quit. Then he could concentrate full-time on his music. His day would come. All the hard work, all the sacrifice and patience would be rewarded. 'Sometimes the road gets rough. Sometimes you feel like giving up. But you've got to keep on believing, no matter what,' he said.

'You must have faith,' said the girl.

'Faith,' said the boy. 'And love.'

Back on the street, it was still raining. Mist had descended, so thick, such a deep and dirty yellow, that the whole Strip seemed shot in sepia. But none of the performers in the doorways had moved.

Between 6th and 7th, we passed a serious bar. 'Refreshments are served,' said Tu Sweet, and he led me inside a long, dark room, warm and snug as a neon womb.

It smelled strong of jail. The room was jammed full of hustlers – dealers, strong-arms, salesmen of all descriptions. Transvestites clustered round the jukebox, miming to Donna Summer. A white man with hairy legs who wore a plaid miniskirt, peroxide wig and ankle socks stood by the telephone, weeping. And two solemn blacks sat in a far corner, with heads close together, discoursing in conspiratorial undertones.

These men were immense. They must have weighed 270 pounds apiece and were built like defensive tackles. The face of one was crisscrossed by so many scars, it looked like a ghetto road map. As for the other, he had known Tu Sweet in jail.

Understandably, Tu Sweet showed deference. 'Didn't mean to interrupt your conference,' he said. 'We just chanced to be passing.'

'No interruption. None at all,' said his friend, whose name was Luke. 'Me and Junior, we was just discussing the best way to cook a veal. I said rolled in bread crumbs, real thin slices, then pan-fry and serve *al limone*.'

'Sweet wine sauce is better,' said Junior. 'Just take your tender milk-fed meat, sweet and soft as virgin pussy. Then add Marsala wine. Right there, you got heaven.'

'Or maybe stuffed with ham and melted cheese, cordon bleu,' said Luke. 'That ain't so shabby, neither.'

But Tu Sweet was not impressed. His face turned sour, as if his Grand Marnier had suddenly turned to Angostura bitters. 'Gourmet jive,' he said. 'What's wrong with pork chops and sweet potatoes, gravy, hot biscuits, maybe just a mite of collards on the side?'

Luke looked him over, without expression. So did Junior. Between them, weighing more than a quarter ton, they made Sonny Liston look like Barry Manilow. There was an icy silence. Then Luke pronounced judgement. 'Medallions, scallopine, sautéd with mushrooms,' he said. 'That is my final ruling.'

Out on the Strip, the crowds overspilled the sidewalks. Every few yards, we passed a sneak game of cards, played on a cardboard box. But Tu Sweet was not tempted. 'That Luke,' he said, 'he gives me disgust.'

'How's that?'

'The nigger's lost his soul. When we was upstate, he'd have eaten slop. But now that he's out, his hat's run away with his head. Sautéd with mushrooms! Veal cordon bleu! Just because he's a faggot, he thinks he's Jackie Onassis.'

'What was he in for, anyhow?' I inquired.

'He grew unruly with a hatchet.'

Next we went to Show-World, a sexual bazaar on Eighth. Outside, posters advertised the forthcoming attraction, a show called *Bizarre Burlesque*, starring Pregnant Polly, the Enema Queen, and Tina Toilet Tonsils.

The interior was modern, bright-lit, spacious. Among the regulars on the Strip, so Tu Sweet informed me, it was considered a palace, its standing second to none. 'Clean floors, fair prices, and women wall to wall,' he said. 'What more could one man desire?'

Almost everything cost a quarter. For that token fee, you locked yourself in a closet the size of a telephone booth and watched home movies. Somewhere above your head, tapes played simulated orgasms over and over again. Then there were magazines to browse through, all kinds of toys to be examined. More especially, there were peep shows upstairs, where you peered through a porthole at two ladies, one white, one black, who contorted themselves to music. Reclining on a circular bed, naked, they spread their sexes wide open, alternatively simpering and yawning. If you showed approval, one of them rewarded you by rubbing herself up against your porthole. Meanwhile, reflected in the back mirror were the faces of twenty men in a semi-circle, twenty heads bobbing, forty eyes staring, each man trapped behind a porthole of his own, like so many goldfish in bowls.

That was not all. For another dollar in quarters, you could also pick up a phone and talk to a Real Live Woman who sat behind a plate-glass window and served as your personal slave. Whatever you told her to do or say, within reason, she obeyed. So long as you did not get violent, she performed without question, and her smile never wavered.

The prospect was not soothing. Suddenly, lost in this sea of sideshows, I was flooded by nightmares of long-ago funfairs. All through my childhood, my greatest dreads were Ferris Wheels, Tilter Whirls, and roller coasters, which I knew were created to destroy me. Yet, time after time, I would force myself to endure them, eyes shut and stomach lurching, white hands clutching the rail. The thought of a Real Live Woman gave me much the same sensation.

There was no question of escape. I had my duty to perform, my promises to keep. So I went inside a booth and put my money in the slot. Beneath my feet, as I locked the door, I felt something wet and sticky. The smell made me gag.

After a moment, a blind was raised, like a plastic portcullis, and I was faced by a muscular blonde, some twenty pounds overweight, with eyelashes like windscreens and a vivid pink scar on her stomach. She looked serene, benign, cowlike. Waiting for me to begin, she smiled encouragement and blew out gum in a bubble, like a miniature bladder.

That was when I froze. Instead of picking up the phone and delivering terse instructions, I could not move or make any sound. Plunged back to age eight, imprisoned in a different form of Ghost Train, all I could do was shut my eyes tight and hold my breath, blotting out the pink gum, the pink scar, the spread pink sex.

For a long time, it seemed, I remained in darkness and silence. Then I opened my eyes, and the blonde was gone. The plastic blind had shut her out. Shaking, I stumbled out into the passage, where Tu Sweet was waiting. He said I'd been gone for two minutes, no more. But I did not believe him. 'I aged in there,' I said.

'That could be; I don't deny it,' he replied. 'When a man is less than a man, he grows old fast.'

It was barely three o'clock; only six hours had passed, and already I felt used up. For $10 cash, back on the Strip, I bought some cocaine from a man with a walleye. When I tried it out, bent double in a hallway, it revealed itself as lactose mixed with chalk.

The hours dragged slow. Aimless, we kept cruising, nothing else to do. We mooched up and down in the rain, examining the stills outside the dirty movies. It grew dark and the neon came on. Still the performers in the doorways did not change.

Close to the 7th Avenue subway, there was a preacher called Sister Pearl. Big, black and possessed, she rocked her body in frenzy, she hollered and spoke in tongues. Except for a few 'Hallelujahs', hardly any of her words could be deciphered. It did not matter. Nobody stopped to listen.

Afterwards, when the preaching was done and her soul had been soothed, she leaned up against the subway railing to gather her breath. In repose, all hysteria left her; her smile oozed lazy and slow. Nothing bothered her, not public indifference, not the wet and cold, not even her own incoherence: 'What's the use in making sense?' she said. 'Far better to just burn. Fan the flame or the fire will die. Then the Lord spews you forth from his mouth.'

A patrol car sped by, siren shrieking. Wiping off her hands on her black dress, Sister Pearl hung her purse on her wrist, disappeared inside the subway, and we went back to floating. This was the rush hour; Saturday night was just warming up. Outside the Super-Fly Boutique, a youth in a yellow-spotted bandanna barged hard against my shoulder, hoping to pick my pocket. In jumping clear, I blundered into a mongoloid, who cowered against a wall, a dog about to be kicked. I told him I was sorry. But he did not see or hear me.

Human flotsam spilled everywhere, swarming, devouring, like Triffids. We sought refuge in a luncheonette. Lounging against the counter, devouring hot dogs with mustard, three lawmen were discussing Farrah Fawcett-Majors, her assets and debits, her sorrows, her joys, her nipples. The jukebox played 'My Way', and the dealers offered cocaine, mescaline, speed.

We moved on through the crush. We struggled, we shoved. For perhaps the twentieth time since morning, we passed the lines of sailors and midnight cowboys, the weight lifters in black leather, the hookers in their hot pants. 'What next?' asked Tu Sweet.

'I need to be drunk.'

'Fan the flame. Or the fire will die,' he said, and we set to work in earnest. We drank brandies in a Chinese restaurant, bourbon and beer in the Golden Dollar Topless. Upstairs at the Roxy Burlesk, we sat by the edge of the stage and drowned ourselves in rye. A few inches in front of our faces, assorted bodies coupled, gymnastic and inexhaustible. But now I hardly noticed. Blurred in repetition, sex had already turned into background, a style of human Muzak.

Outside, a street photographer stopped me and took my picture. He said he came from North Africa. His father was a big man in Algiers, an international sky-dealer. This did not sound correct, but I didn't care to argue. 'Sky-dealing. That must be nice,' I said.

'Nothing can be better,' said the photographer.

While my image was developing, he whistled 'Feelings', all smiles. But when the picture emerged, he winced. 'You no smiling,' he protested. 'Mister, you sick?'

'I'm dying.'

'In that case,' said Tu Sweet, cutting in fast, 'let me show you the Terminal Bar.'

He did not jest. On the corner of 8th and 41st, right across from the Port Authority, there was a bar of just that name, and its title proved well earned. Everywhere that you looked, there was loss, stock symbols of booze and despair. Faded boxing pictures in the windows, rank stench outside the rest room, broken glass on the floor. A painted sign, announcing TAKEE OUTEE. Grime thick as axle grease. Men drinking in a line, seeing nothing, alone.

The man behind the bar, very large and very black, had once played professional football. Even in retirement, he could crush rocks with his handshake alone. 'This man, he so tough,' Tu Sweet said, 'he chews pig iron for breakfast and spits it out as razor blades.'

We drank whisky, we drank rum. For purposes of research, moving left to right along the bar, we then progressed to vodka, tequila, gin. Tu Sweet spoke of his schemes, his dreams, his hopes, his fears, and I thought about Gertrude, my prize sow. Somewhere behind our backs, an altercation started. There was a dispute about Ireland. Voices were raised, obscenities exchanged. In due course, fists were raised. There was a dull thud. Then a yelp of pain. Then a crash. 'It's late. We really should be going,' I said. But Tu Sweet was already gone.

Later on, when I asked him why he'd fled, he told me that violence always made him think of his mother. 'As soon as I hears breakage, I just got to run down-town and call her, to tell her how much I love her,' he said. 'You might call it a prime-evil need.'

'I might?'

'You could look it up.'

Left alone, I drifted without looking. Every doorway that I passed, I entered automatically. Some contained sex. The rest were filled with alcohol.

In time, progressions, grew blurred. Time kept jumping, and only fragments survived. In the bathroom of some all-night cinema, exactly that strange bathroom that Tu Sweet had warned me against, I purchased some black pills, some red pills, and some green pills, and I swallowed them in a handful. Mixed all together, they made me dizzy, and then they made me laugh. Sitting in the foyer, I started to make noise. Someone told me to keep quiet. Rising, I tried to punch him, but I missed and fell down instead.

Midnight came. The Strip did not slacken its pace. Of all the morning performers, only the lawmen and evangelists had abandoned their posts. No one else could afford defeat.

I rambled, I got lost. When I tried to play cards, across a cardboard box, I kept forgetting the rules. So I sheltered in Starship Discovery 1, close to the corner of 9th. The man on the door told me that this was the biggest and hottest, the most prestigious discotheque in all Manhattan. But when I went inside, everyone came from Jersey.

It was just another disco. There was din and heat and flashing lights, a dance floor like a football scrimmage, universal uproar. Instantly exhausted, I slumped in a corner, where I tried to recover focus. My eyes hurt; I could not breathe. Then a girl wandered by, wearing drawstring pants, mirror glasses, open-toed sandals. Her skin was bad, and she had no chin. In any case, she spilled her drink in my lap, and I was grateful.

She said her real name was Charlene, but I could call her Libra. She had myopic green eyes, passion-pink toenails. I suggested we catch a plane, maybe to Vegas, to play 21. Or else to Acapulco, where she could scuba dive. She said that was real neat, but first she must go to the bathroom. I promised I'd wait for ever. Then she was gone, and I forgot.

I walked. I kept on drinking. When that was done, I went to Nathan's, on Times Square, to straighten up and let time pass. I piled a tray high with hot dogs and chilli dogs, onion rings, fries, and proceeded to gorge myself in ritual self-punishment. Two o'clock came and went. Against all odds, I started to feel stronger. Then an Arab approached in a three-piece silk suit, with a diamond tie-pin and serious gold on his fingers. He called himself Ahmed and swore that he could provide me with anything, absolutely anything, that my heart desired. 'Your wish is my command,' he said. 'Just name your dream, and I will make it come true.'

'Oblivion,' I said.

'Alas, that is not possible,' he replied. 'But I can find you cocaine, mescaline, speed.'

Back on 42nd, *Looking for Mr Goodbar* was playing at the New Amsterdam. Given the time and place, I could think of no more suitable film. So I paid my money; I entered. And I found myself in a fantasia, a truly heroic madness. According to the doorman, it had been the home of *The Ziegfeld Follies*. Now it had fallen on scuffling times. The décor was much scarred, and so was the clientele. But the magnificence was indestructible. There were massive, carved, bronze elevators; sculpted stone frescoes of scenes from Shakespeare and Wagner; green marble stairways, soaring to the empyrean; floors of patterned marble; nymphs, satyrs, wizards, elves; walls gilded or bronzed; a granite fireplace the size of a small house. Every inch of available space, it seemed, had been embellished, in some way transmuted. Door handles turned into centaurs, and light holders became Egyptian goddesses. Junkies slumped on baronial thrones.

I went upstairs and sat in the balcony. Everybody around me was black. Discarded hot dogs, cigarettes and soft drinks formed a swamp underfoot. Somewhere far above me, I could just discern a vast vaulted ceiling. But the aisles were dark and rank, and I took the first seat I found, close to the back, where I could not be trapped.

The film was almost over. In any case, the action left me baffled. For reasons which escaped me, everyone on the screen kept screaming and yelling. This confused and alarmed me, and made my head ache. So I went to hide in the bathroom.

When I returned, my seat had been usurped. In the darkness, it was impossible to make out the intruder in any detail, but I sensed something female, and white. Too weakened to protest, I sat down beside it and dragged my attention back to the screen. Nothing made sense; my confusion only deepened. Then a hand touched my knee, paused for a moment, and started to climb my thigh, very soft. It disturbed my concentration, and I moved away. Shortly afterwards, the film reached an end.

The lights went up; I looked along the row. Sure enough, my neighbour had been female and white. From this distance, she looked about forty, small and well dressed, essentially demure. She wore white gloves, and she looked straight ahead, as if I no longer existed. She seemed to be waiting.

All around her there were blacks at jive. But she did not move and she did not seem to notice. After a few seconds, a white man appeared at her side. He was tall and muscular, and he wore a dark uniform, complete with peaked cap, like a chauffeur. Reaching out his right hand, he placed it behind the woman's back; one hand curled beneath her armpit. Then, without the smallest sign of effort, he lifted her up, cradled in the crook of his elbow. Her head lay against his shoulder, and he carried her away. She had no legs.

It was almost three; at last, the Strip was winding down. From now on, the main action took place in the all-night movies, and the street itself thinned out. Only one game of cards was left. Half the doorways stood empty. Even so, cars still cruised in a steady stream, their windows lowered halfway. The eyes that peered out were impassive. Surveying the remaining performers, they checked, judged, priced, discarded, all in the same instant. No desire was involved; no possibility of pleasure. Like sexual accountants, they merely made their calculations, balanced their books, and moved on.

Right next to the Amsterdam, I saw a sign that said CHESS AND

CHECKERS CLUB OF NEW YORK. It sounded restful. So I walked down another deserted hallway, and I climbed one more flight of stairs. When I reached the top, I found sanctuary.

I entered a room that was large and bright and clean, the image of decorum. Beneath a glass counter, there was a collection of antique cakes and sandwiches, neatly wrapped. Coffee was also served. On the walls, there were pictures of sunlit valleys, of grasslands and of blue skies.

Scattered about the room, men sat at Formica-topped tables, pondering the complexities of backgammon, Scrabble, chess. Most of them wore suits and ties, and none of them was young. Sages, elders, they spoke only when they had to, and then in undertones. Nobody laughed, no one swore. These were serious men.

Close beside the glass counter, a wino slouched in an upright chair, half asleep. I sat down beside him and watched the play. Cards slapped on the tables, setting up irregular rhythms; dice rattled like snakes; the players murmured, droned. In time, lulled by these calm rituals, I lapsed into semi-stupor.

When I came to, it was past five. None of the players had changed position, and none of the games were resolved. In this room, which never closed, time seemed suspended. You came, you played, you remained. Outside, on the Strip, there was madness. Here you were kept safe.

Once again, I went back on the street. The rain had stopped, but it was cold; the wind whipped harsh. All the bars were closed; only the hardiest performers, or the most despairing, clung on. I couldn't face another all-night movie, and I would freeze if I stayed out-doors. So I shambled back to Show-World, where I locked myself in a booth with *Oriental Lesbians*. They smiled nicely; their bodies were not deformed; they offered no threat. Therefore, I did not leave them. Speed-racked, close to tears, I ran and reran their loop, for comfort and companionship, until my last quarter was gone.

Afterwards, there was nothing left but the Port Authority. I dragged myself down 8th very slow. Apart from a few drunks, the sidewalks were deserted. Every door was locked, ever window barred. I was alone.

According to Tu Sweet, these blocks are known as the Minnesota Pipeline on account of the numberless mid-Western girls who clamber down off Greyhounds, suitcases in hand, $20 in their purses, and go straight to work in the doorways, because there is nowhere else to go, nothing else in the world they can do.

True enough, just as I reached the corner of 41st, I was stopped by a girl's voice, coming out of semi-darkness. 'Mister,' it said, 'why don't you enjoy some fun?'

The girl could have been eighteen, twenty at the most. She looked underfed and anaemic, inescapably plain, with thin reddish hair and too much mascara. She wore a white plastic raincoat, tightly belted, but her legs were bare underneath. Her nose had been reddened by the cold. She said that her name was Cindy.

She led me to the Hotel Elk, right next to Starship Discovery. It was a squat brownstone, overlooking Ninth. We toiled up many flights of stairs, past a sign that said NO VISITORS. The light was dim. A small girl sat on the stairway, outside her room, waiting for her parents to finish making love. Three radios played clashing music. We kept on climbing, and we reached a brown door. Cindy took me inside.

She lived in a small, oblong room, which contained a bed and a bedside table, two chairs, one of which had a broken leg, and a washbasin. The blind, cracked and ripped, had been permanently lowered. There was a broken mirror.

All of this made Cindy feel embarrassed. She was new in town, she said, and had yet to find a sponsor. If she had had any choice, she would not have lived like this; it was not her natural style. But she could afford nothing better. 'It's cheap,' she said. 'So am I.'

She took off her clothes. She lay on the bed and waited.

'Where do you come from?' I asked.

'I was born in Kansas. Then I was raised in Ohio.'

'What made you leave?'

'I got too old to stay.'

Conversation did not come easy. Cindy was polite; clearly, she meant to please. But she suffered from some inner cancellation, a curious blankness, almost like a sleepwalker. Her voice was toneless, as if she were forever repeating lessons, and all her answers came out in subtitles, staccato, no more than a few words long. If I closed my eyes, she sounded like a recorded message.

Outside, it was just starting to get light. In the next room, a man woke up and started swearing, methodically, without inflection.

'New York gets cold. Not as cold as Ohio. But cold,' Cindy said. 'Sometimes it gets so cold, I can't even sleep.'

'You could move somewhere warmer.'

'I couldn't. To move, you have to be protected. But I'm not protected. Every girl is protected by someone. But I'm not protected.'

'It's true,' I said. 'New York can be hard.'

'It's so large. So large.'

'It is.'

'It's the biggest place I ever was in.'

'Don't you have any friends?'

'Friends cost money.'

For $25, she let me stay until morning. Stretched out across the bed, she lay on her back, eyes wide open, looking up at the ceiling. I tried to sleep but couldn't. Feverish, I tossed and rambled, I sweated. Cindy never stirred.

When the time came to leave, she kissed me on the cheek, very chaste. Make-up was smeared across her eyelids and mouth; her nose was still red from the cold. 'I hope you enjoyed your fun. Please come again,' she said.

'Thank you.'

'You're welcome.'

One last time, I walked up the street, back towards Times Square. It was Sunday morning, when bars do not open till noon, and there was nobody around. The Strip itself was abandoned, a tenderloin *Marie Celeste*. Of all yesterday's performers, that massed throng, not one remained.

My twenty-four hours were up. In celebration, I bought myself some coffee and a jelly doughnut, takee outee, to go. Then I made my final tour of duty, from Nathan's to the Terminal Bar, from the Amsterdam to Show-World, via the Roxy Burlesk and Golden Dollar Topless and Super-Fly Boutique. Everything was shut or deserted. I had outlasted them all. Now I was free to go home.

I stood on the corner of 8th, waiting for a cab. Washed up on the curb like sea wrack, there were the same abandoned pamphlets, the ones that said 'You don't have to be Jewish to love Jesus.' I stooped to study the small print. As I did so, Tu Sweet appeared, emerging from the subway, right across the street.

He looked indecently rested. Freshly laundered, showered, shaved, he sported a flash plaid jacket, knife-edged flannels, patent pumps. When he reached my side, he slapped me five. 'What's the action?' he asked.

'Nothing much. Just a little sky-dealing,' I said.

'Is that a fact? I thought you perished for sure. Me and your young lady, we spent the whole night on our knees, lighting candles. We even planned the wake.'

'I hate niggers,' I said.

Together, we trundled up the avenue. Pale sunshine was breaking through the grey; the cold had begun to ease. As we strolled, the first few performers emerged, greeting the new day. It looked like another lazy Sunday.

I started to feel better. I was still carrying my coffee and jelly doughnut, safe in a large paper bag, and I let myself dream of breakfast. Just for a moment, I relaxed. And that was my final undoing.

The kayo, when it came, was a one-punch job, swift, clean, and total. Outside a Blarney Stone, a drunken woman was sitting on the doorstep, her head clasped in her hands. As we passed, she seemed to be staring into space, oblivious. Then somehow her eye caught mine, and she jumped to her feet, incensed.

Red-faced with fury, hands shaking in wildest outrage, the woman pointed at my face, and then at my paper bag. 'Imposter! Fraud!' she cried. 'You've got nothing in that bag. And, may God be my witness, you never will.'